Lecture Notes in Artificial Intelligence   8863

Subseries of Lecture Notes in Computer Science

Yang Sok Kim   Byeong Ho Kang
Deborah Richards (Eds.)

Knowledge Management and Acquisition for Smart Systems and Services

13th Pacific Rim
Knowledge Acquisition Workshop, PKAW 2014
Gold Cost, Qld, Australia, December 1-2, 2014
Proceedings

 Springer

Volume Editors

Yang Sok Kim
University of Tasmania, Hobart, TAS, Australia
E-mail: yangsok.kim@utas.edu.au

Byeong Ho Kang
University of Tasmania, Hobart, TAS, Australia
E-mail: byeong.kang@utas.edu.au

Deborah Richards
Macquarie University, Sydney, NSW, Australia
E-mail: deborah.richards@mq.edu.au

ISSN 0302-9743   e-ISSN 1611-3349
ISBN 978-3-319-13331-7   e-ISBN 978-3-319-13332-4
DOI 10.1007/978-3-319-13332-4
Springer Cham Heidelberg New York Dordrecht London

Library of Congress Control Number: 2014954090

LNCS Sublibrary: SL 7 – Artificial Intelligence

© Springer International Publishing Switzerland 2014

Typesetting: Camera-ready by author, data conversion by Scientific Publishing Services, Chennai, India

Printed on acid-free paper

Springer is part of Springer Science+Business Media (www.springer.com)

Preface

The Pacific Rim Knowledge Acquisition Workshop (PKAW) has provided a forum for presentation and discussion of all aspects of knowledge acquisition research. In particular, the study of knowledge acquisition has enormous importance currently, because the unprecedented data, called big data, are available today and knowledge acquisition mainly aims to extract useful knowledge from vast and diverse data as well as directly from human experts.

PKAW has evolved to embrace and foster advances in theory, practice, and technology not only in knowledge acquisition and capture but also in all aspects of knowledge management including reuse, sharing, maintenance, transfer, merging, reconciliation, creation, and dissemination. As many nations strive to be knowledge economies and organizations seek to maximize their knowledge assets and usage, solutions to handle the complex task of knowledge management are more important than ever before. This volume contributes toward this goal.

This volume seeks to disseminate the latest solutions from the International Workshop on Knowledge Management and Acquisition for Smart Systems and Services (PKAW 2014), held on the Gold Coast, Australia, during December 1–2, 2014, in conjunction with the Pacific Rim International Conference on Artificial Intelligence (PRICAI 2014).

The workshop received 69 submissions from 11 countries. From these, we accepted 18 papers (26%) as regular long paper and 4 papers as regular short paper (6%). All papers were reviewed by at least two members of the PKAW/PRICAI Program Committee. The papers demonstrate a balance of theoretical, technical, and application-driven research, many papers incorporating all three foci.

The workshop co-chairs would like to thank all those who were involved with PKAW 2014, including the PRICAI 2014 Organizing Committee, PKAW Program Committee members, those who submitted papers and reviewed them and of course the authors, presenters, and attendees. PKAW is made possible by the generous support of our sponsors - Air Force Office of Scientific Research (AFOSR) and Asian Office of Aerospace Research and Development (AOARD).

We warmly invite you to participate in PKAW 2014 anticipated to be held in Gold Coast, Queensland in conjunction with PRICAI 2014.

December 2014

Yang Sok Kim
Byeong Ho Kang
Deborah Richards

Organization

Program Committee

Ghassan Beydoun	University of Wollongong, Australia
Ivan Bindo	University of Tasmania, Australia
Xiongcai Cai	The University of New South Wales, Australia
Kyung Jin Cha	KeiMyung University, Korea
Paul Compton	The University of New South Wales, Australia
Richard Dazeley	University of Ballarat, Australia
Saurabh Garg	University of Tasmania, Australia
Byeong Ho Kang	University of Tasmania, Australia
Mihye Kim	Catholic University of Daegu, South Korea
Yang Sok Kim	University of Tasmania, Australia
Masahiro Kimura	Ryukoku University, Japan
Alfred Krzywicki	University of New South Wales, Australia
Maria Lee	Shih Chien University, Taiwan
Kyongho Min	University of New South Wales, Australia
Toshiro Minami	Kyushu Institute of Information Sciences and Kyushu University Library, Japan
Luke Mirowski	University of Tasmania, Australia
James Montgomery	University of Tasmania, Australia
Hiroshi Motota	Osaka University, Japan
Kouzou Ohara	Aoyama Gakuin University, Japan
Ulrich Reimer	University of Applied Sciences St. Gallen, Switzerland
Deborah Richards	Macquarie University, Australia
Kazumi Saito	Univesity of Shizuoka, Japan
Shuxiang Xu	University of Tasmania, Australia

Sponsoring Organizations

Air Force Office of Scientific Research (AFOSR)

Asian Office of Aerospace Research and
Development (AOARD)

University of Tasmania

Table of Contents

Machine Learning and Data Mining

Incremental Knowledge Acquisition

Web-Based Techniques and Applications

Domain Specific Knowledge Acquisition Methods and Application

Regular Short Papers

Academic Performance in a 3D Virtual Learning Environment: Different Learning Types vs. Different Class Types

Nader Hanna[1], Deborah Richards[1], and Michael J. Jacobson[2]

[1]Computing Department, Macquarie University, NSW 2109, Australia
{nader.hanna,deborah.richards}@mq.edu.au
[2]Centre for Computer Supported Learning and Cognition
The University of Sydney, NSW 2006, Australia
michael.jacobson@sydney.edu.au

Abstract. The last decade has seen an increasing interest in the use of 3D virtual environments for educational applications. However, very few studies investigated the influence of the learning context, such as class type and learning type, on learners' academic performance. This paper studied the impact of class type (i.e. comprehensive or selective) classes, as well as learning type (i.e. guided or challenge and guided), on students' level of usage of a Virtual Learning Environment (VLE) as well as on their academic performance. The results showed that, unlike class type, there is a significant difference between learners' in their usage of the VLE. Moreover, the results showed that the levels of using a VLE significantly correlated with learners' academic performance.

Keywords: 3D Virtual Environment, Learning Analytics, Academic Performance, Guided Learning, Comprehensive Class.

1   Introduction

In the traditional classroom, learning is a teacher-centered process. Interactions go from the main source of knowledge who is the teacher to the students. Physical monitoring and tests were typically used to assess the learners' academic performance. The learning process involved students statically interacting with their teachers in the class environment. Advances in technology have led to the creation of many exciting new approaches to student learning. However, despite these advances the traditional classroom model has remained largely unchanged in the last 20 years. In particular, the use of Virtual Learning Environments (VLEs) is underutilized and absent from most classrooms. VLEs offer the promise of experiential and constructivist learning, allowing students to learning by doing. In recent years, the dramatic growth in hardware capacity and drop in prices have made it possible to run 3D Virtual Environments (VEs) on personal computers [1]. With the versatility of VEs, various applications have emerged. These applications include training, entertainment, and learning. A number of studies (e.g. [2], [3]) stress the impact of using VE on learning performance. However, a number of challenges need to be addressed before VLEs become a common learning approach.

Y.S. Kim et al (Eds.): PKAW 2014, LNCS 8863, pp. 1–15, 2014.

Learning analytics (LA) is a branch of knowledge that uses data collected from a learning situation to uncover the student's current level of understanding and tune the learning process for the individual student. LA was defined as "the measurement, collection, analysis and reporting of data about learners and their contexts, for purposes of understanding and optimizing learning and the environments in which it occurs" [4]. The definition of LA focuses on the data collection and the context of learning. Although there are many studies that explored different Learning Management Systems (LMS), few studies addressed the influence of different context of learning on the collected data. LA emerges from two converging trends: 1) the evolving use of LMS in educational institutions, 2) the application of data mining techniques to business intelligence processes in organizational information systems. LA has moved beyond analysis of data related to student assessment and activity in a LMS to social network analysis [5], cloud computing [6], and virtual environment [7]. LA applications utilize data generated as a result of learner activities, such as learner participation in discussion board or computer assisted formative assessments [8]. The results of LA could be directed to learners [8], instructors or managers [9].

Many studies have investigated learning in 3D virtual worlds [10] [11]. These studies focused either on factors in the physical world such as student-student or student-teacher interaction [7]; while other studies explored interactions which may reflect the information exchanges between students and the system via the VLE interface, which they called student-system interaction [12]. Few studies explored management factors such as class management or how the learning instructions are presented in VLEs.

To address this gap in the literature, this paper addresses an uncovered topic about the impact of class type, i.e. comprehensive (range of academic abilities) or selective (high academic achievers) classes, as well as learning type, i.e. guided (provided with goal/problem and instructions) or challenge and guided (provided only with the goal/problem) learning type, on students' levels of using a VLE and the influence of level of VLE usage on their academic performance.

In addition, the paper investigates the impact of the level of learners' exposure to the learning material in a VLE on learners' continuous learning performance, on one hand, and the final academic achievement, on the other hand. Exposure to the learning material refers to the amount of time a student spends in the VLE. Continuous learning performance means their progressive learning overtime, often measured via formative assessment. In contrast, academic achievement refers to the final academic student outcome in the form of a mark awarded to the summative assessment task. To achieve these aims, we propose the following research questions:

1. Does learning type (guided learning vs. challenge and guided learning) correlate with learners' exposure to the learning material in VLE?
2. Does class type (comprehensive vs. selective) correlate with the learners' exposure to the learning material in VLE?
3. Does learners' exposure to the learning material in VLE correlate with their continuous learning performance? Moreover, which level of exposure leads to better performance?

4. Does learning type (guided learning vs. challenge and guided learning) correlate with learners' continuous learning performance.
5. Does learners' continuous learning performance relate to their final academic achievement?

2   Literature Review

The learning analytics research community defines learning analytics as the analysis of log files [13], learning resources [14] and learning designs [15] in order to predict and advise people's learning. In order to achieve this goal learning analytics provides a recommendation to predictive models [16] . Learning analytics has many benefits to learning and education administration [17]. Many learning analytics studies investigated the influence of different learning sources (e.g. forum, dashboard, VLE, etc.) on students' academic achievement. In an investigation of the impact of students' performance on some activities that affected their final grade, it was found that students' participation in a discussion forum was the best predictor of their final grades [18]. In [19] data such as login frequency, site engagement, student pace in the course, and assignment grades were used to predict learners' outcome in a course. In [20] the number of discussion messages read and number of discussion replies posted were utilized to predict learner's achievement. [21] used the number of attempts at doing homework, time spent on a problem, and reading of material to predict final grades.

With the emerging use of virtual environments (VEs) in the classroom, learning analytics relies on data sources and logs generated from usage of the VE [7]. Among the studies that used data from VLE to understand learners academic achievement, Agudo-Peregrina et al. [22] studied different interactions in VLEs and its impact on students' academic performance. They investigated three types of interactions associated with learning: student-student interactions, student-teacher interactions and student-content interactions. The results found no relation between the different class interactions or student-content interactions and final academic achievement. Lee et al [23] investigated the impact of a VE-based learning environment on the academic performance of learners with different learning styles. They adopted a classification of learning styles into accommodator learning and assimilator learning. Their results showed that there was no significant difference in the cognitive and affective learning outcomes for students with different learning styles in the VR-based learning environment.

3   A VLE Case Study: Omosa

To answer the research questions a VLE was used. This VLE is an ecosystem for a fictitious island called Omosa created to help school students to learn scientific knowledge and science inquiry skills, see Fig. 1. Omosa Virtual World has been implemented using Unity3D. The goal is to determine why the fictitious animals, known as Yernt, are dying out.

The island of Omosa consists of four different locations the learner can visit. In each location there is a virtual agent waiting for the learner's visit. The learner can ask each agent a set of questions (between seven and nine questions). At the end of the session with that agent, the agent will provide the learner with evidence that supports their viewpoint concerning the problems on the island. Learners have to explore the island and visit four different locations. The four locations are the village, the research lab, the hunting ground and the weather station. In the village, the student will meet both the firestick agent and the hunter agent. In the research lab, the students can meet the ecologist agent. In the weather station, the students can meet the climatologist agent. Each agent has a list of questions that the user can ask about the agent and each agent will present an alternative view on why the Yernt are dying out.

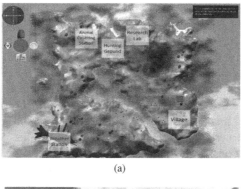

(a)

(b)

Fig. 1. (a) A Snapshot to the map of Omosa virtual world, (b) A snapshot to one of the four locations the users have to visit

In addition to encountering various agents and getting evidence to determine the possible causes for the Yernt's increased death rates, the students will have to collect multiple notes to get more details and facts that could be used to compare the current and past states of Omosa and deduce the cause of the problem. There are four sets of notes the students can pick up; the first set of notes are rainfall notes located in the weather station that contains information about temperature and rain level readings in different periods. The second set of notes is village field notes located in the village that contains information about the activities of the people in Omosa during the last period. The third set of notes is tree ring notes located in research lab that contains information about the internal structure of the stems of the trees on the island. The fourth set of notes is ecologist notes located in the research lab and they contain notes about the changes in the ecology system of Omosa Island.

After exploring the virtual world and collecting notes, data and evidence from the imaginary island, students are asked to answer a daily question in a workbook. On the last day of exploration, students are required to create a presentation that summarizes their conclusion about what is the cause of the changes in the ecosystem of the island Omosa and what is the reason the imaginary animal Yernt are dying out.

3.1   Participants

The reported data is from a classroom study carried out in 2013. The study was conducted in an Australian public secondary school in two science classes: a comprehensive class, and a selective class. Selective and comprehensive classes are types of classes that exist in some states in Australia, including the state of New South Wales where this study was conducted. Selective classes are comprised of students who have sat a voluntary statewide exam in their final year of primary school and achieved at a high level. Comprehensive classes are comprised of students who have not chosen to sit the selective class exam or who did not achieve the level required. Comprehensive classes may also be streamed based on student academic performance or they may have a full range of academic abilities in one class. Nine 50-minute class periods were available. The study was conducted at the end of the first half of the 2013 academic year.

Fifty-five and 45 students from selective and comprehensive classes were invited to participate in the study. Twenty-six students from both selective and comprehensive used the VLE enough to provide data that could be visualized and completed the workbook, and 37 students finished the final presentation slides.

3.2   Procedures

Nine 50-minute class periods were available. Each class period was considered a new day in the student's workbook where they were given a task to do. The study was conducted at the end of the first half of the 2013 academic year. The participants were divided into two groups; the first group was given a guided workbook (Guided Learning), while the other group was given an unguided workbook (Challenge and guided Learning). The students were free to navigate the VLE to be able to answer the task in the workbook. Guided Learning (GL) and Challenge and guided Learning (CGL) differ in the level of support or scaffolding provided to the student as s/he tries to solve a problem or achieve a goal. CGL presents the student with the problem but does not assist them in solving the problem. Earlier research on CGL used the term productive failure [24], that reflected that even though students failed initially and needed to go through one or more rounds of trial and error, in the end they were more productive in terms of understanding of the concepts and achieving the intended learning outcomes.

Guided Learning

The Guided Learning (GL) group was given a workbook with instructions designed to direct learners while navigating the VLE. The instructions were in the form of a series of checkpoints. In each checkpoint, the learner was asked to go and visit a particular location, ask the virtual character in the target location some questions, and pick up notes in the VLE that contained useful information to help to draw conclusion.

Challenge and Guided Learning

The Challenge and guided Learning (CGL) group was given a workbook with no guided instructions. Students had to discover the VLE system themselves and decide where to go to find clues about what happened in the VLE. In addition, learners have to decide whether to talk with virtual characters or not and which questions to ask and which notes to collect. For brevity and clarity, we also refer to this type as unguided in the discussion.

4   Materials and Method

4.1   Data Collection

To conduct studies on VEs, it is critical to collect participant related data quickly and accurately [25]. Hanna et al [26] provided a taxonomy of techniques to collect data from VEs. In this study, the following three data collection techniques were used.

Log Files

Logging users' activities in a VE to interpret their engagement is not new research [27]. Students' navigations across VLE leave a trace of breadcrumbs which may be collected to build a composite picture of activities while learning [28]. To keep track of students' learning activities, three log files for each participant were collected: 1) position log file; 2) virtual agents the user met and which questions were asked and 3) the notes the user picked up. The position log file is used to register the path the user takes while navigating the VE.

Workbook Marks

A student workbook was developed to provide learners with information about how to use the Omosa VE. For eight classes/days, the student workbook included assignments and activities to do each day. Learners' answers to the daily assignment were registered; later, answers were coded and marked. The marks awarded for each of the workbooks were used to measure each student's continuous learning.

Final Presentation Marks

After completing the daily tasks, students were asked to create presentations using Microsoft PowerPoint. In these presentations, students were asked to conclude their understanding of the learning material by performing scientific inquiry to deduce a reason behind the dying out of the virtual animal. The marks awarded for the presentation were used to measure the learners' final academic achievements.

4.2   Visualizing Quantitative Measures of Users' Interactions in Omosa VLE

Visualization was used to display the analytics information in a more meaningful way [29] [30]. The aim of this study was to investigate the impact of users' exposure to the learning content of a VE on the progress of their learning performance and later on their academic achievement. The first step is to evaluate users' usage of VLE and rank their interaction. A case-by-case evaluation of the log files that recorded users' activities was conducted. A number of factors were considered to evaluate users' experience. These factors included the numbers of days the learners used the VLE, the navigated distance in the VLE, the number of virtual characters that learners talked with, and the number of objects that were collected. Using these factors, learners' exposure was sorted into three levels: low, medium and high. Figure 2(a, b, c) shows examples for different levels of learner participation. As an example of a high level of VLE usage, Figure 2(a) depicts the distance navigated in each day of the four days and the collected learning notes from Omosa VLE (ecology notes and tree ring data). An example of a learner with a medium level of VLE usage is shown in Figure 2(b). The learner's activity was coded as medium, because the learner visited the VLE only on one day and no learning material in the VLE was collected. Figure 2(c) demonstrates an example of low-level usage of the VLE. This learner was coded as low level because two locations in were not visited and no notes were collected.

5   Results

This study aimed to investigate the influence of different class types as well as learning types on learners' level of exposure to the VLE. Additionally, the paper studied the impact of learners' exposure to VLE on learners' continuous learning performance and the final academic achievement. To answer research questions, study variables were tested for normality. The result of Shapiro-Wilk normality test showed that study variables were normality (p-value<0.05).

To answer the first research question about the influence of learning type, the results, see Table 1, showed that there was a significant difference between the students in the guided learning type versus the students in the challenged learning type on the levels of using VLE, [$F(1, 24) = 7.53$, $p < 0.05$, $\eta^2=0.24$]. To further understand which learning type led to more exposure to the learning content of VLE, the mean of each group was calculated. The results, see Fig. 3, showed that average usage of VLE by guided learners was 2.2 and standard deviation was 0.79, while the average of challenge and guided learners was 1.37 and standard deviation was 0.72.

To the second research question about the influence of class type, the average VLE usage for students in the comprehensive and selective classes were 1.7 and 1.67, respectively with standard deviation 0.80 and 1.04, respectively. The result of ANOVA test revealed that there was no significant difference, see Table 2, between students who were in comprehensive or selective classes and their usage level of the VLE.

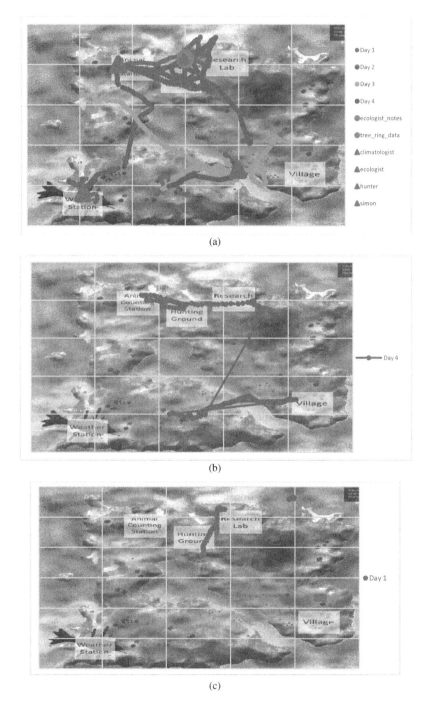

Fig. 2. Visualization of different level of using Omosa, (a) high level of usage, (b) medium level of usage, (c) low level of usage

Table 1. Summary of one-way ANOVA to show signifcant difference between learning type and VLE usage (Q1)

	Sum of Squares	df	Mean Square	F	Sig.
Between Groups	4.188	1	4.188	7.530	0.011
Within Groups	13.350	24	0.556		
Total	17.538	25			

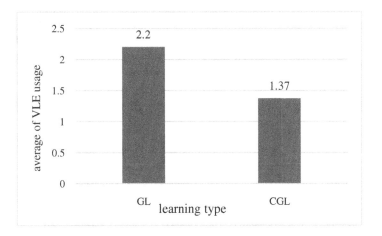

Fig. 3. Average of VLE usage for each learning type

Table 2. One-way ANOVA to show difference between class type and VLE usage (Q2)

	Sum of Squares	df	Mean Square	F	Sig.
Between Groups	0.005	1	0.005	0.007	0.934
Within Groups	17.533	24	0.731		
Total	17.538	25			

Table 3. Summary of one-way ANOVA to show signifcant difference between VLE usage and workbook grades (Q3)

	Sum of Squares	df	Mean Square	F	Sig.
Between Groups	46.17	1	46.17	9.22	0
Within Groups	250.38	50	5.01		
Total	296.56	51			

To answer the third research question about the impact of learners' exposure to the learning material in VLE on their continuous leaning progress, the results, see Table 3, showed that there was a statistically significant difference between the levels of using VLE on the learning progress as represented in students' workbook marks [$F(1, 50) = 9.22$, $p < 0.01$, $\eta^2=0.16$]. To further understand which exposure level led to higher learning performance, the mean of learners in each level was calculated as demonstrated in Fig. 4. The results showed that the average mark of low exposure students was 3.21 (SD=3.37), 4.33 (SD=3.61) was the average of medium exposure learners and 3.67 (SD=1.70) was the average of high exposure learners.

The fourth research question asked whether there is a correlation between guided/unguided learning in the VLE and learners' academic performance. Although the results did not show a statistically significant difference between guided and unguided students in their workbook grade, see Table 4, the mean grade of unguided learning students was higher than that of guided students.

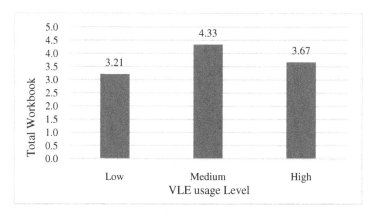

Fig. 4. Average workbook grade for each VLE usage

Table 4. Summary of one-way ANOVA to show signifcant difference between learning type and workbook grades (Q4)

	Sum of Squares	df	Mean Square	F	Sig.
Between Groups	26.496	1	26.496	3.082	0.092
Within Groups	206.35	24	8.598		
Total	232.846	25			

Finally, the fifth research question inquired whether there is a relation between the learners' continuous performance based on their daily workbook marks and their final academic achievement as shown in the presentation mark. A paired T-test was used to determine whether there was a significant difference between the average values of learners' scores for the workbook and their scores in the final presentation. The results, see Table 5, showed that there was no significant difference between students' workbook results and presentation result.

6   Discussion

This study aimed to investigate the influence of different class types (comprehensive vs. selective) as well as learning types (guided learning vs. challenge and guided learning) on the learners' level of exposure to the VLE. In addition, the paper investigated the impact of the different level of learners' exposure to the learning material in a VLE on 1) learners' continuous learning performance, and 2) learners' final academic achievement.

The first research question asked whether different learning types, guided learning or challenge and guided learning, correlates with VLE usage level. The results showed that there was a significant difference between the students who had guided learning versus the students who had challenge and guided learning on VLE usage level of these students. This result reveals the importance of learning type to stimulate learners to explore the learning material included in a VLE. In this study, guided learning may direct learners to explore the VLE more and encourage them to follow the instructions to talk with virtual characters or pick up the virtual notes. A number of studies (e.g. [31]) investigated the effect of guided and unguided learning to stimulate users' attention and the level to explore VE content more. This finding is consistent with other studies that suggested that discovery learning with guidance can be more effective than discovery learning with no guidance in enabling students to apply their knowledge to new problems [32]. Another study on discovery learning suggested that discovery learning accompanied by guidance in the form of coaching is more effective than unguided discovery learning [33]. Goo et al. [34] proposed that the tasks in a VE which begin with unguided followed by guided learning style was more effective to simulate users than the tasks which begin with guided followed by unguided learning style.

Table 5. Summary of Paired Samples T-Test between workbook and presentation grades (Q5)

	Paired Differences							Sig. (2-tailed)
				95% Confidence Interval of the Difference				
	Mean	Std. Deviation	Std. Error Mean	Lower	Upper	t	df	
workbook - presentation	0.875	4.17172	0.73746	-0.62906	2.37906	1.187	31	0.244

The results of the second research question inquire whether there is a relationship between learners' class type and their usage level of the VLE. The results showed that there is no significant difference in exploring the VLE between students in comprehensive and selective classes. These findings along with the finding of the first research question suggest that what really matters in discovery learning is how the learning material is presented to the learners regardless of their academic ability.

The third research question investigates the impact of learners' exposure to the learning material in VLE on their continuous learning progress. The results showed that learners' with a low level of exposure to VLE content had the poorest average marks in their daily workbook. The learners demonstrating a medium level of exposure to VLE achieved the highest mark. An unexpected result was the finding that students with highest VLE usage did not achieve the highest workbook scores.

To further understand the result of high VLE usage students, a qualitative analysis of the high VLE usage students (level 3) showed that some of these students outwardly used the VLE; however their usage does not reflect real engagement at a cognitive level with the learning content. For example, some students superficially navigated around the VLE; however, these traversals were aimless and did not explore the learning material. Other students in this level asked many questions of the virtual character, however, many of these questions were repeated and hence asking questions did not build towards an increase in their understanding of the situation. The finding highlights the importance of estimating the student's meaningful usage of VLE so that their activity builds towards the learning target.

Many research studies reported the positive impact of VLE on learners' academic performance compared to traditional learning [31]; however, research studying the relation between guided/unguided learning in a VLE have reported mixed conclusions. Although our study did not show significant differences between guided and unguided learning in VLE, many studies [35] reported that although learners preferred unguided VLE, learners who have the guided VLE (teacher-demonstrated based or TDB) learning significantly outperformed their peers who had unguided learning (Student Co-navigated Based or SCB). Another study [36] indicated that students who received the Guided Inquiry Learning approach performed significantly higher than those who received the tutorial approach.

The finding related to the last research question suggested that learners' continuous learning performance in daily assignments is consistent with their final academic achievement. This confirms the value of early monitoring of learner performance and possible automated intervention via alerts and encouragement to change behaviour or recognition of achievement to encourage continued performance.

7   Conclusion and Future Work

This study aimed to investigate the relationship between class type, comprehensive or selective, as well as learning type, guided or challenge and guided, and the level of exposure to the learning content in VLE, on one hand, and on the continuous academic performance and final learning achievement, on the other hand. The results showed that class type had no significant relationship with learners' level of using the VLE, while learning type had a significant relationship with learners' level of using the VLE. Learners who had the guided learning experience showed more willingness to use the designed VLE.

Our findings promote active student participation as a lever to improve the learning outcomes. In other words, learners' engagement with the learning content of VLEs is a fundamental element in continuous academic performance and final achievement. However, this participation should be monitored to be sure that it is moving the learner toward the learning goal and not just aimless exploration. This finding necessitates the implementation of a run-time LA that measure learners' positive participation in the content of VLEs.

Among the findings of this study, learners' usage of VLEs was found to correlate with their continuous academic performance and their final achievement. The Challenge and Guided Learning activities are based on Kapur's productive failure theory [37], which has an "idea generation and exploration" phase (Challenge) and a "consolidation" phase (Guided Learning). What is reported in this paper is only looking at learner behaviors in the virtual environment in the first phase. In other work looking at the results for the second phase, both learning type conditions showed the same learner behaviors.

As future work, an objective evaluation of the learners' level of exposure to the learning content of VLEs is needed to be designed. This objective evaluation will help in monitoring learners and drawing a picture of their behaviour in early stages of learning. Understanding student performance and behaviour will potentially allow teachers and/or the VLE to provide just-in-time support according to the needs and context of the learner.

References

1. Tsai-Yen, L., Hung-Kai, T.: An intelligent user interface with motion planning for 3D navigation. In: Proceedings of Virtual Reality, pp. 177–184. IEEE (2000)
2. Goldberg, H.R., McKhann, G.M.: Student Test Scores are Improved in a Virtual Learning Environment. Advance Physiological Education 23, 59–66 (2000)
3. Demian, P., Morrice, J.: The Use of Virtual Learning Environments and their Impact on Academic Performance. Engineering Education 7, 11–19 (2012)
4. Romero, C., Ventura, S., García, E.: Data Mining in Course Management Systems: Moodle Case Study and Tutorial. Computers & Education 51, 368–384 (2008)
5. Koulocheri, E., Soumplis, A., Xenos, M.: Applying Learning Analytics in an Open Personal Learning Environment: A Quantitative Approach. In: 16th Panhellenic Conference on Informatics (PCI), pp. 290-295 (2012)
6. Murnion, P., Helfert, M.: Learning Analytics and Cloud Computing. In: Jovanovic, J., Chiong, R. (eds.) Technological and Social Environments for Interactive Learning, pp. 419–447. Informing Science Press, Santa Rosa (2013)
7. Fernández-Gallego, B., Lama, M., Vidal, J.C., Mucientes, M.: Learning Analytics Framework for Educational Virtual Worlds. Procedia Computer Science 25, 443–447 (2013)

8. Tempelaar, D.T., Rienties, B., Giesbers, B.: Computer Assisted, Formative Assessment and Dispositional Learning Analytics in Learning Mathematics and Statistics. In: Kalz, M., Ras, E. (eds.) CAA 2014. CCIS, vol. 439, pp. 67–78. Springer, Heidelberg (2014)

9. Kapros, E., Peirce, N.: Empowering L&D Managers through Customisation of Inline Learning Analytics. In: Zaphiris, P., Ioannou, A. (eds.) LCT 2014, Part I. LNCS, vol. 8523, pp. 282–291. Springer, Heidelberg (2014)

10. Gutl, C., Pirker, J.: Implementation and evaluation of a collaborative learning, training and networking environment for start-up entrepreneurs in virtual 3D worlds. In: 14th International Conference on Interactive Collaborative Learning (ICL), pp. 58-66 (2011)

11. Richards, D., Jacobson, M.J., Porte, J., Taylor, C., Taylor, M., Newstead, A., Kelaiah, I., Hanna, N.: Evaluating the Models and Behaviour of 3d Intelligent Virtual Animals in a Predator-Prey Relationship. In: The 11th International Conference on Autonomous Agents and Multiagent Systems (AAMAS 2012)-, Valencia, Spain, vol. 1, pp. 79–86 (2012)

12. Hillman, D.C., Willis, D.J., Gunawardena, C.N.: Learner–Interface Interaction in Distance Education: An Extension of Contemporary Models and Strategies for Practitioners. American Journal of Distance Education 8, 30–42 (1994)

13. Hanna, N., Richards, D., Jacobson, M.J.: Automatic Acquisition of User Models of Interaction to Evaluate the Usability of Virtual Environments. In: Richards, D., Kang, B.H. (eds.) PKAW 2012. LNCS, vol. 7457, pp. 43–57. Springer, Heidelberg (2012)

14. Niemann, K., Schmitz, H.-C., Scheffel, M., Wolpers, M.: Usage Contexts for Object Similarity: Exploratory Investigations. In: Proceedings of the 1st International Conference on Learning Analytics and Knowledge, pp. 81–85. ACM, Banff (2011)

15. Lockyer, L., Dawson, S.: Learning Designs and Learning Analytics. In: Proceedings of the 1st International Conference on Learning Analytics and Knowledge, pp. 153–156. ACM, Banff (2011)

16. Fancsali, S.E.: Variable construction for predictive and causal modeling of online education data. In: Proceedings of the 1st International Conference on Learning Analytics and Knowledge, pp. 54–63. ACM, Banff (2011)

17. http://www.educause.edu/ero/article/penetrating-fog-analytics-learning-and-education

18. Falakmasir, M.H., Habibi, J.: Using Educational Data Mining Methods to Study the Impact of Virtual Classroom in E-Learning. In: The 3rd International Conference on Educational Data Mining (EDM 2010), Pittsburgh, PA, pp. 241–248 (2010)

19. Smith, V.C., Lange, A., Huston, D.R.: Predictive Modeling to Forecast Student Outcomes and Drive Effective Interventions in Online Community College Courses. Journal of Asynchronous Learning Network 16, 51–61 (2012)

20. Macfadyen, L.P., Dawson, S.: Numbers are not Enough: Why e-learning Analytics Failed to Inform an institutional Strategic Plan. Educational Technology & Society 15, 149–163 (2012)

21. Manaei-Bidgoli, B., Kashy, D.A., Kortmeyer, G., Punch, W.: Predicting student performance: An application of data mining methods with an educational web-based system (LON-CAPA). In: ASEE/IEEE Frontiers in Education Conference. IEEE, Boulder (2003)

22. Agudo-Peregrina, A.F., Hernandez-Garcia, A., Iglesias-Pradas, S.: Predicting academic performance with learning analytics in virtual learning environments: A comparative study of three interaction classifications. In: 2012 International Symposium on Computers in Education (SIIE), pp. 1–6 (2012)

23. Lee, E.A.-L., Wong, K.W., Fung, C.C.: Learning with Virtual Reality: Its Effects on Students with Different Learning Styles. In: Pan, Z., Cheok, A.D., Müller, W., Zhang, X., Wong, K. (eds.) Transactions on Edutainment IV. LNCS, vol. 6250, pp. 79–90. Springer, Heidelberg (2010)

24. Pathak, S.A., Jacobson, M.J., Kim, B., Zhang, B., Deng, F.: Learning the Physics of Electricity with Agent-Based Models: The Paradox of Productive Failure. In: Chan, T.-W., Biswas, G., Chen, F.-C., Chen, S., Chou, C., Ja-cobson, M., Kinshuk, F.K., Looi, C.-K., Mitrovic, T., Mizoguchi, R., Nakabayashi, K., Reimann, P., Suthers, D., Yang, S., Yang, J.-C. (eds.) International Conference on Computers in Education, pp. 221–228 (2008)

25. Zhang, Y., Yu, X., Dang, Y., Chen, H.: An Integrated Framework for Avatar Data Collection from the Virtual World. IEEE Intelligent Systems 25, 17–23 (2010)

26. Hanna, N., Richards, D., Jacobson, M.J.: Automatic Acquisition of User Models of Interaction to Evaluate the Usability of Virtual Environments. In: Richards, D., Kang, B.H. (eds.) PKAW 2012. LNCS, vol. 7457, pp. 43–57. Springer, Heidelberg (2012)

27. Callaghan, M., McShane, N., Gomez Eguiluz, A.: Using game analytics to measure student engagement/retention for engineering education. In: 2014 11th International Conference on Remote Engineering and Virtual Instrumentation (REV), pp. 297-302 (2014)

28. Retalis, S., Papasalouros, A., Psaromiligkos, Y., Siscos, S., Kargidis, T.: Towards Networked Learning Analytics – A Concept and a Tool. In: The 5th International Conference on Networked Learning Lancaster University (2006)

29. Mazza, R., Milani, C.: Exploring Usage Analysis in Learning Systems: Gaining Insights from Visualisations. In: AIED 2005 Workshop on Usage Analysis in Learning Systems, pp. 65–72 (2005)

30. Schmidt, M., Laffey, J.: Visualizing Behavioral Data from a 3D Virtual Learning Environment: A Preliminary Study. In: 45th Hawaii International Conference on System Science (HICSS), pp. 3387–3394 (2012)

31. Piccoli, G., Ahmad, R., Ives, B.: Web-Based virtual learning environments: a research framekwork and a preliminary assessment of effectiveness in basic IT skills training. MIS Q. 25, 401–426 (2001)

32. Shulman, L.S., Keislar, E.R.: Learning by Discovery: a Critical Appraisal. Rand McNally, Chicago (1966)

33. Mayer, R.: Should there be a three-strikes rule against pure discovery learning? The case for guided methods of instruction. American Psychologist 59, 14–19 (2004)

34. Goo, J.J., Park, K.S., Lee, M., Park, J., Hahn, M., Ahn, H., Picard, R.W.: Effects of Guided and Unguided Style Learning on User Attention in a Virtual Environment. In: Pan, Z., Aylett, R.S., Diener, H., Jin, X., Göbel, S., Li, L. (eds.) Edutainment 2006. LNCS, vol. 3942, pp. 1208–1222. Springer, Heidelberg (2006)

35. Lin, M.-C., Tutwiler, M.S., Chang, C.-Y.: Exploring the relationship between virtual learning environment preference, use, and learning outcomes in 10th grade earth science students. Learning, Media and Technology 36, 399–417 (2011)

36. Umar, I.N., Maswan, S.: The Effects of Guided Inquiry Approach in a Web-based Learning Environment on the Achievement of Students with Different Cognitive Style. In: 6th International Conference on Advanced Learning Technologies, pp. 959–963 (2006)

37. Kapur, M.: Productive Failure. Cognition and Instruction 26, 379–424 (2008)

The Performance of Objective Functions for Clustering Categorical Data[⋆]

Zhengrong Xiang[1] and Md Zahidul Islam[2]

[1] College of Computer Science, Zhejiang University, China
zolaxiang@gmail.com
[2] School of Computing and Mathematics, Charles Sturt University, Australia
zislam@csu.edu.au

Abstract. Partitioning methods, such as k-means, are popular and useful for clustering. Recently we proposed a new partitioning method for clustering categorical data: using the transfer algorithm to optimize an objective function called within-cluster dispersion. Preliminary experimental results showed that this method outperforms a standard method called k-modes, in terms of the average quality of clustering results. In this paper, we make more advanced efforts to compare the performance of objective functions for categorical data. First we analytically compare the quality of three objective functions: k-medoids, k-modes and within-cluster dispersion. Secondly we measure how well these objectives find true structures in real data sets, by finding their global optima, which we argue is a better measurement than average clustering results. The conclusion is that within-cluster dispersion is generally a better objective for discovering cluster structures. Moreover, we evaluate the performance of various distance measures on within-cluster dispersion, and give some useful observations.

Keywords: Objective Function, Clustering, Categorical data, Transfer algorithm.

1 Introduction

Clustering is an important task in data mining [1,2]. A basic idea is that objects in the same cluster are similar to each other. Usually clustering is for discovering natural structures in data. There are also utility reasons like compression or summarization. Among different clustering schemes, partitioning methods such as k-means [3] and k-medoids [1] are extremely popular in practice. They define objective functions to be the goal of clustering, and they have heuristic algorithms to optimize the objective. In this paper, the objective functions we discuss are all from partitioning methods.

Clustering for categorical data can be different from numerical data, because the distance measures for categorical data has a different nature. For example,

---

[⋆] The second author would like to thank the Faculty of Business Compact Fund R4 P55 in Charles Sturt University, Australia.

Y.S. Kim et al (Eds.): PKAW 2014, LNCS 8863, pp. 16–28, 2014.
© Springer International Publishing Switzerland 2014

the definition of center in k-means does not directly apply for categorical data. In this regard, k-modes [4] is designed specifically for categorical data in the framework of partitioning methods. It has a different definition of center than k-means, but the optimization algorithm is similar.

Recently another partitioning method [5] for clustering categorical data is proposed. The objective function is called within-cluster dispersion, and it emphasizes pairwise similarities between objects in a cluster. The optimization method is a version of transfer algorithm [6], which is a general procedure for optimizing any form of objective functions. This method is as efficient as k-modes but produces clustering results with better average quality.

In this paper, we focus on comparing the performance of three major objective functions for categorical data: k-medoids, k-modes and within-cluster dispersion. We analyze what kind of cluster structures those objectives define and experiment on how good they cluster real data sets. We measure the performance with respect to global optima, which we argue is a more convincing way to decide the goodness of objective functions.

One advantage of the within-cluster dispersion objective is that it can be used with any distance measures. In practice, it gives flexibilty for users. We can use different measures to achieve multiple clustering results [7]. Then we can either choose a best result or learn from different perspectives. It will be interesting to know how different distance measures affect clustering results when using this objective.

Another reason for evaluating performance of distance measures is the lack of study in this topic. For numerical data, the distance measure is usually Minkowski distance. For categorical data, it remains a open question. There has been a study [8] comparing distance measures on the task of outlier detection, but no study has been conducted on the task of clustering. In this paper, we show within-cluster dispersion is an objective function of good quality, thus evaluating distances on this objective is something significant to carry out.

Contributions of this paper are:

1. For partitioning methods in clustering categorical data, we analyze the quality of three objective functions: k-medoids, k-modes and within-cluster dispersion. The main conclusion is that within-cluster dispersion discovers structures better than the other two.
2. Various benchmark data sets are used to evaluate the performance of the three objective functions. We compare the global optima rather than average clustering results, to make the comparison more convincing. The results are consistent with our analysis.
3. On the within-cluster dispersion objective, we evaluate the performance of various data-driven distance measures and provide some useful observations.

2   Related Work

The objective functions we discuss here are from partitioning relocation clustering methods. They are highly efficient, and easily explainable because of clear goals defined by objective functions. K-means is most popular and typical, which is usually for numerical data. For categorical data, three major algorithms are k-medoids, k-modes and the transfer algorithm.

The algorithm of k-medoids [1] has the same structure as k-means, except that the centers of clusters are medoids. A medoid is defined to be the object whose sum of distances to other objects is minimal. One advantage of k-medoids over k-means is that the medoid can be computed with respect to any distance measures.

K-modes [4,9] is also a k-means-like algorithm, but it's specifically used for categorical data. The center here is called mode. It takes the same form as an object, with each attribute value being the most frequent value in the cluster.

Recently another method is proposed to use transfer algorithm for clustering categorical data [5]. The objective, called within-cluster dispersion, is traditionally a cluster evaluation measure [10]. With the appropriate design of the transfer algorithm, the objective can be locally optimized as efficient as k-modes. The average of clustering results shows that this method discovers more real structures than k-modes.

For numerical data, there have been empirical performance evaluations of various objective functions. Some evidence suggest that the classical k-means objective performs better than others, although the k-means objective tends to result in clusters of approximately the same size and shape [3].

For performance evaluation of data-driven distance measures of categorical data, there is some good work in [8]. They bring together fourteen distance measures, and evaluated them in the task of outlier detection.

Books on cluster analysis [2,10] usually do not include these data-driven distance measures. They discuss more about measures for binary data that are independent from data sets, while data-driven distances use helpful information from data sets.

Some clustering algorithms define distance measures based on neighbors [11,12]. Definition of neighbor uses simple distance measures like the simple matching distance. The distances we use here are different, in that they directly calculate the distances between two objects.

3   Quality Analysis of Objective Functions

3.1   Perspective of Cluster Structures

For the objective function of k-means, there is an equivalence as follows:

$$\sum_{k=1}^{K} \sum_{i \in C_k} \left(x_i - \overline{x}^{(k)} \right)^2 = \sum_{k=1}^{K} \frac{1}{2n_k} \sum_{i \in C_k} \sum_{j \in C_k} (x_i - x_j)^2 \tag{1}$$

In the equation, K is the number of clusters, x_i is the ith object of a data set. For the simplicity of notations, we assume the data is one-dimensional. $\overline{x}^{(k)}$ is the mean of cluster k. n_k is the number of objects in cluster k.

The left side of the equation is based on centers, while the right side of the equation computes all pairwise distances between objects in the same cluster. Because the k-means algorithm is closely related to centers (assign objects to nearest cluster center and update centers), the perspective reflected by the right side of the equation is often neglected. It's actually an important perspective and a basic idea of cluster definition: objects in a cluster are similar with each other. This definition is obviously very useful because k-means has been proved to be very successful in discovering structures in many applications.

The objective of within-cluster dispersion is the same as the right side of equation (1), except that it replaces the squared Euclidean distance with a general distance measure for categorical data. See equation (2). So within-cluster dispersion also defines clusters by calculating pairwise similarities between all objects in a cluster (Figure 2).

$$Dispersion = \sum_{k=1}^{K} \frac{1}{n_k} \sum_{i \in C_k} \sum_{j \in C_k} d(x_i, x_j) \tag{2}$$

Now let's check k-medoids and k-modes from this perspective. Their objective functions have a same form:

$$\sum_{k=1}^{K} \sum_{i \in C_k} d(x_i, m_k) \tag{3}$$

Where m_k is medoid and mode respectively for the kth cluster. For k-medoids, the medoid is defined to be one of the objects that minimizes the sum of distances, thus its objective function sums over much less number of distances than all pairwise distances (see the comparison between Figure 1 and Figure 2).

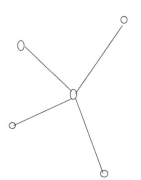

Fig. 1. Star Structure of K-medoids

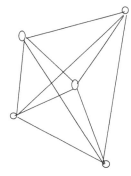

Fig. 2. Net Structure of Within-cluster Dispersion

For k-modes, the way objects connect with each other is a little more complicated. The mode is not necessarily a real object like a medoid, but a virtual object: each attribute of a mode can take any value from that attribute. The mode is chosen to minimize the sum of distances from objects in the respective cluster to the mode. On each attribute of a mode, the value minimizes the sum of distanes between values of objects and the value of the mode. So for each attribute, k-modes is like doing a one-dimensional k-medoids (except that some one-dimensional objects are duplicated).

In the following example, we assume the data has two attributes. In Figure 3, assume object x_1 and object x_2 have a same attribute value. Also reasonably assume that this value is the most frequent value on the first attribute, thus it's the minimizer. So all other objects are connected to these two objects because these pairs of distances are included in the objective function. We used dashed lines to represent a "partial connection" because the connection is only on one attribute rather than both attributes. In Figure 4, x_2 and x_3 have the minimizer value on the second attribute, and dashed lines are similarly connected. In Figure 5, we add the effects of two attributes together to get the whole picture of how objects interact. For a pair of objects, if there are dashed lines in both Figure 3 and Figure 4, a solid line is plotted in Figure 5 meaning that they have full connection. From Figure 5, we can see that the k-modes considers only a part of the pairwise distances as in the case of within-cluster dispersion.

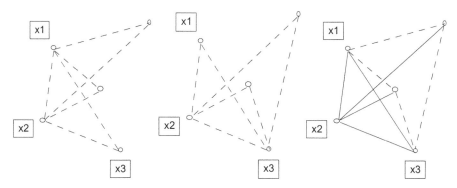

Fig. 3. K-modes on the First Attribute

Fig. 4. K-modes on the Second Attribute

Fig. 5. Adding up Figure 3 and Figure 4: Partial-Net Structure of k-modes

We have presented the different cluster structures that three objectives define. Now the question is which cluster structure is more dominant in real data sets, because in exploratory data analysis, we want to find the natural structures in data. In the fully connected net structure, all objects are supposed to be similar with each other. It's a more compact cluster than k-modes and k-medoids. If real-life clusters are such good quality clusters, then within-cluster dispersion is better suited to discover them. One way to know what real-life clusters are like is to look at k-means. K-means defines clusters to be the net structure and k-means is widely recognized as being successful.

Another argument from us is that the net structure is more dominant because that's how objects in natural clusters interact with each other. For populations of plants, pollination happens to all adjacent plants. For a human society, people are constantly moving and communicating with others. Objects interact with many others that are near them, not with only one "central" object. In this reasoning, within-cluster dispersion also performs better than k-modes, and k-modes better than k-medoids.

In the experiment section, we show the superiority of within-cluster dispersion at discovering structures in real data sets.

3.2   Perspective of Informativeness

In this perspective, we compare how informative the objective functions are in terms of describing clusters. From the discussion of cluster structures, we can see that the computation of within-cluster dispersion involves the most amount of distances/similarities. Obviously, the more distances computed, the more information an objective provides.

We can also reach this conclusion by comparing the centers of the objective functions. Within-cluster dispersion can also be written in a center-based form. We use simple matching distance to illustrate. Simple matching distance between objects x and y on d attributes is defined as:

$$d(x,y) = \sum_{j=1}^{d} d_j(x_j, y_j) \quad d_j(x_j, y_j) = \begin{cases} 0 & \text{if } x_j = y_j \\ 1 & \text{otherwise} \end{cases} \tag{4}$$

If we transform the categorical data into binary data, and treat the binary data as numerical data, then within-cluster dispersion on the original data is equivalent to the objective function of k-means on the transformed data. This is because simple matching distance is essentially equivalent to Euclidean distance on 0/1 data. So the center of k-means is our virtual "center" for within-cluster dispersion. Obviously, the dimension of the center is the same as the number of all attribute values, and the entry on each dimension is proportional to the number of objects taking the respective attribute value:

$$\left(\frac{f(A_{11})}{N}, ..., \frac{f(A_{1p_1})}{N}, ..., \frac{f(A_{d1})}{N}, ..., \frac{f(A_{dp_d})}{N} \right) \tag{5}$$

Where A_{ij} denotes the jth value of the ith attribute, and $f(A_{ij})$ is the number of objects taking value A_{ij}, N being the total number of objects, p_d being the number of values in attribute A_d.

This center obviously has more information than the centers of k-modes and k-medoids. For each attribute, k-modes takes the attribute value with the biggest entry in vector (5), while k-medoids restricts the values to be from one real object. So although mode and medoid both have the same dimension as the number of attributes, mode has more significant information. If we see objective functions as a measure for the information in clusters, the more informative an objective is, the better. In this sense, within-cluster dispersion is the best, and k-modes better than k-medoids.

Informativeness means how well an objective can distinguish the quality of a cluster. If a distance between two objects is not reflected in the objective, changing it might not affect the value of the objective. Thus the two clusters before and after change are not distinguished by the objective. In practice, lacking the ability to distinguish between clusters can result in a problem: for a single objective value, several different structures are found. If this objective value is the minimum and chosen to be the best result, there are no apparent ways to choose one structure among several options.

Note that there is no way to strictly prove that one objective function is better than another one. The reason is that clustering in real data sets can be arbitrary. That's why there are so many different clustering methods that define different concepts of clusters. For one data set, say an objective function A finds structure S_A, and it's better than S_B found by objective B. However, we can always change the data labels to something else (creating a new data set), so that B performs better than A. So to summarize this section, the argument we are trying to make is: within-cluster dispersion is "generally" better than the other two objectives.

4   Distance Measures

One advantage of within-cluster dispersion over k-modes is that it doesn't define a specific distance measure. Since within-cluster dispersion is a very good objective function, it is useful to evaluate how different distance measures affect its clustering performance. In this section, we introduce the distance measures [8] we use for evaluation.

The limitation of the simple matching distance is that it treats all categorical values the same. Data-driven measures use the characteristics from a particular data set to define distances. For example, if an attribute of two objects has the same categorical value, and that value is rare in the data set, it might be a good idea to decide that this rare match shows more similarity (less distance).

Assume a data set has N objects, each has d attributes, $A_1, ...A_d$. Then we can use the following information from the data set:

n_k: The number of attribute values for attribute A_k.

$f_k(x)$: The number of times (frequency) attribute value x appears in attribute A_k.

$\hat{p}_k(x)$: The sample probability of attribute A_k takes value x, given by: $f_k(x)/N$.

$p_k^2(x)$: Another probability measure of attribute A_k takes value x, given by:

$$p_k^2(x) = \frac{f_k(x)(f_k(x) - 1)}{N(N - 1)} \tag{6}$$

From Boriah [8], some of the measures are distance measures in the original form. They can be directly applied here. For others, we use a simple but effective way to transform similarity measures into distance:

$$distance = 1 - similarity \tag{7}$$

All the measures are calculated by summing over per-attribute distances:

$$d(X, Y) = \sum_{k=1}^{d} d_k(X_k, Y_k) \tag{8}$$

The measures are listed in Table 1. They have different ideas of how to incorporate the characteristics of a data set. For example, IOF says that mismatches between higher frequency values are stronger, thus a larger distance is assigned. Some of the measures from [8] are too complicated and they have similar ideas about how to use the information in data sets. These measures are not included in our study. Note that for all these measures, the transfer algorithm can be carried out in a time complexity that is linear to data size N.

5   Experiments

5.1   Quality of Objective Functions

In Section 3, the conclusion of the analysis is that the within-cluster dispersion discovers better (more real) structures than k-medoids and k-modes. In this section, the goal is to evaluate the objective functions with real data sets. If the structures an objective discovered fit well with the real clusters, then it's a good objective.

The data sets we use are from UCI machine learning repository [13]. Their characteristics are listed in Table 2. There are more than 5 categorical data sets in UCI repositary. We didn't include more data sets to the experiment because real data sets can be hard for all three objective functions to handle. For example, if objects in a real cluster (class) are hardly similar with others, any clustering methods don't work. The 5 data sets we do have are more or less suitable for the task of cluster analysis, but they are not deliberately chosen in favor of any of the three objectives.

In this paper we compare the quality of different objective functions when their global optima are reached. One other option is to compare average clustering results, which means the average of any optima (global or local) when the algorithms converged. We argue that global optimum is a better criterion for deciding the goodness of objective functions. There are two reasons. One is that the quality of local optima depends on the optimization algorithm. For example, in k-means, Hartigan's method finds better optima than the common Lloyd's method [14,15]. However, the thing we want to find out is how good the objective function is, not the goodness of the optimization algorithm. Global optimum is the result that an objective function can provide at its best. The other reason is, for heuristic algorithms like k-means, the standard way is to run the algorithm multiple times (say 1000) and pick the result with the minimum

Table 1. Distance Measures For Categorical Data

$Measures$	$d_k(X_k, Y_k)$
$Eskin$	$= \begin{cases} 0; & if\ X_k = Y_k \\ \frac{2}{n_k^2}; & otherwise \end{cases}$
IOF	$= \begin{cases} 0; & if\ X_k = Y_k \\ \log f_k(X_k) log f_k(Y_k); & otherwise \end{cases}$
OF	$= \begin{cases} 0; & if\ X_k = Y_k \\ \log \frac{N}{f_k(X_k)} log \frac{N}{f_k(Y_k)}; & otherwise \end{cases}$
$Goodall1$	$= \begin{cases} \sum_{q \in Q} p_k^2(q); & if\ X_k = Y_k \\ 1; & otherwise \end{cases}$ $\{Q \subseteq A_k : \forall q \in Q, p_k(q) \leq p_k(X_k)\}$
$Goodall2$	$= \begin{cases} \sum_{q \in Q} p_k^2(q); & if\ X_k = Y_k \\ 1; & otherwise \end{cases}$ $\{Q \subseteq A_k : \forall q \in Q, p_k(q) \geq p_k(X_k)\}$
$Goodall3$	$= \begin{cases} p_k^2(X_k); & if\ X_k = Y_k \\ 1; & otherwise \end{cases}$
$Goodall4$	$= \begin{cases} 1 - p_k^2(X_k); & if\ X_k = Y_k \\ 1; & otherwise \end{cases}$
$Gambaryan$	$= \begin{cases} 1 + \hat{p}_k(X_k) \log_2 \hat{p}_k(X_k) + \\ (1 - \hat{p}_k(X_k)) \log_2 (1 - \hat{p}_k(X_k)); & if\ X_k = Y_k \\ 1; & otherwise \end{cases}$

Table 2. Characteristics of Benchmark Data Sets

	Mushroom	Congress	Promoter	Soybean	Splice
Number of Objects	8124	435	106	47	3190
Number of Attributes	22	16	58	35	61
Number of Classes	2	2	2	4	3

objective value. As the computing power grows in modern days, the best result from thousands of runs is very likely to be the global optima [16].

In our experiment, in order to increase the chance of finding the global optima, we run the algorithms for as many times as possible. Note that we use random initial conditions to make the clustering results as diverse as possible. Although we can not be 100% sure that global optima are found, but it's very likely to be true: for all data sets the optima we get from 1000 runs are already highly duplicated.

The results are shown in Table 3 and Table 4. In Table 3, different numbers of clusters are set on the Mushroom data set. In Table 4, the number of clusters of the four data sets is the same as the number of true clusters(classes). The performance measure is purity [10] (also called accuracy in literature like [17]), which measures how well cluster results correspond to real structures in data sets. a_k is the number of objects from the most dominant class in cluster k.

$$Purity = \frac{\sum_{k=1}^{K} a_k}{N} \qquad (9)$$

From the results, we can see that within-cluster dispersion outperforms the other two, which is consistent with the analysis in Section 3. We can also see that in most cases, k-modes outperforms k-medoids. This is also reflected in our analysis: k-modes defines a more real cluster structure than k-medoids.

Table 3. Clustering Performance of Three Objectives on Mushroom Data Set

	k=2	k=3	k=4	k=5	k=6
k-medoids	0.879	0.772	0.854	0.85	0.855
k-modes	0.891	0.719	0.856	0.888	0.888
Dispersion	**0.892**	**0.894**	**0.894**	**0.894**	**0.894**

Table 4. Clustering Performance of Three Objectives on Four Data Sets

	Soybean	Promoter	Congress	Splice
k-medoids	0.936	0.864	0.509	0.519
k-modes	1	0.864	0.528	0.519
Dispersion	1	**0.880**	**0.623**	**0.845**

In Section 3.2, we mentioned that due to the uninformativeness of k-modes and k-medoids, different clustering structures can have a same value of objective function. This problem is exposed in the experiments on real data sets. For example, using k-modes in the Mushroom data set (number of clusters set to 2), for a local optimum of 62534, some results have an accuracy of 0.871, others have an accuracy of 0.884. In practice, if this kind of local optimum happens to be the minimum after some runs, it's a problem for users to choose among different clusterings.

5.2   Evaluation of Distance Measures

We evaluated nine data-driven distance measures on the five benchmark data sets in Table 2. The results are shown in Table 5 and Table 6. Again, the goodness of discovered structure is measured by purity. In Table 5 the results are averaged from 1000 runs, while in Table 6, the results are recorded when global optima are achieved. Although the number of data sets is not quite big, but we can still make some interesting observations:

1. For one data set, different distance measures can have significantly different performances in discovering structures. For example, for the Mushroom data set, Eskin is a lot worse than IOF. So it's important to choose a suitable measure for a particular data set.

2. For data sets of a similar nature, distance measures can have consistent performances. For example, Goodall4 is good for two gene data sets (Promoter and Splice). OF is not good for the two plant data sets (Mushroom and Soybean in Table 6). So in practice, we can use the knowledge from previous data sets to make the choice of an appropriate distance.

3. Distances with opposite philosophies have significantly different results over one data set. For example, the performance of Goodall3 and Goodall4 on data set Splice. This is easily expected and in practice, if one measure doesn't work well, it's a good idea to choose an "opposite" one.

4. No distance measure performs badly across all data sets. For example, OF has bad performance on most data sets. But for the Congress data set, it is the best measure. This implies that these various distance measures can all somehow be useful, and they are worth a try in practical clustering tasks.

Table 5. Average Performance of Different Distance Measures

	Mushroom	Congress	Promoter	Soybean	Splice
SMD	0.7534	0.8805	0.8022	0.9650	0.8392
Eskin	0.7856	0.8805	0.8035	0.9122	0.8384
IOF	0.8182	0.8805	0.8160	0.9656	0.8687
OF	**0.8352**	**0.8828**	0.5881	0.8875	0.5972
Goodall1	0.7435	0.8805	0.7874	0.9350	0.7523
Goodall2	0.7404	0.8805	0.7663	0.9192	0.7430
Goodall3	0.7580	0.8805	0.7761	**0.9698**	0.7415
Goodall4	0.7480	0.8805	**0.9528**	0.9600	**0.8919**
Gambaryan	0.7652	0.8805	0.8226	0.9583	0.8707

Table 6. Performance of Different Distance Measures with Respect to Global Optima

	Mushroom	Congress	Promoter	Soybean	Splice
SMD	0.8922	0.8805	0.6226	1	0.8445
Eskin	0.8385	0.8805	0.6226	1	0.8455
IOF	**0.8987**	0.8805	0.6226	1	0.8774
OF	0.8469	**0.8828**	0.6226	0.8511	0.6009
Goodall1	0.8978	0.8805	0.6321	1	0.7520
Goodall2	0.8936	0.8805	0.6226	1	0.7508
Goodall3	0.8954	0.8805	0.6226	1	0.7455
Goodall4	0.8865	0.8805	**0.9528**	1	0.8928
Gambaryan	0.8912	0.8805	0.6226	1	**0.8962**

6   Conclusions

In this paper, we focused on the performance of objective functions for clustering categorical data. First, we analyzed the quality of three objective functions, by presenting what kind of structures each of them define, and how informative they are to measure cluster quality. Our conclusion is that within-cluster dispersion is generally better than k-medoids and k-modes for discovering structures. In experiments on benchmark data sets we measure the performance of objectives functions with respect to their global optima, and the results are consistent with the previous analysis. Secondly, for the objective of within-cluster dispersion, we evaluated how various distance measures affect the performance of clustering results. Experiments exposed several interesting insights for the practice of cluster analysis.

References

1. Kaufman, L., Rousseeuw, P.J.: Finding groups in data: an introduction to cluster analysis. John Wiley & Sons (2009)
2. Everitt, B.S., Landau, S., Leese, M., Stahl, D.: Cluster Analysis, 5th edn. John Wiley & Sons (2011)
3. Steinley, D.: K-means clustering: a half - century synthesis. British Journal of Mathematical and Statistical Psychology 59(1), 1–34 (2006)
4. Huang, Z.: Extensions to the k-means algorithm for clustering large data sets with categorical values. Data Mining and Knowledge discovery 2(3), 283–304 (1998)
5. Xiang, Z., Ji, L.: The use of transfer algorithm for clustering categorical data. In: Motoda, H., Wu, Z., Cao, L., Zaiane, O., Yao, M., Wang, W. (eds.) ADMA 2013, Part II. LNCS, vol. 8347, pp. 59–70. Springer, Heidelberg (2013)
6. Banfield, C.F., Bassill, L.C.: Algorithm AS 113. A transfer algorithm for nonhierarchical classification. Applied Statistics 26, 206–210 (1977)
7. Muller, E., Gunnemann, S., Farber, I., et al.: Discovering multiple clustering solutions: Grouping objects in different views of the data. In: 2012 IEEE 28th International Conference on Data Engineering (ICDE), pp. 1207–1210. IEEE (2012)
8. Boriah, S., Chandola, V., Kumar, V.: Similarity measures for categorical data: A comparative evaluation. Red 30(2), 3 (2008)
9. Chaturvedi, A., Green, P.E., Caroll, J.D.: K-modes clustering. Journal of Classification 18(1), 35–55 (2001)
10. Pang-Ning, T., Steinbach, M., Kumar, V.: Introduction to data mining. Library of Congress (2006)
11. Guha, S., Rastogi, R., Shim, K.: ROCK: A robust clustering algorithm for categorical attributes. In: Proceedings of 15th International Conference on Data Engineering, pp. 512–521. IEEE (1999)
12. Palmer, C.R., Faloutsos, C.: Electricity based external similarity of categorical attributes. In: Whang, K.-Y., Jeon, J., Shim, K., Srivastava, J. (eds.) PAKDD 2003. LNCS (LNAI), vol. 2637, pp. 486–500. Springer, Heidelberg (2003)
13. Bache, K., Lichman, M.: UCI Machine Learning Repository. University of California, School of Information and Computer Science, Irvine (2013), http://archive.ics.uci.edu/ml

14. Telgarsky, M., Vattani, A.: Hartigan's Method: k-means Clustering without Voronoi. In: International Conference on Artificial Intelligence and Statistics, pp. 820–827 (2010)
15. Slonim, N., Aharoni, E., Crammer, K.: Hartigan's K-means versus Lloyd's K-means: is it time for a change? In: Proceedings of the Twenty-Third International Joint Conference on Artificial Intelligence, pp. 1677–1684. AAAI Press (2013)
16. Steinley, D.: Local optima in K-means clustering: what you don't know hurt you. Psychological Methods 8(3), 294 (2003)
17. Ng, M.K., Li, M.J., Huang, J.Z., et al.: On the impact of dissimilarity measure in k-modes clustering algorithm. IEEE Transactions on Pattern Analysis and Machine Intelligence 29(3), 503–507 (2007)

Modeling of Operating Photovoltaic Module Temperature Using Hybrid Cuckoo and Artificial Neural Network

Shahril Irwan Sulaiman[1], Nur Zahidah Zainol[1], Zulkifli Othman[1], and Hedzlin Zainuddin[2]

[1] Faculty of Electrical Engineering, Universiti Teknologi MARA, 40450 Shah Alam, Selangor, Malaysia
shahril_irwan2004@yahoo.com
[2] Faculty of Applied Sciences, Universiti Teknologi MARA, 40450 Shah Alam, Selangor, Malaysia

Abstract. Photovoltaic (PV) module temperature is an important parameter in PV system operation as the system output power decreases as the module temperature increases. Therefore, the modeling of operating PV module temperature is crucial to understand the climatic factors which contribute to the variation of the PV module temperature. This paper presents the modeling of operating PV module temperature from a Grid-Connected Photovoltaic (GCPV) system located at Green Energy Research Centre (GERC), Universiti Teknologi MARA, Malaysia. An Artificial Neural Network (ANN) was developed to model the operating PV module temperature with solar irradiance and ambient temperature set as the ANN inputs. In addition, Cuckoo Search (CS) was introduced to search for the optimal number of neurons of ANN hidden layer, learning rate and momentum rate such that the Mean Absolute Percentage Error (MAPE) of the modeling process could be minimized. The results showed that CS had outperformed an Artificial Bee Colony (ABC) algorithm for the ANN training optimization by producing lower MAPE.

Keywords: Operating photovoltaic module temperature, modeling, Artificial Neural Network, Cuckoo Search, Mean Absolute Percentage Error.

1 Introduction

Solar energy is reported to be one of the fastest growing types of renewable energy worldwide [1]. The usage of solar energy in electricity generation is executed using photovoltaic (PV) modules which have become the primary component of a PV system. A PV module basically consists of solar cells that are commonly connected in series to provide the required voltage and current. These cells convert sunlight into DC electricity which will be later channeled to either an inverter in a Grid-Connected Photovoltaic (GCPV) system for power conditioning purpose or both storage and power conditioning in a Stand-Alone Photovoltaic (SAPV) system.

Y.S. Kim et al (Eds.): PKAW 2014, LNCS 8863, pp. 29–37, 2014.

As solar irradiance increases throughout the day, the ambient temperature correspondingly increases and this subsequently heats up the cells in a PV module. The heating of these solar cells causes the operating PV module temperature, MT to rise gradually. Increasing MT would result in decreasing output voltage of the PV module, and thus reducing the output power from the module. Due to the significant role of MT, several studies had been conducted to model the MT. A review of different mathematical models for MT had been presented [2]. These models were developed based on different factors, i.e. the thermal and physical properties of PV modules, the solar irradiance and other weather parameters, as well as the heat transfer coefficient due to wind. As a result, every model is only applicable for specific conditions covered by the specific factors [3]. Apart from that, these models were formulated using linear mathematical relationship, thus limiting the practicality of the models because any change in MT does not occur instantaneously since any changes in temperature frequently lags behind the changes in solar irradiance [4].

Due to the limitations described earlier, an Artificial Neural Network (ANN) for modeling MT is presented in this study. ANN is a modeling tool which is inspired by biological nervous system. The execution of ANN is unique such that no mathematical models or pre-assumptions are required in its development [5]. Therefore, this feature would offer strong advantage in modeling of MT since no information regarding the thermal and physical properties of PV modules, and the heat transfer coefficient due to wind are required for the modeling process. In addition, ANN is also capable for both linear and non-linear modeling [6]. Hence, the modeling of MT can be performed merely using solar irradiance and other weather parameters without knowing the mathematical relationship among these weather parameters.

Although ANN possesses distinctive advantages compared to conventional mathematical models, one of the difficulties in ANN implementation is the selection of the optimal training parameters such as the number of neurons in the hidden layer, the learning rate and the momentum rate. These parameters are commonly determined using trial-and-error method that can be tedious and time consuming [7]. Therefore, different Computational Intelligence (CI) had been introduced to facilitate the search for these optimal ANN training parameters [8-9]. In this study, a Cuckoo Search (CS) had been used to search for the optimal number of neurons in hidden layer, the optimal learning rate and the optimal momentum rate such that the modeling error could be minimized.

2   Methodology

The CS-ANN was implemented in a few stages. Firstly, an ANN model was created for modeling the MT of a PV array from a GCPV system. Then, the input and output data of the ANN were collected for the learning process. Later, a hybrid CS-ANN was developed to optimize the ANN training parameters. Finally, the CS-ANN was compared with an Artificial Bee Colony (ABC)-ANN in terms of modeling error for benchmarking purpose.

2.1   Multi-Layer Feedforward Neural Network

In this study, the Multi-Layer Feedforward Neural Network (MLFNN) with a single hidden layer had been selected as the ANN architecture since it has been used to solve many complex problems of industry [10]. The inputs to the ANN were set to be the solar irradiance (SI) in Wm^{-2} and ambient temperature (AT) in °C while operating PV module temperature (MT) in °C was set to be the output of the MLFNN, as illustrated in Fig. 1. The MLFNN was developed in two stages, i.e. the training and testing processes, which were performed in Matlab.

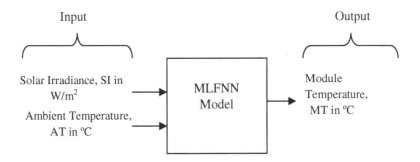

Fig. 1. MLFNN for modeling operating PV module temperature

During training of MLFNN, the number of neurons in the hidden layer, the learning rate, the momentum rate and the learning algorithm are often determined using heuristic method. The heuristic method requires these parameters to be empirically determined using trial-and-error method which can be time consuming and tedious. Therefore, unlike in the heuristic method, these parameters were optimally determined using the CS in this study. Apart from that, different types of learning algorithm were applied in the MLFNN training to determine the most suitable algorithm for the learning scheme. Besides that, the type of activation function at the hidden layer and the output layer were set to be logarithmic sigmoid (LOGSIG) and purely linear (PURELIN) respectively.

2.2   Data Collection

All data comprising SI, AT, MT and Pac were collected from a GCPV system located at the Green Energy Research Centre (GERC), Universiti Teknologi MARA, Shah Alam, Selangor, Malaysia. The system comprises 6 kWp poly-crystalline PV array and a 4.6 kW inverter. The irradiance and temperature sensors were connected to a built-in data logger inside the inverter while all data were recorded at five-minute interval. 70% of the collected data or 2359 data patterns were allocated for MLFNN training whereas the remaining 30% of the collected data or 1010 data patterns had been utilized for the testing process. A summary of the GCPV system specifications is shown in Table 1.

Table 1. System specifications

Parameters	Specification
Type of PV module	Poly-crystalline
PV array configuration	2 string with 13 modules per string
PV array power	6kWp
Type of mounting	Retrofitted
Type of inverter	1 unit X SB5000TL

2.3   Cuckoo Search - ANN

As the routine plan of MLFNN requires far-reaching work and experimentation strategy in figuring out the number of neurons, a hybrid CS-ANN is proposed in this study. CS is a meta-heuristic algorithm inspired by the obligate brood parasitic behavior of a few species of a bird family called Cuckoo [11]. It is a population-based methods derived by emulating the reproduction strategy of cuckoos. Cuckoos commonly lay their eggs in the nests of other birds from different species. Moreover, these cuckoos even tend to destroy the host bird eggs such that the hatching probability of their own eggs increases. Once their own eggs hatch inside the host bird nest, the chicks will be fed by the host birds. However, if the host bird discovered the alien eggs inside its nest, it is most likely abandon the nest or discards the alien eggs from the nest. As a result, cuckoo undergoes an evolution by mimicking the nature of the host birds such that it has better chances to survive in the host bird nest. CS has been successfully used to solve various engineering optimization tasks [12].

In CS, every egg laid by the cuckoo represents a potential solution to an optimization problem. The CS algorithm is developed using three idealized rules:

• Each cuckoo lays only one egg at a time and drops the egg in a randomly chosen nest.
• The best nests with the better quality of eggs will be transcribed to the next generation.
• The probability of an alien egg is discovered by the host bird is from 0 to 1 and the number of available nests is fixed.

The algorithm of CS in an optimization problem [13] can be described as follows:

Step 1: Initialize population of host nests, $x_{i,k}$ where i = 1,2,3,...m, k is the decision variable number, and m is the population size. In addition, the probability of alien egg discovery, Pa and maximum number of iterations are also defined.

Step 2: While maximum number of iterations has not been achieved, move a random cuckoo i from the population via Levy flights. The new position of the cuckoo, x'i,k(t+1) is calculated using

$$x'_{i,k}(t+1) = x_{i,k}(t) + \alpha \oplus Levy(\lambda) \tag{1}$$

where $x_{i,k}(t)$ is the initial position of the cuckoo. α is a positive step size parameter which controls the scale of a random search and is dependent on optimization problem under study. α is determined using

$$\alpha = \alpha_o \left(x_{j,k}(t) - x_{i,k}(t) \right) \tag{2}$$

where $x'_{j,k}(t)$ is the initial position of random cuckoo for k-th decision variable and α_o is a constant.

The symbol $\oplus$ means entry-wise multiplications. Levy flight provides a random walk derived based on Levy distribution:

$$Levy \sim u = t^{1-\lambda} \tag{3}$$

where λ is set between 1 to 2. In this study, λ is set at 1.5.

Step 3: Evaluate the fitness value of the cuckoo i at the new position, F_i.

Step 4: Randomly choose a nest j among the m nests. If fitness of cuckoo j, F_j is worse than F_i, replace cuckoo j with cuckoo i together with the corresponding fitness value.

Step 5: Abandon a fraction of the worse nest with probability P_a while keeping the remaining nests as potential solutions. Then, new nests by the same fraction are built at new locations via Levy flights.

Step 6: Evaluate the fitness value of the new nests.

Step 7: Rank all nests according to the fitness value and determine the current best nest.

Step 8: Repeat step 2 until maximum number of iterations are achieved.

Step 9: Determine the optimal nest based on the best nest from all iterations.

The CS was later hybridized with an ANN for modeling the operating PV module temperature of a GCPV system. CS was used to search for the optimal number of neurons in the hidden layer, the learning rate, the momentum rate and the learning algorithm, which are defined as the decision variables for the optimization problem. On the other hand, the objective function for the optimization problem is to minimize the Mean Absolute Percentage Error (MAPE) of the MT. MAPE is calculated as follows:

$$MAPE = \frac{1}{n} \sum_{p=1}^{n} \left| \frac{A_p - P_p}{A_p} \right| \times 100\% \tag{4}$$

where p is the data pattern number, n is the total number of data patterns, Ap is the actual value of the MT and P_p is the modeled or predicted value of MT.

Upon completion of training process, the network underwent testing process. Then, the performance of the hybrid CS-ANN was compared with the performance of an Artificial Bee Colony (ABC)-ANN for benchmarking purpose.

3   Results and Discussions

The development of CS-ANN for modeling MT was completed in different stages. The first stage involved the investigation of the optimal population size for Cuckoo. The population of Cuckoos was varied from 10 to 100 at 10 increment and the results are shown in Fig. 2. The best population size is 100 as it produced the lowest MAPE of 2.5659 % for the modeling process. In contrast, population of 30 cuckoos produced the highest MAPE of 2.5997 %.

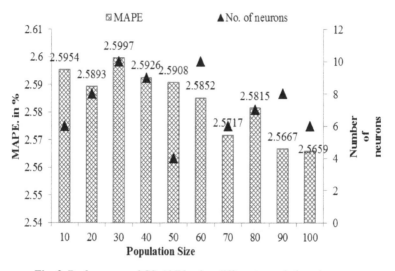

Fig. 2. Performance of CS-ANN using different population size

After determining the population size, the CS-ANN was tested using different learning algorithm to determine the best algorithm for the learning process in ANN. Levenberg-Marquardt algorithm (trainlm), scaled-conjugate gradient algorithm (trainscg), quasi-Newton backpropagation (trainbfg) and resilient backpropagation (trainrp) were used in this investigation and the performance of the CS-ANN with these algorithms are shown in Fig. 3. The learning algorithm which produces the lowest MAPE of 2.5659 % is trainlm, followed by trainbfg, trainscg and trainrp.

Apart from that, the performance of the CS-ANN was compared with the performance of an ABC-ANN for the similar training task. The results of the hybrid ANN training is shown in Table 2. CS-ANN was found to outperform ABC-ANN in terms of producing lower MAPE by approximately 14.76%. In addition, the CS-ANN also requires lower computation time when compared to ABC-ANN. CS-ANN is approximately 1.80 times faster compared to ABC-ANN.

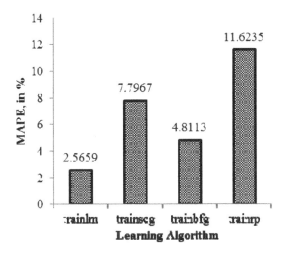

Fig. 3. Performance of CS-ANN using different learning algorithms

Table 2. Optimal ANN parameters and computation time for different hybrid ANNs

Parameters	CS-ANN	ABC-ANN
Optimal number of neurons in hidden layer	6	4
Optimal learning rate	0.4217	0.6382
Optimal momentum rate	0.1000	1.000
Minimum MAPE, in %	2.5659	2.9445
Computation time, hours	2.98	5.36

During testing process, the performance of the CS-ANN and ABC-ANN were again compared in terms of MAPE. A summary of the performance of CS-ANN and ABC-ANN during training and testing is shown in Fig. 3. Similarly, during testing, the CS-ANN had outperformed ABC-ANN by yielding MAPE which is approximately 26.22 % lower compared to ABC-ANN.

Since CS-ANN had produced lower MAPE compared to ABC-ANN during both training and testing stages, CS was discovered to be a more accurate optimizer as compared to ABC in the ANN learning. In fact, CS is also a faster search algorithm when compared to ABC during the hybrid training.

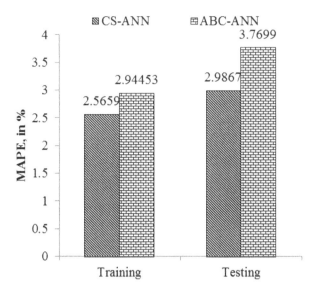

Fig. 4. Performance of CS-ANN and ABC-ANN during training and testing

4   Conclusion

This paper has presented a hybrid CS with ANN for modeling the operating PV module temperature from a PV array of a GCPV system. CS had successfully been used to determine the optimal number of neurons in hidden layer, the learning rate and the momentum rate such that the MAPE of the modeling could be minimized. When compared with the performance of ABC-ANN, the CS-ANN had outperformed the ABC-ANN by yielding a lower MAPE during both training and testing. Moreover, CS-ANN was also found to require lower computation time than ABC-ANN during the optimization task.

Acknowledgment. This work had been supported in part by the Fundamental Research Grant Scheme, Ministry of Education, Malaysia (Ref: 600-RMI/FRGS 5/3 (34/2012) and Ref: FRGS/1/2014/TK06/UITM/02/2)) and Universiti Teknologi MARA, Selangor, Malaysia.

References

1. Tyagi, V.V., Rahim, N.A.A., Rahim, N.A., Selvaraj, J.: Progress in solar PV technology: research and achievement. Renewable and Sustainable Energy Reviews 20, 443–461 (2013)
2. Skoplaki, E., Palyvos, J.A.: On the temperature dependence of photovoltaic module electrical performance: A review of efficiency/power correlations. Solar Energy 83, 614–624 (2009)

3. Dubey, S., Sarvaiya, J.N., Seshadri, B.: Temperature dependent photovoltaic (PV) efficiency and its effect on PV production in the world – a review. Energy Procedia 33, 311–321 (2012)
4. Armstrong, S., Hurley, W.G.: A thermal model for photovoltaic panels under varying atmospheric conditions. Applied Thermal Engineering 30, 1488–1495 (2010)
5. Srivastava, S., Malone, B., Sukhija, N., Banicescu, I., Ciorba, F.M.: Predicting the flexibility of dynamic loop scheduling using an artificial neural network. In: IEEE 12th International Symposium on Parallel and Distributed Computing, pp. 3–10 (2013)
6. Abyaneh, H.Z.: Evaluation of multivariate linear regression and artificial neural networks in prediction of water quality parameters. Journal of Environmental Health Science & Engineering 12, 2–8 (2014)
7. Hussain, T.N., Sulaiman, S.I., Musirin, I., Shaari, S., Zainuddin, H.: A hybrid artificial neural network for grid-connected photovoltaic system output prediction. In: IEEE Symposium on Computers & Informatics, pp. 96–99 (2013)
8. Sulaiman, S.I., Muhammad, K.S., Musirin, I., Shaari, S.: Hybridization of meta-evolutionary programming and artificial neural network for predicting grid-connected photovoltaic system output. In: IEEE Tencon-Spring, pp. 475–479 (2013)
9. Sulaiman, S.I., Muhammad, K.S., Musirin, I., Shaari, S.: Hybridization of meta-evolutionary programming and artificial neural network for predicting grid-connected photovoltaic system output. In: IEEE Tencon-Spring, pp. 475–479 (2013)
10. Zhang, G., Patuwo, B.E., Hu, M.Y.: Forecasting with artificial neural networks: the state of the art. International Journal of Forecasting 14, 35–62 (1998)
11. Kumar, S.R., Ganapathy, S.: Cuckoo search optimization algorithm based load frequency control of interconnected power systems with GDB nonlinearity and SMES units. International Journal of Engineering Inventions 2, 23–28 (2013)
12. Soneji, H.R., Sanghvi, R.C.: Towards the improvement of cuckoo search algorithm. International Journal of Computer Information Systems and Industrial Management Applications 6, 77–88 (2014)
13. Sapra, U.: Solving combined economic and emission dispatch using cuckoo search. International Journal of Engineering Trends and Technology 4, 2544–2549 (2013)

l_p-norm Multiple Kernel Learning with Diversity of Classes

Dayin Zhang[1,2] and Hui Xue[1,2,3,*]

[1] School of Computer Science and Engineering, Southeast University,
Nanjing, 210096, P.R. China
[2] Key Laboratory of Computer Network and Information Integration
(Southeast University), Ministry of Education, Nanjing, 210096, P.R. China
[3] State Key Laboratory for Novel Software Technology, Nanjing University,
Nanjing, 210093, P.R. China
{zhangdayin,hxue}@seu.edu.cn

Abstract. Multiple Kernel Learning (MKL) can learn an appropriate kernel combination from multiple base kernels for classification problems. It is often used to handle binary problems. However, multi-class problems appear in many real applications. In this paper, we propose a novel model, l_p-norm multiple kernel learning with diversity of classes (LMKLDC), for the multi-class multiple kernel learning problem. LMKLDC focuses on diversity of classes and aims to learn different kernel combinations for different classes to enhance the flexibility of our model. LMKLDC also utilizes l_p-norm $(0 < p \leq 1)$ to promote the sparsity. However, LMKLDC boils down to a non-convex optimization problem when $0 < p < 1$. In virtue of the constrained concave convex procedure (CCCP), we convert the non-convex optimization problem into a convex one and present a two-stage optimization algorithm. Experimental results on several datasets show our model selects fewer kernels and improves the classification accuracy.

Keywords: Multiple kernel learning, Multi-class classification, Diversity of classes, l_p-norm.

1 Introduction

So far, Multiple Kernel Learning (MKL) has attracted much attention from the community of machine learning. MKL helps users to select the most suitable kernel for learning problems at hand. Besides, MKL can deal with one case in which there are many heterogeneous data sources, especially in bioinformatics. Related researches include Lanckriet et al. (2004), Bach et al. (2004), Rakotomamonjy et al. (2008), Kloft et al. (2009), Xu et al. (2010) and Xu et al. (2013).

MKL methods above can be applied to the binary learning problem. However, we often face multi-class learning problems in the real world. So it is necessary to design effective MKL algorithms to solve multi-class problems. Such a MKL

---

* Corresponding author.

Y.S. Kim et al (Eds.): PKAW 2014, LNCS 8863, pp. 38–47, 2014.

algorithm is called MCMKL. Zien et al. (2007) proposed a model of MCMKL based on the joint feature maps (Tsochantaridis et al. 2004) and the multi-class loss function (Crammer et al. 2002). Ye et al. (2008) decomposed a multi-class problem into multiple binary problems via some kind of coding. Kumar et al. (2012) converted the classification problem in the original input space into the binary classification problem in the proposed K-space. Recently, Cortes et al. (2013) introduced the notion of multi-class kernel margin and constructed the corresponding MCMKL model. However, most of these MCMKL methods learn the same weights of combining kernels for all classes. When there exists the diversity of classes, doing so seems unreasonable. Especially, as mentioned in (Zien et al. 2007), if the user is only interested in which kernel can distinguish one class from the rest, disadvantages of sharing a common feature space for all classes arise. Hence, it is obvious that learning the same weights for all classes restricts the flexibility of the model and will decrease its classification performance.

In addition, there are some researchers who are interested in enhancing the sparsity of MKL models by constraining different norms of the weights of combining kernels. The sparsity can lower the complexity of MKL models to improve the generalization performance and save the computation cost. In (Lanckriet et al. 2004), (Bach et al. 2004), (Rakotomamonjy et al. 2008) and (Xu et al. 2013), they directly or indirectly used the l_1-norm (it has a better sparsity than l_2-norm) of the weights. In Bach et al. (2008), the equivalence between group lasso and MKL is demonstrated. Szafranski et al. (2010) and Nath et al. (2009) combined MKL with the mixed-norm, still using l_1-norm to promote the sparsity. Basically, many MKL methods constrain l_1-norm of the weights to improve the sparsity of models. However, using l_p-norm $(0 < p < 1)$ can get a better sparsity than using l_1-norm in plenty of computational studies (Chartrand 2007; Chartrand et al. 2008; Xu et al. 2012). So it is worth trying combining MKL and l_p-norm $(0 < p \leq 1)$.

In this paper, we expand MKL to multi-class problems and propose a novel algorithm LMKLDC which considers diversity of classes. LMKLDC learns different weights of combining kernels for different classes to improve the flexibility of the model. Meanwhile, LMKLDC also utilizes l_p-norm $(0 < p \leq 1)$ to promote the sparsity, which can reduce the computation cost. However, LMKLDC boils down to a non-convex optimization problem when $0 < p < 1$. Unlike (Rakotomamonjy et al. 2011), separately solving optimization problems for $p = 1$ and $0 < p < 1$, we present an unified method to solve relevant optimization problems, no matter what the value of p takes. We apply the two-stage approach to find the classifier's parameters and the weights of combining kernels. We utilize the constrained concave convex procedure (CCCP) (Smola et al. 2005) to transform the non-convex optimization problem into a convex one, which is a quadratic programming and can be solved by the existing toolbox CVX.

The rest of the paper is organized as follows. In section 2, we discuss the multi-class kernel-based learning problem. Section 3 presents the proposed LMKLDC. Section 4 shows the experimental results and conclusions are drawn in Section 5.

2 Multi-Class Kernel-Based Learning (MCKL)

Given the multi-class data $x \in \mathbf{X}$ and the labels $y \in \mathbf{Y} = \{1, ..., m\}$, $m > 2$ and (x, y) is from some unknown distribution P over $\mathbf{X} \times \mathbf{Y}$. According to the Represent Theorem (Girosi 1998; Schölkopf et al. 2001) as well as the previous research of (Grammer et al. 2002), the output function for multi-class problems can be formulated as below,

$$f(x) = \left(\sum_{i=1}^{n} c_{r,i} k(x, x_i) \right), r = 1, ..., m, \tag{1}$$

where k is a kernel function that is positive definite. Then, the corresponding decision function is

$$\hat{y}(x^*) = \arg\max_{r=1}^{m} \left\{ \sum_{i=1}^{n} c_{r,i} k(x^*, x_i) \right\}, \tag{2}$$

where x^* is a new example. That implies that the predicted label for a new example x is the one that gets the largest score $\sum_{i=1}^{n} c_{r,i} k(x, x_i)$.

Based on the results above, we can cast the multi-class kernel-based learning into the following optimization problem,

$$\min_{C} \sum_{i=1}^{n} \sum_{r=1}^{m} l(y_r(x_i) f_r(x_i)) + \gamma \|C\|_2^2, \tag{3}$$

where l is a loss function and $f_r(x_i)$ denotes the rth element of $f(x_i)$. The matrix $C \in \mathrm{R}^{m \times n}$ is the parameters of the classifier, which is consisted of $(c_{r,\cdot})$, $r = 1, ..., m$ and $c_{r,\cdot} = (c_{r,1}, ..., c_{r,n}) \in \mathrm{R}^n$. γ is the regularization parameter. $\|\cdot\|_2$ denotes the l_2-norm of a matrix. And $y_r(x_i)$ is 1 if $r = y_i$ and -1 otherwise.

In the paper, we use the smooth quadratic hinge loss $l(z) = \max(0, 1-z)^2$ so that Eq. (3) is convex. So, we can solve the optimization problem via letting the derivation about C of Eq. (3) to be zero to get the stable point, that is the optimal solution.

3 l_p-norm Multiple Kernel Learning with Diversity of Classes (LMKLDC)

3.1 Multi-class Multiple Kernel Learning with l_p-norm

Now, we can generalize the multi-class kernel-based learning to the multi-class multiple kernel learning. Unlike the general MKL algorithms which often learn the same weights of combining kernels for all classes, we take the diversity of classes into consideration. LMKLDC will learn different weights of combining kernels for each class. So, we can generalize the output function Eq. (1) to be

$$f(x) = \left(\sum_{i=1}^{n} c_{r,i} \sum_{k=1}^{q} \beta_{r,k} k_k(x, x_i) \right), r = 1, ..., m \ . \tag{4}$$

Here $\beta_{r,\cdot} = (\beta_{r,1}, ..., \beta_{r,q}) \in R^q$ is the weights of q base kernels for the rth class. As usual, we add the simplex constrain for $\beta_{r,\cdot}$, $r = 1, ..., m$. That is,

$$\forall r, \beta_{r,\cdot} \in \Delta_1 := \left\{ \beta_{r,\cdot} \middle| \forall k : \beta_{r,k} \geq 0, \sum_{k=1}^{q} \beta_{r,k} = 1 \right\} .$$

Correspondingly, the decision function becomes

$$\hat{y}(x^*) = \arg\max_{r=1}^{m} \left\{ \sum_{i=1}^{n} c_{r,i} \sum_{k=1}^{q} \beta_{r,k} k_k(x^*, x_i) \right\} . \tag{5}$$

Moreover, the regularization term in LMKLDC is in the form of the l_p-norm ($0 < p \leq 1$) to promote the sparsity. As a result, the optimization problem of multi-class multiple kernel learning with l_p-norm is

$$\min_{B,C} \sum_{i=1}^{n} \sum_{r=1}^{m} l(y_r(x_i) f_r(x_i)) + \alpha \|B\|_{p,2}^2 + \gamma \|C\|_2^2$$
$$s.t. \ \forall r : \beta_{r,\cdot} \cdot e = 1, \tag{6}$$
$$\forall r : \forall k : \beta_{r,k} \geq 0,$$

where $B = [\beta_{r,k}]_{r=1,...,m;k=1,...,q} \in R^{m \times q}$, $p \in (0,1]$ and α and γ are regularization parameters. $e \in R^q$ is a column vector whose elements are 1. $\|\cdot\|_{p,2}$ is a matrix norm defined as (Wang et al. 2013).

Considering diversity of classes, LMKLDC can learn different weights of combining kernels for each class to cater to the feature space of each class. Unfortunately, the objective function in Eq. (6) happens to be non-convex when $p \in (0,1)$, which makes it difficult to solve Eq. (6). Hence, it is necessary to design an efficient algorithm to solve Eq. (6) with $p \in (0,1]$.

3.2 Optimization Method

At first, the objective function of Eq.(6) can be rewritten as

$$\sum_{r=1}^{m} \min_{\beta_{r,\cdot}, c_{r,\cdot}} \sum_{i=1}^{n} l(y_r(x_i) f_r(x_i)) + \alpha \|\beta_{r,\cdot}\|_p^2 + \gamma \|c_{r,\cdot}\|_2^2, \tag{7}$$

so we can decompose the initial optimization problem Eq.(6) into m small optimization problems as follows,

$$\min_{\beta_{r,\cdot}, c_{r,\cdot}} \sum_{i=1}^{n} l(y_r(x_i) f_r(x_i)) + \alpha \|\beta_{r,\cdot}\|_p^2 + \gamma \|c_{r,\cdot}\|_2^2$$
$$s.t. \ \beta_{r,\cdot} \cdot e = 1, \tag{8}$$
$$\forall k : \beta_{r,k} \geq 0,$$

with $r = 1, ..., m$. Substituting the smooth quadratic hinge loss into Eq. (8), we can get

$$
\min_{\beta_{r,\cdot}, c_{r,\cdot}} \sum_{i=1}^{n} [\max(0, 1 - y_r(x_i) f_r(x_i))]^2 + \alpha \|\beta_{r,\cdot}\|_p^2 + \gamma \|c_{r,\cdot}\|_2^2
$$
$$
s.t. \quad \beta_{r,\cdot} \cdot e = 1,
$$
$$
\forall k : \beta_{r,k} \geq 0 .
$$
(9)

So, the key to solving Eq. (6) is to solve the optimization problem Eq. (9). We apply a two-stage approach to solve the optimization problem Eq. (9). Firstly, initialize $\beta_{r,\cdot}$.

Since knowing $\beta_{r,\cdot}$, we can yield the value for $c_{r,\cdot}$ by solving Eq. (9). Once getting $c_{r,\cdot}$, $\beta_{r,\cdot}$ can be updated by solving Eq. (9). The process is repeated until $\beta_{r,\cdot}$ and $c_{r,\cdot}$ converge.

Optimize $c_{r,\cdot}$. After fixing the vector $\beta_{r,\cdot}$, Eq. (9) degenerates to the following unconstrained optimization problem,

$$
\min_{c_{r,\cdot}} g(c_{r,\cdot}) := \frac{1}{\gamma_1^2} \sum_{i=1}^{n} [\max(0, 1 - y_r(x_i) f_r(x_i))]^2 + \|c_{r,\cdot}\|_2^2
$$
(10)

where $\gamma_1^2 = \gamma$.

It can be found that the objective function of Eq. (10) is a convex function. So, we can work out the stable point about $c_{r,\cdot}$, that is just right the optimal solution.

Firstly, the partial derivative about $c_{r,\cdot}$ of $g(c_{r,\cdot})$ can be calculated as

$$
\frac{\partial g(c_{r,\cdot})}{\partial c_{r,\cdot}} = \frac{1}{\gamma_1^2} \sum_{i=1}^{n} 2 y_r(x_i)^2 \cdot c_{r,\cdot} \cdot K(x_i) \cdot \beta_{r,\cdot}^T \cdot \beta_{r,\cdot} \cdot K(x_i)^T
$$
$$
- \frac{1}{\gamma_1^2} \sum_{i=1}^{n} 2 y_r(x_i) \cdot \beta_{r,\cdot} \cdot K(x_i)^T + 2 c_{r,\cdot}
$$
(11)

Here, $K(x) := \begin{bmatrix} k_1(x, x_1) & k_2(x, x_1) & ... & k_q(x, x_1) \\ k_1(x, x_2) & k_2(x, x_2) & ... & k_q(x, x_2) \\ .. & ... & ... & ... \\ k_1(x, x_n) & k_2(x, x_n) & ... & k_q(x, x_n) \end{bmatrix} \in R^{n \times q}$.

Then, by letting Eq. (11) to be zero, we can get

$$
c_{r,\cdot} = \beta_{r,\cdot} \sum_{i=1}^{n} y_r(x_i) K(x_i)^T \cdot \left(\sum_{i=1}^{n} K(x_i) \beta_{r,\cdot}^T \beta_{r,\cdot} K(x_i)^T + \gamma_1^2 I_n \right)^{-1},
$$
(12)

where I_n denotes unit matrix.

Optimize $\beta_{r,\cdot}$. As above, fixing the vector $c_{r,\cdot}$ makes Eq. (9) become

$$\min_{\beta_{r,\cdot}} h(\beta_{r,\cdot}) := \frac{1}{\gamma_2^2} \sum_{i=1}^{n} [\max{(0, 1 - y_r(x_i)f_r(x_i))}]^2 + \|\beta_{r,\cdot}\|_p^2$$

$$s.t. \ \beta_{r,\cdot} \cdot e = 1,$$
$$\forall k : \beta_{r,k} \geq 0, \tag{13}$$

where $\gamma_2^2 = \alpha$ and $p \in (0, 1]$.

No matter what the value of p takes, we always convert Eq. (13) into a convex optimization problem via CCCP (Smola et al. 2005). The concrete steps are: (1) get an initial value x_0 for $\beta_{r,\cdot}$, which satisfies the simplex constrain; (2) calculate the 1th order Taylor expansion $T_1 \left\{ \|\beta_{r,\cdot}\|_p^2, x_0 \right\} (\beta_{r,\cdot})$ of $\|\beta_{r,\cdot}\|_p^2$ at location x_0, that is

$$T_1 \left\{ \|\beta_{r,\cdot}\|_p^2, x_0 \right\} (\beta_{r,\cdot}) = \|x_0\|_p^2 + \left\langle \beta_{r,\cdot} - x_0, \frac{\partial \|\beta_{r,\cdot}\|_p^2}{\partial \beta_{r,\cdot}} \Big|_{\beta_{r,\cdot} = x_0} \right\rangle$$

$$= \|x_0\|_p^2 + \left\langle \beta_{r,\cdot} - x_0, 2 \|x_0\|_p^{2-p} \cdot \Psi_p(x_0) \right\rangle . \tag{14}$$

Here, $\Psi_p(\cdot)$ is defined as $\Psi_p(x) := \left(x_1^{p-1}, ..., x_q^{p-1} \right)$ with $x \in R^q$. (3) approximate $\|\beta_{r,\cdot}\|_p^2$ using its 1th order Taylor expansion.

Now, we substitute Eq. (14) into Eq. (13) and obtain the following optimization function

$$\min_{\beta_{r,\cdot}} h(\beta_{r,\cdot}) := \frac{1}{\gamma_2^2} \sum_{i=1}^{n} [\max{(0, 1 - y_r(x_i)f_r(x_i))}]^2 + \|x_0\|_p^2$$

$$+ \left\langle \beta_{r,\cdot} - x_0, 2 \|x_0\|_p^{2-p} \cdot \Psi_p(x_0) \right\rangle \tag{15}$$

$$s.t. \ \beta_{r,\cdot} \cdot e = 1,$$
$$\forall k : \beta_{r,k} \geq 0 .$$

We can find that Eq. (15) is a QP, which can be solved by the efficient solver. In the implementation, we use CVX with the solver SeDuMi for QP.

4   Experimental Results

In the section, to evaluate the performance of our proposed model, LMKLDC, we compare it with the SimpleMKL (Rakotomamonjy et al. 2008) and the unweighted MKL for multi-class classification, which corresponds to LMKLDC with the same weights of combining kernels for every class and for each base kernel. We perform some experiments on a toy dataset and UCI[1] datasets. The detailed experimental setting and analysis of results are presented as below.

---

[1] The dataset is available from 'http://www.ics.uci.edu/ mlearn/MLRepository.html'

4.1   Toy Dataset

In the toy problem, we construct a toy dataset to test the effectiveness of
LMKLDC. The toy dataset has three classes and the data of every class is
respectively from a two-dimensional Gaussian distribution. Every class has 100
examples. The toy dataset is shown in Figure 1. *mu* and *sigma* respectively denote the average value and the covariance matrix of a Gaussian distribution. We
randomly split the toy dataset into 70% training and 30% test set. And the process is repeated ten times. Like SimpleMKL, base kernels include the Gaussian
kernels with the bandwidths $\{0.5, 1, 2, 5, 7, 10, 12, 15, 17, 20\}$ and the polynomial
kernels with the degrees $\{1, 2, 3\}$. The average results of ten splits are reported.

We set the same parameters $\gamma_1 = 2^{-7}$, $\gamma_2 = 2^2$ and $p = 0.5$ for our algorithm
and the unweighted MKL. If LMKLDC is effective, it should learn a different
kernel combination for each class and has a better classification performance.
The weights of combining kernels for each class of LMKLDC are presented in
Figure 2. From the figure, we can find our algorithm does select a few different
base kernels for each class. Class 2 and Class 3 select the similar base kernels,
but the weights of these base kernels are different. Compared with Class 2 and
Class 3, Class 1 selects entirely different base kernels. Besides, we compare our
algorithm with the unweighted MKL about the classification accuracy. The result
is reported in Table 1. We can find that LMKLDC gets a better classification
accuracy. It implies that when the weights of combining kernels for all classes are
restricted to be the same, the classification performance of MCMKL algorithms
is decreased. Hence, considering diversity of classes in MCMKL algorithms is
necessary.

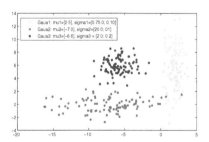
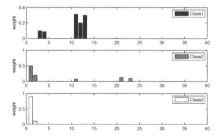

Fig. 1. Toy dataset

Fig. 2. The weights of combining kernels
for each class of LMKLDC. The x-axis denotes the base kernels.

4.2   UCI Dataset

In the subsection, we perform a serial of experiments to evaluate the performance of the LMKLDC algorithm. Eight UCI datasets are used in our experiments. They include *Balance (3,4,625), Iris (3,4,150), Soybean (4,35,47), Lenses*

Table 1. Accuracy of two algorithms on the toy dataset

Dataset	LMKLDC	Unweighted MKL
toy dataset	0.9833	0.9778

(3,4,24), Wine (3,13,178), Tae (3,5,151), Ecoli (6,6,332) and Cmc(3,9,1473), where the number of classes, the dimension and number of samples are listed in the bracket. Likewise, for every dataset, we randomly split it into 70% training and 30% test set. And the process is repeated ten times. The regularization parameters γ_1 and γ_2 are tuned via grid searching in the set $\{2^{-10}, 2^{-9}, .., 2^9, 2^{10}\}$ and p in the set $\{0.25, 0.5, 0.75, 1\}$. Similarly, we select the Gaussian kernels with the bandwidths $\{0.5, 1, 2, 5, 7, 10, 12, 15, 17, 20\}$ and the polynomial kernels with the degrees $\{1, 2, 3\}$ as base kernels. The average results of ten splits are reported in the experiments.

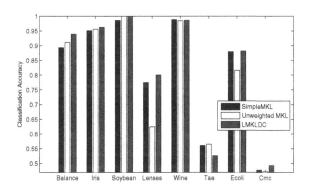

Fig. 3. Classification accuracy of algorithms on UCI datasets

For every dataset, we report the average classification accuracies of these compared algorithms in Figure 3. From the figure, it can be seen that our algorithm gets a better classification accuracy on most of datasets. Though the accuracy of SimpleMKL is higher than the accuracy of LMKLDC in Wine and Tae, LMKLDC selects fewer base kernels than SimpleMKL. And in Tae, the unweighted MKL, which is a special case of LMKLDC, gets the highest accuracy. In a sense, that also shows the superior classification performance of LMKLDC.

Moreover, we also perform an experiment to examine the sparsity of our model, which is measured by the number of kernels selected from base kernels. Considering our model learns different kernel combinations for each class, we use the average number of selected kernels of all classes as the final number of selected kernels for our model. The corresponding result is presented in Table 2. Kernels whose weight is greater than 0.0001 are selected. It is obvious that our model selects the less number of kernels from the base kernels than SimpleMKL.

It indicates the superiority of l_p-norm ($0 < p \leq 1$). Especially in Balance, Iris, Soybean, Wine and Cmc, the sparsity of LMKLDC makes it select far fewer base kernels than SimpleMKL. Hence, our algorithm LMKLDC can get a better classification accuracy and the sparsity simultaneously.

Table 2. The percentage of selected kernels from base kernels

Dataset	SimpleMKL	LMKLDC
Balance	7.69% (5/65)	2.56% (1.667/65)
Iris	7.69% (5/65)	1.54% (1/65)
Soybean	39.87% (181/454)	0.39% (1.75/454)
Lenses	4.62% (3/65)	4.10% (2.667/65)
Wine	10.43% (19/182)	1.10% (2/182)
Tae	6.41% (5/78)	5.13% (4/78)
Ecoli	10.99% (10/91)	4.76% (4.333/91)
Cmc	60.00% (78/130)	1.54% (2/130)

5   Conclusion

In this paper, we combine MKL with the multi-class classification and propose an effective algorithm LMKLDC. It considers the diversity of classes and utilizes the sparsity of l_p-norm ($0 < p \leq 1$) to promote the computational efficiency. Some experiments demonstrate its superiority.

In the paper, LMKLDC employs positive definite kernels as base kernels. How to expand LMKLDC with indefinite kernels as base kernels becomes an interesting issue for future work.

Acknowledgements. This work was supported in part by National Natural Science Foundations of China (Grant Nos. 61375057 and 61300165), Natural Scinence Foundation of Jiangsu Province of China (Grant No. BK20131298), and the Scientific Research Startup Project of New Doctorial Faculties of Southeast University.

References

Lanckriet, G.R.G., Cristianini, N., Bartlett, P., Ghaoui, L.E., Jordan, M.I.: Learning the kernel matrix with semidefinite programming. The Journal of Machine Learning Research 5, 27–72 (2004)

Bach, F.R., Lanckriet, G.R.G., Jordan, M.I.: Multiple kernel learning, conic duality, and the SMO algorithm. In: Proceedings of the Twenty-first International Conference on Machine Learning, vol. 6. ACM (2004)

Rakotomamonjy, A., Bach, F.R., Canu, S., Grandvalet, Y.: SimpleMKL. Journal of Machine Learning Research 9(11) (2008)

Kloft, M., Brefeld, U., Sonnenburg, S., Laskov, P., Müller, K.R., Zien, A.: Efficient and accurate l_p-norm multiple kernel learning. NIPS 22(22), 997–1005 (2009)

Xu, Z., Jin, R., Yang, H., King, I., Lyu, M.R.: Simple and efficient multiple kernel learning by group lasso. In: Proceedings of the 27th International Conference on Machine Learning, ICML, pp. 1175–1182 (2010)

Xu, X., Tsang, I.W., Xu, D.: Soft margin multiple kernel learning. IEEE Transactions on Neural Networks and Learning Systems 24, 749–761 (2013)

Zien, A., Ong, C.S.: Multiclass multiple kernel learning. In: Proceedings of the 24th International Conference on Machine Learning, pp. 1191–1198. ACM (2007)

Tsochantaridis, I., Hofmann, T., Joachims, T., Altun, Y.: Support vector machine learning for interdependent and sturcutured output spaces. In: Proceedings of the 16th International Conference on Machine Learning (2004)

Crammer, K., Singer, Y.: On the algorithmic implementation of multiclass kernel-based vector machines. The Journal of Machine Learning Research 2, 265–292 (2002)

Ye, J., Ji, S., Chen, J.: Multi-class discriminant kernel learning via convex programming. The Journal of Machine Learning Research 9, 719–758 (2008)

Kumar, A., Niculescu-Mizil, A., Kavukcuoglu, K., Daumé, H.: A binary classification framework for two-stage multiple kernel learning. arXiv preprint arXiv:1206.6428 (2012)

Cortes, C., Mohri, M., Rostamizadeh, A.: Multi-Class Classification with Maximum Margin Multiple Kernel. In: Proceedings of the 30th International Conference on Machine Learning, ICML, pp. 46–54 (2013)

Bach, F.R.: Consistency of the group lasso and multiple kernel learning. The Journal of Machine Learning Research 9, 1179–1225 (2008)

Szafranski, M., Grandvalet, Y., Rakotomamonjy, A.: Composite kernel learning. Machine Learning 79(1-2), 73–103 (2010)

Nath, J.S., Dinesh, G., Raman, S., Bhattacharyya, C., Ben-Tal, A., Ramakrishnan, K.R.: On the Algorithmics and Applications of a Mixed-norm based Kernel Learning Formulation. In: NIPS, pp. 844–852 (2009)

Chartrand, R.: Exact reconstruction of sparse signals via nonconvex minimization. IEEE Signal Processing Letters 14(10), 707–710 (2007)

Chartrand, R., Yin, W.: Iteratively reweighted algorithms for compressive sensing. In: IEEE International Conference on Acoustics, Speech and Signal Processing, ICASSP 2008, pp. 3869–3872. IEEE (2008)

Xu, Z., Chang, X., Xu, F., Zhang, H.: $L_{1/2}$ regularization: A Thresholding Representation Theory and a Fast Solver. IEEE Transaction on Neural Networks and Learning Systems 23(7) (2012)

Rakotomamonjy, A., Flamary, R., Gasso, G., Ganu, S.: l_p-l_q penalty for sparse linear and sparse multiple kernel multitask learning. IEEE Transactions on Neural Networks 22(8), 1307–1320 (2011)

Smola, A., Vishwanathan, S.V.N., Hofmann, T.: Kernel methods for missing variables (2005)

Girosi, F.: An equivalence between sparse approximation and support vector machines. Neural Computation 10(6), 1455–1480 (1998)

Schölkopf, B., Herbrich, R., Smola, A.J.: A generalized representer theorem. In: Proceedings of the 14th Annual Conference on Computational Learning Theory, pp. 416–426 (2001)

Wang, L., Chen, S.: $l_{2,p}$-Matrix norm and its application in feature selection. arXiv preprint arXiv:1303.3987 (2013)

Design of Technology Value Analysis System Based on Patent Big Data

Youngkon Lee[1] and Ukhyun Lee[2]

[1] e-Business Department, Korea Polytechnic University,
2121 Jeongwangdong, Siheung city, Korea
yklee777@kpu.ac.kr
[2] School of IT Convergence Engineering, Shinhan University,
233-1 Sangpae dong, Dongducheon city, Korea
uhlee@shinhan.ac.kr

Abstract. Research and development in a company suggests a direction, along which the company can live on in the future and it is the most important activity for a company to survive in the competition. Recently, a few methodologies and systems analyzing the trend of future technology are being studied. Especially, there are some studies, which explore future technology by huge patent documents. However, the existing systems for it have limitation issues in performance and accuracy. In order to complement existing methods, this study approaches patent documents by technology-unit instead of utilizing related information by patent-unit. This study draws core keywords through data mining and suggests a method detecting User Defined Technology Trend Discovery (UDTTD).

Keywords: future technology, patent document, SNA, UDTTD, IPC, TF-IDF, SKOS, ontology RDF, technology trend analysis.

1 Introduction

Research and development in a company suggests a direction, along which the company can live on in the future and it is the most important activity for a company to survive in the competition. At present, the success rate of domestic research and development of private companies and government do not reach 1% of project planning stage. In order to resolve the difficulty in domestic research and development, private companies and government have been developing various systems, which can analyze core technology owned by self and predict future technology trend [1]. Recently, many methodologies and systems analyzing the trend of future technology are being studied in major advanced countries including United States, Japan and Germany. Especially, there are many studies, which explore future technology by huge patent documents. However, the existing systems have many issues as following.

First, the existing systems use SNA (Social Network Analysis) skill by utilizing related information by patent-unit; however, it is difficult to provide with information

Y.S. Kim et al (Eds.): PKAW 2014, LNCS 8863, pp. 48–58, 2014.

required by users by simple related information only. On the contrary, it can raise confusion in research and development policy decision-making by bringing in excessive and huge amount of information to users. Second, in order to use a system which predicts the future of technology by using existing patent documents, one should have the knowledge on patent documents as well as domain knowledge on the core technology owned by self.

In order to complement existing methods, this study approaches patent documents by technology-unit instead of utilizing related information by patent-unit. This study draws core keywords through data mining and suggests a method detecting User Defined Technology Trend Discovery (UDTTD). In Chapter 2, related studies, information about patent analysis solutions being globally used is reviewed so that the difference between existing analysis solutions and the system suggested in this study would be explained. In Chapter 3, the development methodology of this system is stated from the viewpoint of realization. In Chapter 4, the result of empirical analysis on the result realized by the web system is given.

2   Related Studies

2.1   Aureka (MicroPatent, the Thomson Corporation)

This solution for patent analysis was developed by MicroPatent [2]. At present, Thomson Reuter owns it. It expresses the keyword clustering result as a visual contour map. The information processing method of Aureka consists of following 4 steps.

- Step 1: Draw keywords from the abstract of the object patent document sought by a user
- Step 2: The keywords drawn in Step 1 go through refining and selection process. Keyword selection uses TF (term frequency) and IDF (inverted document frequency).
- Step 3: Documents are grouped by using clustering naive bays algorithm and the visualization work is prepared in advance by performing reduction, layout and density estimation using SOM algorithm.
- Step 4: The solution enables a user visually distinguish 'blue ocean' and 'red ocean' by showing a visual contour map. It draws and suggests 1~3 words, which have high frequency at each contour.

Aureka suggests a direction required by future research and development to a user using contour map visualization method utilizing the keywords of a simple patent document through above 4 steps. The following Figure 1 is the result screen capture drawn in Aureka system.

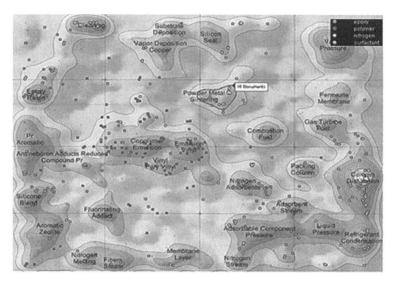

Fig. 1. The analysis result screen of Aureka system

However, Aureka has following limitations. First, Aureka makes actually-necessary information extraction difficult by showing a system-user too many data in a limited UI and results in excessive information effect. Second, since there is no technical meaning in the horizontal axis and vertical axis of technology map, it is not possible to assume the related technology of an area. Third, the empty area in Aureka is just a visually empty area and it has no relation with other surrounding keywords. Therefore, it is difficult to use Aureka as a research and development decision-making tool from the viewpoint of research and development planning.

2.2   PIAS (Patent Information Analysis System) of KIPO (Korea Intellectual Property Office)

The PIAS (patent information analysis system) provided by KIPO is a patent data analysis solution which collects various patent information and knowledge related to science and technology in systematic way, provides with data and supports various analyses [3]. The solution had been developed by KIPO and is being provided to users free of charge; however, it is not favored by users because of following issues; though it has multiple merits. First, a technology from the viewpoint of a user cannot be defined. The system analyzes patent applicants based on subclass step, which is the topmost step of IPC class code provided by the system as default. However, the scope of patent data technology lower than the subclass is too diverse that the subclass cannot be defined as a technology level. A small and medium-sized company, which is doing specialized technology research and development, wants to know the trend of that specific technology; however, PIAS does not meet this needs. It is believed that this issue should be improved. Second, there is a difficulty in securing latest patent data. PIAS was produced as a client-side program and it does patent data search and analysis by user's search word. However, it does not guarantee the quality of service when querying huge patent data. To set up a direction for a company or an institution to go forward by analyzing latest patent data trend from the viewpoint of a research and development planner, the system should provide with service by securing service quality on latest data in real-time.

3   Development Environment

This study used the patent documents of United States, which country is more technically advanced than Korea, as the raw data of technology trend analysis in Korea. In order to analyze 'technology'-focused patent documents suggested in this study for the analysis of future technology trend, a significant definition on 'technology' is necessary first. In this study, technology means a set of patent. The concept of technology is established by IPC (Internet Patent Code), which is an international classification code [4]. Two hypotheses were set up to define technology by utilizing data, which can be analyzed from IPC section. First, in a section lower than subclass which is mapped with patent data by industry, the number of lower section should not be lopsided on specific technology level. As seen in following Table 1, in IPC section, there are 7 topmost sections from A to H.

Table 1. Hierarchical structure of IPC

Section	Content
A	Living necessities
B	Processing organization; transportation
C	Chemistry; metallurgy
D	Textile; paper
E	Fixed structure
F	Mechanical engineering; lighting; heating; weapon; explosion
G	Physics
H	Electricity

Figure 2 shows the process and modules for analyzing big patent data to obtain technology value and trend. The system is composed of patent DB, ontology translator, inference engine, and simulator. The system extracts the technology relationship data by calculating the technology distance based on patent ontology and neural network. We borrowed the keyword reference group from SKOS framework, by which we classified the keywords used frequently in patents and calculate grades by technology distance by weight factor [5][6].

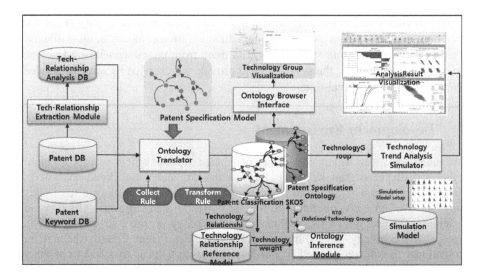

Fig. 2. Components for Technology Value Analysis System

4   Design and Realization

4.1   Keyword Drawing Algorithm and Methodology

The technology value analysis system is based on neural network, which evaluates the technology value by the frequency of main keyword on the respect of technology fusion, technology promising, and technology influence (see Fig. 3). The keyword extraction algorithm is composed with 3 steps. First is the keyword analysis module utilizing TF-IDF algorithm. Second is the synonym/equivalence refining process utilizing a thesaurus. Third is the 'stopword' refining process. TF-IDF (term frequency - inverse document frequency) is a representative keyword drawing algorithm of text mining. It expresses the importance of arbitrary core keyword in a document group made of N ea of document as statistical value through weight based on vector space model [7] by employing MapReduce mechanism, simplified data processing on large clusters [8]. When drawing keywords from diverse documents, grouping is required to classify the documents in accordance with their characters.

Since the keyword drawn from claim is the keyword having same character with the word drawn from patent document which has same IPC class code, the synonym/equivalence refining process by word is essential. A thesaurus is absolutely necessary for the vocabulary refining process between the words. The raw data to be entered into vocabulary dictionary database is English version vocabulary dictionary in the format of SKOS (simple knowledge organization system) downloaded from Wikipedia. The SKOS vocabulary dictionary file is in RDF structure, in other words, it is in the data expression structure of ontology form [9].

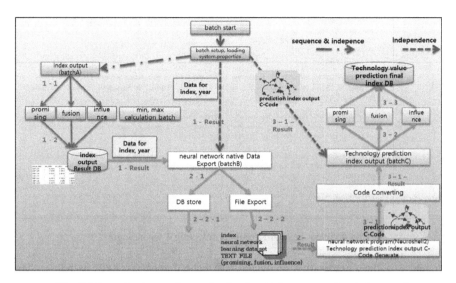

Fig. 3. The technology value evaluation by the frequency of main keyword

4.2 Technology Analysis System Realization Plan

The major function of technology analysis system consists of "lower level technology trend analysis", "technology trend analysis between technologies" and "user group technology trend analysis". In this study, the definition of technology is the subgroup of IPC code. The system suggested by this study supports technology trend analysis between technologies by enabling analysis through selecting up to 5 technologies for an IPC subgroup technology. The trend analysis between technologies is done by selecting upper level technology and lower level technology at the "technology selection tree" and moving keywords with interest to analysis information by the relevant keyword set.

4.3 Empirical Analysis

The final product of the system developed by this study consists of five areas. First, the system produces selected technology keyword analysis set. When multiple products are observed in actual process, it is possible to query a technology keyword group, which was taken as an analysis object by self.

개요	• G06F 17/10 (특정한 수치적 연산) • G06B 17/20 (자 어 거 처리) • G06F 17/30 (전 그 겁 의 이 를 위 한 디 데 베이스 구조) • G06F 17/40 (데 터 특 성 측 기 기 저 장)
키워드	• G06F 17/10 output signa , digital filter , filter coefficients , adaptive filter , computer implemented , machine readable medium , impulse response , central processing Unit , FIR filter , computer readable medium , computer system , integrated circuit , Finite Impulse Response , finite element , control unit , filter coefficient , computer program product • G06B 17/20 user interface , natural language , machine readable medium , computer system , target language , data processing , handheld electronic device , language model , medium having computer readable , translated text , data processing system , text string , recording medium , character string , speech recognition , operating system , character set , language text , input device • G06F 17/30 file system , search query , user interface , readable medium having computer , web page , computer readable , data set , readab e medium , computer program product , search engine , medium having computer readable , management system • G06F 17/40 machine readable medium , computer implemented , data processing system , management system , control unit , data processing , event data , received data , sensor data , output signal , time series , health care , central processing unit , user device , readable medium , computer program product , user interface , computer readable

Fig. 4. Select keyword group by selecting 4 technologies

Figure 4 is the comparative analysis of 4 technologies at G06F or below. The screen shows 15 or more object keywords drawn by each technology. To analyze future trend of a technology, the past trend of the technology should be learned. The system analyzed future technology trend through past data 10 years, from 2000 to 2009. The system enables the learning of technology trend by year by showing two kinds of chart on past data such as technology keyword trend and technology patent trend.

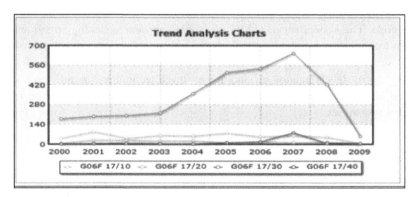

Fig. 5. Technology keyword trend

As seen in Figure 5, the technology keyword trend shows the query frequency of previous selected technology keyword in the patent of relevant technology as an index for each year. It is possible to roughly learn current linear S curve step of each technology by reviewing the yearly status of patent related to the keyword selected by a user at the technology keyword trend.

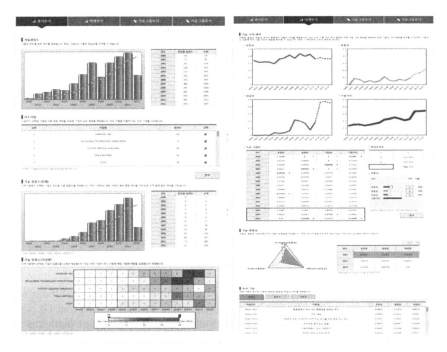

Fig. 6. Technology patent trend of G06F 17/00

As seen in Figure 6, the technology patent trend is a chart, which shows the number of lower level patent application of the technology selected by a user by each year. It is possible to find the relationship between the keyword selected by self and the number of actual patent by above two technology trend analyses and give technical significance to it. Since there are too many variables in the market, it is difficult to analyze technology trend in the market by patent data and the keyword of technology. However, it is believed that the data would become substantially significant from the viewpoint of research and development, if quantitative assumption value of future technology value measured data would be available by analyzing past data using the system suggested by this study.

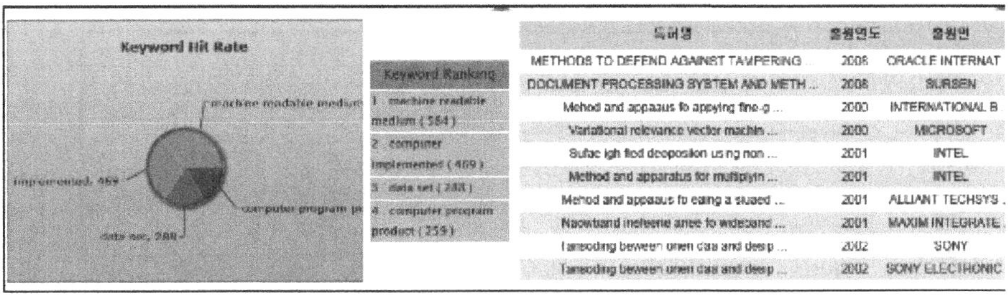

Fig. 7. Keyword distribution analysis

Figure 7 is the screen showing the upper 10% of keyword determined by the trend analysis and the representative patent including the relevant keyword. Analyzing the patent applicant of a patent document including core keywords selected by a company during technology trend analysis process is an important element in the research and development achievement of the company.

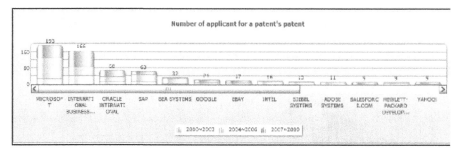

Fig. 8. Analysis of technology trend applicants

As seen in Figure 8, it was possible to know by analyzing past data that there were 193 patent applications by Microsoft, 166 patent applications by IBM and 68 patent applications by Oracle on the two technologies of G06F 17/10 (complex mathematical calculation) and G06F 17/30 (information search: database structure for it).

This study performed the tests by 3 candidate groups when selecting the keyword, which would become the entry value (refer to Figure 9.10). In the first test group, single noun and compound noun were entered together as entry values. In the second group, only single noun was selected as entry value. In the third test group, only compound noun was selected as entry value. The result of the third test suggested that the increase/decrease rates of the control group and entry value become contrary to each other in specific year in approximately 20 technologies. Since the raw data of the system is the keywords, it had been expected that it would become similar to the number of patent increase/decrease rate; however, when compound noun was selected as entry value, the trend between technologies showed different trend from the control group.

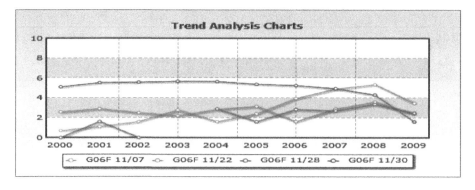

Fig. 9. Technology trend analysis of compound noun standard value

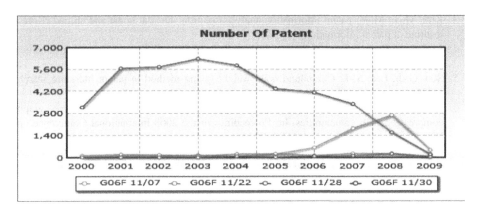

Fig. 10. Number of patent trend analysis of compound noun standard value

The reason for above result is believed that the technical meaning of a compound noun keyword, which is the raw data of entry value, has higher quality level meaning than a single noun keyword because of the word characteristic. By way of above results, it was possible to obtain the conclusion that analyzing technology trend by a keyword related to the technology desired by a user in the patent is more significant work than analyzing technology trend by way of simple difference in the number of patent increase/decrease rate.

5   Conclusion and Contemplation

This study suggested a technology trend analysis method using patent documents, stated the technology trend analysis algorithm which can utilize the suggested method and reviewed the applicability of the system suggested by this study through empirical analysis. The significance of this study is in the suggestion of a systematic quantitative methodology, which overcomes the limitation of existing qualitative studies, by predicting overall technology trend through utilizing patent information. Since the section (classification system) covers various viewpoints, the suggested system has higher probability in finding a significant technical set. It is expected that the suggested system has wide utilization scope as an element in future technology trend analysis when finding the relationship between certain technologies using F-TERM during technology trend analysis. Studies on the utilization of F-TERM and IPC would be the future required study tasks based on this study.

References

1. Jeon, Y.-S., Kim, Y.-H., Jeong, Y.-J., Ryu, J.-H., Maeng, S.-H.: Language model for technology trend detection from patent document text and clue-based mechanical study method. Software and Application 5 (May 2009), Book 36
2. http://thomsonreuters.com/scholarly-scientific-research/

3. Kim, M.-J.: Major patent information analysis solution status at home and abroad (Korea institute of patent information) (2006)
4. Jo, J.-S.: A study on convergence analysis of IPC and utilization plan of it in the evaluation and judgment. Industrial Property Right 38 (June 2012)
5. Son, G.-J., Lee, S.-J.: Compound noun weight giving method in patent literature search (2005)
6. Buehrer, G., Chellapilla, K.: A scalable pattern mining approach to web graph compression with communities. In: Proceedings of the 2008 International Conference on Web Search and Data Mining. ACM (2008)
7. Jeon, H.-W., Jeong, C.-H., Song, S.-G., Choi, Y.-S., Choi, S.-P., Jeong, H.-M.: Building of technology-related word bundle for technology trend analysis. Korean Internet Information Association Summer Conference Journal 1 (2012), Book 13
8. A Study on the efficient noise removal during patent data analysis and patent technology level evaluation with improved reliability. Technology Innovation Academy Journal 1, 105–128 (March 2012), Book 15
9. Dean, J., Ghemawat, S.: MapReduce: simplified data processing on large clusters. Communications of the ACM 51(1), 107–113 (2008)

Problems Detected by a Ripple-Down Rules Based Medication Review Decision Support System: Are They Relevant?

Ivan Bindoff, Colin Curtain, Gregory Peterson, Juanita Westbury, and Tristan Ling

School of Medicine, University of Tasmania, Tasmania, Australia
{Ivan.Bindoff,Colin.Curtain,G.Peterson,Juanita.Westbury,
Tristan.Ling}@utas.edu.au

Abstract. A ripple-down rules based clinical decision support system to detect drug-related problems (DRPs) has been previously designed and discussed. A commercial implementation of this system (MRM) was evaluated to determine how many additional DRPs would be identified by the reviewing pharmacist when supported by MRM, and whether these additional DRPs were clinically relevant. The DRPs identified by pharmacists were compared against those found by MRM on a dataset of 570 medication review cases, MRM found 2854 DRPs, pharmacists found 1974 DRPs, yet only 389 of the problems that MRM found were also found by the pharmacist. A sample of 20 of these cases were assessed by an expert panel to determine if the DRPs found by each source were clinically relevant. It was determined that DRPs found by both sources were clinically relevant. It is estimated that a pharmacist supported by MRM will find 2.25 times as many DRPs.

Keywords: ripple down rules·multiple classification ripple down rules·rdr·mcrdr· drug related problems·DRP·medication review·clinical relevance·clinical decision support systems·DSS·CDSS.

1   Introduction

Clinical decision support systems (CDSS), an increasingly popular tool to use in a wide variety of healthcare settings, are designed to alert the professional to potential therapeutic problems with their patients. One popular application for clinical decision support systems is detecting drug-related problems (DRPs), due to the potentially high value of preventing adverse events from occurring [1, 2], and the relative accessibility of the data required to detect the problems (patient's medical conditions, medications, and pathology results)[3, 4].

In 2007, Bindoff et al. reported on the development of a multiple classification ripple-down rules (MCRDR) based clinical decision support system designed to assist pharmacists in performing medication reviews, an expert process wherein a trained pharmacist attempts to detect and make recommendations for the resolution of DRPs for a high-risk patient.

Y.S. Kim et al (Eds.): PKAW 2014, LNCS 8863, pp. 59–68, 2014.
© Springer International Publishing Switzerland 2014

Like other MCRDR systems, this system functions by allowing the expert user to enter the details of their patient, then indicate which DRPs are present on the case. In each instance, the system will prompt the user to justify their finding by indicating the relevant features of the case that led them to detect that DRP. In subsequent cases where these same features are present, the system will automatically detect the DRP for the user. In instances where the system incorrectly identifies a DRP, the expert is asked to refine that rule by indicating the features that make this case different to the past cases on which the rule was correctly applied. This approach is comprehensively detailed in past publications [5, 6].

This system, like many other MCRDR systems before and since, was evaluated in terms of its internal performance [7-12]. Typical measures, such as rules per case, classifications per case, and number of avoided missed classifications per case, were reported [5, 6]. These results were highly promising, with estimates from this data indicating that the prototype system, which was trained on only 244 medication review cases, was able to identify approximately 90% of the DRPs for a case, and was able to reduce the incidence where the expert reviewer missed a DRP from 43% to 4% [3].

However, using these standard measures it remained unknown whether the additional DRPs being identified due to this system were clinically relevant or not. It was known that the expert pharmacist using the system believed the identified DRPs were correct and was willing to let the system retrospectively add them to the case, but it was not known if they were important. It was thought that if the expert reviewer missed them on their first pass, perhaps it was because they didn't think they were very important at the time.

Since the past analysis, the approach described in [5, 6] has been adopted by a commercial medication review system, Medscope Medication Review Mentor[1] (MRM). This system has since been used to successfully assist tens of thousands of medication reviews in Australia, and had a knowledge base consisting of approximately 1800 rules at the time this research was conducted.

The aim of this research is to determine how many additional DRPs might be detected when using this MCRDR-based medication review system, and critically, whether these additional DRPs are clinically relevant.

2   Methodology

Several sub-studies were undertaken to determine the quality of problems identified by the commercial medication review system, MRM. Two of the sub-studies most relevant to the research question of this paper are described here.

Both sub-studies were undertaken using data from a selection of 570 Australian medication review cases for patients aged 65 years and older. These cases were extracted from an existing dataset that was collected in 2008 [13]. This dataset included details such as patient's birth date, gender, height, weight, medical diagnoses, medication regimen and laboratory test results, as well as all the DRPs identified by the accredited pharmacists who originally reviewed the cases. Since MRM did not launch

---

[1] http://www.medscope.com.au/

until 2009, the DRPs identified in these cases by the original reviewing pharmacist could not have been influenced by MRM.

These cases were then input into the MRM system, and the identified DRPs and recommendations for resolution were recorded, so that both the original pharmacist's set of findings and MRM's equivalent findings were available for each case.

2.1   Sub-Study 1: Comparison of DRPs Identified between Pharmacists and MRM

To determine which problems pharmacists were identifying and which problems MRM was identifying, and the overlap across both groups, a comparison was necessary. Since each knowledge source used their own language to describe essentially identical DRPs, it was necessary to convert the DRPs identified by each source to a common lexicon. An iterative process was used to do this, that is described in detail in [14]. Each of the individual classifications was also grouped under broad headings, shown in Figure 1.

Examples of DRPs that were successfully mapped to a common lexicon can be seen in Table 1.

Table 1. Examples of successfully mapped DRPs

MRM	*Pharmacist*	*Mapped to*
Patient has elevated triglycerides and is only taking a statin. Additional treatment, such as a fibrate, may be worth considering.	Patient's cholesterol and triglycerides remain elevated despite Lipitor. This may be due to poor compliance or an inadequate dose.	Hyperlipidaemia undertreated
Heart failure with calcium channel blocker: Patient has a history of heart failure and is taking either verapamil or diltiazem. These agents can worsen signs and symptoms of systolic heart failure. Alternative agents should be considered if possible.	Diltiazem may adversely affect patients with heart failure	Heart failure and concurrent verapamil or diltiazem

Descriptive classifications were compared by frequency and type between pharmacists and MRM. Analysis of classifications was mainly descriptive, presenting classification frequencies found by MRM or pharmacists and by those found in common. Classifications were considered to be 'in common' if the same classifications could be identified by a pharmacist as well as MRM in the same patient.

The basic unit of analysis was the number of *distinct* classifications found in each case. The number of distinct classifications found in each case may differ from the number of actual DRPs found in each case. An example may be a patient using both atorvastatin and simvastatin, both statins. If statins are contraindicated due to risk of myopathy, each of these DRPs were assigned the classification *statin myopathy risk*. These two DRPs were then collated into only one distinct classification, since the end goal was to determine if pharmacist or software was able to detect this central therapeutic problem in this patient, with no extra credit being given for finding essentially the same problem multiple times.

2.2   Sub-Study 2: Expert Panel Assessment

An expert panel was coordinated to review a random selection of 20 of these cases. Fourteen experts in pharmacology were recruited to independently complete this review.

During the mapping process described earlier, several DRP categories were identified that the expert panel would not be able to assess, because they were based on pharmacist-only data that was not available in the digital representation of the patient case. For the purposes of the expert panel analysis these DRPs were excluded. Examples of these DRPs included:

- Communication breakdown
- Documentation insufficient
- Compliance – confusion about therapy
- Compliance – using too little medication
- Compliance – using too much medication
- Cost of therapy concern
- Difficulty using dosage form
- Eligible for Department of Veterans Affairs funded dose administration aid
- Medication expired
- Medication regimen complicated

Each expert was presented the cases in a random order and was asked to review the case data, as well as each DRP identified by both the original pharmacist reviewer, and those identified by MRM. The reviewer was blind to the source of each DRP, although in practice they may have been able to determine which source was human and which was from MRM due to repetition in the wording used by MRM when encountering the same problem in multiple cases.

For each DRP the reviewer was asked to indicate both the clinical relevance and the appropriateness of the recommendations made to resolve the DRP. These measures were assessed using a 5-point Likert agreement response to the following assessment statements:

- "The DRP is clinically relevant in this case, i.e. if unresolved the DRP would have resulted in a suboptimal outcome (e.g. under treatment, patient harm)"
- "The recommendation for resolving this DRP was appropriate"

Normality was assessed using Shapiro-Wilk tests and Bartlett's test for homogeneity of variance. Between group Likert item responses were analysed using Wilcoxon Rank-Sum Tests. Quantitative data analysis was performed using R (R Foundation for Statistical Computing, Vienna[2]).

---

[2] http://www.R-project.org/

3   Results

3.1   Sub-Study 1: Comparison of DRPs

MRM identified a total of 2953 DRPs in the 570 cases. These were mapped to 2854 classifications, representing 100 different types of problem. One hundred and forty-eight pharmacists identified 1726 DRPs which were mapped to 1680 classifications representing 113 different types of problem. Overall, MRM identified 70% more DRPs than pharmacists.

MRM found 389 classifications in common with the original reviewing pharmacists (23%). MRM identified a total of 2465 DRPs that the original pharmacists did not identify, while the original pharmacists identified 1585 DRPs that MRM did not. This means that MRM identified 56% more unique DRPs than the original reviewing pharmacist. The total number of unique DRPs that were identified when both sources were combined was 4439, of which MRM alone identified 2465, pharmacists alone identified 1585, and both identified 389.

In an attempt to determine if there was any particular type of DRP that a source excelled at detecting, the DRPs identified by each source were depicted in terms of classification category. Fig. 1 shows that MRM and pharmacists were both

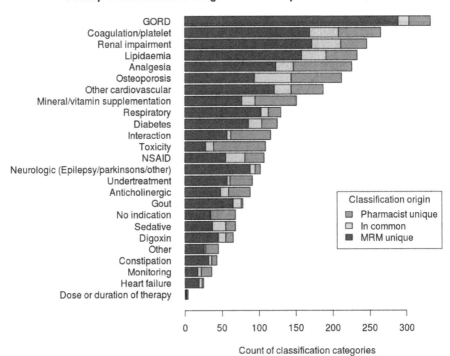

Fig. 1. Classification categories in common or unique to MRM or pharmacists. (GORD = gastro-oesophageal reflux disease, NSAID = non-steroidal anti-inflammatory drug)

identifying DRPs in a broad variety of classification categories, and the level of over-lap in each category was generally quite low.

3.2   Sub-Study 2: Expert Panel Assessment

Emails were sent to 41 general practitioners (primary care physicians), pharmacists accredited to perform medication review services, and specialist physicians. Fourteen experts consented to participate – two specialist physicians, two general practitioners, and 10 accredited pharmacists. Of these, 12 experts completed the assessment of all 20 cases, while two (a general practitioner and a pharmacist) did not complete any cases.

From the 570 cases, 294 pharmacist-only DRPs that could not be assessed for re-levance or appropriateness were removed.

The random 20 cases that were assessed by the expert panel were tested to deter-mine if they were representative of the larger sample of 570, as shown in Table 2. Independent samples t-test (equal variances not assumed) showed there was no signif-icant difference in patient ages between the panel cases and the remaining cases ($p=0.641$). Similarly, there was no difference in the number of medications recorded ($p=0.229$), or the number of diagnoses recorded ($p=0.527$).

Table 2. Demographics of patients assessed by the expert panel

Demographic	*Panel cases (N = 20)*	*Dataset (N = 570)*
Age (years)	79 ± 8	80 ± 7
Gender	Male 9 (45%) : Female 11 (55%)	Male 225 (41%) : Female 325 (59%)
Laboratory tests	With 13 (65%) : Without 7 (35%)	With 442 (80%) : Without 108 (20%)
Number of medications	13.6 ± 6.0	12.0 ± 4.3
Number of diagnoses	10.0 ± 6.2	9.1 ± 5.2

Chi-square tests for independence were conducted for the factors gender and labor-atory tests (with/without). There were no significant differences between the groups for either of these factors (gender $p=0.893$, laboratory tests $p=0.162$).

Across the 20 cases there were 73 DRPs identified by pharmacists and 125 identi-fied by MRM, totaling 198 DRPs. Each of these DRPs was assessed by 12 experts resulting in 2376 total opinions collected.

The expert panel responses concerning the clinical relevance of the DRPs are shown in Table 3. A similar spread is seen for both the DRPs identified by MRM and by pharmacists. There was no statistically significant difference between these two groups (W=674591, $p=0.212$).

Table 3. Opinions on clinical relevance of DRPs

	Pharmacists	MRM
Strongly Agree	116 (13%)	165 (11%)
Agree	529 (60%)	927 (62%)
Neutral	162 (18%)	272 (18%)
Disagree	67 (8%)	121 (8%)
Strongly Disagree	2 (0%)	15 (1%)

Similar results were seen for the appropriateness of recommendations question, as seen in Table 4. However, in this case there was a significant difference between pharmacists and MRM (W=568346, $p<0.001$), with recommendations proposed by MRM showing slightly higher levels of agreement than the original pharmacist's findings.

Table 4. Opinions on appropriateness of recommendations for resolution of DRPs

	Pharmacists	MRM
Strongly Agree	82 (9%)	141 (9%)
Agree	380 (43%)	853 (57%)
Neutral	244 (28%)	335 (22%)
Disagree	146 (17%)	151 (10%)
Strongly Disagree	24 (3%)	20 (1%)

To delve deeper into the question of whether the additional DRPs that MRM finds are clinically relevant, a subset of DRPs was analyzed where the DRP was identified by MRM but not by the pharmacist, and vice versa. This is shown in Table 5. Both were typically considered relevant, and there was no significant difference between the two groups (W=409246, $p=0.304$).

Table 5. Opinions on clinical relevance of DRPs missed by one source and not the other

	Pharmacist DRPs missed by MRM	MRM DRPs missed by pharmacist
Strongly Agree	80 (12%)	120 (10%)
Agree	397 (59%)	716 (60%)
Neutral	142 (21%)	230 (19%)
Disagree	51 (8%)	108 (9%)
Strongly Disagree	2 (0%)	14 (1%)

The same subset analysis was performed for the appropriateness of recommendations. This can be seen in Table 6. Again, there was a significant difference between the two groups (W=349218, $p<0.001$), with the missed MRM recommendations being preferred over the missed pharmacist recommendations.

Table 6. Opinions on appropriateness of recommendations missed by one source and not the other

	Pharmacist DRPs missed by MRM	MRM DRPs missed by pharmacist
Strongly Agree	62 (9%)	108 (9%)
Agree	294 (44%)	674 (57%)
Neutral	186 (28%)	261 (22%)
Disagree	112 (17%)	128 (11%)
Strongly Disagree	18 (3%)	17 (1%)

4   Discussion

The first sub-study made it clear that the MCRDR-based MRM system can detect a broad variety of DRPs, with a similar, but not as comprehensive scope as a human pharmacist. However, MRM identified substantially more DRPs than the human pharmacists, 2854 vs. 1974.

The surprising finding from this study was the level of overlap, where the same DRPs were identified in the same case by both sources. Overall, MRM only found 389 (23%) of the DRPs that pharmacists also found. However, MRM also found an additional 2465 DRPs that pharmacists did not find, and pharmacists also found an additional 1585 DRPs that MRM did not.

Yet, when we delve into the results of sub-study 2, it is clear that the DRPs identified by both sources are, in the vast majority of instances, thought to be clinically relevant by the expert panel. We can infer that of the 2465 additional DRPs that MRM found, 70% of them were clinically relevant (1725 relevant DRPs). Likewise, of the 1974 DRPs that pharmacists found without MRM support, 73% of them were relevant (1441 relevant DRPs). This translates to an average of 3.03 additional relevant DRPs per case when the pharmacist is supported by MRM (2465*0.7/570=3.03), on top of the 2.53 relevant DRPs that pharmacists would find without MRM support (1974*0.73/570=2.53). Overall, this means 2.20 times as many clinically relevant DRPs will be found when the pharmacist is supported by MRM.

It is clear that the MCRDR-based MRM system and the human pharmacist are complementary. The human finds problems that MRM cannot or does not, and MRM finds problems that the human cannot or does not. Both these sets of DRPs are generally thought to be relevant, and the total number of DRPs that can be identified with these two sources working together is far greater than the number of DRPs either of these sources is capable of identifying alone.

This does raise the question of whether the MRM system can be further improved, so as to find more of the relevant problems that it still failed to detect. The answer to this is mixed. It is thought that a substantial portion of the problems MRM failed to detect were "undetectable", in that they involved data that MRM could not possibly have access to. These are things that come out through the patient interview, but are not encoded in their medical data, such as the list included in section 2.2. Beyond this, there is another segment of problems that MRM has failed to detect due to poor design choices. For example, it is not capable of handling combination therapies in an intelligent way – so it will fail to detect that a patient is taking too much of a particular medication if it is delivered as part of a combination therapy. These design issues are addressable, although at this stage significant cost and effort would be expended to do so, for marginal improvement. The third segment of problems that it failed to detect are those that are detectable, but where the rules simply did not exist to cover it. Due to the incremental knowledge acquisition approach of RDR, these problems should eventually be addressed, and indeed may have already been addressed since the time this study was done, assuming that the experts using the system are aware of them.

Considering that MRM is a clinical decision support system that is designed to assist pharmacists when they are conducting medication reviews, and it is not intended to be a stand-alone solution, it is clear that MRM is a highly valuable support tool for medication review pharmacists. It can be reasonably expected to provide substantial additional value for the patient, beyond that which the reviewing pharmacist could provide without its support. The figures suggest approximately 2.25 times as many DRPs will be detected by pharmacists using MRM than those who act without its support, and of these extra DRPs, 70% of them would be clinically relevant, resulting in 2.20 times as many clinically relevant DRPs being found. This supports the estimates produced by Bindoff et al. in their earlier work [3].

An additional benefit of MRM appears to be its ability to generate good recommendations for the resolution of DRPs, since its recommendations were rated more highly by the expert review panel than those provided by the human pharmacists. These results suggest that not only does MRM assist pharmacists by significantly reducing the number of missed, clinically relevant DRPs, and providing good recommendations for their resolution; MRM is also likely to offer the pharmacist slightly better approaches to resolving DRPs than the pharmacist would normally consider. It is difficult to speculate as to why this is the case. Manual inspection suggests that the recommendations MRM made were both more in line with clinical guidelines, and more comprehensive – including more detail and being generally more confident and assured in tone. However, to date, no robust analyses of the qualitative differences between the recommendations has been undertaken.

Additional analyses of MRM have been performed, including a usability and satisfaction survey delivered to MRM users, and a comparison with a range of popular prescribing criteria. However, for the sake of brevity and clarity, these will not be discussed in this paper, but are discussed at length in other publications by the authors.

5   Conclusions

The MCRDR-based MRM clinical decision support system for performing medication reviews is a highly valuable support tool for accredited pharmacists performing medication review services. It detects DRPs with greater frequency than, and equivalent clinical relevance to, human pharmacists acting without its support.

It is expected that pharmacists performing medication reviews with the support of MRM will identify 2.20 times as many clinically relevant DRPs as they would if they were acting independently.

The only further work that remains for this project is to quantify the clinical impact of this tool, by performing a health economics analysis to determine what impacts MRM has in terms of patient quality of life and healthcare expenditure. This analysis would be valuable, as it is still unclear in some instances whether standard medication reviews are a cost effective healthcare service to provide [13, 15]. It is possible that the additional DRPs that MRM can detect for very little additional cost would help to establish clear cost-effectiveness of the service.

References

1. Routledge, P.A., O'Mahony, M.S., Woodhouse, K.W.: Adverse drug reactions in elderly patients. Br. J. Clin. Pharmacol. 57(2), 121–126 (2004)
2. Karnon, J., et al.: Modelling the expected net benefits of interventions to reduce the burden of medication errors. J. Health Serv. Res. Policy 13(2), 85–91 (2008)
3. Bindoff, I., et al.: The potential for intelligent decision support systems to improve the quality and consistency of medication reviews. J. Clin. Pharm. Ther. 37(4), 452–458 (2012)
4. Peterson, G.M.: The future is now: the importance of medication review. Australian Pharmacist 21(4), 268–274 (2002)
5. Bindoff, I., Kang, B.-H., Ling, T., Tenni, P., Peterson, G.: Applying MCRDR to a multi-disciplinary domain. In: Orgun, M.A., Thornton, J. (eds.) AI 2007. LNCS (LNAI), vol. 4830, pp. 519–528. Springer, Heidelberg (2007)
6. Bindoff, I., et al.: Development of an intelligent decision support system for medication review. Journal of Clinical Pharmacy and Therapeutics 32(1), 81–88 (2007)
7. Compton, P., et al.: Experience with ripple-down rules. Knowledge Based Systems 19(5), 356–362 (2006)
8. Deards, E.A.: MCRDR Applied to Email Classification. Department of Computer Science (2001)
9. Kang, B.: Validating knowledge acquisition: multiple classification ripple-down rules. In: Computer Science and Engineering. University of New South Wales, Sydney (1995)
10. Kang, B., Compton, P., Preston, P.: Multiple Classification Ripple Down Rules: Evaluation and Possibilities. AIII-Sponsored Banff Knowledge Acquisition for Knowledge-Based Systems (1995)
11. Kang, B., et al.: Help desk system with intelligent interface. Applied Artificial Intelligence 11(7-8), 611–631 (1997)
12. Park, S., Kim, Y., Kang, B.H.: Personalized Web Document Classification using MCRDR. In: Pacific Knowledge Acquisition Workshop, Auckland (2004)
13. Stafford, A.C.: A clinical and economic evaluation of medication reviews conducted by pharmacists for community-dwelling Australians, University of Tasmania (2012)
14. Curtain, C., et al.: An investigation into drug-related problems identifiable by commercial medication review software. The Australasian Medical Journal 6(4), 183 (2013)
15. Zermansky, A.G., Freemantle, N.: Is medication review by pharmacists of any use? Pharmacoeconomics 25(2), 91–92 (2007)

Incremental Schema Mapping

Sarawat Anam[1,2], Yang Sok Kim[1], and Qing Liu[2]

[1] School of Computing and Information Systems,
University of Tasmania, Sandy Bay, Tasmania, Australia
{Sarawat.Anam,YangSok.Kim}@utas.edu.au
[2] Intelligent Sensing and Systems Laboratory,
CSIRO Computational Informatics, Hobart, Tasmania, Australia
Q.Liu@csiro.au

Abstract. Schema mapping that provides a unified view to the users is essential to manage schema heterogeneity among different sources. Schema mapping can be conducted by machine learning or by knowledge engineering approach. Machine learning approach needs training data set for building models, but usually it is very difficult to obtain training datasets for large datasets. In addition, it is very difficult to change the model by human knowledge. Knowledge engineering approach encodes human knowledge directly, such that the knowledge base can be constructed with limited data, but it needs time consuming knowledge acquisition. This research proposes an incremental schema mapping method that employs Ripple-Down Rules (RDR) with the censored production rules (CPR). Our experimental results show that RDR approach shows comparable performance with the machine learning approaches and RDR knowledge base can be expanded incrementally as the cases classified increase.

Keywords: Schema mapping, incremental knowledge acquisition techniques and machine learning techniques.

1 Introduction

Schema mapping takes as input of two schemas/ontologies, each consisting of a set of discrete entities, and determines as output the relationships holding between these entities [1]. Schema mapping is necessary when data comes from various sources for the following reasons: 1) to improve the quality of data by checking and removing errors, 2) to delete inconsistencies and redundancies in data, and 3) to provide a unified view to the users. Schema mapping is used in many application domains such as data integration, data exchange, data warehousing and schema evolution [2]. Schema mapping can be conducted by schema matching systems, which combine different mapping algorithms with a mapping selection module [3]. Schema matching can be done in the element level and structure level. While the element level matching considers only names of the schemas, the structure level matching uses the result of element level matching for matching the full graph. There are two problems of schema matching: false positives and true negatives which are needed to be solved by the incremental schema mapping approaches.

Y.S. Kim et al (Eds.): PKAW 2014, LNCS 8863, pp. 69–83, 2014.

Many schema mapping systems [4-7] are developed by machine learning and knowledge engineering approaches. Though machine learning techniques are promising for predicting element similarity, but these techniques need training dataset which are got manually. However, for large datasets in various domains, getting training datasets is not feasible. In addition, the model created by the machine learning algorithms cannot be modified by human insight/knowledge. Knowledge engineering approach encodes human knowledge directly, such that the knowledge base can be constructed with limited data. However, the conventional knowledge engineering approaches generally require time consuming knowledge acquisition process, which is called 'knowledge acquisition bottleneck' problem.

Ripple-Down Rule (RDR) has been proposed to address this problem and has been successfully applied in many application domains [8]. There are several versions of RDR methods, including Single Classification RDR (SCRDR), Multiple Classifications RDR (MCRDR), and Nested RDR. Since the research aims to find matching relationship of schema (matched or not-matched), SCRDR is chosen for this research. In RDR methods, each rule can be either a standard production rule (SPR) or a censored production rule (CPR). While SPR has the form $p \rightarrow c$, which is interpreted as "**if** a case satisfies condition p **then** do action a", CPR has the form $p \rightarrow a \neg c$, which is interpreted as "**if** a case satisfies condition p **then** do action a **unless** the case does not satisfy the censor conditions c." Kim et al [9] suggest RDR with CPR which is useful, since the experts can refine the new rule by adding conditions until all incorrect cases are removed. This approach also can provide multiple cornerstone cases that satisfy the main condition clause (positive cornerstone cases) as well as the censored condition clause (negative cornerstone cases).

The main contributions of our research are the followings:

- We design a knowledge-based schema mapping tool using a CPR based RDR. Even though Kim et al. [9] suggested theory of the censored RDR, there is no existing application so far. Therefore, this is the first case study that uses the censored production rules in RDR. It can handle two problems of schema matching, false positives and true negatives using incremental knowledge acquisition techniques.
- We compare the performance of CPR based RDR and machine learning techniques for schema mapping.

2   Related Works

Machine learning techniques have been used in the context of schema matching. Learning Source Descriptions (LSD) [10] is a schema mapping system and the extension of LSD is GLUE [6] which creates ontology mapping. Both systems use machine learning techniques like Multi-strategy learning approach as base learner, Naïve Bayes for classifying text, and Meta learner for finding matching among a set of instances. Marie and Gal [7] develop Schema Matcher Boosting (SMB) approach based on Boosting. They combine more than 30 individual matchers into ensembles and measure performance of the matches over a real world data of 230 schemata. They show that the performance of combined matcher outperforms individual matchers.

Embley et al. [11] develop an approach based on learning rules of decision trees for discovering hidden mapping among entities. In the approach, rules are used for matching terms in WordNet. However, the decision trees are not used for choosing the best match algorithms. In machine learning techniques, training dataset is needed which is got manually and the techniques cannot easily change its conclusion without sufficient data. In our research, we use rule based approach and we provide a comparative analysis of rule based approach to machine learning techniques.

Some systems have already used rule based techniques for schema matching. Among them, COMA/COMA++ [4, 5] is a generic schema and ontology matching systems where simple, hybrid and reuse oriented matchers are used. In the systems, schemas are internally encoded as DAGs (Directed Acyclic Graphs) and are analyzed using string matching algorithms. Different aggregation functions such as average, minimum, maximum and weighted sum, and rule based techniques are used in the systems for obtaining combined match results. However, in COMA/COMA++, determining best combination of matcher is not easy. YAM [12] is a rule based schema matching factory. In the learning phase, YAM considers users' requirement such as a preference for recall or precision, provided expert correspondences. It uses a Knowledge Base (KB) that consists of a set of classifier, a set of similarity measures, and pairs of schemas which have already been matched. In the matching phase, KB is used to match unknown schemas. However, in the system, appropriate classifier is selected by users or to use a default classifier learned over a huge mapping knowledge base. In our rule based system, KB is empty in the beginning, and it is filled by rules incrementally when rules are created to match schemas.

Traditional rule-based systems need time consuming knowledge acquisition as in those systems a highly trained specialist, the knowledge engineer, and the time-poor domain expert are necessary in order to analyze domain [8]. In order to solve the problem of time consuming knowledge acquisition, we adopt RDR (Ripple Down Rule) [13], a well-known incremental knowledge acquisition method. RDR has been successfully applied in many practical knowledge-based system developments and RDR is extended to MCRDR (Multiple Classification Ripple Down Rules) in order to solve problems in some domains, e.g., pathology, text/web document classification, help desk information retrieval and medication review [8]. The success of RDR does not depend on representational differences; rather it largely depends on its distinctive operational semantics on standard production rules (SPR). RDR systems in general process cases sequentially and whenever the current knowledge base suggests wrong conclusions, new rules are added. Whenever a new rule is created, it is necessary to validate the rule normally by checking whether or not the future cases are given the correct classifications. If any case is wrongly classified by a rule, then RDR systems acquire exception rules for this particular rule. In this case, the expert directly refines the new rule adding conditions until all incorrect cases are removed. However, it is not easy to construct this kind of rule with resource constraints such as limited time and information. We use CPR (censored production rules) based RDR [9], to be used for acquiring exceptions when a new rule is created using censor conditions. This approach is useful when we have a large number of validation cases at hand.

3   Methods

3.1   RDR with Censored Production Rule

Ripple down rules (RDR) [13] is an approach that allows the user to incrementally build the knowledge base while the system is in use, with no outside assistance or training from a knowledge engineer. The knowledgebase (KB) of RDR is designed as a binary tree with a rule at each node. A rule consists of conditions and conclusion, like IF [condition] THEN [conclusion]. A conclusion is a classification or an interpretation. The value of the conclusion part of a rule can be null. This rule, called stop rule, is added to stop the application of the current fired rule. Many rules in RDR are exceptions to other rules. The RDR inference operation is based on searching the KB represented as a decision list with each decision possibly refined again by another decision list. Once a rule is satisfied by any case, the inference is terminated. In order to solve some problems, RDR is extended to Single Classification Ripple Down Rules (SCRDR) [14] and Multiple Classification Ripple Down Rules (MCRDR) [15]. Most RDR uses standard production rules and exception rules. With sequential processing, RDR acquires exception rules for a particular rule only after the rule wrongly classifies cases. In order to validate a large number of cases, the rules of RDR has been modified as ordered CPR (Censored Production Rules) [9] where censored conditions are added to create exception rules. Most of the features of CPR based RDR [9] is developed based on MCRDR [15]. In CPR based RDR, a rule is fired as long as none of its exception rules are fired like MCRDR.

Knowledge Base (KB) of CPR Based RDR. The Knowledge Base (KB) of CPR based RDR is designed as an n-tree. Each node of the tree is a rule and each rule consists of IF [conditions] THEN [conclusion] UNLESS [censor-condition].

Inference of CPR Based RDR. The inference process is based on searching the KB represented as a decision list with each decision possibly refined again by another decision list. Once a rule is satisfied by any case, the process evaluates whether or not the censor conditions are matched to the given case. If any censor rule is not satisfied, then the process stops with one path and one conclusion. However, if any censor rule is satisfied, other rules below the rule that was satisfied at the top level is evaluated. The process stops when none of the rules can be satisfied by the case in hand.

Knowledge Acquisition (KA). Knowledge acquisition is a process which transfers knowledge from human experts to knowledge based systems. Knowledge acquisition of CPR based RDR is necessary to handle the incorrect or missing classifications. Knowledge acquisition process can be divided into three parts. Firstly, a correct classification should be decided by the expert. Secondly, new rules' locations should be specified by the system. Thirdly, new rule's condition should be decided by the expert. If the current knowledge base suggests wrong classification, it is necessary to add a censor rule that has NULL as classification. If the current knowledge base suggests no classification for any case, a new rule should be added as an alternative rule, which is added as a child rule of the root node of the knowledge base.

Cornerstone Case (CB). The cases which are used for creating rules are called cornerstone cases and these cases are used in consequent knowledge acquisition [14]. The only difference between conventional RDR and CPR based RDR in managing cornerstone cases is that the CPR based RDR approach maintains non-conforming cases as well as conforming cases for creating a new rule while the conventional RDR approach only maintains conforming cases for a new rule.

3.2   Machine Learning Techniques

In this research, we use five machine learning techniques: decision trees such as J48, RandomForest and ADTree, rules such as DecisionTable, and Bayesian Network, Naïve Bayes. These are supervised classification algorithms. Classification algorithms input a collection of records (training set) where each record contains a set of attributes, and one of the attributes is the class. The purpose of training a dataset is to build up a model for class attribute as a function of the values of other attributes. A test set is used to determine the accuracy of the model.

Decision Tree J48. J48 classifier is a simple C4.5 [16] decision tree for classification. It divides a dataset into smaller subsets and creates a binary decision tree with decision nodes and leaf nodes. A decision node has more than one branch, and the top most decision node corresponds to the best predictor called root node. A leaf node represents a classification or a decision. For a given dataset, one or more decision rules are created that describe the relationships between inputs and targets. Decision rules can predict the value of new or unseen cases if the cases match with the inputs.

Random Forest. Random Forest [17] consists of many individual trees to operate quickly over large datasets. In order to build each tree in the forest, the forest can be diverse by using random samples. A tree is constructed as [18]: (1) bagging takes samples from datasets with replacement for training set and selects small amount of data to be used for tree construction, (2) a random number of attributes is chosen from the bagging data and the one with the most information gain is selected to comprise each node, (3) all the nodes of the tree is traversed until no more nodes can be created due to information loss, and (4) bagging error is estimated by running dataset through tree and measuring its correctness.

ADTree. Alternating decision tree (ADTree) [19] is a generalization of decision trees, voted decision trees and voted decision stumps. It consists of decision nodes and prediction nodes, where decision nodes specify a predicate condition and prediction nodes contain a real valued number. It always has prediction nodes as both root and leaves. In ADTree, an instance defines a set of paths, and the instance is classified by following all paths for which all decision nodes are true and summing any prediction nodes that are traversed.

Decision Table. Decision table represents a conditional probability table and it stores input data based on a selected set of attributes [20] where each entity is associated with class probability. In learning decision table, attributes are selected based on the maximum performance of cross-validation. In cross-validation, the structure of decision table does not change if some instances are inserted or deleted, only the class is changed which is associated with the entities [20].

Naïve Bayes. The Naive Bayes algorithm is a simple probabilistic classifier applied to a classification task [21] . It uses probability based on Bayes Theorem, and inputs a

node F_i for each of the feature and a class variable C. It assumes all attributes to be independent given the value of the class variable.

4 Experimental Design

4.1 Datasets

Four XDR schemas of purchase order domain, such as EXCEL, CIDX, NORIS, and PARAGON, obtained from www.biztalk.org are used for this evaluation study. We denote the schema datasets EXCEL, CIDX, NORIS and PARAGON by E, C, N, and P respectively. These schema datasets are used for some schema matcher evaluation [4]. These schema datasets contain different types of features such as identical words, combined words, abbreviated words and synonym words. Each schema dataset contains 35 (E), 30 (C), 46 (N), and 59 (P) schema names.

4.2 Experimental Procedure

In this research, we experimented five matching tasks one by one using all combinations of four schema datasets such as E-C (first matching task is to deal with two datasets, EXCEL and CIDX), E-N, E-P, C-N, and N-P. We took the Cartesian product of the schema datasets for five matching tasks separately. The sizes of Cartesian product of the matching tasks are 1050 (E-C), 1610 (E-N), 2065 (E-P), 1380 (C-N), and 2714 (N-P) entity pairs. In order to use the datasets for classification and to give proper knowledge to the users for creating rules, we compute attributes as follows:

Attribute Computation. In order to give proper knowledge to the users, attributes are computed in three steps:

- The input schema names (source and target);
- Application of text processing approaches such as tokenization, abbreviations and acronyms expansion, and synonym lookup on the features of input. In tokenization and word separation, schema names containing multiple words are split into lists of words by a customizable tokenizer using punctuation, uppercase, special symbols, whitespace and digits. For instance, "contactEmail" is split into "contact" and "Email". Abbreviations and acronyms are expanded by using external resources such as a dictionary and/or a thesaurus. For instance, "tel" is expanded into its original form "telephone". For this, we use the abbreviation file created for COMA [4]. Synonym processing is applied to use semantically identical schema names to

measure similarity (e.g., 'Invoice' is semantically same as 'Bill' in purchase order domain). We use the synonym file created for COMA [4].

• Application of the string similarity metrics on the features of the attributes computed from step 1 and 2, which creates another attributes. We use string similarity metrics developed by two open source project. For Levenshtein, JaroWinkler, Jaro Measure, TFIDF and Jaccard, we use open source library SecondString[1] and for Monge-Elkan, Smith-Waterman, Needleman-Wunsch, Q-gram and Cosine we use SimMetric open source library[2]. Similarity values are normalized, such that the value within from 0 to 1, where 0 means strong dissimilarity and 1 means strong similarity. The threshold values for deciding schemas matching (true/false) are increased with 0.1 from 0 to 1.We also provide class level (true or false) manually which creates another attribute. In such a way we get 73 attributes by using schema information of two datasets (one matching task). Computed attributes represent knowledge about a relation between attributes, operator or process patterns. After preparing the attributes and the data contents under the attributes, all these are fed in to the rule based technique, CPR based RDR and machine learning techniques.

Schema Mapping by CPR based RDR. A simple GUI (Graphical User Interface) is created which can select any datasets from repository. The attributes that are created by the above steps of *attribute computation* are represented in a "**Case Browser**" to provide sufficient knowledge to the users (**Fig. 1**). The system works in two phases: learning phase and testing phase. In the learning phase, "**Add Classification**" of **Fig. 1** is used. In the testing phase, "**Classify**" button of **Fig. 1** is used.

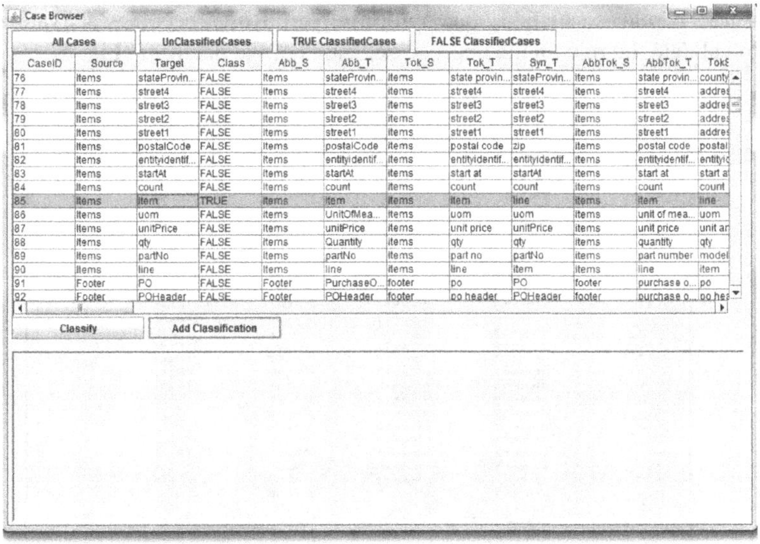

Fig. 1. GUI represents 73 attributes with schema names

---

[1] http://secondstring.sourceforge.net
[2] http://sourceforge.net/projects/simmetrics

In **Fig. 1**, "**Add Classification**" button add classification for a selected case. For adding classification, the Knowledge Acquisition GUI is displayed **in Fig. 2**.

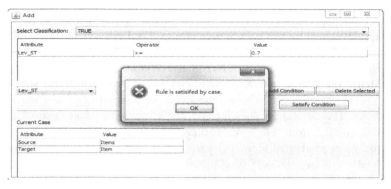

Fig. 2. Knowledge Acquisition GUI for adding rules

In **Fig. 2**, first, the classification of the rule is selected. This can be done using the drop down box at the top, which lists TRUE or FALSE classifications for this domain. Having selected the classification, the rule conditions are added. For each condition in the rule, the attribute, operator, and value are selected from the drop down boxes, which list all the attributes. After selecting condition, "**Add Condition**" adds condition. It is possible to add more than one condition and delete condition using "**Delete Selected**" button if users think that the added condition is not suitable. "**Satisfy Condition**" button helps to look at whether the rule is satisfied by the selected case or not. If rule is satisfied, the "**Validate New Rule**" becomes activate and this helps to validate the rule on the unprocessed cases of the database (**Fig. 3**).

CaseID	Source	Target	ReportedM...	Algorithmic...
32	Header	POHeader	TRUE	TRUE
85	Items	Item	TRUE	TRUE
235	Item	Item	TRUE	TRUE
297	unitPrice	unitPrice	TRUE	TRUE
398	partNumber	poNumber	FALSE	TRUE
483	Contact	Contact	TRUE	TRUE
759	contactName	contactName	TRUE	TRUE
761	contactName	contactEmail	FALSE	TRUE
762	contactName	contactPhone	FALSE	TRUE
827	street4	street4	TRUE	TRUE
828	street4	street3	FALSE	TRUE
829	street4	street2	FALSE	TRUE
830	street4	street1	FALSE	TRUE
857	street3	street4	FALSE	TRUE
858	street3	street3	TRUE	TRUE
859	street3	street2	FALSE	TRUE
860	street3	street1	FALSE	TRUE
887	street2	street4	FALSE	TRUE
888	street2	street3	FALSE	TRUE
889	street2	street2	TRUE	TRUE
890	street2	street1	FALSE	TRUE
917	street1	street4	FALSE	TRUE
918	street1	street3	FALSE	TRUE
919	street1	street2	FALSE	TRUE
920	street1	street1	TRUE	TRUE
946	stateProvince	stateProvince	TRUE	TRUE
981	postalCode	postalCode	TRUE	TRUE
1005	country	country	TRUE	TRUE
1014	country	count	FALSE	TRUE
1033	city	city	TRUE	TRUE

Fig. 3. Rule validation

In **Fig. 3,** *Reported Match* shows the manual matching results and *Algorithmic Match* shows the results calculated from rules. The "**Save Rule**" button helps to save rule in the rule database (KB) and case in the case database. "**Edit Classification**" button helps to refine the wrong classified cases by adding new conditions until all incorrect cases are removed or creating another new rule using knowledge Acquisition GUI. Classification for the censor rule is always "**NULL**". The refined cases and the deleted miss-classified cases from the satisfied cases list are seen in **Fig. 4**.

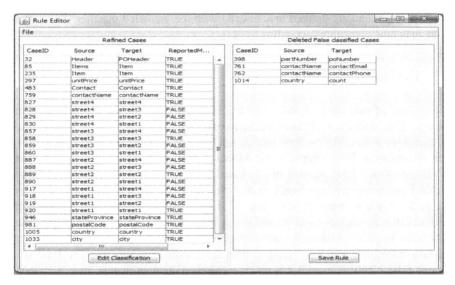

Fig. 4. GUI for refined cases and the deleted cases

In **Fig. 4,** the "**Save Rule**" button saves the censor rule in the rule database (KB) as censor node and the deleted cases in the case database as NULL classification. If there are more wrong classified cases, the rule can be refined by adding other censor rules. Then to classify the "NULL' classified cases, the alternative rules are added by "**Add Classification**" button of **Fig. 1**. The alternative rules are added as parent rules in the KB. In the testing phase, "**Classify**" button of **Fig. 1** classifies test cases using the rules created by the above procedure.

Schema Mapping by Machine Learning Techniques. In order to determine similarity between two datasets, we train one dataset using decision trees such as J48, RandomForest and ADTree, rules such as DecisionTable and Bayesian Network, Naïve Bayes. The attributes which are created by the above steps of *attribute computation*, are used as training sample to build a model. The purpose of building a model is to classify whether a given entity pair of schema names is matched or not based on their feature similarity measure. For all machine learning techniques, we consider 10-fold cross validation. 10-fold cross validation means that the data is split into 10 groups where nine groups are considered for training and the remaining one group is considered for testing. This process is repeated for all 10 groups. For matching entity pair of schema names using the algorithms, we provide the attributes created from another datasets. Finally, we get the results.

4.3   Evaluation Metrics

As this task is a classification task, we use the following conventional metrics: precision $= \frac{TP}{TP+FP}$, recall $= \frac{TP}{TP+FN}$ and F-measure $= \frac{2*precision*recall}{precision+recall}$, where TP is True Positive (hit), FP is False Positive (false alarm, Type I error) and FN is False Negative (miss, Type II error). For a specific threshold value, we calculate TP, FP and FN by comparing manually defined matches (R) with the predicted matches (P) returned by the matching algorithms according to [22].

5   Evaluation Results

Performance of rule based system and machine learning techniques depend on the features of the datasets such as identical words, combined words, abbreviated words and synonym words. The performance of rule based system also depends on the efficient rule creation. For example, if the datasets which are used for training and creating rules contain a large number of combined words, but the testing datasets do not contain large number of combined words, then performance becomes low. We compute performance in terms of precision, recall and F-measure. Precision estimates the reliability of the match predictions and recall specifies the share of real matches. During schema mapping, manually matching schemas of two heterogeneous data sources and false identified matches by algorithms are handled by humans. The burden of deleting false identified matches is much easier than creating manual matches among thousands of schemas [23]. As for calculating recall value, manually identified matches are necessary, so recall value is very important. Only precision or recall cannot estimate the performance of match algorithms [24]. So it is necessary to calculate the overall performance or F-measure of rule based system and machine learning techniques using both precision and recall. For this, we determine the best performing classification system based on the optimized F-measure [7] for almost all experimental datasets. For all experiments using machine learning techniques, we use WEKA [25] data mining and machine learning toolbox. For all experimental results, we denote Performance Metric, CPR based RDR Rule based schema mapping system, decision tree J48, RandomForest, ADTree, DecisionTable and Naïve Bayes by PM, RDR, J48, RF, AT, DT and NB respectively.

5.1   Schema Mapping Results with One Training Dataset

We use E-C for creating rules using RDR and we create 12 rules in order to be satisfied by cases. The detail rule creation process is explained in **Section 4.2**. We also use E-C to feed in to the machine learning techniques, for training. We use other datasets, E-N, E-P, C-N, and N-P for testing. The performance of rule based system and machine learning techniques is summarized in **Table 1**. The results indicate that using RDR, the performance is high in terms of precision and F-measure for E-N, E-P and N-P datasets. DT shows the same precision for E-P dataset and Random Forest shows the same F-measure for N-P dataset. The performance of Random Forest is high in terms of precision and F-measure for C-N dataset. Though the performance of Naïve Bayes algorithm is very low according to precision and F-measure, but is higher according to recall compared to other algorithms. The reason of high precision means less false positive values, and high recall means that the false positive numbers are very high [7]. As the features of C-N dataset is different from other dataset, so the performance of C-N dataset is lower compared to others.

Table 1. Performance Comparison with one training dataset

Datasets	PM	RDR	J48	RF	AT	DT	NB
	Precision	**0.94**	0.91	0.92	0.81	0.81	0.50
E-N	Recall	0.97	0.91	0.94	0.94	0.94	**1.00**
	F-measure	**0.96**	0.91	0.93	0.87	0.87	0.67
	Precision	**0.98**	0.85	0.97	0.87	**0.98**	0.52
E-P	Recall	0.95	0.95	0.81	0.91	0.93	**1.00**
	F-measure	**0.97**	0.90	0.89	0.87	0.95	0.68
	Precision	**0.97**	0.77	0.90	0.87	0.92	0.41
N-P	Recall	0.85	0.85	0.92	0.85	0.85	**1.00**
	F-measure	**0.91**	0.81	0.91	0.86	0.88	0.58
	Precision	0.79	0.78	**0.84**	0.74	0.60	0.44
C-N	Recall	0.93	0.89	0.93	0.93	0.89	**1.00**
	F-measure	0.85	0.83	**0.88**	0.83	0.71	0.61

In order to increase the performance, it is necessary to do further processing. In this research, we combine two datasets, E-C and N-P and train for creating a model and use other datasets for testing. The results are summarized below.

5.2   Schema Mapping Results with Two Training datasets

Table 2 summarizes the schema mapping results when two datasets, E-C and N-P are combined and trained using machine learning techniques and other datasets E-N, E-P, N-P, C-N are tested. However, for rule based system, we do not create rules for E-C and N-P datasets from the very beginning. We use the 12 rules which are created for E-C dataset in the first experiment in **Section 5.1** for classifying N-P dataset. We find that some cases are not classified correctly by the existing rules. For this, we add censor rules to make the classification NULL and add alternative rules to classify the cases correctly and this process incrementally builds the knowledge base. Then we use all the 13 rules to classify the datasets. We also find that some cases are not classified correctly. We add another rule in order to solve the problem of wrong classification. Finally, we use all the 14 rules to get the result. In **Table 2**, we find that the performance of Rule based system and almost all algorithms is improved in terms of precision, recall and F-measure. However, the performance of Naive Bayes is decreased according to precision and F-measure. Recall of Naive Bayes is always high because it can match all the true cases and it can match many cases which are not actually true. The results indicate that the performance of RDR is high for E-N dataset according to precision, recall and F-measure. Random Forest shows better performance for two datasets, E-P and N-P. The performance of AT is higher than others in terms of precision and F-measure.

Table 2. Performance Comparison with two training datasets

Datasets	PM	RDR	J48	RF	AT	DT	NB
	Precision	**0.92**	0.89	0.90	0.85	0.89	0.41
E-N	Recall	**1.00**	0.91	0.97	0.94	0.94	**1.00**
	F-measure	**0.96**	0.90	0.93	0.89	0.92	0.58
	Precision	0.98	0.98	**1.00**	0.98	0.97	0.44
E-P	Recall	0.98	0.93	0.98	0.93	0.88	**1.00**
	F-measure	0.98	0.95	**0.99**	0.95	0.93	0.61
	Precision	0.97	0.97	**0.98**	0.97	0.95	0.33
N-P	Recall	0.95	0.95	**1.00**	0.97	0.95	**1.00**
	F-measure	0.96	0.96	**0.99**	0.97	0.95	0.50
	Precision	0.79	0.77	0.74	**0.89**	0.74	0.36
C-N	Recall	0.96	0.93	0.93	0.89	0.89	**1.00**
	F-measure	0.87	0.84	0.83	**0.89**	0.81	0.53

5.3   Prune Tree and Knowledge Base

As an example of prune tree for training one dataset (left) and two datasets (right) using J48 is given in Fig. 5. It is found that the prune tree for training one dataset is different from the prune tree of training two datasets.

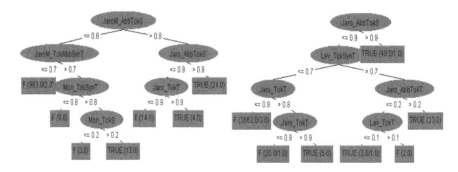

Fig. 5. J48 Prune Tree for training one dataset (left) and two datasets (right)

The Knowledge Base (KB) of RDR which is created for one dataset and two datasets is given in **Table 3**. In **Table 3,** rule 1 is always true. We use rules 2 to 13 for classifying cases of E-C dataset. We apply rules 2 to 13 to classify other datasets. In order to solve missclassification and incorrect classification of N-P dataset, we create rules 14 and 15 which incrementally increase the knowledge base.

Table 3. Knowledge Base (KB) for creating rules for one dataset and two datasets

RuleID	ParentRuleID	Condition	Conclusion	ClassifiedCaseID
1	0			0
2	1	Lev_ST == 1.0	TRUE	1033
3	1	Source== AbbT	TRUE	1
4	1	Lev_SynT == 1.0	TRUE	240
5	1	Lev_TokS == 1.0	TRUE	204
6	1	Lev_TokT== 1.0	TRUE	489
7	1	Lev_ST == 0.9	FALSE	828
8	1	Lev_AbbTokS >= 0.9	TRUE	269
9	1	Lev_TokSynT >= 0.9	TRUE	125
10	9	Mon_AbbTokS == 0.2	NULL	699
11	1	Lev_ST == 0.8	TRUE	85
12	1	Lev_TokSynT == 0.8	TRUE	90
13	1	Lev_ST <= 0.7	FALSE	2
14	1	Lev_TokSynT== 1.0	TRUE	383
15	1	Lev_AbbS == 0.8	TRUE	1183

In **Table 3,**   Lev, S, T, AbbT, SynT, TokS, TokT, AbbTokS, TokSynT, Mon, AbbS means Levenshtein function, source schema, target schema, abbreviation of target, synonym of target, tokenization of source, tokenization of target, abbreviation and tokenization of source, tokenization and synonym of target, Monge-Elkan function, abbreviation of source respectively. The values 1.0, 0.9, 0.2 are thresholds. For example, Lev_ST==0.8 means if the value of Levenshtein function applied on source and target equals to the threshold value 0.8, then the conclusion is TRUE.

6   Discussion

In order to achieve high match accuracy, it is necessary to handle two problems of schema matching: incorrect matching where irrelevant matching among schemas is found as relevant (false positive matching), and missing correct matching where relevant matching among schemas is found as irrelevant (true negative matching) [7]. The advantage of CPR based RDR rule based schema mapping system compared to machine learning techniques is that it can incrementally build knowledge base by adding rules to solve schema matching problems. Though we have been able to delete some false positive values and solve the problem of true negative values using CPR based RDR rule based schema mapping system, but in the results, there are still some false positive values. Though F-measure is high for almost all datasets, but for C-N dataset, the performance is not high. In order to improve the performance, we will add structure level matching with our element level matching.

7   Conclusion

In this research, we have computed attributes from the input schemas as well as from the application of text processing techniques and string similarity metrics on the schema names. We have designed a schema mapping tool and use the attributes in order to create rules using CPR based RDR. It can handle two problems of schema matching, false positives and true negatives using incremental knowledge acquisition techniques. We have also used the attributes to feed into machine learning techniques, and have compared the performance of CPR based RDR and machine learning techniques for schema mapping. We have found that our CPR based RDR schema mapping system shows comparable performance with machine learning techniques. In this research, we have only considered element level matching, but accurate results of this element level matching should be a premise to work in the next step with structure level matching. In structure level matching, more wrongly suggested match candidates (false positive values) will be handled for increasing the performance of schema mapping system.

Acknowledgement. The Intelligent Sensing and Systems Laboratory and the Tasmanian node of the Australian Centre for Broadband Innovation are assisted by a grant from the Tasmanian Government which is administered by the Tasmanian Department of Economic Development, Tourism and the Arts.

References

1. Cate, B. T., Dalmau, V. and Kolaitis, P.G.: Learning schema mappings, in Proceedings of the 15th International Conference on Database Theory, ACM: Berlin, Germany, p. 182-195 (2012).
2. Glavic, B., Alonso, G., Miller, R. J. and Hass, L. M.: TRAMP: Understanding the behavior of schema mappings through provenance, in Proceedings of the VLDB Endowment, 3(1-2): p. 1314-1325 (2010).
3. Ngo, D., Bellahsene, Z. and Todorov, K.: Opening the Black Box of Ontology Matching, in The Semantic Web: Semantics and Big Data, Springer, p. 16-30 (2013).
4. Do, H. H. and Rahm, E.: COMA: a system for flexible combination of schema matching approaches, in Proceedings of the 28th international conference on Very Large Data Bases, VLDB Endowment: Hong Kong, China, p. 610-621 (2002).
5. Aumueller, D., Do, H. H., Massmann, S. and Rahm, E.: Schema and ontology matching with COMA++, in Proceedings of the ACM SIGMOD international conference on Management of data, ACM (2005).
6. Doan, A., Madhavan, J., Domingos, P. and Halevy, A.: Learning to map between ontologies on the semantic web, in Proceedings of the 11th international conference on World Wide Web, ACM (2002).
7. Marie, A. and Gal, A.: Boosting schema matchers, in On the Move to Meaningful Internet Systems: OTM 2008, Springer, p. 283-300 (2008).
8. Richards, D.: Two decades of ripple down rules research, The Knowledge Engineering Review, 24(02): p. 159-184 (2009).

9. Kim, Y. S., Compton, P. and Kang, B. H.: Ripple-down rules with censored production rules, in Knowledge Management and Acquisition for Intelligent Systems, Springer, p. 175-187 (2012).

10. Doan, A., Domingos, P. and Halevy, A.Y.: Reconciling schemas of disparate data sources: A machine-learning approach, in ACM Sigmod Record, ACM (2001).

11. Embley, D. W., Xu, L. and Ding, Y.: Automatic direct and indirect schema mapping: experiences and lessons learned, ACM SIGMod Record, 33(4): p. 14-19 (2004).

12. Duchateau, F., Coletta, R., Bellahsene, Z. and Miller, R. J.: Yam: a schema matcher factory, in Proceedings of the 18th ACM conference on Information and knowledge management, ACM (2009).

13. Compton, P., Edwards, G., Kang, B., Lazarus, L., Malor, R., Menzies, T., Preston, P., Srinivasan, A. and Sammut, S.: Ripple down rules: possibilities and limitations, in Proceedings of the Sixth AAAI Knowledge Acquisition for Knowledge-Based Systems Workshop, Calgary, Canada, University of Calgary (1991).

14. Compton, P. and Jansen, R.: A philosophical basis for knowledge acquisition, Knowledge acquisition, 2(3): p. 241-258 (1990).

15. Kang, B., Compton, P. and Preston, P.: Multiple classification ripple down rules: Evaluation and possibilities, in The 9th knowledge acquisition for knowledge based systems workshop (1995).

16. Quinlan, J. R.: C4.5: programs for machine learning, California Morgan kaufmann (1993).

17. Breiman, L.: Random forests, Machine learning, 45(1): p. 5-32 (2001).

18. Pater, N.: Enhancing random forest implementation in WEKA, in Machine learning conference paper for ECE591Q. (2005).

19. Freund, Y. and Mason, L.: The alternating decision tree learning algorithm, in ICML (1999).

20. Hall, M. and Frank, E.: Combining Naive Bayes and Decision Tables, in FLAIRS Conference (2008).

21. Sahami, M., Dumais, S., Heckerman, D. and Horvitz, E.: A Bayesian approach to filtering junk e-mail, in Learning for Text Categorization: Papers from the workshop (1998).

22. Jimenez, S., Becerra, C., Gelbukh, A. and Gonzalez, F.: Generalized mongue-elkan method for approximate text string comparison, in Computational Linguistics and Intelligent Text Processing, Springer. p. 559-570 (2009).

23. Stoilos, G., Stamou, G. and Kollias, S.: A string metric for ontology alignment, in Proceedings of the 4th international conference on The Semantic Web, Springer-Verlag: Galway, Ireland, p. 624-637 (2005).

24. Cheng, W., Lin, H. and Sun, Y.: An efficient schema matching algorithm, in Knowledge-Based Intelligent Information and Engineering Systems, Springer (2005).

25. Hall, M., Frank, E., Holmes, G., Pfahringer, B., Reutemann, P. and Witten, I. H.: The WEKA data mining software: an update, ACM SIGKDD explorations newsletter, 11(1): p. 10-18 (2009).

Linked Production Rules: Controlling Inference with Knowledge

Paul Compton[1], Yang Sok Kim[2], and Byeong Ho Kang[2]

[1] School of Computer Science and Engineering, The University of New South Wales
Sydney 2052, Australia
[2] School of Computing and Information Systems, The University of Tasmania
Hobart 7005, Australia
compton@cse.unsw.edu.au,
{yangsok.kim,byeon.kang}@utas.edu.au

Abstract. A key insight in artificial intelligence, which has been the foundation of expert systems and now business-rule systems, is that reasoning or inference can be separated from the domain knowledge being reasoned about. We suggest that the knowledge acquisition and maintenance problems that arise, might result from too great a separation of knowledge and inference. We propose Linked Production Rules, where each rule evaluated directs the next step of inference and the inference engine has no meta-heuristics or conflict resolution strategy. We suggest that this loses none of the power of conventional inference but may greatly improve knowledge acquisition and maintenance since various Ripple-Down Rule knowledge acquisition methods, which have had some success in facilitating knowledge maintenance can be described as specific instances of Linked Production Rules. Finally the Linked Production Rule approach suggests the possibility of a generalized Ripple-Down Rule method applicable to a wide range of problem types.

Keywords: inference engine, declarative knowledge, conflict-resolution, problem-solving methods, Ripple-Down Rules.

1   Introduction

A crucial insight in the history of artificial intelligence was that domain knowledge should not be embedded in procedural code, but that knowledge and reasoning can be separated. This insight resulted in the classic idea of a rule-based expert system, composed of a knowledge base, working memory and an inference engine. However, the inference engine itself contains knowledge embedded in procedural code: not only different reasoning strategies, but ad hoc conflict resolution strategies.

While there has been some research on specifying the knowledge used in controlling inference e.g. [1], it is probably fair to say that most business-rule systems, the latest incarnation of the expert system idea use the same sort of inference engine and conflict resolution strategies developed over 30 years ago for expert systems. The aim of this paper is to revisit the way in which domain knowledge and inference have

Y.S. Kim et al (Eds.): PKAW 2014, LNCS 8863, pp. 84–98, 2014.

been separated in expert systems, and now business rule systems, and question whether this is the best approach to building these systems. The discussion here is restricted to forward-chaining propositional production rule systems, as these are the dominant form of rule-based technology.

Typically [2] a production rule is described as having two components a condition part and an action list

```
if [condition] then [action-list]
```

This rule representation does not contain any information about which rule should be evaluated next as this is determined by the inference engine. In practice there may be other information specified with the rule such as salience but this only gives the rule a priority to be used in determining whether a rule should be evaluated. In contrast we propose an approach where each rule contains information that determines which rule will be evaluated next rather than this being determined by the inference engine using its conflict resolution heuristics.

In our proposal for **Linked Production Rules**, there are three types of component: [condition], [**case** action-list] and [**inference** action]. Inference actions do not change the case (working memory), but specify which rule is to be evaluated next and only a single rule can be specified. Case actions change the case in the conventional way. We use the term case rather than working memory to emphasise that rule-based systems process and add further facts to cases where a case is a group of data from the world (e.g. a partial patient record). The rule-based system reasons about the case and if possible adds to the case (e.g. a diagnosis or patient management plan).

In the Linked Production Rule approach inference actions are specified for every rule both for when the rule is satisfied and when it is evaluated but fails. This gives the following structure:

```
if [condition] then [case action-list],

[inference action]
      else [inference action]
```

In this representation there is a single specific inference action for whether the rule fires or fails to fire.

The paper contains: a review of the problems with rule-based systems; a discussion of the simplicity of knowledge acquisition with Ripple-Down Rules and how this arises because they are instances of Linked Production Rules and finally an outline of how Linked Production Rules can be used for rule-based systems in general.

2   Issues with Rule-Based Systems

After the initial euphoria over the possibilities with expert systems, it became clear that they were harder to build and maintain than hoped. XCON, one of the most successful early expert systems, was very expensive to maintain. It took over a year of training before DEC engineers could maintain XCON, then a system with 1,000 rules, and its maintenance demands meant they were unable to also maintain other expert systems introduced from CMU to DEC [3]. XCON eventually had 6,500 rules with 50% changed every year – a major maintenance challenge [4].

It has been argued that the situated nature of knowledge is the underlying problem in knowledge acquisition (e.g. [5]). Clancey in particular argued that knowledge is not something in the head to be mined – a common metaphor – but is constructed in particular contexts. From experience maintaining an early medical expert system, it was argued that human expertise does not provide reasons why conclusion X is correct in any absolute sense, but why it is a better hypothesis than other conclusions in the context [6]. This parallels the qualification problem [7]: that it is impossible to enumerate every factor that might alter the outcome of an action.

Situated cognition explained why experts cannot readily justify conclusions out of context, but we suggest that the separation of knowledge and inference in rule-based systems has compounded the difficulties of acquiring, and particularly maintaining, knowledge. As suggested by the qualification problem, and as observed (e.g [8]), there always seem to be errors and omissions that need fixing; however, one does not readily know how changes in knowledge will interact with the inference engine and its conflict resolution strategies acting on top of domain knowledge and exerting procedural control over how the domain knowledge is used. "Changing a knowledge base of an expert system built with typical current technology requires a knowledge engineer who understands the design of the system and the structure of the knowledge base thoroughly; most often, this means only the original author of the system"[9]. In a study of expert systems for industrial applications, in which less that half the apparently successful systems were actually functioning, Bachmann et al noted: "Parts of the problem solving strategy applied by experts in the field of configuration or machinery diagnosis are not represented in the knowledge base of the system but in its inference engine. This is totally ignored if highly specified ready-made shells are used". [10]

Various researchers have identified that expert systems addressed different kinds of tasks e.g. [11,12]. This led to comprehensive software engineering approaches where the nature of the problem, and hence the appropriate problem-solving method, were identified prior to acquiring specific domain knowledge (e.g. [13]). One would expect such methods, as with any systematic software engineering, to increase the likelihood that a successful system will result; however, it is unclear whether this reduces the maintenance problems due to the separation of knowledge and inference, or whether these remain because the knowledge embedded in the inference engine is not under the control of the domain expert. In a recent survey of developers of rule-based systems, using a range of tools and methods, the major problem identified was knowledge debugging i.e. dealing with the difficulties in making changes to a knowledge base [14]. It seems clear that these debugging problems are precisely because the developer often does not know how a change in the knowledge base will be handled by the inference engine without trial and error.

Our focus here is on rule-based systems because of their re-emergence as business rule systems. A central assumption behind business rule systems is again that declarative knowledge in the form of rules is much more maintainable than procedural code in data base triggers [15] – the expert system insight revisited. A web search suggests that these systems are largely based on inference techniques deriving from work on RETE networks [16] and the conflict resolution strategies used in early expert systems. There is also interest in sequential inferencing for business rules, but aimed at improving performance for a given rule set rather than improving knowledge maintenance e.g. [17]. The general idea of a strict inference sequence is part of the OMG standard [2]; what we propose here is a particular way structuring the sequence.

One conflict resolution strategy, salience, relates to our proposal. Salience and the more formally defined Courteous Logic [1] allow the expert or knowledge engineer to specify the relative priority between pairs of rules. Such approaches are of increasing importance and Courteous Logic is part of RuleML [18]. These techniques are an option the expert or knowledge engineer may apply to some rules, to help resolve between which rule to fire if both are candidates. In contrast, the Linked Production Rule approach requires that the next rule to be evaluated be explicitly specified by the current rule being evaluated. Possibly this full specification of inference paths could be implemented with Courteous Logic, or other forms of labeled logic, but the starting point of these approaches is to determine between candidate rules which should be evaluated next, whereas with Linked Production Rules, each rule that is evaluated (whether true or false) specifies the next rule to be evaluated.

3   Ripple-Down Rules (RDR)

In this section we briefly outline some of the successes of Ripple-Down Rules (RDR). Since, as will be shown, RDR are an example of Linked Production Rules, the utility of RDR demonstrates or at least suggests the utility of Linked Production Rules. The two most common forms of RDR, single and multiple classification, will be presented as Linked Production Rule systems below.

3.1   RDR Introduction

RDR were developed in response to the maintenance problems of expert systems [19]. The essential feature of RDR is that rules are added to deal with specific cases (generally while the system is already in operational use). That is, a case has been processed by the system with a specific inference sequence and has failed to give the correct output. New rules to give the correct output for the case are added into the inference sequence. This rule placement is automatic and outside the control of the expert (or knowledge engineer). Since there is no knowledge structuring by the expert or knowledge engineer and no requirement to understand the knowledge base as a whole, rules can be added by domain experts. Greater detail of these algorithms will be shown using the linked rule representation below.

The strict inference sequencing in RDR enables a second type of knowledge acquisition support. An expert may add a rule for the case that is overly specific, but they can only introduce an error affecting the previous knowledge base by adding a rule that is too general, so that cases previously processed by the same sequence may now incorrectly fire the new rule. Such cases can be shown to the expert who either makes their rule more specific to exclude the cases, or accepts that the rule should apply to these cases. Suitable cases can be provided by saving the cases for which rules are added, known as 'cornerstone cases'.

3.2   RDR Experience

The first RDR system in routine use, using SCRDR inference (see below), was a 2000 rule system for chemical pathology [20]. Later pathology systems in routine use were based on MCRDR (see below). In a study of these systems, chemical pathologists from one laboratory added about 16,000 rules across 20 knowledge bases over a 29 month period, at an median speed of 77 secs per rule [21]. Since rules are only added for cases, 77 secs is the time to call up a case, add a rule and test the rule against other cases. The case has already been identified as requiring a new conclusion – a standard pathologist task. The median time of 77 secs covers the purely knowledge engineering task of selecting and verifying conditions for the rule, or rules against past cases. In a more recent larger study the median time to add a rule across 17 laboratories, 256 knowledge bases and about 56,000 rules was 78 secs [22]. About 46% of the rules were added after the systems had been in use for more than a year and the median time to add these rules was 91 secs. This on-going and very rapid rule acquisition strongly suggest that experts found it still easy to add rules more than a year after the system had been introduced. This contrasts with the comments that the whole knowledge base needs to be understood [9]. There are no directly comparable data on the time to add rules to a conventional knowledge base, but Zacharias' study implies the average time to add a rule is more like half an hour to five hours [14].

RDR are used commercially in other areas apart from medicine. For example Ivis [23] and Erudine [24] use technology based on RDR for marketing and software engineering respectively, while IBM offers data a cleansing product based on RDR [25]. The point of these references is to demonstrate that RDR, which we will now describe in terms of Linked Production Rules, is a commercially successful approach to building rule-based systems, and which as the results from pathology demonstrate, allows very rapid and simple rule addition throughout the life of the system.

3.3   RDR as Linked Production Rules

SCRDR Inference. Table 1 shows an example of a single classification RDR (SCRDR) knowledge base as linked rules. The same SCRDR knowledge base is shown in Fig 1 using a more conventional RDR tree representation. SCRDR was the first RDR system proposed [19] and used in the first RDR pathology system [20]. An SCRDR knowledge base is a binary tree, but in practice such trees are very unbalanced since rules tend to be added as new rules or new corrections to a rule rather than deeper and deeper corrections.

Table 1. an SCRDR knowledge base as Linked Production Rules. Inf. action is an abbreviation for inference action. The rule numbers indicate the order in which rules were added. Inference starts with rule 1 and terminates when an exit is reached. For illustration, the conclusions are identified by the number of the rule which asserts them. In practice some of the conclusions may be identical as different inference paths may give the same conclusion.

Rule no	Case actions	Inf. action (true)	Inf. action (false)
1	assert conc 1	exit	to rule 2
2	assert conc 2	to rule 3	to rule 4
3	retract conc 2 assert 3	exit	to rule 6
4	assert conc 4	to rule 5	exit
5	retract conc 4 assert 5	exit	to rule 7
6	retract conc 2 assert 6	exit	exit
7	retract conc 4 assert 7	exit	exit

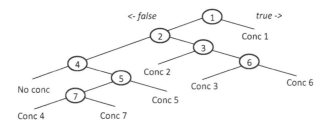

Fig. 1. the same knowledge base as Table 1, but shown as a binary tree. The rule numbers are in circles. If a rule fires the right hand link is traversed, if it fails to fire the left hand link is traversed. The rule numbers indicate the order in which rules were added.

Table 2 shows examples of extra rules being added to the knowledge base in Table 1. Rule 8 is added for a case where no conclusion was given. The false branch of rule 4, the former exit point for the case, links to rule 8. Rule 9 is added because rule 6 has given the wrong conclusion and so the rule 6 inference action for true, links to rule 9. Rule 10 is added since rule 4 gave the wrong conclusion, and no correction rule fired (i.e rules 5 & 7). The false branch inference action for rule 7, links to rule 10 giving the same sequence of 4 true, 5 & 7 false whenever 10 is evaluated.

Table 2. The three rules that have been added to Table 1 are shown, as well as the three rules whose inference action was changed to link to the new rules. New rules are in *italics* and changed actions are **bold**.

4	assert conc 4	to rule 5	**to rule 8**
6	retract conc 2 assert 6	**to rule 9**	exit
7	retract conc 4 assert 7	exit	**to rule 10**
8	*assert conc 8*	*exit*	*exit*
9	*retract conc 6 assert 9*	*exit*	*exit*
10	*retract conc 4 assert 10*	*exit*	*exit*

These changes to inference actions are not under the control of the expert, but automatically determined by the inference sequence for the case for which a rule is being added. The case action for a rule is not changed; only the inference action.

MCRDR Inference. Multiple classification RDR (MCRDR) was introduced to allow multiple conclusions for a case, e.g multiple diagnoses [26] and is widely used in pathology [22]. MCRDR has an n-ary tree structure; i.e. at the top level all rules are evaluated and if a rule fires all its correction rules are evaluated and so on; however, since rules are always evaluated one-by-one, the order can be made explicit. MCRDR papers do not specify the order of sibling rule evaluation but of course a specific order is implemented by the person programming the MCRDR system. Since the whole sequence must be specified with Linked Production Rules, we specify that older siblings should be evaluated before newer - which we believe has been the actual common practice. The difference here is that the sequence is specified in the knowledge base, rather than being part of the inference engine implementation.

Table 3. An MCRDR knowledge base as Linked Production Rules; same formatting as Table 1

Rule no	Case actions	Inf. action (true)	Inf. action (false)
1	assert conc 1	to rule 2	to rule 2
2	assert conc 2	to rule 3	to rule 4
3	retract conc 2 assert 3	to rule 4	to rule 6
4	assert conc 4	to rule 5	exit
5	retract conc 4 assert 5	to rule 7	to rule 7
6	retract conc 2 assert 6	to rule 4	to rule 4
7	retract conc 4 assert 7	exit	exit

Table 4a. Addition of rule 8 giving an extra conclusion

4	assert conc 4	to rule 5	**to rule 8**
7	retract conc 4 assert 7	**to rule 8**	**to rule 8**
8	*assert conc 8*	*exit*	*exit*

Table 4b. Addition of rule 8 and then rule 9. Rule 9 is a correction to rule 6

4	assert conc 4	to rule 5	**to rule 8**
6	retract conc 2 assert 6	**to rule 9**	**to rule 9**
7	retract conc 4 assert 7	**to rule 8**	**to rule 8**
8	*assert conc 8*	*exit*	*exit*
9	*retract conc 6 assert 9*	*to rule 4*	*to rule 4*

Table 4c. Addition of rules 8, 9 and 10. Rule 10 is a further correction to rule 4

4	assert conc 4	to rule 5	**to rule 8**
6	retract conc 2 assert 6	**to rule 9**	**to rule 9**
7	retract conc 4 assert 7	**to rule 10**	**to rule 10**
8	*assert conc 8*	*exit*	*exit*
9	*retract conc 6 assert 9*	*to rule 4*	*to rule 4*
10	*retract conc 4 assert 10*	*to rule 8*	*to rule 8*

Table 3 shows an MCRDR knowledge base as Linked Production Rules with a parent before child and older child before new child sequence. The difference from the SCRDR KB in table 1 is that inference passes to a sibling rule rather than exiting after a conclusion is decided, resulting in potentially many conclusions. Tables 4a-c show how further MCRDR corrections are made; they are shown cumulatively, with one extra rule being added in each table.

The SCRDR and MCRDR Linked Production Rule representations in Tables 1 and 3 provide a complete description of SCRDR and MCRDR inference and how new rules are added. Because with RDR the rules are at least implicitly linked, RDR knowledge acquisition results in a new rule or rules being automatically linked into the inference sequence, as shown in the examples above. This allows for very simple rule addition, with the rule then being checked using the case differentiation support normally provided by RDR. That is, if any previous case can fire the new rule, then the expert needs to select further features from the current case to be added to the rule to distinguish the cases, or alternatively the expert may decide the conclusion from the new rule should apply to the previous case. The normal practice with RDR is to store and check the cases which have prompted the addition of a rule, so-called cornerstone cases. For SCRDR only the case for the parent rule needs to be considered, while for MCRDR the case for the parent rule, and the cases from sibling rules to the new rule need to be considered. A rule added at the top level of an MCRDR tree requires that all cases be checked, but in practice the expert only considers 2 or 3 cases before the rule is sufficiently precise to exclude all previous cases.

It is beyond the scope of this paper to consider other RDR methods and the range of RDR research (reviewed by [27]), but all RDR methods implicitly have a fixed inference path and a fixed way of adding new or correction rules into the inference path, and also check new rules against some sort of selection of past cases.

4   Production Rule Systems in General

Colomb and Chung have proved that any propositional production rule expert system is equivalent to and can be converted into a decision table [28]. Although this conversion is a simple in theory, it can produce unmanageably large decision tables. Colomb's solution, inter alia, is to use a set of cases known to be processed by the expert system to remove unused rows [29]. If as we suggest here the system is built as a decision table, with rows (rules) added only to deal with specific cases, the explosion in the number of rows will not arise.

Since the order of inference for the rows (rules) in a decision table is not defined, there is no loss of generality in specifying a particular order, e.g. from the first to the latest row or rule added. If a new rule is required for a case it is added at the end. Table 5 shows an example where rule 3 has given the wrong conclusion. It is retracted by rule 3.1 and a rule with the same body, but giving the new conclusion, is added at the bottom. The expert simply provides the rule to give the new conclusion, and this is used for both. As with RDR, (cornerstone) cases are used to check if cases from earlier rules fire rule 6, and the rule is made more specific if necessary.

Although the structure in Table 5 is one of many possible, it has a particular feature: that if an expert adds a rule to retract a conclusion this is automatically linked to the rule whose conclusion is to be retracted. I.e. rules that retract conclusions are not added as standard rules as normally allowed, but always linked to the rule being corrected. Such rules are *composite rules* [30] and have also been described as censored production rules for use in data mining [31]. The difference between this approach and the RDR systems described above is that rules now have only one level of correction, and these corrections do not provide a conclusion to replace a previous conclusion, but simply stop the conclusion being given, with a new rule used to add the new conclusion. In fact in the first experiments with MCRDR using simulated experts, this particular structure was used with the correction rules called stopping rule [32].

Table 5. A decision table where rule 3 gives the wrong conclusion and should be replaced by the rule 6 conclusion

Rule no	Case actions	Inf. action (true)	Inf. action (false)
1	assert conc 1	to rule 2	to rule 2
2	assert conc 2	to rule 3	to rule 3
3	assert conc 3	**to rule 3.1**	to rule 4
3.1(6)	*retract conc 3*	*to rule 4*	*to rule 4*
4	assert conc 4	to rule 5	to rule 4
5	assert conc 5	**to rule 6**	**to rule 6**
6	*assert conc 6*	*exit*	*exit*

The inference considered so far has been simple one-pass inference. Intermediate conclusions, to reduce the amount of knowledge required, are widely used in expert systems [12]. The use of intermediates generally requires that inference is repeated over the whole knowledge base, which of course results in rules that use the raw data to provide some intermediate conclusion, being evaluated before rules that need these intermediate conclusions to reach further conclusions – perhaps further intermediate conclusions. Since all rules are repeatedly considered for evaluation, a RETE network is often used to improve efficiency [16], with inference finally stopping when no further conclusions are made.

Table 6. A flat rule structure with repeat inference

Rule no	Case actions	Inf. action (true)	Inf. action (false)
1	assert conc 1	to rule 1	to rule 2
2	assert conc 2	to rule 1	to rule 3
3	assert conc 3	to rule 1	to rule 4
4	assert conc 4	to rule 1	to rule 5
5	assert conc 5	to rule 1	exit

We use the following to provide structure inference: knowledge acquisition or maintenance takes place because a case is identified as needing a new or corrected conclusion. This happens only after inference on the case is complete; i.e. all inference cycles have been completed. If a new rule is added at the bottom, like rule 6 in Table 5, this should be processed after the previous repeat inference for the case is complete so rule 6 is reached after the same inference sequence giving the same wrong conclusion. If this applies to all rules as they are added we end up with the structure shown in Table 6, where after each rule satisfied, inference returns to the first rule. Table 7 shows an example of where a correction rule is added for a repeat inference. Two correction rules are added to illustrate the links.

Table 7. A flat rule structure with repeat inference with two correction rules to retract the conclusion of rule 3, when the conclusions of rule 6 or 7 should be given instead.

Rule no	Case actions	Inf. action (true)	Inf. action (false)
1	assert conc 1	to rule 1	to rule 2
2	assert conc 2	to rule 1	to rule 3
3	assert conc 3	**to rule 3.1**	to rule 4
3.1(6)	retract conc 3	to rule 4	to rule 3.2
3.2(7)	retract conc 3	to rule 4	to rule 1
4	assert conc 4	to rule 1	to rule 5
5	assert conc 5	to rule 1	to rule 6
6	assert conc 6	to rule 1	to rule 7
7	assert conc 7	to rule 1	exit

To stop endless repeat inference the inference engine does not re-evaluate any rule that has already been satisfied (even if its conclusion has been retracted by one of its refinements). When inference is directed to such a rule the inference action of the false branch is followed. For problems such as configuration, where a solution has multiple components, with dependencies between them, but only one value for each component, we further constrain inference. If a component is already part of the case (from the original data or added by a previous rule) any further rule assigning a value for that component is bypassed (i.e. its false branch is followed). If components in the solution need to be added to or changed, they are fixed in the order in which they are inferred. That is, the first component is fixed (by adding and/or stopping a rule) and the case is rerun and the next error fixed – perhaps newly introduced by the first correction, and the case is rerun again and so on. Because of the way the rules are linked, no earlier conclusion for a case can be altered by a later change, so this approach guarantees that the maximum number of changes to fix a case (i.e. the number of rules added) is no more than the number of components that make up the overall conclusion for the case. Each fix, or addition to the inference sequence, should take the same minimal time as with RDR.

It is beyond the scope of this paper to provide detailed examples of Linked Production Rules for other problem types; however, the approach outlined is essentially a problem solving method that builds a solution for a case one component at a time, regardless of whether it is a classification or a construction problem. Errors in particular components are corrected by knowledge acquisition rather than by reasoning as in problem solving methods such as Propose and Revise.

A final question is computational efficiency because inference is repeated each time a conclusion is reached. Considered very simplistically: if there are n components to a solution and the rules that infer these components are scattered randomly through the m rules, on average m x n/2 rules will need to be evaluated, with m x n as the worst case. If we consider a conventional system in the same simplistic way, all rules are evaluated on each pass for the conflict resolution to determine which satisfied rule will be acted on. The means at least m x n rules will be evaluated. Of course a RETE network or other techniques can be used to speed the process – but such techniques, which essentially maintain an index of rules that have fired and rules that could fire, should be able to be applied to Linked Production Rules, suggesting a general Linked Production Rule system should be at least as efficient as a conventional system.

4.1   Ontologies and Linked Production Rules

A key aspect of the system described is that inference can only change a case by adding some fact or conclusion to it. Inference cannot retract a fact or conclusion that has already been reached, not can it change data provided initially. Putting this generally: whatever the status of the case (or working memory), when a rule fires it only adds to the case, it does not change or retract what is already part of this case whether a rule conclusion or part of the data supplied to the system. If an incorrect conclusion is made this is fixed by having an exception rule, which prevents that conclusion being added to the case in the first place. If the original data includes an error, again the system does not change this, although of course it may output a conclusion that the data should be re-checked. That is, it is not the responsibility of a rule to correct a prior error, whether made by a rule or in the original data; the source of the error should be corrected so that the error is not made in the first place, and this can be easily done through on-going rule addition as with Ripple Down Rules.

We have described initially a system where a conclusion is a simple Boolean, so that once a conclusion is asserted it can't be retracted, but then for configuration we have assumed a number of parameters each of which can take a single value, so that once a value for a particular parameter has been assigned no other rule can assign a different value for that parameter. If one were to assume a taxonomy was specified, then once a diagnostic conclusion was reached about a type of leaf disease, for example, another rule should not make a conclusion about a type of liver disease, because leaf disease implies the data is about a plant, while liver disease implies that data is about an animal. This is a far fetched example but we can use it to generalize the constraint that a case can only be added to, not changed: I.e. a conclusion cannot be asserted which has ontological implications that conflict with the ontological implications of a conclusion that has already been asserted or of the original data. This relates to term-subsumption systems such as KL-ONE [33] (some of which include a Ripple-Down Rule representation [34]). In such systems one can reason both by inheritance and by rules, whereas here we propose that the ontology simply provides constraints to ensure that rules can only add to a case not change it. Although the broad principle of not allowing rules to fire which would alter the case, either explicitly or implicitly via an ontology, seems reasonable, we have not explored how this would work with more complex ontologies. It is also beyond the scope of this paper to consider the relationship of the ideas presented here to the wide range of modern semantic reasoners proposed for the Semantic Web.

5   Discussion

The Linked Production Rule system proposed is not necessarily the only general linked rule system possible. Our aim has been simply to demonstrate that such a system is possible. Since the rule acquisition task of adding a rule into a sequence is essentially the same as for RDR, each change should take no more than a minute or two. This contrasts greatly with comments about expert systems in general [9].

Conversely there seems to be no advantage in the various conventional conflict resolution strategies over Linked Production Rules. Linked Production Rules with a strict rule ordering, replace position-in-text rule ordering and salience etc. In particular salience, or the more recent Courteous Logic, is an ad hoc ordering or prioritising imposed by the knowledge engineer for some rules. Linked Production Rules impose a total ordering, but determined by the order in which rules are added and corrected. In particular Linked Production Rules replaces the conflict resolution strategy of selecting the more specific rule. The exception rules used in Linked Production Rules (e.g. 3.1 & 3.2 in Table 7) require the parent rule also to be satisfied, but once the conclusion is retracted, replacement rules such as 6 & 7 do not need to be more specific. Strategies such as recency and data ordering are also covered by the linked rule approach, rather than being some arbitrary function of the inference engine.

Our approach has similarities with work on verification e.g [35,36] and refinement knowledge acquisition techniques [37], as these techniques are based on identifying inference paths; however, this is done after the knowledge is assembled, whereas we propose to build all rules with a linked structure from the outset.

The early assumptions with expert systems were that you simply added knowledge and built a system. Of course it turned out to be much more difficult than this, and one of the major insights was that in fact there were many different problem types [38] which needed to be thought about in different ways and for which different problem solving methods were appropriate. This sort of analysis started with Clancey's recognition that many expert systems used a method that he called heuristic-classification [12] and led on to careful descriptions of families of problem-solving methods [39] and methods for managing the overall process of building a knowledge-based system, including selecting the problem-solving method [13]. If with Linked Production Rules, the domain expert can build up a set of rules case by case, to provide the solution for the case and the process of adding and correcting rules (by adding retraction or correction rules) itself determines the inference path through the knowledge base, what is the problem-solving method?

One of course might say that linked-production rules are a problem-solving method, particularly when including heuristics such as:

- Errors are corrected by adding exception to clauses to rules, preventing the error.
- Intermediate conclusions can be used as in heuristic classification
- Inference returns to the first rule after each conclusion is asserted
- Once a particular conclusion is added it cannot be deleted or its value changed
- New conclusions cannot be added which conflict with the ontological implications of previous conclusions.

However, these heuristics are not really about reasoning or inference, but about managing knowledge acquisition, and reflecting the knowledge acquisition that has occurred. Returning inference to the first rule after a conclusion is asserted ensures that inference follows the same path for any case for which the expert has added rules. Not allowing conclusions to be changed by inference is a way of forcing changes to be made by the domain expert adding specific knowledge.

Traditionally problem-solving methods have been ways of inferring over some knowledge. In contrast Linked Production Rules as a problem-solving method, are a way of managing knowledge acquisition, so that the sequence of knowledge acquisition provides the sequence of inference. Although this may make it easier to add knowledge to a knowledge-based system, one must remember that many of the difficulties identified by methods like CommonKADS remain:

- One must develop a clear understanding of the problem to be addressed,
- and develop an appropriate representation and terminology for the domain,
- and issues of interfacing to other information system as well as appropriate user interfaces are critical if a system is to have any chance of success.

6   Conclusion

We have proposed Linked Production Rules as a replacement for general production rule systems and their conflict resolution strategies. Nothing seems to be lost in this approach, but knowledge acquisition and maintenance should be greatly facilitated. Although the approach closely links domain knowledge and inference, the expert is only required to provide domain knowledge; the inference actions providing the links are added automatically. The expert or knowledge engineer can completely ignore this structure, rather than trying to control the hidden decisions of inference heuristics.

Acknowledgement. This research was supported by an Australian Research Council Discovery Grant.

References

1. Grosof, B.: Prioritized conflict handling for logic programs. In: Logic Programming: Proceedings of the 1997 International Symposium, pp. 197–211 (1997)
2. OMG: Production Rule Representation (PRR). Object Management Group (2009), `http://www.omg.org/spec/PRR/1.0`
3. Polit, S.: R1 and Beyond: AI Technology Transfer at Digital Equipment Corporation. AI Magazine 5(4), 76–78 (1984)
4. Soloway, E., Bachant, J., Jensen, K.: Assessing the maintainability of XCON-in-RIME: coping with the problems of a VERY large rule base. In: Proceedings of AAAI 1987, Seattle, pp. 824–829. Morgan Kaufmann (1987)
5. Clancey, W.J.: Situated Cognition: On Human Knowledge and Computer Representations (Learning in Doing - Social, Cognitive and Computational Perspectives). Cambridge University Press (1997)
6. Compton, P., Jansen, R.: A philosophical basis for knowledge acquisition. Knowledge Acquisition 2, 241–257 (1990)
7. McCarthy, J.: Epistemological problems of artificial intelligence. In: International Joint Conference on Artificial Intelligence, January 1, pp. 1038–1044 (1977)
8. Compton, P., Horn, R., Quinlan, R., Lazarus, L.: Maintaining an expert system. In: Quinlan, J.R. (ed.) Applications of Expert Systems, vol. 2, pp. 366–385. Addison Wesley, London (1989)
9. Jacob, R., Froscher, J.: A software engineering methodology for rule-based systems. IEEE Transactions on Knowledge and Data Engineering 2(2), 173–189 (1990)
10. Bachmann, R., Malsch, T., Ziegler, S.: Success and failure of expert systems in. different fields of industrial application. In: Ohlbach, H.J. (ed.) GWAI 1992. LNCS, vol. 671, pp. 77–86. Springer, Heidelberg (1993)
11. Stefik, M., Aikins, J., Balzer, R., Benoit, J., Birnbaum, L., Hayes-Roth, F., Sacerdoti, E.: The organization of expert systems, a tutorial* 1. Artificial Intelligence 18(2), 135–173 (1982)
12. Clancey, W.J.: Heuristic classification. Artificial Intelligence 27, 289–350 (1985)
13. Schreiber, G., Akkermans, H., Anjewierden, A., de Hoog, R., Shadbolt, N., Van de Velde, W., Wielinga, B.: Knowledge Engineering and Management: The CommonKADS Methodology. MIT Press, Cambridge Mass. (1999)
14. Zacharias, V.: Development and Verification of Rule Based Systems — A Survey of Developers. In: Bassiliades, N., Governatori, G., Paschke, A. (eds.) RuleML 2008. LNCS, vol. 5321, pp. 6–16. Springer, Heidelberg (2008)
15. Date, C.J.: What, not how: the business rules approach to application development. Addison Wesley, Reading (2000)
16. Forgy, C.R.: A fast algorithm for the many pattern/many object pattern match problem. Artificial Intelligence 19, 17–37 (1982)
17. Linear Inferencing: High Performance Processing. An Oracle White Paper (February 2009)
18. Grosof, B.: Representing e-commerce rules via situated courteous logic programs in RuleMl. Electronic Commerce Research and Applications 3, 2–20 (2004)
19. Compton, P., Jansen, R.: Knowledge in context: A strategy for expert system maintenance. In: Barter, C.J., Brooks, M.J. (eds.) Canadian AI 1988. LNCS, vol. 406, pp. 292–306. Springer, Heidelberg (1990)

20. Edwards, G., Compton, P., Malor, R., Srinivasan, A., Lazarus, L.: PEIRS: a pathologist maintained expert system for the interpretation of chemical pathology reports. Pathology 25, 27–34 (1993)
21. Compton, P., Peters, L., Edwards, G., Lavers, T.G.: Experience with Ripple-Down Rules. Knowledge-Based System Journal 19(5), 356–362 (2006)
22. Compton, P., Peters, L., Lavers, T., Kim, Y.-S.: Experience with long-term knowledge acquisition. Paper presented at the Proceedings of the Sixth International Conference on Knowledge Capture, KCAP 2011, Banff, Alberta, Canada (2011)
23. Sarraf, Q., Ellis, G.: Business Rules in Retail: The Tesco.com Story. Business Rules Journal 7(6) (2006), http://www.BRCommunity.com/a2006/n2014.html
24. Benham, A., Read, H., Sutherland, I.: Network Attack Analysis and the Behaviour Engine. In: 2013 IEEE 27th International Conference on Advanced Information Networking and Applications (AINA), pp. 106–113. IEEE (2013)
25. Dani, M.N., Faruquie, T.A., Garg, R., Kothari, G., Mohania, M.K., Prasad, K.H., Subramaniam, L.V., Swamy, V.N.: Knowledge Acquisition Method for Improving Data Quality in Services Engagements. In: IEEE International Conference on Services Computer (SCC), Miami, pp. 346–353. IEEE (2010)
26. Kang, B.H., Compton, P.: Knowledge acquisition in context: the multiple classification problem. In: Proceedings of the 2nd Pacific Rim International Conference on Artificial Intelligence, Seoul, pp. 847–853 (1992)
27. Richards, D.: Two decades of Ripple Down Rules research. The Knowledge Engineering Review 24(2), 159–184 (2009), doi:10.1017/S0269888909000241
28. Colomb, R., Chung, C.: Strategies for building propositional expert systems. International Journal of Intelligent Systems 10(3), 295–328 (1995)
29. Colomb, R.M.: Representation of Propositional Expert Systems as Partial Functions. Artificial Intelligence 109, 187–209 (1999)
30. Crawford, E., Kay, J., McCreath, E.: IEMS - the intelligent mail sorter. In: Sammut, C., Hoffmann, A. (eds.) Proceedings of the Nineteenth International Conference on Machine Learning (ICML 2002), Syndey, pp. 83–90. Morgan Kaufmann (2002)
31. Kim, Y.S., Compton, P., Kang, B.H.: Ripple-Down Rules with Censored Production Rules. In: Richards, D., Kang, B.H. (eds.) PKAW 2012. LNCS, vol. 7457, pp. 175–187. Springer, Heidelberg (2012)
32. Kang, B.: Multiple Classification Ripple Down Rules (PhD thesis). UNSW (1996)
33. Brachman, R.J., Schmolze, J.G.: An Overview of the KL-ONE Knowledge Representation System. Cognitive Science 9(2), 171–216 (1985)
34. Gaines, B.R.: Integrating Rules in Term Subsumption Knowledge Representation Servers. In: AAAI, pp. 458–463 (1991)
35. Nguyen, T., Perkins, W., Laffey, T., Pecora, D.: Checking an expert systems knowledge base for consistency and completeness. In: Proceedings of the 9th International Joint Conference on Artificial Intelligence, pp. 374–378 (1985)
36. Preece, A.D., Shinghal, R., Batarekh, A.: Principles and practice in verifying rule-based systems. The Knowledge Engineering Review 7(2), 115–141 (1992)
37. Craw, S.: Refinement complements verification and validation. International Journal of Human Computer Studies 44, 245–256 (1996)
38. Chandrasekaran, B.: Towards a taxonomy of problem solving types. AI Magazine, 9–17 (Winter/Spring 1983)
39. Puppe, F.: Systematic introduction to expert systems: Knowledge representations and problem-solving methods. Springer, Berlin (1993)

Using a Domain Expert in Semi-supervised Learning

Angela Finlayson and Paul Compton

School of Computer Science and Engineering,
The University of New South Wales Sydney 2052, Australia
{angf,compton}@cse.unsw.edu.au

Abstract. Semi-supervised learning requires some data to be labeled but then uses this in conjunction with a large amount of unlabeled data to learn a model for a domain. Since the labeled data should be representative of the range of unlabeled data available, the aim of this research is to identify which data should be labeled. An approach has been developed where a domain expert starts to label unlabeled data and also writes rules to classify such data. The labeled data are also used as machine learning training data. If the expert rules and the rules developed by machine learning agree on a label for an unseen datum, the label is accepted and the case automatically added to the training data for learning, otherwise the case is checked by the expert and if the label from the rules is wrong, the expert provides the correct label and a rule to correctly classify the case. Further data is then processed in the same way. Results from a number of datasets using a simulated expert as the domain expert suggest that this method produces more accurate knowledge bases than other semi-supervised methods using similar amounts of labeled data and the resultant knowledge bases are as accurate as having all the data labeled.

Keywords: Semi-supervised learning, active learning, knowledge engineering, ripple-down rules.

1   Introduction

Semi-supervised learning is concerned with trying to learn from a dataset which contains unlabeled data and a relatively small amount of labeled data [1,2]. The main focus of semi-supervised learning research has been to find synergies between the labeled and unlabeled data for learning. For example, one might use the varying distribution of a large volume of unlabeled data to find possible clusters and then use labeled data within the clusters to label the unlabeled data. A wide range of interesting techniques have been developed for combining labeled and unlabeled data [1] (this review updated in 2008).

One approach to semi-supervised learning is to exploit disagreements between learners [3]. Disagreement-based learning arose out of research in co-training [4], where two learners can learn from two different views or aspects of the labeled data, (e.g. web page headings versus web page text). If one learner is more confident of correctly labeling some unlabeled data the label it assigns can then be used by the

Y.S. Kim et al (Eds.): PKAW 2014, LNCS 8863, pp. 99–111, 2014.

weaker learner. Similarly one can exploit the differences between different learning algorithms even when using data from a single view [5]. Active learning has also been used together with semi-supervised learning to identify which data in the unlabeled data would it be most useful to have labeled by a domain expert [6,7]. Parsazad et al use an evolutionary approach motivated by the idea of generating antibodies to antigens to identify which data should be labeled [8].

In a method such as that of [8] all the data is available and the goal is to see which of this data should be labeled by a domain expert. A different problem is where there is a stream of incoming data and one needs to decide which data needs to be referred to a domain expert for labeling.

2   Aim

The aim of the research here was to develop techniques to identify which data in a data stream should be labeled by a domain expert to facilitate semi-supervised without considering data that is as yet unseen. We [9] and others e.g. [10] have previously considered a number of techniques for identifying when a data stream contains a case different from those seen previously and one of these is the basis of the approach here. Two different knowledge bases are used to process incoming cases, one built manually and the other built by machine learning. If they both agree on the label for some unlabeled data, that classification is accepted otherwise the data is checked by a domain expert and if the case was not labeled correctly by the manual knowledge base, the expert provides the correct label and also a rule to correct the knowledge base so it will assign this label to the case.

As will be described below the domain expert used in the experiments here is a simulated expert. This is not a part of the proposed semi-supervised method, as in industrial applications a human domain expert would be used; however, using a simulated expert makes it possible to carry out multiple repeat studies and investigate a number of domains.

3   Methods

3.1   Summary

The data we stream in these experiments as unlabeled data comes from already labeled data sets. The simulated expert is a knowledge base built from the initially labeled data using machine learning. This includes all the data used for training or testing, as the simulated expert is meant to be an oracle who can correctly label any case in the domain. To ensure this, any cases misclassified by the machine-learning knowledge base built from all the data are removed from the training data used for later semi-supervised learning. For example pruning may result in training cases being misclassified. We call this knowledge base a "simulated expert" since it can correctly classify any of the cases that will be later used in the training part of the experiments and can also provide a classification rule for a given case using a selection of conditions from its rule trace for that case.

With the simulated expert built, the data is then split into 50% test data and 50% training data with cases the simulated expert can't correctly classify removed from the training data, but not the test data. We include all data in the test data to allow comparison with other methods. Two knowledge bases are then developed, one built from rules provided by the domain expert (the simulated expert) and one built by machine learning using all the training data which has been labeled to date. The process can start with both knowledge bases empty, or with some cases initially labeled and for which rules have been acquired from the expert. An unlabeled case is passed to both knowledge bases. If both the manually built knowledge base and the machine learning knowledge base give the same classification for the unlabeled case, then that label is attached to that case regardless of whether it is the correct label or not. If the two knowledge bases disagree, or neither is able to assign a label to the data, then the (simulated) domain expert is consulted to provide the correct label for that case and to add a rule to correctly assign the correct label. Rules are added to the knowledge base, using the Ripple-Down Rule knowledge acquisition method discussed below. A number of different experiments have been carried out using different initial labeling strategies, or having no cases labeled initially.

When all the stream of training data has been processed the manually built knowledge base and the machine-learning-built knowledge base are tested on the 50% of the data kept as test data. Note that the test data used included data the simulated expert could not correctly classify to allow for comparison with other methods. For comparison we also tested the performance of the machine learning using number of different selections of cases to be labelled. All studies were repeated 10 times with the selection of data randomized between test and training data. The results shown are average of the 10 experiments ± one standard deviation.

3.2   Datasets Used

We report here on the use of the technique on 13 different datasets; with the results of one dataset presented in detail and the others in summary. The detailed study uses data that comes from the Garvan Institute of Medical Research. The dataset used is a larger version of the thyroid dataset available from the UCIrvine Machine Learning Repository. It contains 43,472 records dating from 1979 to 1990. As with the UCIrvine data, this data had been run through the medical expert system GARVAN-ES1 [11] to ensure consistent classifications were provided for the data. However, in the studies here the full range of the 56 classes provided by Garvan-ES1 (and Garvan endocrinologists) were used, whereas for the UCIrvine data, the data was classified into fewer more coarse-grained classes. It is likely that differences between some of the 56 classes is small, but the endocrinologists expected the expert system to emulate the way in which they distinguished such classes, so we used the full 56 classes to provide a difficult real-world domain. The distribution of classes is very skewed with 16 classes covering 95% of the cases (with the top class covering 69% of cases) and the bottom 13 classes covering less than 10 records each. Another difficulty is that if one selects different subsets from the 11 years of patient records for machine learning, quite different knowledge bases are produced [12]. Although using GARVAN-ES1 to classify the records, ensured consistent classification, the population distribution probably varied over time because the records available depend on the patterns of referral and investigation by clinicians, particularly specialist endocrinologists who requested the bulk of the thyroid tests.

The dataset contains 7 numerical fields providing laboratory results, and fields for patient age and sex, the name of referring clinician or clinic and the referring clinician's (brief) clinical notes. The fields for age, sex, referral and clinical notes were preprocessed by the GARVAN-ES1 expert system, so that data used in this experiments consist of 8 numerical fields (including age) and 21 Boolean attributes extracted from the preprocessed data. There is a large amount of missing data in the dataset. The missing data for the laboratory test results range from 15% missing for one laboratory test to 95% missing for another. On average a patient record includes 3.6 laboratory results out of a possible 7. This is not because the data has been lost, but because clinicians will only request those tests that they think are relevant to their particular diagnostic hypothesis or patient management query. As well about half the records do not contain clinical notes. In summary this is a fairly difficult real-world dataset for machine learning. Of particular significance is that the UCIrvine Garvan data is seen as too skewed for semi-supervised learning [13]. The Garvan data used here is even more skewed because of the inclusion of classes with very few representatives.

The other datasets used are standard datasets from the UCIrvine dataset repository.

3.3   The Domain Expert

In the experiments carried out the domain expert built hundreds of different knowledge bases to explore different options. It is clearly impossible to carry out such large numbers of knowledge acquisition experiments with a human expert, and in the knowledge acquisition literature there are virtually no repeat experiments using a human expert. To make the experiments possible a simulated expert was used. The task for the simulated expert was to correctly classify data and also to provide a rule to give that classification. Any classification expert system for a domain that also provides a rule trace could be used as this sort of simulated expert. A selection of the conditions from the rule trace can be used as if they were the conditions an expert might provide for a rule to give the desired classification. This sort of simulated expert has long been used for evaluating various Ripple-Down Rule algorithms [14]. In previous work various selections of conditions from the rule trace have been used, as a crude way of simulating levels of expertise; here 75% of the conditions in the rule trace were selected randomly, (with standard numerical rounding used where required to specify the number of conditions in the rule). We do not wish to suggest that this sort of simulated expert creates the same sort of rules as a human expert; however for the purpose of the experiments here it does provide a useable rule. In particular human experts will probably identify the most important and discriminatory conditions for a rule, even if these are not complete, whereas as a random selection of conditions from a rule trace may select less relevant conditions.

The simulated expert was built with J48 and using all the data to be used later as training or test data in the semi-supervised learning experiments. Any data that was misclassified by the resulting knowledge base, because of pruning etc was discarded from the data to be used as training data in the semi-supervised learning experiments. This meant that although the simulated expert could correctly label all the cases in the training data for semi-supervised learning. However, whether its rules were good rules or not is a different question. This corresponds with normal practice with a domain expert, where one expects the domain expert be able to correctly classify items in the domain, but may or may not provide optimal rules to give these classification. Although not necessary the simulated expert was relearned for each run of the semi-supervised learning experiments and more importantly a different randomization of test and training data was created for each run. The use of a simulated expert is not intrinsic to the proposed semi-supervised learning method; it is purely to make repeat experiments feasible, which would not be possible with a human expert.

3.4   Ripple-Down Rules

Other types of knowledge-based technology could be used, but Ripple-Down Rules (RDR) are ideal for this application as rules are added case by case, whenever a case is given the incorrect conclusion (perhaps no conclusion) by the knowledge base. There is a fixed structure into which new rules are automatically located, so the domain expert is only concerned with the rule being added, not the overall structure of the knowledge base. The new rule is either a refinement correcting a previous rule, or a rule covering a new type of case. The new rule is tested against previous stored cases and if it gives the wrong conclusion for these cases, further conditions are add to refine the rule. In practice an expert only has to see two or three such cases before the rule is sufficiently precise to exclude all previous cases. Using the simulated expert, if the initial rule provided is not precise enough, further conditions are randomly selected from the rule trace and added to the rule until previous cases are excluded.

RDR are fairly widely used in industry, particularly for interpreting medical laboratory data and log data shows that across 10s of 1000s of rules and many knowledge bases, the median time pathology experts take to add a rule and exclude past cases is 78secs [15]. A number of companies use RDR for various applications including, IBM where RDR are used for data cleansing [16].

Richards provides a detailed review of a number of different RDR techniques, but all with the key features outlined above [17]. In the experiments below simple Single Classification RDR (SCRDR) is used. In SCRDR the knowledge base is constructed as a binary tree, with a rule at each node and the classification provided by the last satisfied rule. A new rule added to give the correct classification for a case is added at the end of the rule evaluation path for that case. Since it is then the last satisfied rule, the new rule will thus provide the conclusion for the case, rather than the previous rule that gave the wrong classification. If no rule had previously fired, the new rule will be added at the end of the all-false branch and is only evaluated if no other previous rule is satisfied by the data. Generally most rules are added to the end of the all-false branch giving a very unbalanced tree. There are a number of other RDR structures, but all with the same essential features as SCRDR [17]. The most common structure used industrially is so-called Multiple-Classification RDR where an n-ary tree is produced; however SCRDR is very simple and appropriate for the studies here using standard datasets where cases have only a single label.

We should emphasize that the use of RDR or any particular version of RDR is not essential to the idea of using a domain expert in disagreement-based semi-supervised learning; however, RDR is a very convenient way of building a knowledge base case by case as required in our proposed method. Secondly, data from many knowledge bases in industrial use show that an expert can add a rule to an RDR system in a couple minutes (median 78 secs), making the approach we suggest quite feasible for industrial use [15]. Thirdly, RDR also leads to more consistent labeling, as the expert is required to distinguish the current case from previous cases given a different label [18].

3.5   Machine Learning

The machine-learning algorithm used was J48 from the WEKA machine tool bench [19] which is an open-source implementation of the C4.5 algorithm. The reason for using J48 or C4.5 is that a decision tree learner proceeds by selecting the feature which best partitions the data into subsets and then recursively splits the subsets by further feature selection until a subset contains a single class, or there is no further information gain from any feature. This contrasts significantly with RDR which for each case writes a rule to correctly classify that case. That is, the rule is an attempt to specify the particular pattern of which that case is an instance. Since we are seeking to exploit disagreement between the two knowledge bases, we expect that the two approaches of dealing with a class at a time versus selecting features to best separate classes as whole, may be useful in identifying disagreement. There are a number of machine-learning algorithms which learn RDR, including RIDOR from WEKA based on Induct[12] but it seemed more appropriate to use a learning method with perhaps more chance of disagreement. We used the default pruning settings for J48.

4   Results

The essential feature of the proposed method is that a sequence of cases is processed and the (simulated) expert consulted to check any case where the manually developed rules assign a different label to the case than the knowledge base developed using J48, or if neither has assigned a label. If both knowledge bases agree on the label, that label is used for the case regardless of whether it is right or wrong.

In the following experiments we also evaluated various scenarios in which the simulated expert labels and provides rules for some initial cases independent of whether there is a difference between the expert rules and the J48 knowledge base. This provides some priming for the learning. One strategy is to require the expert to check a number of initial cases for each rule, before using those cases for learning.

If the rule misclassified a case, another rule would be added as above. The idea is that each rule represents a certain data pattern and you need a few correct examples of each data pattern before J48 can be expected to learn that pattern. Fig. 1 shows the errors on the test data for no data initially labeled and requiring the expert to see either 5 or 10 cases which have been covered by a each rule before using cases covered by that rule for learning. Fig. 1 and the following figures also show other comparative data. The red line shows the error from the RDR rules on the test data for the different initial priming strategies. The orange line shows the J48 error on the test data when the only data used for learning are the cases actually referred to the simulated expert for checking. These will be correctly labeled, but there are far fewer than when the automatically labeled cases are also included. The grey line shows the J48 error on test data when the training data has the same number of cases as referred to the expert, but selected randomly from correctly labeled training data. The final point on this grey line is when all training data with the correct labels are used for learning. The green line also uses all the training data, but with the labels assigned during the semi-supervised learning process. I.e. some of the labels will have been correctly assigned because of disagreement between the knowledge bases, or because neither can classify the case, but the majority will have be automatically assigned because both knowledge bases agreed on the classification, regardless of whether their agreed classification was right or wrong. Finally the blue line is the number of cases referred to the expert for label assignment and therefore also the number of cases used for the machine leaning experiments shown by the orange and grey lines.

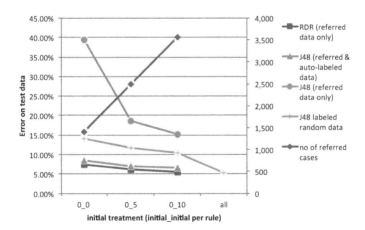

Fig. 1. Inductive learning results for different initial labeling of cases

In Fig. 1 the RDR errors are similar to but slightly less than the J48 errors using all the data labeled by the experimental protocol, no doubt because J48 is likely to prune small classes. Because the RDR errors are smaller we tend to focus on these as the best measure of the proposed method in the following discussion. Using an initial 10 cases per rule labeled by the expert and then cases referred by the method (0_10 on the figure) Fig. 1 shows that the RDR achieve an accuracy (5.44% ± 1.48%,) on the test data. This is not significantly different (P<.0.05) from the accuracy (5.13% ± 0.15%) using all the (correctly labeled) training data (21,178 cases). The method may seem to require a lot of training data with 3,558 cases labeled by the expert, but for this difficult dataset when 3,558 correctly labeled cases are randomly selected from the training data, there is a much higher error of 10.40 ± 0.52%. Even if no initial cases are referred to the expert (0_0), and the flagging of cases to be manually labeled by expert depends entirely on the semi-supervised method the RDR error is only 7.49% ± 1.99%, with 1,410 cases seen. Applying J48 to a random selection of 1,410 correctly labeled cases results in much greater errors, 14.09% ± 0.91%. Clearly using the proposed method to select the cases to be labeled by a domain expert gives much better results than the expert labeling a random selection of data. It is interesting to note that using only the actual referred cases as training data gives much worse errors than randomly selecting the same number of cases. This is no doubt because the method tends to select more anomalous cases rather than cases representing the population distribution. Even requiring the first 5 or 10 cases seen by each rule to be correctly labeled by the expert is unlikely to produce the same distribution of cases as in this very unbalanced dataset as a whole.

We applied a further priming strategy of requiring an overall initial number of cases to be labeled by the expert as well as the initial cases per rule strategy. Fig. 2. shows the results using this approach. The most obvious difference from Fig. 1 is that using the actual referred cases produces a much better result for larger numbers of initial referrals as the initial selection is more likely to represent the population distribution. For more than 1000 initial cases and 10 initial cases per rule, and then using the method for further cases, J48 performance using only referred cases exceeds selecting the same number of correctly labeled cases randomly. RDR accuracy exceeds the accuracy of using all the training data labeled, from group 1000_5 upwards. Again we assume the reason is that RDR is likely to be better for patterns with small number of representatives. A rule can be written for a single case, but J48 learning requires sufficient examples for each pattern.

The overall pattern of results for the Garvan data is shown in Table 1. In this table the numbers of labeled training cases are shown in increasing order in the first column. The second column shows the J48 errors (± 1SD) on the 21,736 test cases when the correctly labeled training cases were randomly selected. The bottom entry in this column is the error when J48 was used on all the training data. The third column shows the protocol used in semi-supervised learning. E.g. 5_500 means that the first 500 cases were all correctly labeled by the expert and if necessary rules added, then the first 5 cases seen by each rule were correctly labeled and if necessary rules were added, and finally any cases flagged by the semi-supervised method were correctly labeled and if necessary rules were added. The total number of cases in column 1, used in each of the experiments where chosen from the number of cases labeled by the expert both initially and by the semi-supervised process specified in column 2. The fourth column shows the J48 error on test data using all the training cases from the semi-supervised learning, i.e. cases actually referred to the expert (numbers in column 1) and also the cases automatically labeled during the semi-supervised process because the J48 and

RDR knowledge bases agreed. The final column shows the error of the RDR knowledge base on the test data. The RDR were built by the expert adding a rule when a case referred for labeling was not given the correct label by the RDR knowledge base.

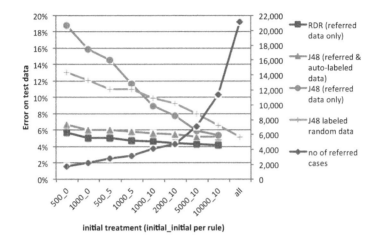

Fig. 2. Inductive learning results for different initial labeling of cases

Table 1. Summary of error against number of expert-labeled training data

No of training cases	J48 error (training cases randomly selected)	Initial cases (semi-supervised)	J48 error (semi-supervised training cases)	RDR error (semi-supervised training cases)
1,410	14.09% ± 0.91%	0_0	8.44% ± 2.22%	7.49% ± 1.99%
1,765	11.78% ± 0.57%	0_500	7.03% ± 1.78%	5.71% ± 0.42%
2,209	10.97% ± 0.46%	0_1000	6.51% ± 1.34%	5.09% ± 0.21%
2,500	13.07% ± 0.67%	5_0	6.65% ± 0.44%	6.14% ± 1.86%
2,831	11.02% ± 0.48%	5_500	6.02% ± 0.24%	5.05% ± 0.28%
3,169	10.40% ± 0.39%	5_1000	6.00% ± 0.27%	4.78% ± 0.21%
3,558	12.13% ± 0.524%	10_0	5.77% ± 0.15%	5.44% ± 1.48%
4,153	9.97% ± 0.61%	10_1000	5.65% ± 0.13%	4.63% ± 0.17%
4,768	9.24% ± 0.35%	10_2000	5.49% ± 0.13%	4.44% ± 0.12%
7,159	7.95% ± 0.27%	10_5000	5.21% ± 0.12%	4.25% ± 0.12%
11,365	6.62% ± 0.20%	10_10000	5.19% ± 0.14%	4.15% ± 0.11%
21,178 (all)	5.13% ± 0.15			

Table 1 shows that regardless of the number of correctly labeled training cases, the semi-supervised protocol always produces smaller (J48 or RDR) errors than randomly selecting the same number of correctly labeled training cases. Also the RDR knowledge base always has a smaller error than the J48 knowledge base, and the results for the last four protocols were smaller than J48 learning from all the training data. Even for 500 initial cases and 5 per rule (5_500), with a total of 2,831 expert-labeled training cases the error is smaller than J48 learning from all 21,178 cases correctly labeled by the expert. This is no doubt because an RDR rule can be written for a single instance of a data pattern where J48 needs a number of examples – a problem with this very unbalanced dataset, even with very large numbers of training examples. Using the method to label only 10.4% of the cases (the 0_1000 protocol) gives the same accuracy as the expert labelling all the data, while randomly selecting the same number of cases of cases doubles the error.

Table 2. Summary of error against number of expert-labeled training data for various datasets

Dataset	Total Training data nos.	J48 error using total training data	Partial training data nos.	J48 errors using random partial data	RDR errors using selected partial data
mushroom	4062	0.0%	23 (0.6%)	12.9%	0.8%
vote	211	5.0%	14 (6.6%)	9.6%	5.0%
breast-w	342	4.9%	24 (7%)	10.0%	3.7%
breast cancer	109	25.2%	8 (7.3%)	31.5%	25.9%
iris	73	8.0%	9 (12.3%)	30.7%	17.3%
pima	322	23.2%	41(12.7%)	27.9%	19.8%
diabetes	321	22.1%	42 (13.1%)	26.3%	19.0%
balance scale	282	19.8%	42 (14.9%)	30.0%	18.8%
ionosphere	174	11.4%	28 (16.1%)	23.9%	5.1%
soya bean	328	11.7%	81 (24.7%)	32.5%	10.2%
liver (BUPA)	146	32.4%	38 (26.0%)	41.0%	26.6%
sonar	101	29.8%	37 (36.6%)	37.5%	12.5%

We also investigated a number of other datasets as shown in Table 2. The same semi-supervised strategy has been used for each dataset and for simplicity does not include any initial referral of cases to the expert as this may vary between datasets. The datasets shown in the first column all come from the UCIrvine data repository. 50% of the data was used for training and 50% for testing and again for each of the 10 repeat studies the data was randomised. The total numbers of training data are shown in the second column, which excludes the cases pruned when building the simulated expert, as discussed above. The third column is the error on test data using a J48 knowledge base built on all the training data. The fourth column shows the numbers of training cases referred to the expert for labeling by the method, and also as a percentage of the total training data. The fifth column shows errors on test data using a J48 knowledge base built using the same number of training cases as in column four, selected randomly from the training data correctly labeled. The sixth column shows errors on test data for the RDR knowledge base built by the semi-supervised process.

The errors using the RDR knowledge bases are closely similar to or smaller than the error using J48 with all the labeled training data for every dataset except Iris. The semi-supervised method also requires far fewer cases to be labeled to achieve the same results. Across the 12 datasets an average of 14.8% of the data needed to be labeled by an expert using the semi-supervised process. For the Iris dataset, the error was worse for the RDR system than for J48 with all the training data labeled (12.3% vs 8.0%). When we used an initial priming for the Iris dataset of requiring the first 2 cases seen by each rule to be referred to the expert, the RDR error dropped to 4.0 %, with the number of cases the expert needed to see rising from 9 to 11. We used a number of initial priming strategies for all the datasets, but only the Iris dataset required this to achieve the same error as using all the training data.

5   Discussion

We have described a technique for semi-supervised learning which identifies data to be labeled by a domain expert: A domain expert and machine learning are used to build two knowledge bases to classify unlabeled cases one by one. If both agree on the classification for that data, that classification is accepted as the label and the case is added to the labeled training data and the machine learning knowledge base rebuilt. Otherwise the domain expert is asked to provide the correct label and if necessary to add a rule to correctly classify that case. The now correctly labeled case is added to the training data, the machine learning knowledge base rebuilt and more unlabeled cases processed.

As shown with a number of datasets, this approach greatly reduces the amount of data need to be labeled by a domain expert to produce a knowledge base of the same accuracy as the expert labeling all the data; for some datasets in Table 2 only a few percent of the data needed to be labeled.

Although we divided datasets into training and test data, in practice the process could easily be ongoing, as industrial evidence shows it only takes a couple of minutes to add rule – even across thousands of rules [15]. It should also be noted that the method here introduces an extra error by training the system only on cases the simulated expert can correctly classify, but testing it on data that included cases the simulated could not correctly classify. This was done only to enable comparison with other methods' results and the error it introduces would not occur in an industrial setting.

For the Garvan and Iris datasets, as well as the data identified by the semi-supervised method, some initial data had to be seen by the domain expert in order to produce the same accuracy as labeling all the data. It is only with hindsight that we know that this was not necessary for other domains. For new unknown domains it would probably be important to have some sort of initial labeling strategy. Other strategies warrant investigation, for example such as having less confidence in nodes of the J48 decision tree where cases have been pruned. This would enable a probabilistic decision to be made about the number of cases to be initially checked manually.

Comparing our results with an empirical study of various semi-supervised methods [13], our method produced more much accurate knowledge bases across the nine datasets in common (P<0.005, paired t-test). The average accuracy of our method was 89.5% ± 8.83% vs 80.5% ± 10.99% for the best results from [13] for the same datasets. 75% of the data was used for training in [13] while we used 50%, so that the fixed 10% of the training data selected for training in [13] would be equivalent to 15% of our 50% training data. The average amount labeled training data we used was 14.8% and for 8 of the 12 datasets in Table 2 less than 15% of the data needed to be labeled. Our method also produces equivalent accuracies to having all the data labeled. Very skewed datasets such as the Garvan data were excluded in [13], whereas with our method using 10.4% of the Garvan data achieved the same accuracy as having all data labeled. In general our proposed method seems to produce better accuracies for the same amount of training data than the methods included in [13]. The possibly superior performance of our method is perhaps because the method uses a significant source of extra information in the rules provided by the expert. Using a different approach [8] also identified which cases to label. With two datasets in common, our method produced a higher accuracy for fewer cases for Iris (0_2 method), while for Soyabean the method in [8] produced higher accuracy with fewer cases. Semi-supervised methods like [8] and those in [13] use all the training data in a batch mode, for example to identify clusters of unlabeled data associated with labeled instances. Our method deals with individual cases as they occur in a data stream.

The most distinctive feature of the method we propose is that when an expert labels a case they may also be required to provide a rule to classify the case. Ripple-Down Rules are a convenient way of adding rules case by case, but other methods could be used and also other machine learning methods than J48.

Acknowledgment. This research was supported by an Australian Research Council Discovery Grant.

References

1. Zhu, X.: Semi-supervised learning literature survey. TR1530. Computer Science, University of Wisconsin-Madison (2005)
2. Chapelle, O., Schölkopf, B., Zien, A.: Semi-supervised learning. MIT Press, Cambridge (2006)
3. Zhou, Z.-H., Li, M.: Semi-supervised learning by disagreement. Knowledge and Information Systems 24(3), 415–439 (2010)
4. Blum, A., Mitchell, T.: Combining labeled and unlabeled data with co-training. In: Proceedings of the Eleventh Annual Conference on Computational Learning Theory, pp. 92–100. ACM (1998)
5. Goldman, S., Zhou, Y.: Enhancing supervised learning with unlabeled data. In: ICML 2000 Proceedings of the Seventeenth International Conference on Machine Learning, pp. 327–334 (2000)

6. Tur, G., Hakkani-Tür, D., Schapire, R.E.: Combining active and semi-supervised learning for spoken language understanding. Speech Communication 45(2), 171–186 (2005)
7. Zhu, X., Lafferty, J., Ghahramani, Z.: Combining active learning and semi-supervised learning using gaussian fields and harmonic functions. In: ICML 2003 Workshop on the Continuum from Labeled to Unlabeled Data in Machine Learning and Data Mining, pp. 58–65 (2003)
8. Parsazad, S., Saboori, E., Allahyar, A.: Data Selection for Semi-Supervised Learning. arXiv preprint arXiv:1208.1315 (2012)
9. Finlayson, A., Compton, P.: Run-time validation of knowledge-based systems. In: Proceedings of the seventh International Conference on Knowledge Capture, pp. 25–32. ACM (2013)
10. Dazeley, R., Park, S.S., Kang, B.H.: Online knowledge validation with prudence analysis in a document management application. Expert Systems With Applications 38(9), 10959–10965 (2011)
11. Horn, K., Compton, P.J., Lazarus, L., Quinlan, J.R.: An expert system for the interpretation of thyroid assays in a clinical laboratory. Aust. Comput. J. 17(1), 7–11 (1985)
12. Gaines, B., Compton, P.: Induction of Ripple-Down Rules Applied to Modeling Large Databases. Journal of Intelligent Information Systems 5(3), 211–228 (1995)
13. Guo, Y., Niu, X., Zhang, H.: An extensive empirical study on semi-supervised learning. In: 2010 IEEE 10th International Conference on Data Mining (ICDM), pp. 186–195. IEEE (2010)
14. Compton, P., Preston, P., Kang, B.: The Use of Simulated Experts in Evaluating Knowledge Acquisition. In: Gaines, B., Musen, M. (eds.) Proceedings of the 9th AAAI-Sponsored Banff Knowledge Acquisition for Knowledge-Based Systems Workshop, Banff, Canada, pp. 12.11–12.18. University of Calgary (1995)
15. Compton, P., Peters, L., Lavers, T., Kim, Y.-S.: Experience with long-term knowledge acquisition. Paper Presented at the Proceedings of the Sixth International Conference on Knowledge Capture, KCAP 2011, Banff, Alberta, Canada, pp. 49–56. ACM (2011)
16. Dani, M.N., Faruquie, T.A., Garg, R., Kothari, G., Mohania, M.K., Prasad, K.H., Subramaniam, L.V., Swamy, V.N.: Knowledge Acquisition Method for Improving Data Quality in Services Engagements. In: IEEE International Conference on Services Computer (SCC), Miami, pp. 346–353. IEEE (2010)
17. Richards, D.: Two decades of Ripple Down Rules research. The Knowledge Engineering Review 24(2), 159–184 (2009)
18. Wang, J.C., Boland, M., Graco, W., He, H.: Use of ripple-down rules for classifying medical general practitioner practice profiles repetition. In: Compton, P., Mizoguchi, R., Motoda, H., Menzies, T. (eds.) Proceedings of Pacific Knowledge Acquisition Workshop PKAW 1996, Coogee, Australia, pp. 333–345 (1996)
19. Hall, M., Frank, E., Holmes, G., Pfahringer, B., Reutemann, P., Witten, I.H.: The WEKA data mining software: an update. ACM SIGKDD Explorations Newsletter 11(1), 10–18 (2009)

Impacts of Linked URLs in Social Media

Preliminary Analysis of Linked URLs
for Health-Related Social Media Postings

Kyongho Min[1], William H. Wilson[1], and Yoo-Jin Moon[2]

[1] School of Computer Science and Engineering
University of New South Wales, Sydney, Australia
{min,billw}@cse.unsw.edu.au
[2] Management Information Systems,
Hankuk University of Foreign Studies, Korea
yjmoon@hufs.ac.kr

Abstract. This paper describes preliminary analysis of health-related social media postings in Twitter. We classified Tweets two ways: those (A) with and (B) without linked URLs, and similarly for users, those commonly posting Category A Tweets and users commonly posting Category B Tweets. The Tweet user groups and the two categories of Tweets show different characteristics in use of user-defined hash-tag terms, the impact of expanded URLs through social media community, and posting period of the two Tweet categories. One user among the top 25 most frequent posters in each user group only posted both Category A and B Tweets. Seven hash-tag terms from the top 25 hash-tag terms obtained from each category were used for both Category A and B. Tweets with and without linked URLs show different characteristics in terms of user groups, hash-tag terms, and the posting period of the linked URLs.

Keywords: social media analysis, Tweet analysis, tiny URLs.

1   Introduction

The mobile internet accelerates real-time information generation, sharing, and access by social media network communities, for example, Twitter. Compared to other social media, Twitter specifically contributes rapid spread of information to its community users anywhere in the world, if they were connected by the internet or the mobile internet – almost with real time pervasion. Each posting, called a Tweet, has a constraint on the length of its content (140 characters) but it may include various types of information, for example, personal opinions, live events or accidents, or new information and news. In the context of the health-related postings studied in this paper, some Tweets include health-related URLs (e.g. tiny URLs) that may point to the internet web pages whose content would not be reliable as the pages may not be certified by health-care professionals, and so might contain misinformation.

Y.S. Kim et al (Eds.): PKAW 2014, LNCS 8863, pp. 112–125, 2014.
© Springer International Publishing Switzerland 2014

Past research has discussed the use of Tweets for information extraction, text mining, information detection and surveillance, and education. For example, Tweets have been used for health-related research topics such as syndromic or disease surveillance [1, 2, 3, 4, 5], health education [6], dissemination of health information [7], and health policy decision-making [8]. Gold et al. [9] discussed the health behavior change interventions where social media contributed to positive intervention for health problems such as smoking cessation [10], sexual health promotion [9], breast cancer screening dialogues [11], and public health monitoring [12]. However, many Tweets were not relevant to the recommended health behavior or showed misunderstanding of medications, such as antibiotics [7], or of concussion [13].

Recent work has discussed research for automatic processing or analysis of Tweets in many areas including a health and medical area. Health-related Tweets were categorised into 7 ailment topics using probabilistic models [2] or used for global health event detection [1]. For automatic processing of Tweets, various natural language processing methods were applied to Tweets analysis, including an N-gram method [2], [3], [14], a shallow parsing method [15], and an SVM method [2, 3]. However, this paper focuses on the characteristics of Tweets with or without linked URLs in users, user-defined hash-tag terms, the posting period of expanded URLs including the content analysis of linked URLs. We shall investigate filtering out unwanted information such as spam Tweets [16] in future work.

In Section 2, the design of the system and implementation of data analysis will be discussed. The section 3 will discuss preliminary analysis of Tweets in relation to users, hash-tag terms, and expanded URLs and discussion and conclusions follows.

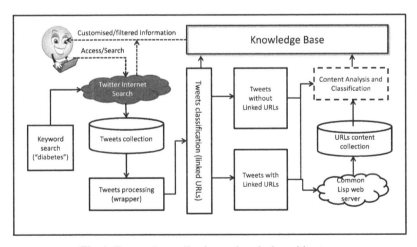

Fig. 1. Tweets data collection and analysis architecture

2   Design and Implementation

This section describes the methodology of data collection, especially Tweets related to health information – diabetes, properties of Tweet-specific data, and the approaches to data management to extract valid information from Tweets for knowledge acquisition between health-related Tweets and its linked URLs.

2.1   Data Collection

The Tweets were collected by using Twitter's internet search API and the search term was a health-related term, diabetes. Instead of using commercially available datasets provided by Twitter, Twitter HTML search results were collected from May 2012 to June 2013 – 81 sets collected on 81 days.

Table 1. Number of collected Tweets

Collection month	Data set(days)	Total Tweets	Tweets with linked URL	Tweets without linked URL	Total words
May 2012	8	6620	4182	2438	98266
Jun 2012	2	3255	1672	1583	47612
Jul 2012	8	7705	4106	3599	111862
Aug 2012	10	18085	7766	10319	271907
Sep 2012	7	10050	4876	5174	149249
Oct 2012	3	8737	3614	5123	128240
Jan 2013	5	8738	3767	4971	128939
Feb 2013	13	22525	9665	12860	325626
Mar 2013	14	36320	16496	19824	539115
Apr 2013	5	24993	11120	13873	365603
May 2013	4	6124	2791	3333	90282
Jun 2013	2	3306	1519	1787	49463
Total	**81**	**156,458**	**71,574** **(45.7%)**	**84,884** **(54.3%)**	**2,306,164**

The 81 data sets had 156,458 Tweets and the Tweets were classified into two types: those including a tiny URL (Category A Tweet) and those that did not include a tiny URL (Category B Tweet). Table 1 shows that 45.7% Tweets are Category A Tweets and their linked URLs showed various types of contents such as news, personal blogs, announcements, new information about diabetes, events, or advertisements. Tweets are limited to 140 characters, and each Tweet in the Table 1 included 14.7 words on average. Due to this limitation, a tiny URL, for example http://t.co/X12345, may be used to get more text into the Tweet compared with normal internet URLs (e.g. http://www.cse.unsw.edu.au/index.htm).

2.2   Data Features Analysis

The micro-blogging social media system, Twitter, is for posting short texts, Tweets, of various information including health-related information, in real time. The Tweets show Tweet-specific freedom of writing styles using Tweet-specific terms, symbols, and tokens. The terms include user-defined keyword terms starting with the # symbol

(Tweet-specific hash-tag term), for example, #diabetes, a search term enclosed by * symbols, for example *diabetes* or a <strong> HTML tag, a Twitter user account starting with the @ symbol, for example @diabetes (Table 2). The tokens include emoticons (for example, ☺ or :D), acronyms (for example, NHS or AU), and internet jargon (for example, "lol" - laughing out loud).

Other Tweet text characteristics are use of all upper letters (e.g. "HAHAHAHAHAHA") which could indicate emphasis or an acronym, repetition of punctuation marks (e.g. "???????", or "..."), characters, or phrases (e.g. "KKKKKKKKKK", "eat eat eat", "slooooow"), and misspelt words (e.g. "cigaretts", "liek"). In addition, the Tweet-specific hash-tag terms (a user-defined keyword for its Tweet) are not normal terms used for information search in, say, search engines. For example, they might be #ff, #sv, #doc, #livingwithdiabetes..., and #HealthyLiving. These provide another challenge to understanding the meanings of the Tweets tagged by such hash terms by users.

Table 2. Tweet-specific symbols and terms

Symbol	Terms and meaning
Hash (#) symbol	#diabetes – user-defined keyword (Hash-tag term). This is a part of Tweet content.
@ symbol	@user-account (e.g. @diabetes), @place or location (e.g. @Sydney), @URLs (e.g. @www.000.com)
RT	RT this is not the Tweet created by a user but the user posts to his/her followers Tweets posted by another user whom the user follows.
Internet jargon	lol (laughing out loud)
Emoticons	:), :-(, :p, :)), o.o, :=)
Acronyms	Common acronyms (e.g. FDA, UK, NIH), Special group-dependent acronyms (e.g. NIH's *GRADE* study - The Glycemia Reduction Approaches in Diabetes: A Comparative Effectiveness Study, *DTN* pharma news - Defence-Technology News, *2DG - 2-Deoxy-D-glucose*)
Tiny URLs	http://t.co/Abcd12

The Tweets also include ungrammatical, extra-grammatical, and ungrammatical but human-understandable expressions which make another challenge for automatic text processing to acquire relevant information from Tweets (Table 3). Examples of ungrammatical expressions are "then I'ma eat it..." and "i liek you coz its sweet". Tweets also include expressions that would not parsed by normal syntactic knowledge, grammar, and those are called extra-grammatical expressions. Examples of extra-grammatical expressions are "Night shift workers more likely to develop", "... too sleepy all the time", and ""... ur gonna get diabetes". The first extra-grammatical expression would require the verb 'are' between 'workers' and 'more'. Phrases like "Ive bn with my b0yfriend f0r 2 yrs" are ungrammatical but understandable.

2.3   Data Analysis Procedure

This section describes the data analysis process for the Tweet data based on text format with some HTML tags. Data extraction is based on a pattern matching method. The process is composed of: 1) extraction of each Tweet from the set of saved Tweets and classification of Tweets with or without linked tiny URLs, 2) extraction of terms such as hash-tag terms, jargons, and user accounts, and extraction of word frequency, and 3) collection of the expanded URLs (the real internet site) of the linked tiny URLs in the Tweets for the analysis of URLs content using a Common Lisp web server.

Table 3. Grammaticality of Tweets

Grammaticality	Examples
Misspelling	*liek, plsforgive, naaathing, I'ma, sighssss*
All upper case (not acronym)	*NOW* (now), *HAHAHA, NEW ARTICLE,*
Extra-grammatical	*Night shift workers more likely to develop, low levels of melatonin linked to diabetes, Or that burnout book*
Ungrammatical	but *can't cos* of..., the rest is *naaathing*, if i *liek* candy means i *liek* you ...,
Jargon-based extra-grammatical	... check I can *cos* i *dunno* if ..., ... catch *u* on a good day,

Extraction of Each Tweet. Each set of Tweet data collected contains plenty of Tweet blocks. Each Tweet block is composed of Tweet user account, Tweet body, and Tweet functions such as Expand, Reply, etc. The Tweet extraction process identifies Tweet user account, Tweet body, and tiny URLs in the Tweet after removing HTML tagged terms, for example, <http://twitter/search?q=%23Diabetes&src=hash>, which means a hash-tag term. Then each Tweet is classified as Category A or Category B as previously defined. When extracting the linked URLs, it was not considered whether the Tweet is re-Tweeted or directly replied to.

Extraction of Terms. After detecting and extracting each Category A Tweet, named entities in Tweets of both categories are extracted by a pattern matching method and their frequencies are analysed. They are user accounts (preceded by @), user-defined hash-tag term (preceded by #), highlighted terms (bold-face terms, for example, Diabetes in HTML format, *Diabetes* in text format), internet jargon terms, tiny URLs, and tokenised words.

Collection of Expanded URLs. The strength of Twitter would be its rapid dissemination of information to an interested audience. The content of a linked URL in the Tweet would include more detailed information than the Tweet itself. However, users need to access the linked URL's content to identify whether the linked URL is relevant to the user's needs. To evaluate this, the internet sites indicated by the tiny URLs were accessed and their web contents were collected for information extraction and analysis.

3   Preliminary Result of Tweet Data Analysis

Health-related Tweets were collected for 81 days using and the number of Tweets in this dataset is 156,458 (1,931.5 Tweets per day/set on average). The Tweets are classified into two categories: Category A Tweets with linked URLs in the body text and Category B Tweets without linked URLs in the body text. The number of Category A Tweets is 71,574 (45.7%) and the number of Category B Tweets is 84,884 (54.3%). In terms of the analysis of the data we collected, category A Tweets would distribute the latest news or information linked with internet web pages. We use the data to analyse and describe the influence of URLs on users, user-defined hash-tagged keywords, different use of words, and contents of expanded URLs.

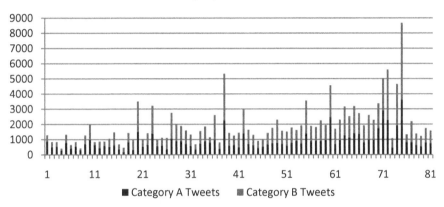

Fig. 2. Daily analysis of total number of Tweets of Category A and B Tweets

3.1   Impacts of URLs in Social Media Postings

As noted earlier, Tweets are used to distribute information, including health-related information that is linked to internet sites (e.g. via tiny URLs). The test data we used for this research showed that 45.7% of Tweets containing the health-related search term "diabetes", included linked URLs. Fig. 2 shows the portion of Category A Tweets for 81 days in 2012 and 2013. The number of Tweets collected per day on average was 1931.6 Tweets (883.6 Category A Tweets and 1048.0 Category B Tweets on average per day).

3.2   Impacts of URLs Posted by Social Media Users

The Tweets data have been analysed for the relationships between linked URLs in Tweets and their users. In addition, the profiles of users who post Tweets with linked URLs could be classified by the contents of the linked URLs, for example, reliable health-related information, spam, announcement, news information, advertisement, etc. In terms of linked URLs in Tweets, users were classified into two groups: User Group A is a group of users who posted Category A Tweets (27,273 users (27.6%) among 98,592 users) and User Group B is a group of users who posted Category B Tweets (69,373 users (70.4%)). There are also users who posted both Category A and B Tweets through the data collection days (1,946 users (2.0%)).

In our data, one user posted 981 Tweets scattered through the 81 data set (965 Category A Tweets and 16 Category B Tweets), the largest number of Tweets posted among the 98,592 users. Among the users, 5,892 users in User Group A (21.6% of the total users in User Group A) posted more than two Category A Tweets and 5,027 users in User Group B (7.2% of the total users in User Group B) posted more than two Category B Tweets. All users (Both Group A and B) combined posted 156,458 Tweets and each user posted 1.6 Tweets on average (0.7 Category A Tweets and 0.9 Category B Tweets).

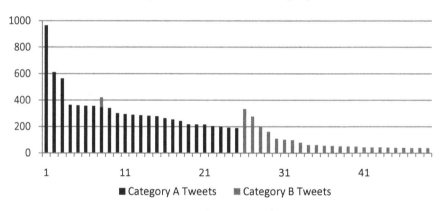

Fig. 3. Accumulated number of Tweets of top 25 users posted either Category A or B Tweets

Fig. 3 shows an analysis of top 25 users who posted Category A or B Tweets and their posting characteristics. As noted above, the most prolific user posted 965 Category A Tweets among their total 981 Tweets but only 16 Category B Tweets. However, another user posted Category B Tweets most frequently: 333 Category B Tweets, but no Category A Tweet. Thus the users could be analysed by profiling their posting characteristics in terms of inclusion of linked URLs in their Tweets. The users who posted Category A Tweets did not post Category B Tweets frequently as the Category A Tweets in relation to the linked URLs would imply more information than the Category B Tweets – for the purpose of information dissemination.

Among the top 25 users in each user group – user group A who posted Category A Tweets and user group B who posted Category B Tweets, 24 users in each user group only posted either Category A or B Tweets and only one user of both user groups posted both Category A and B Tweets over the 81 days. The top 25 users in user group A posted 8,163 Category A Tweets (326.5 Tweets per user on average) and the top 25 users in user group B posted 2,186 Category B Tweets (87.4 Tweets per user on average). Therefore users classified as being in user group A posted Tweets with linked URLs more frequently than those in user group B: 8,163 Category A Tweets vs 2,186 Category B Tweets.

Number of Days Posting Tweets by Top 25 Users of Each Category

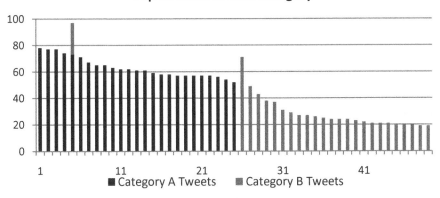

Fig. 4. Accumulated number of posting days of the top 25 users posted Category A or B Tweets (if a user posted both Tweet categories on the same day, then it was considered one day for each Tweet category)

Fig. 4 shows the number of days that each user posted one of both Tweet categories for 81 days. The figure also shows that users in user group A posted Category A Tweets more frequently than users in user group B posted Category B Tweets. One user (the fifth bar from the left) in both user groups posted Category A and B Tweets together on the same or different day(s).

With the data we collected, it could be concluded that the users in user group A who posted Category A Tweets posted or re-posted more Tweets than the users in user group B who posted Category B Tweets. If the contents of the linked URLs in Category A Tweets were analysed, then we could find out the reason Category A Tweets were posted more frequently than Category B Tweets, and content analysis of linked URLs is planned for future research.

3.3 Impacts of URLs to Hash-tag Terms

One of the characteristics of Tweet context is the use of user-defined keyword(s) for the content of the user's Tweet. This is called a hash-tag term as it is preceded by a hash symbol. The most frequently used hash-tag term in the dataset is #diabetes (18,398) and then #health (2,484) and #obesity (901) among the 15,212 unique hash-tag terms (76,150 in total) found from 156,458 Tweets. However, there are some hash-tag terms that would not be common words and not understandable, for example, #ff or #in. The longest hash-tag term in the data, #my…usedtosay…i… give…about, is 50 characters long. Fig. 5 shows the accumulated frequency of hash-tag terms used for Category A and B Tweets. The Fig. 5 also shows the characteristics of hash-tag terms found in both Category A and B Tweets. Among the top 25 hash-tag terms in both Category A and B (43 unique hash-tag terms after merging together), 7 hash-tag terms (16.3% of 43 terms) were used for both Category A and B and the rest 36 hash-tag terms of each category (83.7% of 43 terms in total from both categories) were used for only either Category A or B (41.9% for each category).

Number of Hash-Tag Terms Posted by Top 25 Users of Each Category

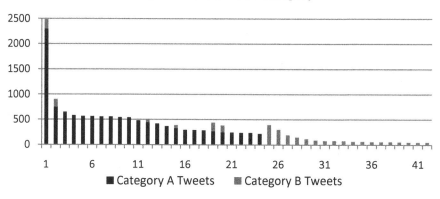

Fig. 5. Accumulated number of top 24 hash-tag terms used in Category A and B Tweets (the most frequent hash-tag term, #diabetes, used for 18,398 times for both Tweet categories – 13,423 times used for Category A Tweets and 4,975 times used for Category B Tweets - was removed for better representation)

In the daily use of hash-tag terms, Category A Tweets used 6911 unique hash-tag terms and each term was posted for 2.6 days on average. Category B Tweets used 9910 unique hash-tag terms and each term was posted for 1.6 days on average.

Fig 6. shows the frequency of the top 25 hash-tag terms of both Category A and B Tweets through 81 days. For example, the hash-tag term #diabetes was used for posting Category A Tweets on all 81 days and also used for posting Category B Tweets on all 81 days whether they are the same days or not (accumulated 162 days in Fig. 6). It shows that Tweets in each category used different hash-tag terms depending on the Tweet category. Among the top 25 hash-tag terms from each category (42 unique hash-tag terms), 8 hash-tag terms were used for both Category A and B Tweets (for example, #diabetes, #health, #diet); and the other 17 hash-tag terms from each category were used only for Category A or only for Category B Tweets

(34 terms in total across both Tweet categories). For example, #healthinfo, #jobs, or #news were only used in Category A Tweets and #sugar, #winning, or #findacure were only used in Category B Tweets. In terms of the analysis in Fig. 6, 19% of 42 terms were used for both Tweet categories and 81% of 42 hash-tag terms were only used for each category of Tweets.

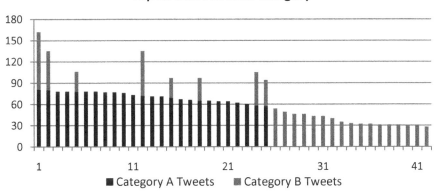

Fig. 6. Accumulated number of posting days of the top 25 hash-tag terms used in Category A or B Tweets (if a hash-tag term is used in both Tweet categories on the same day, then it was considered one day for each Tweet category). Eight hash-tag terms were present in both Category A and B Tweets.

3.4   Impacts of Expanded URLs with Tiny URLs

Tweets are used to post the latest news, information, or events that are linked to the internet sites and the links are represented by tiny URLs. The tiny URLs are too compact and abstract to predict their internet site's characteristics or contents. The collection of expanded URLs indicated by the tiny URLs in Tweets was analysed and in future work we will analyse the Tweets' information quality and relevance to a user's needs. Fig. 7 shows the total frequency of the top 50 expanded URLs in the Category A Tweets. The most frequent internet sites linked to the Tweets are a social media login page that was blocked due to member login request (posted 762 times). The total number of unique expanded URLs is 38,289 sites (posted 1.9 times on average) - in some cases the attempt to retrieve the pages resulted in an access error, or a 'page not found' message. The top 50 expanded URLs were posted 130.6 times on average and 33.6 days on average.

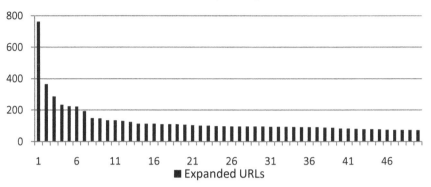

Fig. 7. Total frequency of top 50 expanded URLs in the Category A Tweets

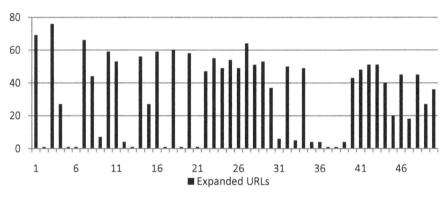

Fig. 8. Number of posting days for the top 50 expanded URLs: the URLs for bar are the same as those of the corresponding bars in Fig. 7

3.5   Impacts of URLs' Life

The linked URLs in the Tweets have varying lifetimes through the collection period: the most frequently posted expanded URL, a social media login site, was posted on 69 days (762 times in total and 11 posting per day on average) (the first bar from the left in Fig. 7 and the first bar from the left in Fig. 8). However, the second most frequently posted expanded URL (364 times in total – the second bar from the left in Fig. 7) was an information portal site (mashable.com) and this URL was posted 364 times in a single day, and not thereafter – the second bar from the left in Fig. 8. The third frequently posted expanded URL (286 times in total) was a blogger's site and it was posted for 76 days (3.8 posts per day on average). Thus the second URLs would have more impact to the social media community than the third expanded URLs. The fifth (224 times in total, edition.cnn.com) and the sixth (222 times in total, bbc.co.uk) frequently posted expanded URLs were also posted for a day as they would have more impact to the social media community than those posted for more days.

The top 50 most frequently posted expanded URLs - see Fig. 8 - show that some linked URLs were posted and distributed through the social media community for one day only and some other URLs with the same or different contents were posted and distributed longer for more days than other expanded URLs. Thus this analysis shows the posted URL's impact to the social media community through time.

4   Discussion

The paper discussed the different characteristics of both Tweet categories: Tweets with linked URLs and Tweets without linked URLs. The characteristics discussed in this paper are classification of Tweets based on inclusion of linked URLs in Tweets, different groups of users, their hash-tag terms, frequency of expanded URLs, and the impact of the expanded URLs through posting days. The Tweet has limited content due to 140-character limit, but the huge number of Tweet data would be useful for the information detection or discovery and surveillance of a specific event. The analysis of Tweet content would be useful for the health-related information extraction, classification, or data mining like surveillance.

The Tweet analysis architecture described by Fig 2 in Section 2 discussed the content classification and analysis and construction of the knowledge base. Future re-search will analyse the content of each Tweet in both categories to classify their topics and characteristics of health-related Tweets. In addition, the content of the expanded URLs indicated by linked URLs will be analysed to identify whether their contents are relevant to the specific health-related topic, for example, diabetes. Its analysis and content classification will be useful to identify more relevant health-related information in Tweets for users in real time.

It is not easy to identify whether Tweets contain trustworthy information, partly because of their short length. Their time-span analysis of users and linked URL domains may help to determine which Tweets have trustworthy information, and which users post trustworthy information. Therefore our future work will focus on extracting relevant and trustworthy health-related information after classifying contents of Tweets and their linked URLs, after filtering out spam users and Tweets.

5   Conclusions

This paper analyses health-related Tweets collected by using Twitter search API using a health-related search term, "diabetes". The Tweets were also classified into two categories: Tweets with linked URLs (Category A) or without linked URLs (Category B). The Tweet users were classified into two groups: user group A usually posting Category A Tweets and user group B usually posting Category B Tweets. The two user groups show different characteristics, posting Tweets with or without linked

URLs. Most users usually posted Tweets either Category A or B Tweets. Only one users from top 25 users in each user group posted both Category A and B Tweets together. In addition, the user group A posted the Category A Tweets more days than the user group B posted the Category B Tweets.

The two Tweet categories show the use of different user-defined hash-tag terms except for one hash-tag term, #diabetes, which was our original search term. Among the top 25 frequently used hash-tag terms from each Tweet category, 8 hash-tag terms were used in both Category A and B Tweets but the other 34 hash-tag terms were only used for either Category A or B Tweets.

The expanded URLs were analysed to identify the impact of the URLs including the life (posting period) of each linked URL as defined below, distribution or influence of each URL in the social media community. One linked URL was posted 346 times in a single day, while another URL was posted 286 times over 76 days. Thus the analysis of the relationship between linked URLs and posting days indicates the impact of the linked URLs posted in Tweets. In addition, this would be useful in ana-lysing degree/scalability of information dissemination through social media commu-nity, say information reachability for social community users, through Tweeting or re-Tweeting linked URL information among users.

References

1. Collier, N., Goodwin, R.M., et al.: An ontology-driven system for detecting global health events. In: 23rd International Conference on Computational Linguistics, pp. 215–222. ACL, Beijing (2010)
2. Paul, J.M., Dredze, M.: You are what you Tweet: analyzing Twitter for public health. In: Proc. of International AAAI Conference on Weblogs and Social Media (ICWSM 2011), pp. 265–272. AAAI Press (2011)
3. Aramaki, E., Maskawa, S., Morita, M.: Witter catches the flu: detecting influenza epidem-ics using Twitter. In: Proc. of Empirical Methods in Natural Language Processing (EMNLP 2011), pp. 1568–1576. ACL (2011)
4. Signorini, A., Segre, A.M., Polgreen, P.M.: The use of Twitter to track levels of disease activity and public concern in the U.S. during the influenza A H1N1 pandemic. PLoS One 6, e19467 (2011)
5. Heaivilin, N., Gerbert, B., et al.: Public Health Surveillance of Dental Pain via Twitter. Journal of Dental Research 90(9), 1047–1051 (2011)
6. Chew, C., Eysenbach, G.: Pandemics in the age of twitter: content analysis of tweets during the 2009 H1N1 outbreak. PLoS One 5, e14118 (2010)
7. Scanfeld, D., Scanfeld, V., Larson, E.: Dissemination of health information through social networks: Twitter and antibiotics. Am. J. Infect. Control. 38, 182–188 (2010)
8. Kamel Boulos, M.N., Sanfilippo, A.P., Corley, C.D., Wheeler, S.: Social web mining and exploitation for serious applications: technosocial predictive analytics and related technol-ogies for public health, environmental and national security surveillance. Comput. Methods Programs Biomed. 100, 16–23 (2010)
9. Gold, J., Pedrana, A.E., et al.: A systematic examination of the use of online social net-working sites for sexual health promotion. BMC Public Health 11, 583 (2011)
10. Prochaska, J.J., Pechmann, C., et al.: Twitter=quitter? An analysis of Twitter quit smoking social networks. Tobacco Control 21(4), 447–449 (2012)

11. Lyles, R., López, C.A., et al.: 5 Mins of Uncomfyness Is Better than Dealing with Cancer 4 a Lifetime: an Exploratory Qualitative Analysis of Cervical and Breast Cancer Screening Dialogue on Twitter. Journal of Cancer Education 28(1), 127–133 (2013)
12. Stoové, M.A., Pedrana, A.E.: Making the most of a brave new world: Opportunities and considerations for using Twitter as a public health monitoring tool. Preventive Medicine 63(0), 109–111 (2014)
13. Sullivan, S.J., Schneiders, A.G., et al.: 'What's happening?' A content analysis of concussion-related traffic on Twitter. British Journal of Sports Medicine 46(4), 258–263 (2012)
14. Agarwal, A., Xie, B., Vovsha, I., Rambow, O., Passonneau, R.: Sentiment analysis of Twitter data. In: Proc. of Workshop on Language in Social Media (LMS 2S); Etzioni, M., Etzioni, O.: Named entity recognition in Tweets: an experimental study. In: Proc. of Empirical Methods in Natural Language Processing (EMNLP 2011), pp. 1524–1534. ACL (2011)
15. Castillo, C., Mendoza, M., et al.: Information credibility on twitter. In: 20th International Conference on World Wide Web, pp. 675–684. ACM, Hyderabad (2011)

Twitter Trending Topics Meaning Disambiguation

Soyeon Caren Han[1], Hyunsuk Chung[1], Do Hyeong Kim[2],
Sungyoung Lee[2], and Byeong Ho Kang[1]

[1] School of Engineering and ICT
University of Tasmania, Sandy Bay, 7005, Tasmania, Australia
{Soyeon.Han,David.Chung,Byeong.Kang}@utas.edu.au
[2] Department of Computer Engineering
Kyung Hee University, Giheng-gu,Youngin, Korea
{dhkim,sylee}@oslab.khu.ac.kr

Abstract. Twitter is one of the most popular social media services that allow users to share and spread information. Twitter monitors their users' postings and detects the most discussed topics of the moment. Then, they publish these topics on the list, called 'Trending Topics'. Trending Topics on Twitter shows the list of top 10 trending topics but each topic consists of short phrase or keyword, which does not contain any explanation of those meanings. It is almost impossible to identify what a trending topic is about unless you read all related tweets. The goal of this paper is finding the most successful method that uses to retrieve the representative contents of trending topics in order to disambiguate the meaning of topics. We first collected the trending topics and tweets related to them. Then, we applied four types of information retrieval approaches (key factor extraction, named entity recognition, topic modelling, and automatic summarization) for extracting the representative contents of trending topics. We conducted human experiments with 20 postgraduate students.

Keywords: Twitter, Twitter Trending Topics, Social Media, Disambiguation.

1 Introduction

The rise of new types of online social media services (Twitter, Facebook, or YouTube) has caused a human communication paradigm shift and the exchange of unprecedented amounts of information on a wide variety of real-world events. The real-world events are not only the small-scaled local events, but also the large-scaled worldwide events. Twitter is one of the popular online social medias that enables post and share information of the local and worldwide events in real time. Twitter users post the message that is an answer of the question "What is happening now?" asked by Twitter. The answer should be limited to 140 characters. These short messages, called tweets, reflect the information of real-world event from the users' point of view. Several previous studies proved

Y.S. Kim et al (Eds.): PKAW 2014, LNCS 8863, pp. 126–137, 2014.

that these tweets are useful for notifying real-world events of different types and scale, regardless of the event types [1,7,12]. This unprecedented amount of events information from users also attracts Twitter's attention. Since then, Twitter has been monitoring and detecting the keywords and hash tags that are most often mentioned and discussed by their users. The detected top 10 popular topics of the moment are published in the list, called "Twitter Trending Topics". The 'trending topics' ist is located on the middle-right side of the Twitter interface, and displays trending topics from several small cities to worldwide. Twitter Trending Topics is now considered as the guide that displays what kind of event information is currently spread on Twitter. Several researchers also regard that the service is very useful for identifying both local and worldwide events [4].

However, there is one big problem in using the Twitter Trending Topics. As trending topics consist of short phrases, keywords, or hash tags, most of them are the term in an ambiguous sense. Lets assume that 'Galaxy' is one of top 10 trending topics. It is very difficult to define whether the topic is about the phone/tablet made by Samsung or a large group of the stars and planets. Without reading and analysing all related tweets of the topic 'Galaxy', it is almost impossible to fully-understand the exact meaning of the topic. In order to solve this issue, several researchers have investigated summarizing trending topics both manually and automatically[10,3,13]. The most popular trending topics summarisation site is 'What the Trend[1]' which provides the interface for users to manually type the explanation of what the trending topic is about. It is like a Wikipedia for Twitter Trending Topics. However, most of trending topics are not explained properly, but filled with spam and irrelevant content. Then, several researchers were applied automatic summarisation approaches to summarize the definition of trending topics. However, they focused on the readability of the summarized sentences, rather than the quality of content for disambiguating the exact meaning of specific topic.

In this paper, we focus on the finding successful method to retrieve the representative contents from related tweets of a specific trending topic for disambiguating the trending topics sense. We examine the ability of trending topics sense disambiguation, not the readability by human. For the evaluation, we selected four successful approaches in information retrieval area, including key factor extraction, named entity recognition, topic modelling, and automatic summarisation. The performance was evaluated by 20 postgraduate students in computing and information systems. Based on the evaluation result, we address the successful approach for twitter trending topics sense disambiguation.

The contributions of this paper are summarized as follows:

- This paper provides the first proper human evaluation results of the Twitter Trending Topic sense disambiguation
- This paper is the step forwards improving the performance of information retrieval research using trending topics as data

---

[1] HootSuite Media, Inc. 2011 http://www.whatthetrend.com/

2   Related Works

Twitter is one of the most popular social media services. It allows users to share and spread their interests in 140-characters short messages. It provides various ways for users to communicate with others by using their unique symbols, including @ or #. Twitter is aware of the value of these social data so they monitor and collect their data. Based on the data, Twitter currently extracts and displays real-time issues and events to the public by providing the service, called 'Twitter Trending Topics'. Twitter is now considered as very useful service for monitoring and detecting real-time events from local to worldwide level. According to this, several researchers are examined Twitter data for their researches as follows.

Event Detection and Extraction in Twitter. As real-time social data on Twitter is opened to the public, many researchers used the data to detect and extract real-time events. Benhardus and Kalita [1] used Twitter data to detect spikes in usage that related to particular topics: short-term, high intensity discussion in response to a recent event by applying statistical techniques, including TFIDF, normalised TF. Naaman et.al [7] developed taxonomy of trends present in the dataset, and then identified the dimensions that could be used to characterize the data. For characterizing tweets, they discovered various features, including content, interactivity, temporal features, participation level, and the level of reciprocity. Weng et al. [12] used Twitter data to detect real-time events by analyzing streams of tweets. They detected real-time events by clustering signals together using modularity-based graph partitioning. TEDAS (Twitter based Event Detection and Analysis System) is the system that analyses spatial and temporal patterns of events and identify their importance [6]. The system used several rules for classifying tweets and predicting the location of events. Although many researchers examined events mining in Twitter, Twitter detect and extract real-time event topics by applying their own algorithm, and provide the list of top 10 trending topics on their interface, and the list is called 'Twitter Trending Topics'.

Trending Topic Summarisation and Classification. It becomes very popular to detect real-time events in Twitter. 'Twitter Trending Topics', real-time event detection service provided by Twitter, attracts a lot of attention. Trending topics in Twitter are the most often mentioned or posted short phrases, words, and hash-tags but no detailed explanation. Because of this, it is almost impossible to fully understand the exact meaning and the content of the event topic. Hence, many researchers aimed to reveal the exact meaning of trending topics. Sharifi [10] applied phrase reinforcement algorithm to summaries related tweets of Twitter Trending Topics. Then, the author conducted evaluation for comparing hybrid TFIDF and phrase reinforcement in use of Trending topics summarising. Inouye [3] also conducted an experiment to compare twitter summarisation algorithms. They found that simple frequency-based techniques produce the best performance in tweets summarisation. Sport events are one of the popular types in twitter trending topics so Nichols summarises the sport events. All researches in trending topics summarisation applied ROUGE (Recall-Oriented Understudy for Gisting Evaluation) metrics, which is extremely popular evaluation method in automatic summarisation area. Those metrics are for evaluating the quality of a summary, such as the coherence, conciseness, grammaticality, or readability. However, they are not very evaluating whether the summary contains enough contents to fully understand what the trending topic is about. Some researchers examined classifying trending topics. Lee et al. [8] classifies trending topics into general 18 categories by labeling and applying machine-learning techniques. Zubiaga et al. [13] aimed to classify trending topics by applying several proposed features and used SVM to check the accuracy. However, those researches aimed to extract the abstract of twitter trending topics but not the exact meaning.

Approaches in Information Retrieval. In order to find successful approach to retrieve the representative contents for twitter trending topics sense disambiguation, we reviewed several well-known approaches in the general information retrieval field. Statistical key factor extraction with term weighting is widely applied to retrieve the important key terms in a document [9]. The representative keywords of a document can be the objects in it. Named Entity Recognition (NER) has been used for labeling the name of objects in a document, such as person, organisation, or location [8]. For this, topic model has been introduced for extracting the abstract topic that in multiple documents, Blei et al. [11] proposed Latent Dirichlet Allocation (LDA), which is a probabilistic model and present it as a graphical model for discovering the topics.

3   Data Collection

For our studies, it is necessary to collect trending topics on Twitter and tweets related to those topics. Twitter provides an API (Application Programming Interface) that allows developers or researchers to crawl and collect the data easily. Through this API service, we collected twitter trending topics in 3 years (until 30th June, 2014)

3.1   Trending Topics

Twitter monitors all users data and detects the popular trending topics that most people are currently discussing about. The detected popular trending topics are displayed on the service 'Twitter Trending Topics'. This trending topic service is located on the sidebar of Twitter interface by default so it is very easy for users to check the current trending topics and discuss about it. It provides top 10 trending topics in real time. Hence, we have collected those top 10 trending topics per hour using Twitter API. In total, we have collected 105354 unique trending topics in 3 years.

Trending topics in Twitter consist of short phrases, words, or hash-tags. Twitter never provides any detailed explanation of trending topics so it is very difficult to identify the meaning of trending topics until you have a look related tweets of those topics. For example, when a missile destroys Malaysian Airlines, the trending topics were 'Malaysia Airlines', 'Malaysian', etc. It is almost impossible to realise what happened to the Malaysia Airlines by only checking the trending topics. In order to reveal the exact meaning of each trending topic, we need to collect not only the trending topics, but also the related tweets of those topics.

3.2 Related Tweets

The goal of this paper is finding novel method to disambiguate the exact meaning and content of trending topics. To achieve this goal, it is necessary to collect the appropriate related tweets of a specific trending topic. The related tweets should not contain the contents that are irrelevant. If the trending topic is 'Malaysia Airline' which is about a missile attack happened on July 18th, we should not collect the related tweets about missing Malaysia Airline occurred on March 8th. It is extremely important to distinguish the tweets that are related to a specific trending topics. Twitter API provides the tweet/search crawling service that allows users to collect the tweets by using the search query. The concept of tweet/search service is same as the search engine. Users can search the tweets that contain the search keyword. The search results contain detailed information of each tweet, including content, username, location, created date-time, and etc. We used this created date-time to extract the appropriate tweets for the trending topics. As we collect the top 10 trending topics in an hourly basis, we search and collect the related tweets that users upload in last one hour. For example, when Malaysia Airline is on the trending topics list at 8pm, we search and collect the related tweets that users upload in last one hour, 7pm to 8pm. This collecting approach prevents irrelevant tweets.

4 Selected Approaches

As mentioned before, the aim of this paper is to find novel method for disambiguating the exact meaning of the trending topics in Twitter. We focused on examining whether the methods are sufficient to extract the appropriate contents that represent the specific trending topics. We experimented with four different methods that are applied in topic-sense disambiguation research field: Key Factor Extraction, Named Entity Recognition, Topic Modeling, and Automatic Summarisation. The philosophies behind these four methods are very different, but each has been shown to be very effective in the information retrieval area.

4.1 Key Factor Extraction: Term Frequency Weighting

The first selected method for twitter trending topic sense disambiguation is the key factor extraction by applying numerical statistic. There are several key factor extraction approaches that are aimed to find the most important keywords in the document by calculating the importance weights of each word.

TF (Term Frequency) weighting is a classic key factor extraction technique for automatic determination of term relevance [9]. The term frequency in the given tweets gives measure of importance of the term within the particular document. TF weighting is a classic approach but still widely used in Information retrieval area. TF can be determined the exact values in various ways, such as raw frequency, boolean frequency, logarithmically scaled frequency, and augmented frequency. We used raw frequency calculation, which is the most classical approach. The TF weighting tf(t,d) can be calculated by counting the number of times each term occurs in a document.

$$tf(t,d) = \frac{f(t,d)}{max\{f(w,d) : w \in d\}} \tag{1}$$

However, like most English sentences do, tweets include several common words, such as 'the' or 'a'. Assume we calculate TF weights for all terms in documents including those extremely common terms. Since the term 'the' is too common, the result will point the term 'the' as the most important word. In order to solve this issue, we eliminate all stop-words from tweets. The list of stop-words we used is based on the 'Full-Text Stopwords in MySQL'. After removing those stop-words, we applied TF weighting to identify the important terms in the related tweets of each specific trending topic.

4.2 Named Entity Recognition: CRF Sequence Model

Named entity recognition (NER) is widely used for labelling the name of objects in documents. It labels sequences of terms, which are about the name of objects, such as person, organisation, or location. By recognising named entities, it can be easy for people to identify what kind of subject/topic the document is discussing about. We applied one of the most popular Named Entity Recognition approach, Conditional Random Field (CRF) sequence model. CRF-based NER are investigated by Stanford NLP lab [8] and it is widely used as a standard NER technique. CRF is a type of probabilitstic sequence model, and it is applied for sequential data labelling. The basic idea of CRF sequence model is as follows. Assume X is a random variable over data sequences to be labelled, and Y is a random variable over corresponding label sequence. The nodes in the model are seperated into two different sets, X and Y. A conditional distribution p(Y—X) with an associated graphical structure will be modeled.

CRF-based NER models are trained by the official sources such as dictionary or WordNet. The applied CRF model for this study is trained on the CoNLL English training data [2]. For extracting the named entities in related tweets, we applied this trained 4 classes CRF model that contains the entity information of person, location, oragnisation and misc.

4.3 Topic Modelling: Latent Dirichlet Allocation

Topic Modelling is the approach that discovers the abstract topics in the multiple documents. The discovered topics consist of a cluster of words that frequently occur. LDA (Latent Dirichlet Allocation) is the most successful approaches in topic modelling area [11]. The concept of LDA can be explained with the following example. If multiple documents are randomly mixed over various types of topics, the topic can be characterized by a distribution over words. LDA is very different from the traditional Dirichlet-multinomial clustering model. Like many other clustering models, traditional clustering model does not allow a document to being clustered with a single topic. However, LDA has three levels, and notably the topic node is sampled repeatedly within the document. Under this model, documents can be associated with multiple topics.

We used LDA approach in Mallet Topic Modelling tool for training and testing the representative content extraction, with all parameter set to their default values.

4.4   Automatic Summarisation: SumBasics

Automatic Summarisation was introduced for people to save the document reading time by providing a summary that retains the most important points of the documents. There are two main approaches, extraction and abstraction, in automatics summarisation. According to the evaluation conducted by Inouye and Kalita [3], most extraction approaches produced better performance; especially SumBasic had the highest scores in ROUGE metrics. SumBasic is a frequency based summarisation system, which uses the following algorithm. First, it calculates the probability distribution over the words in the input data. For each sentence in the input, assign a weight equal to the average probability of the words in the sentence. Then, select the highest scored sentence that contains the best probability word. For each word in the chosen sentence, update the probability. If the desired summary length has not been reached, go back to the first step. In this paper, we applied SumBasics to extract the summary of related tweets of each specific trending topic.

5   Evaluation

5.1   Evaluation Set-up

After collecting data and selecting the approaches to apply, we conducted evaluation to find the most successful approach in twitter topic sense disambiguation. Unlike other studies, we do not focus on the readability or conciseness of extracted content, but examine which approach can extract the most relevant and representative content of a specific trending topic. As mentioned in section 3, we collected 105,354 twitter trending topics and tweets related to them in 3 years. With this in mind, we randomly selected 100 different trending topics and related tweets for each topic. Then, we selected four different types of information retrieval approaches, including Key Factor Extraction (TF), Named Entity Recognition (CRF sequence model), Topic Modelling (LDA), and Automatic Summarisation (SumBasics). Each selected approach disambiguates the sense of trending topics in their own way by using the related tweets.

Table 1 shows the example contents extracted from the related tweets of a trending topic 'Susan Powell'. Those contents display the result of applying four different information retrieval approaches. The trending topic 'Susan Powell' was on the list in 7th February 2012. It was about the following news. Josh Powell, husband of missing Utah woman, killed himself and his two young sons in Washington house fire. He was a murder suspect of his wife. You can find specific information about the topic from the result of KFE with TF.

Table 1. The contexts extracted of a specific topic by applying four algorithms

Approaches	Extracted Contents
KFE with TF	Susan, Powell, Josh, powell, Utah, sons, woman, killed, Cox, boys, doubts, fate, missing, death, PollyDad, Charlie
NER with CRF	[Susan/P, Candlelight/P, Washington/P, Cox/P, Cheyenne/P, Utah/L, Miller/P, It/P, Powell/P, Charlie/P, Husband/P, City/L, Powell/P, Brandon/P, WEST/L, Wash/P, VALLEY/L, Josh/P, Mommy/P, Marc/P, Denise/P, Candlelight/L, Klaas/P, Kids/P, Dad/P, CITY/L, West/L, Valley/L, Tacoma/P]
TM with LDA	susan, family, lovely, watched, flips, middle, black, husband, children, afternoon
AS with SumBasic	josh powell Any doubts about Susan Powells fate should be dispelled in lieu of Josh Powells homicidal binge.

* The trending topics for this example is 'Susan Powell'

For evaluating the performance, extracted contents of each 100 trending topic is assessed by 20 postgraduate students in Computing and Information Systems. All students are trained by attending 2 hours workshop for this evaluation. In the workshop, students are encouraged to understand that the evaluation is focusing on the quality of the extracted contents for trending topics, not the readability of the contents. For this evaluation, we developed the evaluation system as can be seen in the figure 1. Figure 1 displays the user interface after a student logged into the system.

In the workshop, participants are asked to use the evaluation system in the following order:

1. Choose one of the 100 topics on the top left section, Trending Topics
2. After selecting a specific topic, the related tweets will be shown on the top right section, Related tweets
3. Click any related tweet to read. The content of each tweet will be displayed on the middle section. By reading those related tweets, get the point what the trending topic is about.
4. After fully understanding the specific topic, grade based on the content extracted by four different approaches in the sense disambiguation area.

In the evaluation, the grades are given based on Likert scale (from highest to lowest) 1,2,3,4, and 5. The meanings of those five grades are as follows: 1=strong agree, 2=agree, 3=neutral, 4=disagree, 5=strong disagree. By using this grade, student give grades for each extracted contents. If a student agrees with only the output of the KFE with TF, but strong disagree with 3 other results, they can give grade '2' to KFE and '5' to the content of all 3 other approaches. The evaluation was successfully conducted in 10 days.

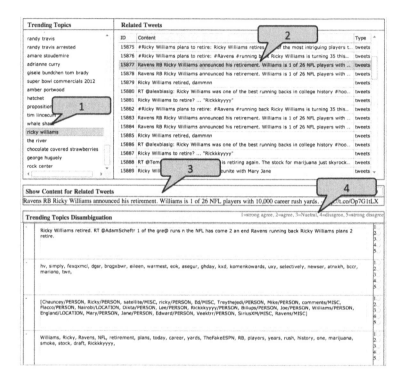

Fig. 1. The human evaluation system interface

5.2   Results

First, we begin the analysis of result with the following question: How much score each approach receives in average? As can be seen in the table 2, the average score for all 4 selected approaches are between 2(agree) and 3(neutral) level.

Table 2. Average Liert Score for each approaches

Approaches	KFE with TF	NER with CRF	TM with LDA	AS with SumBasic
Average score	2.12	2.66	2.90	2.49

It seems all 4 approaches are generally acceptable for twitter trending topics sense disambiguation, and the key factor extraction receives the highest grade among those approaches. However, the average score is not enough to define the successful approach. A graph in figure 2 shows that the distribution of the responses on each approach. The graph clearly indicates that only few participants (less than 10%) strong disagree with the output of sense disambiguation for all evaluated approaches, except topic modelling. The participants roughly understand the meaning of twitter trending topics with the extracted contents of all chosen approaches. As we have seen in the average scores, Keyword Factor Extraction (KFE) got the highest (almost 80%) positive responses (for both strongly agree or agree) and it can be clearly seen from the distribution as well. It is a quite interesting result that the participants provided positive responses with the output of KFE that is extracted based on the classical term frequency weighing technique. However, we found that the contents from Named Entity Recognition (CRF) and Automatic Summarisation (SumBasic) are not clear enough, since the neutral responses took the biggest percentage in those approaches.

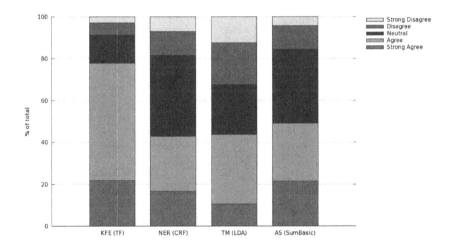

Fig. 2. The grade distribution for four different approaches

Based on the result shown in the above figure, it seems KFE is the good approach to extract the representative contents of the twitter trending topic. However, the KFE result is not fully covered, as there are few amount of neutral and negative response. About this issue, we analysed and found that there is a high correlationship between all four approaches. As you can see from the figure 3, KFE has inverse correlationship with all 3 different approaches in its negative responses (disagree-4 and strong disagree-5). This indicates that other approaches can be used as a substitute of KFE, when the extracted contents are not satisfied. However, this would require an analysis of twitter trending topics to find proper conditions for interchangeability and this is left for our future work.

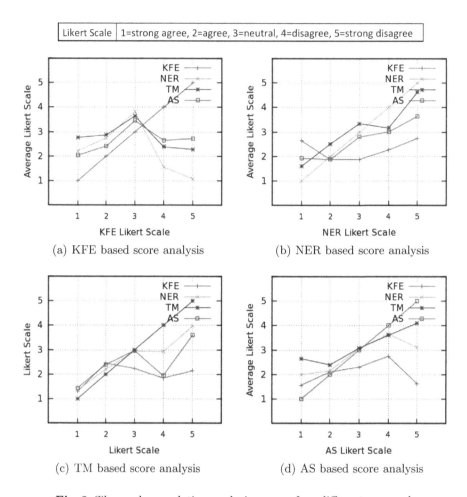

Fig. 3. The grade correlation analysis among four different approaches

6   Conclusion

As mentioned before, the goal of this paper is finding the most successful method
to retrieve the representative contents for twitter trending topics sense disambiguation. In order to achieve the goal, we first collected the trending topics and
tweets related to them. Then, we applied four different information retrieval approaches, including key factor extraction, named entity recognition, topic modelling, and automatic summarisation. We conducted human experiments with
20 postgraduate students. Based on results reported in the paper, the statistical
key factor extraction approach, a classical term weighting technique, provides
the highest performance in retrieving the most representative contents for trending topics sense disambiguation. However, topic modelling does not work well on
finding the topic words from those real-time events information. As mentioned

before, we present the result of the first human evaluation in online trending topic sense disambiguation. We hope the paper is the step forwards improving the performance for any researches using trending topics as a data.

Acknowledgement. This paper was supported by Asian Office of Aerospace Research and Development (AOARD), Japan.

References

1. Benhardus, J., Kalita, J.: Streaming trend detection in twitter. International Journal of Web Based Communities 9(1), 122–139 (2013)
2. Finkel, J.R., Grenager, T., Manning, C.: Incorporating non-local information into information extraction systems by gibbs sampling. In: Proceedings of the 43rd Annual Meeting on Association for Computational Linguistics. Association for Computational Linguistics (2005)
3. Inouye, D., Kalita, J.K.: Comparing twitter summarization algorithms for multiple post summaries. In: 2011 IEEE Third International Conference on Privacy, Security, Risk and Trust (PASSAT) and 2011 IEEE Third International Conference on Social Computing (SocialCom). IEEE (2011)
4. Kwak, H., et al.: What is Twitter, a social network or a news media? In: Proceedings of the 19th International Conference on World Wide Web. ACM (2010)
5. Lee, K., et al.: Twitter trending topic classification. In: 2011 IEEE 11th International Conference on Data Mining Workshops (ICDMW). IEEE (2011)
6. Li, R., et al.: Tedas: A twitter-based event detection and analysis system. In: 2012 IEEE 28th International Conference on Data Engineering (ICDE). IEEE (2012)
7. Naaman, M., Becker, H., Gravano, L.: Hip and trendy: Characterizing emerging trends on Twitter. Journal of the American Society for Information Science and Technology 62(5), 902–918 (2011)
8. Ritter, A., Clark, S., Etzioni, O.: Named entity recognition in tweets: An experimental study. In: Proceedings of the Conference on Empirical Methods in Natural Language Processing. Association for Computational Linguistics (2011)
9. Russell, M.A.: Mining the Social Web: Data Mining Facebook, Twitter, LinkedIn, Google+, GitHub, and More. O'Reilly Media, Inc. (2013)
10. Sharifi, B., Hutton, M.-A., Kalita, J.: Summarizing microblogs automatically. In: Human Language Technologies: The 2010 Annual Conference of the North American Chapter of the Association for Computational Linguistics. Association for Computational Linguistics (2010)
11. Weinshall, D., Levi, G., Hanukaev, D.: Lda topic model with soft assignment of descriptors to words. In: Proceedings of the 30th International Conference on Machine Learning (2013)
12. Weng, J., Lee, B.-S.: Event Detection in Twitter. In: ICWSM 2011, pp. 401–408 (2011)
13. Zubiaga, A., et al.: Classifying trending topics: A typology of conversation triggers on twitter. In: Proceedings of the 20th ACM International Conference on Information and Knowledge Management. ACM (2011)

Utilizing Customers' Purchase and Contract Renewal Details to Predict Defection in the Cloud Software Industry

Niken Prasasti Martono[1,2], Katsutoshi Kanamori[1], and Hayato Ohwada[1]

[1] Department of Industrial Administration, Tokyo University of Science, Japan
[2] Graduate School of Business and Management, Bandung Institute of Technology, Indonesia
niken.prasasti@sbm-itb.ac.id, {katsu,ohwada}@rs.tus.ac.jp

Abstract. This study aims to predict customer defection in the growing market of the cloud software industry. Using the original unstructured data of a company, we propose a procedure to identify the actual defection condition (i.e., whether the customer is defecting from the company or merely stopped using a current product to up/downgrade it) and to produce a measure of customer loyalty by compiling the number of customers' purchases and renewals. Based on the results, we investigated important variables for classifying defecting customers using a random forest and built a prediction model using a decision tree. The final results indicate that defecting customers are mainly characterized by their loyalty and their number of total payments.

Keywords: Customer defection, Cloud software industry, Machine learning, Decision tree, Random forest.

1 Introduction

With the recent increase of Internet use, the cloud software industry has exhibited some very real trends. The cloud software market's 36% compound annual growth is predicted to continue through 2016 [1]. This increasing growth of software is supported by its convenience: it can be used everywhere as long as the users' devices are connected to the Internet. Examples of widely used cloud software are web-based file hosting, social networking, office applications, and security software.

Predicting customer defection is especially important for a fast-growing business with contractual models in order to improve marketing decision-making. Defection refers to a customer's decision to stop using the service or product provided by the company. Defection prediction has been a concern in research and industry, as it is an important measure used to retain customers [2]. In making predictions, most companies collect useful customer data in order to create a predictive model of defection using predictive analytic methods such as data mining and machine learning.

Here, we focus on defection in the cloud software industry. In this study, our case is a security software company. Though we are able to obtain customer data from the company's e-commerce site, predicting customer defection is not a simple task for

Y.S. Kim et al (Eds.): PKAW 2014, LNCS 8863, pp. 138–149, 2014.

four reasons. First, the data features are limited and include only a few customer attributes, unlike several previous works on defection prediction that use typical customer demographics, call logs, and usage details. Second, it is barely possible to gain more customer information by directly approaching each customer, since this company has many customers. Third, in particular, the available data contains simply the records of customer activity in opting-in (continuing) and opting-out (defecting) from one product, while in reality some customers are opting-out to upgrade/downgrade their product. Fourth, with the vast market growth, managing customer defection is an important issue.

This study seeks to tackle these challenges in managing customer defection in one security software company. First, we provide an algorithm in an effort to detect which customers are literally defecting from the company and which are not. Second, from the available data we produce a new feature that can be used as a measure of customer loyalty. Third, using a random forest, we analyze the most important variables that contribute to classifying defecting customers. In addition, we model customer defection using a decision tree, in order to have a visually interpretable result that can be useful for the company as the end user.

The remainder of this paper is organized as follows. Section 2 reviews former works that focus on defection prediction. Section 3 defines the data used in the study. Section 4 describes the data preparation procedures. Section 5 presents the machine-learning procedures in analyzing the important variables and predicting customer defection. Section 6 provides the results of the experiments. Finally, Section 7 discusses the conclusion and future work.

2   Related Works

In recent years, predicting customer defection has increasingly received the attention of researchers. Studies focus on the search for methods and features that most effectively predict defection. The most common methods used for defection prediction are decision tree, regression, Naïve Bayes, and neural network. Most former works focus on customer defection in the telecommunication industry.

Predicting customer defection involves searching for and identifying defecting indicators. Assuming that changes in call patterns may appear as defection warning signals, [3] used call details to extract the features that describe changes in customers' calling patterns. These features are then used as input into a decision tree to build classifiers. Using the same method, a decision tree, [4] discovered that the most significant differentiator between defecting and retained customers are age, tenure, gender, billing amount, number of payment, call duration, and amount of changing information. These findings were obtained using customer demographics, billing information, service status, and service change logs. Other useful features were explored by [5], using data containing customer complaints and service interactions with the operator to predict defection. They also compared the predicting performance of a neural network, a decision tree, and regression.

In [6] we reviewed the applicability of some machine-learning techniques to predicting customer defection using several common techniques such as a decision tree, a random forest, a neural network, and a support vector machine. In a complementary approach in [7], the result of predicting customer defection was applied to calculate the customer lifetime value, considering the strong relationship between customer defection/retention and the predicted customer lifetime value.

As previously mentioned, most former works relied on customer demographics, customer service logs, usage details, complaint data, bills, and payments. A relatively under-investigated source of input for predicting customer defection is the original purchase and renewal data of customers in a contract-based company, because the data often contains unstructured data that is difficult to analyze.

Our data are limited in the number of features and the structure is complicated, but in this study we provide a new system of customer defection management. We propose an algorithm to identify actual customer defection in order to make prediction more reliable and to produce from the available data a new feature that can measure customer loyalty. We subsequently use the results to analyze which variables are important in classifying defecting customers and to build a customer defection prediction model.

3   Data Set

The basic problem of predicting customer defection is finding a good model that can predict customer defection in a company. A quality model to predict defection can be constructed only if quality data is available. In this study, we use two types of data (purchase and auto-renewal data and web log data) and compare them for better prediction of customer defection.

Purchase and auto-renewal data contains six-year records (from 2007 up to 2013) of customer activity in purchasing and renewing their products. It includes the customer's contract ID, the latest status of the renewal flag, the latest date of auto-renewal contract, the total number of purchases and renewals, the type of product base that the customer purchased, the total payment by the customer, the warrant period of the product, whether or not an optional service is used, the type of customer (personal or commercial), and the status of e-mail delivery.

The web log data includes six-month log files (from January to June 2013) that contain total payment by the customer, use of optional service, type of customer (personal or commercial), type of operating system the customer uses, type of browser the customer uses to browse the Internet, number of website page views, number of website visits, number of product views and cart views, and number of orders the customer has made.

The data is originally used to record the details of "opting-in" and "opting-out" activities of each customer after receiving e-mail notification of auto-renewal. Customers who receive the e-mail will be automatically renewed for their current service unless they specifically choose to "opt-out." However, some customers may opt-out from one service of their product and opt-in for another service. Therefore, some new features should be extracted from the original purchase and auto-renewal data for predicting actual defection from the company. In this case, actual defection means the customer does not renew or subscribe to any service from the company.

4   Data Preparation

Data preparation has one important rule that differentiates this study from former studies. The main purpose of data preparation in this study is to determine whether the original data may be used in developing a customer defection prediction model. If it is considered useful, it is necessary to determine which features can be extracted from it and may be useful for machine learning.

Table 1. Original table on the e-commerce site

CONTRACT_ID	NO_PURCHASE	A_1 ... A_n	RENEW_ COUNT	RENEW_ FLAG
1	1		2	0
1	2		1	0
1	3	v_1 ... v_n	1	1
2	4		3	0
2	5	u_1 ... u_n	2	0

Table 1 illustrates the original contents of the table that contains historical records of customer activity collected from the company's e-commerce site, where A_1 ... A_n are the features previously mentioned in Section 2 for each type of data. It contains CONTRACT_ID, which is the ID number of a purchase or renewal that a customer makes. When one customer performs several actions, whether purchasing a new product or renewing the contract for a current product, the data is recorded by the e-commerce site under the same CONTRACT_ID. Thus, if we use the original data from the site without preparing it, the prediction model will not be reliable, since the site can only record data per activity. It does not provide a summary indicating whether the customer is truly defecting from the company or merely defecting from a current product.

To overcome this problem, we first detect actual defection by acquiring CLASS as the actual defection flag attribute of each customer. Second, we produce UPDATE_COUNT as a new measure of customer loyalty, defined as the length of time a customer has stayed with the company, by accumulating that customer's purchasing and renewing frequency. Equations 1 and 2 generally describe how we detect actual defection and calculate UPDATE_COUNT.

$$CLASS = \begin{cases} 0 & if \ \sum RENEW\_FLAG > 0 \\ 1 & if \ \sum RENEW\_FLAG = 0 \end{cases} \tag{1}$$

UPDATE_COUNT

$$= \begin{cases} \sum RENEW\_COUNT + (n_{rows} - 1) & \text{if } CLASS = 1 \\ \sum RENEW\_COUNT + (n_{rows} - 1) - 1 & \text{if } CLASS = 0 \end{cases} \quad (2)$$

In Eq. 2, UPDATE_COUNT is calculated by summing the frequency of renewals on each purchase and the total number of purchases excluding the first chase ($n_{rows} - 1$). Since we are going to predict customer defection, we subtract one from the total length to yield data to be used for prediction.

The results can be used for prediction. Thus, the final features of the purchase and auto-renewal data that will be used for the prediction are UPDATE_COUNT, total payment by the customer (CC_PRODUCT_PRICE), use of optional service (OPT_FLAG), type of customer (personal or commercial) (ORG_FLAG), status of e-mail delivery (MAIL_STATUS), and the actual defection flag (CLASS).

The final web log data that will be used are UPDATE_COUNT, CC_PRODUCT_PRICE, OPT_FLAG, ORG_FLAG, MAIL_STATUS, operating system used in the gadget (OS), type of browser used (BROWSER), number of page views (PAGE_VIEW), product views (PRODUCT_VIEW), cart views (CART_VIEW), web visiting frequency (VISIT), number of orders the customer has made (ORDER), and CLASS.

5   Machine-Learning Process and Evaluation Criteria

Machine learning is executed in the form of a classifier using two algorithms: C4.5 Decision Tree and Random Forest. The advantage of classification using a decision tree is that it can be easily interpreted and is intuitively understandable. Moreover, it provides the ability to make prediction using very large data sets. The decision-tree algorithm selects the best feature for splitting a node based on a statistical measure. The widely used decision-tree algorithm ID3 uses information gain to select the attribute that will categorize the samples into individual classes [8]. However, ID3 does not allow attributes with continuous values, and there are some biases in measur-ing the information gain for attributes with many values. The successor to ID3, C4.5, overcomes these problems by creating a threshold to fit the continuous attributes and avoiding bias in the information gain by using normalization [9].

A random forest is a collection of unpruned decision trees with randomized selec-tion at each split, and outputs the class that is the majority of classes output by indi-vidual trees [10]. Bagging enables random forest to improve prediction accuracy over a single decision tree. Moreover, random forest excels in characterizing and exploit-ing structure in high-dimensional data for classification and prediction [11]. However, the resulting model produced by random forest can be difficult to interpret. One key feature of the random-forest learning algorithm that is used in this study is a novel variable importance measure.

The machine-learning performance must be evaluated to ensure that the model was generated well. In order to assess classification performance, we calculate the following performance criteria: accuracy, recall, precision, and F-measure. Based on the confusion matrix in Table 2, each evaluation criterion is calculated as follows.

- Overall accuracy is measured using the proportion of the total number of predictions that were correct, calculated by $\frac{a_{11} + a_{22}}{a_{11} + a_{12} + a_{21} + a_{22}}$.
- Precision or positive prediction value is calculated by $\frac{a_{11}}{a_{11} + a_{12}}$.
- Recall or true positive rate is calculated by $\frac{a_{11}}{a_{11} + a_{21}}$.
- F-measure or F-score is calculated by $\frac{2\ (Precision\ x\ Recall)}{Precision + Recall}$.

Table 2. Confusion matrix

		Predicted	
		Defect	Not defect
Actual	Defect	a_{11}	a_{12}
	Not defect	a_{21}	a_{22}

Table 3. Number of examples of the initial data set

	Purchase and renewal data		Web log data	
	Positive	Negative	Positive	Negative
Low price	273,339	117,748	5,694	4,401
Middle price	1,172,951	729,163	26,709	27,518
High price	386,872	274,437	8,947	13,867

Table 3 lists the total number of examples available from the initial data sets. Positive examples include customers who defect, and negative examples include those who remain. All the examples will be employed in building the prediction model using the C4.5 decision-tree algorithm, with 10-fold cross validation for data splitting to ensure that instances from the original dataset have the same chance of appearing in the training and testing set. However, when analyzing important variables using a random forest, only a subset of purchase and auto-renewal data samples with the same distribution as the initial data set are used due to its limitation in handling large amounts of data.

6   Experimental Results

6.1   Measuring Variable Importance Using Random Forest

For prediction, it is critical to determine the importance of variables in providing predictive accuracy. In this study, we used the variable-importance algorithm in a random forest to obtain the mean decrease in accuracy of each variable. The mean decrease in accuracy of a variable is the normalized difference in classification accuracy for out-of-bag data when the data for that variable is included as observed, and the classification accuracy for out-of-bag data when the values of the variable in the out-of-bag data have been randomly permuted [11]. Higher values of mean decrease in accuracy indicate variables that are more important to the classification. Table 4 gives the number of samples used by a random forest to obtain the importance of each variable on each customer segment.

Table 4. Number of samples used in obtaining the variable importance using random forest

	Purchase and renewal data		Web log data	
	Positive	Negative	Positive	Negative
Low price	48,693	21,037	5,694	4,401
Middle price	43,216	26,784	26,709	27,518
High price	40,632	29,368	8,947	13,867

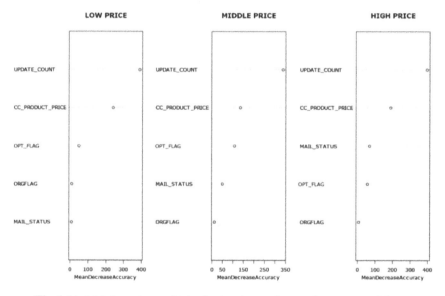

Fig. 1. Variable importance obtained using the purchase and auto-renewal data

For each of the three customer segments, UPDATE_COUNT was identified as the most important variable for classification using purchase and auto-renewal data (Fig. 1). Although we cannot say that variables identified as "important" are right or wrong, the results for a random forest coincide more closely with expectations based on understanding of customer loyalty. The more loyal the customer, described by their period of staying, the less probable their defection.

The results in Fig.2 indicate the variable importance obtained using web log data. Similar to the previous result, UPDATE_COUNT is the most important prediction variable in the Low Price customer segment. For the Middle Price and High Price customer segments, the total payment that each customer has made (CC_PRODUCT_PRICE) appears to be the most important variable. However, there was consistency in the variables identified as the two most important using the entire data set: UPDATE_COUNT and CC_PRODUCT_PRICE.

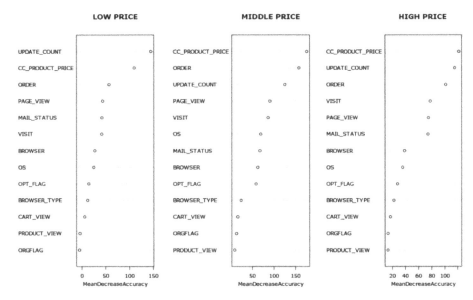

Fig. 2. Variable importance for each customer segment obtained using the web log data

6.2   Prediction Model Using C4.5 Decision Tree

As previously mentioned, one advantage of using the decision tree classifier is convenience in interpreting the results. *R* package supports the process of interpretation by providing tree visualization and tree rules. Decision tree results make it easier for the company or other end user to determine the next action for retaining the customer based on defection prediction. We present an example of the visualization of customer defection prediction in the Low Price customer segment using purchase and auto-renewal data (Fig. 3) and an example of the rules of the defecting customer.

```
Rule number: 7 [RIHAN_FLAG=true cover=137787 (35%) prob=0.98]
    UPDATE_COUNT< 2.5
    CC_PRODUCT_PRICE< 4722
Rule number: 25 [RIHAN_FLAG=true cover=15697 (4%) prob=0.88]
    UPDATE_COUNT< 2.5
    CC_PRODUCT_PRICE>=4722
    UPDATE_COUNT>=0.5
    CC_PRODUCT_PRICE>=4972
Rule number: 13 [RIHAN_FLAG=true cover=70863 (18%) prob=0.84]
    UPDATE_COUNT< 2.5
    CC_PRODUCT_PRICE>=4722
    UPDATE_COUNT< 0.5
```

The rules on node 7 indicate that 35% of customers who have the attributes of UPDATE_COUNT less than 2.5 and make payment on CC_PRODUCT_PRICE less than 4,722 (JPY) have a 98% probability of defecting. Both visualization and rules indicate that the decision tree obtained a model that uses UPDATE_COUNT and total payment or CC_PRODUCT_PRICE is the most powerful predictor. Similarly, it occurs in all customer segments when we use purchase and auto-renewal data. Using web log data (Fig. 4), the status of e-mail delivery appears to be one of the three predictors resulting in predictive accuracy.

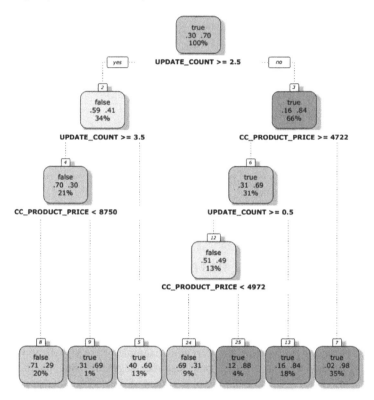

Fig. 3. Visualization of tree on Low Price customer segment based on purchase and auto-renewal data

Performance evaluation of the model on predicting defection using the C4.5 decision-tree algorithm is presented in Tables 4 and 5. The minimum object is set to 40, and the complexity of the tree is set to 0.005. The results indicate that using purchase and auto-renewal data, we can obtain a better prediction model of customer defection and conclude that the new features we acquired in data preparation are useful in predicting customer defection in the case company.

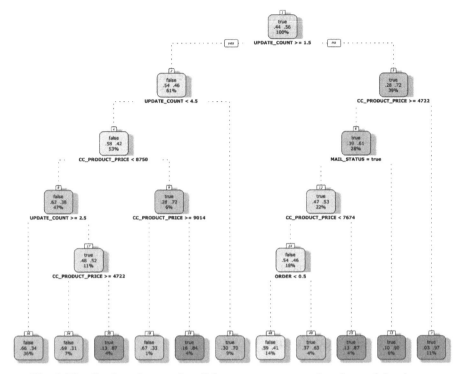

Fig. 4. Visualization of tree on Low Price customer segment based on web log data

Table 5. Predictive accuracy of C4.5 decision tree based on the purchase and auto-renewal data

Data set		Accuracy	Precision	Recall	F-score
Low Price	Baseline	69.7	69.6	49.1	50.5
	C4.5	**82.8**	82.6	82.9	82.7
Middle Price	Baseline	61.6	61.7	38.0	47.1
	C4.5	**72.4**	72.6	72.1	71.8
High Price	Baseline	58.5	58.2	33.9	42.8
	C4.5	**83.3**	82.8	73.8	82.9

Table 6. Predictive accuracy of C4.5 decision tree based on the web-log data

Data set		Accuracy	Precision	Recall	F-score
Low Price	Baseline	56.4	56.4	31.8	40.7
	C4.5	**72.7**	72.7	74.4	72.8
Middle Price	Baseline	50.7	50.7	25.8	34.2
	C4.5	**69.8**	69.8	70.7	69.6
High Price	Baseline	60.8	60.8	36.9	46.0
	C4.5	**73.1**	72.1	79.2	78.4

To summarize and clarify how our methods apply to the case company, we consider several questions and answers that are appropriate based on the experiment results.

1. *Which customers are defecting?*
   If "defecting" is defined clearly based on the original data sets, the answer to this question is straightforward to the number of "opt-outs" that appear in the database query and it is not factual. Thus, analysis using our method clearly indicates that customers who do not have renewal records are actually defecting from the company.

2. *What variables characterize the defecting customer?*
   Defecting customers are characterized mainly by their loyalty attributes: how long they stay with the company, how many purchases they make, and their auto-renewal activity. In addition, the number of total payments the customer has made represents the likelihood that the customer will defect.

3. *Can we determine what strategy may keep a customer from defecting?*
   Based on the previous questions and answers, we can determine what strategy in each customer segment may keep a customer from defecting. For example, since customer loyalty is the main characterizing variable, a company may direct more marketing campaigns toward customers with a low loyalty average.

7   Conclusion and Future Works

One key activity of customer defection management is predicting customer defection. This paper presents several procedures that contribute to resolving some novel problems in predicting defection. We provided an algorithm that is beneficial in determining which customer is truly defecting from the company and produced a new feature (UPDATE_COUNT) from the available data that can be used as a measurement of customer loyalty. Using machine learning, we then identified important variables for classifying defecting customers. Finally, we built a prediction model of customer defection using both purchase and auto-renewal data and web log data.

This study does not capture the dynamic of customer activity and characteristics. Thus, future work will seek to integrate machine learning with a more dynamic approach, such as agent-based modeling and simulation. Agent-based modeling will provide a computational model for simulating interactions between customers from the micro level to a macro level. In addition, machine learning can provide predictive accuracy regarding customer behavior that will be useful for validating the agent-based model.

References

1. Colombus, L.: Predicting Enterprise Cloud Computing Growth. Forbes (April 9, 2013), http://www.forbes.com/sites/louiscolumbus/2013/09/04/predicting-enterprise-cloud-computing-growth/ (accessed July 20, 2014)

2. Huang, B.Q., Kechadi, M.-T., Buckley, B.: Customer Churn Prediction for Broadband Internet Services. In: Pedersen, T.B., Mohania, M.K., Tjoa, A.M. (eds.) DaWaK 2009. LNCS, vol. 5691, pp. 229–243. Springer, Heidelberg (2009)
3. Wei, C., Chiu, I.: Turning telecommunications call detail to churn prediction: A data mining approach. Expert Systems with Applications 23, 103–112 (2002)
4. Yung, S., Yen, D., Wang, H.: Applying data mining to telecom churn management. Expert System with Applications 31, 515–524 (2006)
5. Tiwari, A., Roy, R., Hadden, J., Ruta, D.: Churn Prediction: Does Technology Matter. International Journal of Intelligent Systems and Technologies 1 (2006)
6. Prasasti, N., Ohwada, H.: Applicability of Machine-Learning Techniques in Predicting Customer Defection. In: International Symposium on Technology Management and Emerging Technologies (ISTMET 2014) (2014)
7. Prasasti, N., Okada, M., Kanamori, K., Ohwada, H.: Customer Lifetime Value and Defection Possibility Prediction Model using Machine Learning: An Application to a cloud-based Software Company. In: Nguyen, N.T., Attachoo, B., Trawiński, B., Somboonviwat, K. (eds.) ACIIDS 2014, Part II. LNCS (LNAI), vol. 8398, pp. 62–71. Springer, Heidelberg (2014)
8. Quinlan, J.: Induction of Decision Trees. Machine Learning 1, 81–106 (1986)
9. Xiong, Y., Syzmanski, D., Kihara, D.: Characterization and Prediction of Human Protein-Protein Interaction. In: Biological Data Mining and Its Applications in Healthcare, pp. 237–260 (2014)
10. Breiman, L.: Random Forests. Machine Learning 45, 25–32 (2001)
11. Cutler, D.R., Edwards, T.C., Beard, K.H., Cutler, A., Hess, K.T., Gibson, J., Lawler, J.J.: Random Forest for Classification in Ecology. Ecology 88(11), 2783–2792 (2007)

Multi-robot Coordination Based on Ontologies and Semantic Web Service

Yuichiro Mori, Yuhei Ogawa,
Akatsuki Hikawa, and Takahira Yamaguchi

Keio University
3-14-1, Hiyoshi, Kohoku-ku, Yokohama-city, Kanagawa-ken, Japan
blue-red.7x-v@a5.keio.jp, ogawa@z7.keio.jp,
akatsuki@a2.keio.jp, yamaguti@ae.keio.ac.jp

Abstract. Service robots are currently not able to provide complex services because service robots with physical structures have been developed for a specific service and there is a limit to the tasks a robot can do alone. In this paper, we approach this problem by using multi-robot coordination services in which robots are linked and a wide range of services can be executed using the concept of semantic web service (SWS). SWS facilitates the automation of discovering and combing processes that are multiple web services. Service robots execute a service as a combination of the processes that one or multiple robots can execute. The process can be executed as the combination of multiple program modules. Therefore, we propose a multi-layer architecture. In this case study, we show how to automatically execute coordination services using our architecture and evaluate the usability of our architecture.

Keywords: Multi-Robot Coordination, Semantic Web Service, Ontologies.

1 Introduction

In making social service robots more popular with real human beings, we still face many issues such as human robot interaction (HRI) and system generality, or extension ability from one service to other services. Our previous work approached the former issue by means of multi-modal interaction with Dialog [1], QAs with a large volume of Japanese Wikipedia ontology (JWO) [2] and behavior interaction with Kinect sensing and behavior/kinematics ontologies [3].

This paper addresses the latter issue. In order to perform a task given by a user utilizing multiple robots, our proposed system first plans how to coordinate robots having different functions by means of a semantic web service (SWS) that uses ontologies to automatically create web services (software components) to complete the task assigned by the user. When replacing web services with robots and implementing the planned robot coordination in real life, what difficulties do we face? In this paper, we discuss our proposed system architecture for multi-robot coordination with SWS and ontologies and show how well our proposed system architecture functions by using the case study of RobotCafe.

Y.S. Kim et al (Eds.): PKAW 2014, LNCS 8863, pp. 150–164, 2014.

2   Related Work

2.1   KnowRob and RoboEarth

Tenorth and Beetz use ontologies for intelligent robots. KnowRob (Knowledge processing for Robots) [5][6] is a set of frameworks for robotics, knowledge processing and real-world understanding. Several ontologies are constructed and used in KnowRob for knowledge representation such as general vocabulary [7], task, robot, action, and environment. A robot that works uses KnowRob executes the requested task by linking different items of knowledge. Comparing our work with KnowRob, it is almost the same when it comes to how to use ontologies for robot behavior; however, KnowRob works only for a single robot not for multi-robot coordination. By applying the SWS framework to multi-robot coordination, this paper discusses how to coordinate multiple robots having different facilities in order to perform complex tasks assigned to them by people.

RoboEarth[8] can store and share a vast amount of knowledge among multiple robots using clouds and databases. This system enables robots to learn complex tasks easily.

2.2   Semantic Web Service

A SWS [4] is the server end of a client-server system for machine-to-machine interaction that utilizes the World Wide Web Consortium (W3C). Although web services are standardized by W3C, a hand is needed to achieve cooperation and integration of the Web Wide Web system. To solve this problem and automate the system, SWS uses OWL that makes data machine readable. In order to automatically build a web service, planning functions such as seeking the call sequence of services from semantic matching on IOPE (Input, Output, Prejudge, Effect) is required. IOPE is a basic vocabulary that appears in the planning program.

2.3   Comparison with Our Work

Our purpose is to break down tasks that cannot be performed by one robot into a number of processes using the concept of SWS. By separately executing each process connected to a task, we can execute the required task as a whole.

3   Ontologies

We use ontologies as the technology infrastructure in our study. This is because we think it is quite important for the realization of a HRI that service robots be able to handle machine-readable information. Therefore, in the system architecture shown in the following sections, knowledge data based on ontologies constitute much of the information. In this section, we explain the ontologies that we use and the alignment of ontologies.

3.1   Japanese Wikipedia Ontology

Wikipedia has become popular as a new information resource because it has a rich vocabulary and good updatability. Because Wikipedia has semistructured information resources such as Infobox, the gaps between Wikipedia and ontologies are less than the ones between Wikipedia and free text. Thus many studies have compiled Wikipedia ontologies based on Wikipedia. In particular, Auer and Bizer developed DBpedia, which is a large-scale structured database designed to extract RDF from Wikipedia [9]. In addition, Suchanek developed YAGO, which extends WordNet by using the Conceptual Category of Wikipedia [10].

Table 1. Scale of Japanese Wikipedia Ontology

Resource	#		Relationships	#
Class	87,159		Is-A	93,322
Property	10,769		Class-Instance	421,989
Instance	323,024		RDF Triples	4,867,882
			Property Hierarchy	1,387
			Property Domain	9,486
			Property Range	40,262
			Synonyms	12,558

However, as Wikipedia ontologies mainly come from English Wikipedia, they do not work for human-robot dialogue interactions in Japanese. Therefore we developed a Japanese Wikipedia ontology (JWO), which is a large-scale, general-purpose ontology derived from Japanese Wikipedia. JWO has seven relationships: Is-A (rdfs: subClassOf), class-instance (rdf: type), RDF (Infobox) triple (owl: Object/DatatypeProperty), property hierarchy (rdf: subproperty), property domain (rdfs: domain), and range (rdfs: range) and synonyms.

JWO works for knowledge-level interactions with dialog and fact type QAs. Specifically, we take Is-A, Class-Instance and RDF Triples to do so. Table 1 shows the current scale of JWO. Details of each building method are described in [11].

3.2   Behavior Ontology

Behavior ontology (BO) is a domain ontology specialized into the HRI. The basic concept of BO is the structure of robot behavior and bridging the gaps between human behavior and humanoid robot (the humanoid robot Nao) behavior.

BO works for behavior-level interactions between a user and Nao. BO specifies how behaviors are organized from both the viewpoints of the human body and the robot body. The upper part in BO has a greater relationship with human behavior and the lower part has a greater relationship with robot behavior. BO has 181 classes and 386 instances to date, as shown in Fig. 1.

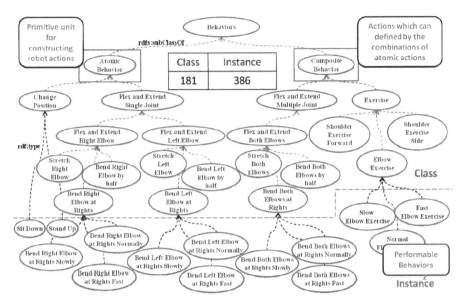

Fig. 1. Behavior Ontology (Excerpt)

The root class "Behavior" is classified into "Atomic Behavior" and "Composite Behavior." Atomic Behavior has been organized based on the primitive behaviors executable by built-in xxx each robot and Composite Behavior consists of two or more Atomic Behaviors. Atomic/Composite Behaviors are furthermore classified by robot body components such as elbow and wrist, directions such as forward and backward, and speed such as fast and slow.

3.3   Robot Kinematics Ontology

A robot has a physical structure that is different from a human, and the structure also differs from robot to robot. A robot's physical components and degree of freedom (DOF) involve the kinematical performance of robot action in a real environment, while devices such as sensors or cameras involve the accuracy or feasibility of a task. We have proposed a special HRI for multi-robot cooperation, for in our approach it is important to assign each robot a suitable task based on its physical characteristics and functions. Therefore we developed what we call robot kinematics ontology (RKO). Each body area instance corresponds to kinematics that are controlled by built-in software.

In this ontology, the fact that a robot has a physical part or device is described by using these "has-joint" or "has-device" properties.

Although their properties might not be complete enough to interpret all the physical structures and functions of a robot, at the point of selecting a robot that can perform a certain task from a group of robot, they work well. The instances in RKO correspond to the instances in BO.

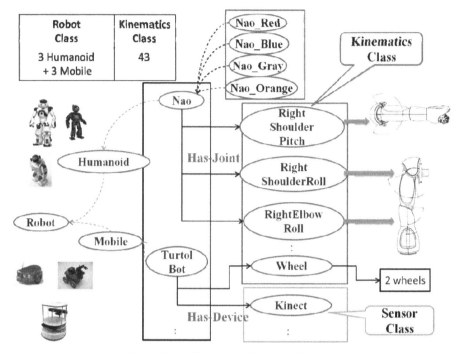

Fig. 2. Robot Kinematics Ontology (Excerpt)

3.4   Ontologies Alignment

By aligning domain ontologies that are specialized robot services (BO, RKO) into a large-scale ontology (JWO), we integrate dialogue knowledge, behavior and built-in software. Here, we show the alignment with JWO and BO as an example of ontologies alignment. Aligning BO with JWO enables Nao to perform behaviors related to dialogue topics. In other words, ontologies alignment functions as a bridge between dialogue and robot behavior. Ontologies alignment was performed manually in this study.

The ontologies alignment enables Nao to understand the situation while performing one or other behaviors—although behaviors are generally nothing more than time-series pose data for Nao. In Fig. 3, when Nao enters into a dialogue on sporting competitions with a user, Nao tells the user that fitness is example of competitions by referring to JWO and then can show the user "Shoulder Elbow Exercise" or "Navy Exercise" through ontologies alignment.

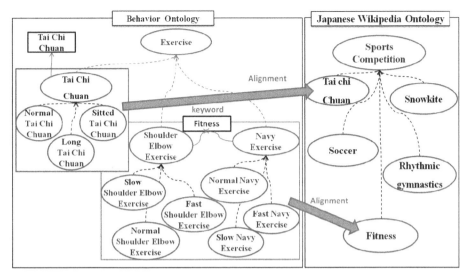

Fig. 3. Ontologies Alignment between JWO and BO

4   System Architecture

4.1   System Architecture for Multi-robot Coordination Service

This section explains the proposed system architecture based on ontologies and SWS to achieve multi-robot coordination and realize a service-efficient construction.

Figure 4 shows a diagram of the architecture hierarchy of the system proposed in our study. This architecture has a five-tier hierarchy. This is included in the processes that make up the contents of a concrete task, and the ontologies that have the necessary data for the needed modules and services using artificial intelligence (AI) technology and existing robotics.

The role of each layer in Fig. 4 is shown below.

- **Task Layer:** This layer is user request. Through interaction with the user, a user request is classified into one task or multiple tasks. A task is realized by performing a number of processes.
- **Process Layer:** This layer contains the processes that need to be conducted to realize a task. For example, "Fact Type QA Task" needs "Question Recognition Process" and "Speech Process" and so on. Process has a flow of modules.
- **Module Layer:** This layer is a software module containing the actual processing units. The software module sorts the particle size considering the reusability of software for multiple robots and devices as well as data and API and external functions and so on.
- **Ontology Layer:** This layer abstracts the data organized as knowledge in the world of words for multi-robot coordination service and interaction with the user

(Fact Type QA Task). Aligning ontologies can realize services by applying the relationship of different regions.

- **Data Layer:** This layer has a data structure in which machines are actually available. Modules have available data such as environment maps that were created manually and skeletons of user data from Kinect   and so on.

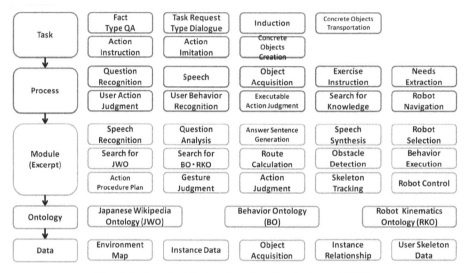

Fig. 4. System Architecture based on Ontologies and SWS

As with constructing SWS, we construct the service by using the necessary processes from the workflow of service. The system constructs the necessary processes for the configuration of the robot service in the system architecture, and each robot executes processes as tasks. In this way, we can realize a multi-robot coordination service.

A process is composed of modules, but we don't implement all modules. Because a module is an advanced research topic for AI, we take advantage of existing research such as natural language processing and data processing by image processing and software that generates the data for the environment map. We implement the required component as the robot service.

The most important objective of this architecture is to break down a task into processes, and each process into modules by using ontologies and data. A task is composed of processes, and each process is executed by a robot. However, each individual process cannot be performed by all robots because each robot has a specific hardware-limit. Therefore, we use Behavior Ontology/Robot Kinematics Ontology (BO/RKO) [3] to determine which robots can perform which process. Using the concept of SWS, it is easy to perform some tasks by recombination of processes.

Of particular note, each module is focused on reusability, which is one of the features of SWS, so it responds flexibly to the robot model and function, and the configurations and changes in the service contents.

4.2   Specific Example of Multi-robot Coordination Service

When applying our system architecture to the service, the sequence of processing is determined, such as how to break down the tasks and how to execute the processes. We show specific example of the processing in the multi-robot coordination service.

Drink Provision Service
In this service, robots receive a drink order and pour the drink and carry the drink to the user. Therefore, this service is a combination of three tasks: "receive drink order," "pour a glass of the drink" and "carry the drink." When we apply this service to our architecture, the three tasks correspond to the following tasks: "Task Request Type Dialogue," "Concrete Object Creation" and "Concrete Object Transportation." We show how each three tasks is executed below.

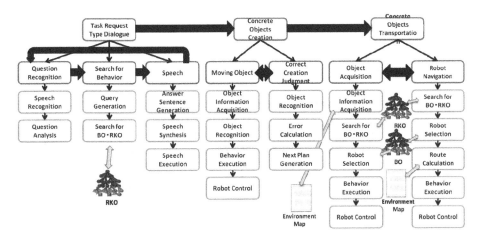

Fig. 5. Drink Provision Service

First, the task receiving drink order is executed by "Task Request Type Dialogue Task." This task is a combination of four processes (Fig. 5). The "Question Recognition Process" consists of the "Speech Recognition Module" and the "Question Analysis Module." If user speech matches the recognition pattern, the flow proceeds to the "Executable Action Judgment Process." Otherwise the flow proceeds to "Speech Process" and the robot asks which task is required. The "Executable Action Judgment Process" consists of the "Query Generation Module" and the "Search for BO/RKO Module." The role of this process is that it converts the requested task into a query and search for a RKO in order to find the executable robot. For example, when the task is to pour a glass of a drink, the robot that has two arms and grippers is selected by searching for RKO. By determining the robot to perform the task, the flow proceeds with the "Speech Process."

Then, the task of pouring a glass of the drink is executed by "Concrete Object Creation." This task is a combination of the "Moving Object Process" and the "Correct Creation Judgment Process," but we cannot use this flow because we are developing the "Object Recognition Module" and "Error Calculation Module." Therefore, we have substituted built-in software for the "Moving Object Process" and the "Correct Creation Judgment Process." Then, the task deliver the drink is executed by "Concrete Object Transportation." This task is a combination of the "Object Acquisition Process" and the "Robot Navigation Process." The "Object Acquisition Process" obtains location information on where there is a glass of drink using the environment map. The "Robot Navigation Process" selects a robot to carry the glass of drink using the "Search for BO Module." When the robot that has a wheel is selected to carry is the drink, the robot carries the glass to the user by referring to the environment map.

QA Service

This service is a QA interaction with the user.

If there is an object relating to the question in the environment map, the robot tells the user that the object is in the room. When the user wants the object brought to her or him, robots take it to the user by multi-robot coordination. A simple dialogue sequence in such a case is shown below.

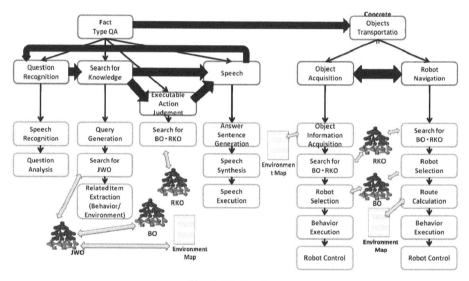

Fig. 6. QA Service

User: What are representative novels of Mr. xxx?

Robot: They are A, B, C, D, E. I have A and B here in RobotCafe. What would you like?

(The robot gets the answers by dealing with SPARQL queries related to representative novels of Mr. xxx with JWO and the environment map.)

Therefore, this service is a combination of the "Fact Type QA Task" and the "Concrete Objects Transportation Task."

The role of the "Speech Recognition Process" and the "Speech Process" in this task is almost same as the "Drink Providing service." The significantly different point from the "Task Request Type Dialogue Task" in the "Drink Providing Service" is that the "Fact Type QA" is an interaction with the user using JWO. The "Search for Knowledge Process" searches for related classes, instances and properties in JWO.

The flow of the "Concrete Objects Transportation Task" is the same as the "Drink Providing Service."

Action Instruction Service
When a user makes a gesture, there is a factor of making the gesture. The role of this service ascertains the needs from the gesture. If the user wants to exercise, the robot instructs the user in exercise and the two perform the exercise together, otherwise the robot continues to interact QA with the user.

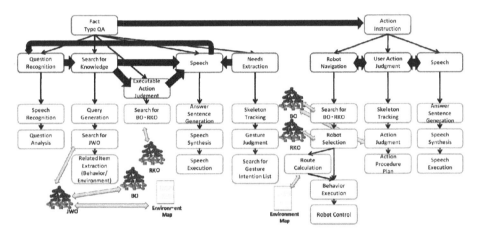

Fig. 7. Action Instruction Service

The "Needs Extraction Process" ascertains the user gesture from Kinect and obtains factor candidates of the gesture from the Gesture Intention List, which we compiled manually. The other processes in the "Fact Type QA Task" are basically the same as the "Fact Type QA Task" in "service that provides something related QA." The points of difference from "service that provides something related QA" are the following: While trying to ascertain the factor, the robot conducts dialogues with the user using the Gesture Intention List. When the factor of performing the gesture is found through dialogue, the robot conducts dialogues with the user using JWO because we are manually mapping the Gesture Intention List and JWO. For example, if the factor of making the gesture is "fatigue," the "Search for Knowledge Process" searches for related classes, instances and properties in JWO. The related class of "fatigue" includes "sports." Moreover, the related action of "sports" is "Navy Exercise" through the ontologies alignment (cf. 3.4). In this way, the service is deployed from the "Fact Type QA Process" to the "Action Instruction Process."

The "Action Instruction Task" gives instruction in a exercise, and the robot and the user perform the exercise together. This task consists of three processes. For example, when executing "Navy Exercise," the "Robot Navigation Process" selects a robot that has Kinect for action judgment and has arms for executing exercise using RKO. The robot that has Kinect moves close to the user and tracks the user skeleton, it then executes the exercise and the robot and the user perform the exercise together. The "User Action Judgment Process" evaluates user behavior by the following flow: The first is atomic behavior judgment based on the parameters for atomic behavior instances. The second is composite judgment, which is a combination of atomic judgments. Nao reviews user performance by timing the single composite behavior in the exercise sequence finishes. The result pattern is classified into the following categories: "Right," "Timing is Off," "Too Much" and "Pose Mismatch" made considering the user's performance. Finally, Nao decides the next interaction based on a user review.

5   Experiments

To show the multi-robot coordination service in action, here we describe the HRI logs of the case study of RobotCafe.

In the following, we use abbreviated notations for robot names.

"NT" stands for humanoid and mobile robot "NaoTorso with Kobuki." This robot has the upper body of NaoTorso upper body and Turtlebot2. This robot is excellent in terms of stability of movement compared to the humanoid robot "Nao."

"N" stands for humanoid robot "NaoOrange" This robot is excellent in dialog and exercise.

"H" stands for the twin-arm robot "HIRONX" [12]. This robot mainly works in the assembly line in Japan. This robot is excellent at handling things.

NT: Welcome to RobotCafe. Will you follow me to your seat?
(Humanoid robot NaoTorso knows where table and chairs are located in RobotCafe by referencing the RobotCafe Environmental Map.)

Fig. 8. NaoTorso guides the user and receives a drink order

Drink Provision Service
NT: What would you like?
U: A glass of orange juice, please.
(At the request of User, expand the service.)
NT: Sure. I'll ask Human Twin-Arm Robot HIRONX to make it.
H: Let me get started with making a glass of orange juice.

(HIRONX opens a refrigerator, takes out a bottle of orange juice and pours a glass of orange juice. HIRONX puts a glass of orange juice on the tray of the carry robot TurtleBot, and TurtleBot carries it to the user's seat.)

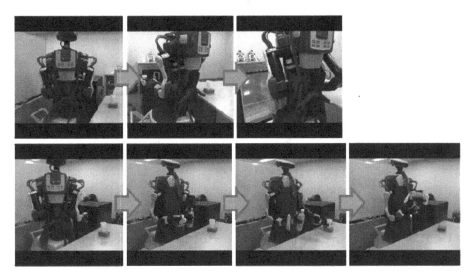

Fig. 9. HIRONX pour a glass of juice

NT: Here's your glass of orange juice.
(The user takes the glass from TurtleBot. TurtleBot leaves the user.)

Fig. 10. TurtleBot carries a glass of juice to the user

QA Service

NT: Do you have any more requests?
U: What are representative novels of Shakespeare?
NT: They are Hamlet, Macbeth, Romeo and Juliet, A Midsummer Night's Dream. I have Hamlet and Romeo and Juliet here in Robot Cafe. What would you like?
(NaoTorso gets the answers by means of SPARQL queries regarding representative Shakespearean novels conducted with JWO)
U: I like Hamlet. Will you bring Hamlet here?
NT: OK. I will ask Pioneer3DX to bring Hamlet here.

(Grip and carrier robot Pinoneer3DX identifies where Hamlet is located in RobotCafe using the environmental map, grips Hamlet and takes the book to the user's seat.)

Fig. 11. As NaoTorso interacts with the user, Pioneer3DX carries the requested book to the user

NT: Now you can read Hamlet. Do you have any more requests?
(User receives the book from Pioneer3DX.)
U: Everything's OK.
NT: Sure. Tell me your requests later.

Action Instruction Service
(Kinect recognizes that a user (a girl) wants to stretch the upper part of her body and transmit the fact to NaoTorso)

Fig. 12. When the user gestures, NaoTorso is interacting with the user

NT: You just stretched the upper part of your body. Is the reason you do so boredom, tiredness, or bad physical condition?
(NaoTorso gets the answers by means of SPARQL queries regarding causes of stretching with JWO.)
U: I'm tired.

NT: The reason is tiredness. Sleep, sports, stretching and Your Favorite Items work to alleviate your tiredness. Do you want to know more?

(NaoTorso gets the answers by means of SPARQL queries regarding alleviating tiredness to with JWO

U: Tell me more about sports.

NT: Sports include field hockey, baseball, and soccer. I can show you Navy Exercise and Tai Chi Chuan. What do you like?

(NaoTorso gets the answers by means of SPARQL queries regarding "Sports" classinstance with JWO and then learns what the robots can perform by dealing with the links between JWO and BO.)

U: Show me Navy Exercise.

NT: OK. I cannot do it, and so I will ask another robot, Ornage Nao, to perform Navy Exercise and also TurtleBot to evaluate how well your exercise goes.

(NaoTorso knows Orange Nao can perform Navy Exercise and that TurtleBot can evaluate human behavior with Kinect by retrieving BO and RKO.)

Fig. 13. OrangeNao exercises with the user

N: First, I'll show you how Navy Exercise is done. Watch me please. Let's do Navy Exercise together.

(Performing together and evaluating user exercise)

N: You are not getting the timing right with Navy Exercise. Let's do it together slowly.

(Performing together and evaluating user exercise again)

N: Well done. That's all.

6   Conclusion

In this paper, we looked at the feasibility of providing services that cannot by executed by one robot, by using multi-robot coordination, which has the concept of SWS. The three services shown in the case study consisted of several processes and often took advantage of the same module, which is included in different processes. Therefore, we were able to show modules of high reusability in our architecture, and this architecture allows a user to adapt another service scene at no extra cost. For example, if the ontology layer has "Care Ontology," which focuses on care, the "Action Instruction Service" in the case study can change to "watch service for elderly" easily.

The service sequence using this architecture is currently limited due to a shortage of tasks and processes. In the future, we will make a great many more tasks and processes to enable several service sequences.

References

1. Kobayashi, S., Tamagawa, S., Morita, T., Yamaguchi, T.: Intelligent Humanoid Robot with Japanese Wikipedia Ontology and Robot Action Ontology. In: Proceedings of the 6th ACM/IEEE International Conference on Human-Robot Interaction (HRI 2011), Lausanne, Switzerland, pp. 417–424 (2011)
2. Japanese Wikipedia Ontology, http://www.wikipediaontology.org/
3. Kobayashi, S., Yamaguchi, T.: Multi-Level Human Robot Interaction by Aligning Different Ontologies. In: 10th International Joint Conference on Knowledge-Based Software Engineering, Frontiers in AI and Applications, vol. 180, pp. 313–322. IOS Press (August 2012)
4. Burstein, M., Bussler, C., Zaremba, M., Finin, T., Huhns, M.N., Paolucci, M., Sheth, A.P., Williams, S.: A Semantic Web Services Architecture. IEEE Internet Computing 9(5), 72–81 (2005)
5. Tenorth, M., Jain, D., Beetz, M.: Knowledge Representation for Cognitive Robots. Künstliche Intelligenz 24 (2010)
6. Tenorth, M., Beetz, M.: Knowledge Processing for Autonomous Robot Control. In: AAAI Spring Symposium on Designing Intelligent Robots: Reintegrating AI (2012)
7. OpenCyc, http://www.cyc.com/opencyc
8. RoboEarth, http://roboearth.org/
9. Auer, S., Bizer, C., Kobilarov, G., Lehmann, J., Cyganiak, R., Ives, Z.: DBpedia: A Nucleus for a Web of Open Data. In: Aberer, K., et al. (eds.) ISWC/ASWC 2007. LNCS, vol. 4825, pp. 722–735. Springer, Heidelberg (2007)
10. Suchanek, F.M., Kasneci, G., Weikum, G.: Yago: A core of semantic knowledge. In: Proceedings of the 16th International Conference on World Wide Web, pp. 697–706. ACM (2007)
11. Tamagawa, S., Sakurai, S., Tejima, T., Morita, T., Izumi, N., Yamaguchi, T.: Learning a Large Scale of Ontology from Japanese Wikipedia. In: 2010 IEEE/WIC/ACM International Conference on Web Intelligence, pp. 279–286 (2010)
12. HIRO, http://nextage.kawada.jp/en/hiro/

Towards Management of the Data and Knowledge Needed for Port Integration: An Initial Ontology

Ana Ximena Halabi-Echeverry[1,2] and Deborah Richards[1]

[1] Department of Computing, Macquarie University
NSW 2109, Australia
[2] Escuela Internacional de Ciencias Económicas y Administrativas, Universidad de La Sabana
Chía (Cundinamarca), Colombia
{ana.halabiecheverry,Deborah.Richards}@mq.edu.au

Abstract. This paper suggests the use of a common ontology to assist with decision making and data-mining in the port domain. Five novel ontological descriptions that demonstrate how to address issues such as conflicts in terminology are presented. The ontology sketches presented in this paper not only provide a vocabulary for the consensual discussion of the port integration decision and to capture the relevant factors and measurement variables that can be used to manage and uncover new knowledge via data mining.

Keywords: ontological descriptions, port integration decision, new knowledge via data mining.

1   Introduction

The synergies resulting from integration between seaports or in general water-based ports can have many positive consequences for a region including: ability to play an important role in the macro-scale economies; rapid growth in international trade; increased capacity to increase wealth and acquire power in the region and increased infrastructure investment in the region. Decision making around how best to integrate ports, such as which ports to connect with and how, is complex and will be aided by the design and development of an intelligent decision making support system (*i*-DMSS) to manage the data and knowledge for the decision and associated choices.

A number of data management issues, such as disparate sources, formats and levels, exist in the port domain [1]. To manage these data integration issues we could use metadata. However, the role of metadata in DSS implementation has been very limited [2, 3]. Additionally, the literature confirms some confusion in defining the terminology used in the port domain. Furthermore, The Tioga Group [4] states that "the data available to modelers often lack explanatory power, and data more directly related to efficiency are inaccessible or confidential…the modelling effort overall [in the port domain] is in an early stage of development (p.109)". Thus, our project seeks to offer a solution to the question:

Y.S. Kim et al (Eds.): PKAW 2014, LNCS 8863, pp. 165–179, 2014.
© Springer International Publishing Switzerland 2014

How can the data produced during capture and modelling of business processes for the decision of port integration be managed?

An important goal of this paper is to show a possible way of assembling data to provide a cohesive body of knowledge for a more accurate and machine interpretable representation of the data capabilities. We want to capture not only the data and its structure but also the semantics behind the data. This paper proposes the use of a common ontology to address this issue. As stated by [5] "it is expected that the use of ontologies will result in building more intelligent applications, enabling them to work more accurately at the humans' conceptual level". An ontology can potentially address the issues of differences in terminology and the different levels of abstraction. To understand both the nature of the problem of managing data in the port integration domain and present some solutions, this paper presents five novel illustrations of a common ontology that reveals inconsistencies in the terminology used in the port domain and suggests an accurate use of terms and links between attributes to allow efficient data mining and consequently decision support process.

In the next section we provide further background to the problem including a review of ontologies in neighbouring domains to the port, suggesting a valid approach to assembling data in a cohesive body of knowledge for a machine interpretable representation for the decision of port integration. This work differs from existing research approaches in that provides a high spectrum of systems (and concepts) linked to the performance of the port which creates a holistic ontology. Section 3 presents the Semantic Web Ontology (OWL) and its subsequent application in decision support systems. Section 4 presents a sketch ontology using OWL particularly supporting key concepts related to port integration. Section 5 provides our conclusions.

2   The Port Domain

The problem of bringing together heterogeneous and distributed data levels is known as the interoperability problem. Kaza and Chen [6] classified the interoperability problem into: a) data and database heterogeneity problems: data is in different structures and b) semantic problem: data in different sources has different meaning. They also state that the interoperability problem is one of the most important and pressing challenges in information sharing. Based on the framework of Kaza and Chen [6], the interoperability problem identified in the port domain includes:

- Data representation: data are recorded in different formats, e.g., rounded decimals or different date formats.
- Data unit conflicts: the units of data differ, e.g. some cargo is sized in metric tons (1,000 kilograms) but some others are expressed as 2204.62 pounds or 0.9842 ton.
- Naming conflicts: the labels of elements differ, e.g., when defining port congestion, Tiwari and ITOH [7] state that port congestion is better referred to the number of vessel calls already high for a port, resulting in a higher volume of TEUs and a negative commercial effect. In its own right, The Tioga Group [4] defines port congestion as the berth utilization and reserve capacity at port indicating a lack of planning and expansion.

- Aggregation conflicts: an aggregation is used to identify some entities in one source but combines attributes in another source, e.g., ports may be aggregated by custom jurisdictions or by coastal borders.

2.1   Review of Ontologies in Neighbouring Domains to the Port Integration

An ontology design is provided in the work of Ruth et al. [8] to utilise a formal semantic description of services in the context of transportation and logistics. The main problem faced by the authors was to find a high number of miscellaneous and heterogeneous tables describing available goods with classifications and qualities difficult to customise in a service-oriented routing solution. Hoxha et al. [9] also offer a formal semantic approach to represent logistic services such as storage and handling. They found a fertile area of ontology application every time a transport service provider require a manually inspection of a parcel, exposing himself to an ambiguous service of classification. Hoxha et al. [9] (p.5) reveal that "the number of available logistics ontologies is very small" as to their revision on the Web Ontology Library Swoogle, DAML and SchemaWeb. Even though, an approach to semantic graphs within the Homeland Port Security domain is provided by   Adam et al. [10]. They use semantic and spatio-temporal contextual relationships among data sources and data flows (events) to identify alerts with potentially dangerous shipments crossing the border of ports and their respective jurisdictions. The authors are able to show a prototype system to the domain ontology known as *Dangerous (chemical) Combinations* and evaluate their approach testing a dataset from US Customs.

3   The Web Ontology Language (OWL)

Ontologies are representations of universals in reality, for this reason the ontology terms describe concepts and relations within the domain of study The most frequently cited definition of an ontology states that "is an explicit specification of a conceptualization…when the knowledge of a domain is represented in a declarative formalism, the set of objects that can be represented is called the universe of discourse [11], (p. 908)". According to Engers et al. [12], (pp.234-236) ontologies are used for five main purposes:

1. Organising and structuring information: this role is describing the domain expressing terms, semantics and sentences that can be used.
2. Reasoning and problem solving: the basic role in this case is to represent knowledge of the domain so that an automated reasoner can represent problems and generate solutions to these problems. The reasoning context consequently limits an ontology's reusability.
3. Semantic indexing and search: this role enables the semantic index of information search for content.
4. Semantics integration and interoperation: the ontology in that case defines the specific vocabulary to be used to interchange information. In a sense these ontologies

function as a semantic information schema and usually reuse parts of ontologies created for other uses.

5. Understanding the domain: this ontology can be viewed as a map that specifies what kinds of knowledge can be identified in the domain and thus may help when making sense of that domain and acquiring relevant knowledge. This type of ontology can be used as a basis for designing more specialised representations.

Kamel et al. [13] suggest that an ontology can be used to answer questions such as:

1. *Where to find data?* answering problems only alleviated by search engines able to match semantic concepts and their relationships.
2. *How to reason with data?* allowing assertions about individuals (instances) and how they relate using a role. Given an individual, we can also determine specific concepts for an individual taking into account any assertions that have been made about themselves. "This is known as DL description logic.
3. *How to label the data collected?* automatically establishing the relationship between the resource and related (tagged) resources.
4. *How to integrate data?* allowing ontologies able to integrate well with other ontologies or o including coding schemes readable by different technologies.

The most recent development in standard ontology languages is The Web Ontology Language (OWL). According to [14] ontologies describe complex concepts out of simpler ones. The fundamental elements of an ontology are: classes, properties, individuals and datatypes. An important challenge in building a common ontology for the port domain is the need for temporal reasoning. "Dealing with information that changes over time is a critical problem for practical Knowledge Representation languages (OWL, RDF)" Preventis [15], (p.10). A time-related relationship must hold as a ternary representation that extends the binary relationship between classes or concepts. Figure 1 gives an example of temporal reasoning.

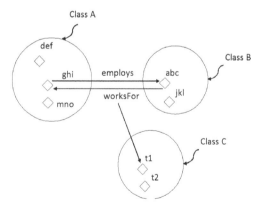

Fig. 1. A schematic representation of a temporal reasoning. Based on [15]

According to Yu et al. [16] three kinds of ontology can be used to generate knowledge from temporal data:

- parameter ontology: used to describe the shape of patterns
- context ontology: used to describe the physical meaning of patterns
- event ontology: used to describe events that happened.

Particular emphasis must be given on keeping the semantics of object and data properties after they are converted to temporal. According to Preventis [15], (p.15) four new objects are introduced in a temporal ontology as depicted in Figure 2:

- *Event*: the class that represents n-ary relation[1]
- *During*: an object that relates the event to the time interval during which it holds.
- *participatesIn*: an object that relates the individuals that participate in an event, to that specific event individual. The object properties that are covered to temporal become sub-properties of this property.
- *Overlaps*: an object property that relates two time intervals. This property implies that those time intervals, in some way overlap each other.

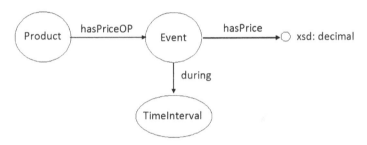

Fig. 2. A schematic representation of a temporal data property. Taken from [16] (p.16)

4   Building the Basis for a Common Ontology in the Port Integration Domain

In this subsection we will seek to motivate an ontology representation for the data-levels that constitute the hierarchical structure presented in Table 1. The Table shows the complex associations among macro-level, meso-level and micro-level data and provides descriptions for the abbreviated attribute names used later. The data-levels

---

[1] **Definition (n-ary relation):** An *n*-ary relation on sets A_1, ..., A_n is a set of ordered *n*-tuples $<a_1, ..., a_n>$ where a_i is an element of A_i for all $i, 1 \leq i < n$. Thus an *n*-ary relation on sets A_1, ..., A_n is a subset of Cartesian product $A_1 \times ... \times A_n$.

Let A1 be a set of names, A2 a set of addresses, and A3 a set of telephone numbers. Then a set of 3-tuples <name, address, telephone number> such as (<Amy Angels, 35 Mediterranean Ave, 224-1357>, <Barbara Braves, 221 Atlantic Ave, 301-1734>, <Charles Cubs, 312 Baltic Ave, 223-9876>), is a 3-ary (ternary) relation.

Illustration taken from http://www.cs.odu.edu/~toida/nerzic/level-a/relation/definition/cp_gen/

Table 1. Abstraction and data aggregation according to levels of complexity

Dimension	Macro-level [N_i]			Meso-level [K_{ij}]	Type	Micro-level [$a,b,c...$]	
	Macro-level (sets)	Source/Repository	Model	Second-level (concepts)		Micro-level (measurements)	Data Description
The strategic dimension of port integration due to transport	ES	US Census Bureau	M1a	Foreign Trade	Continuous	FoTrExpCg	Foreign trade of exports cargo in millions US dollars
	FPT	US Army Corps of Engineers		Port Throughput	Continuous	WtContExp	Annual water transportation of exports by port in twenty-foot equivalent units (TEUs)
	PE	BTS (Bureau of Transportation Statistics)		Selection/Deviation of routes	Continuous	Calls	records of calls service of vessels of 10,000 DWT or greater
	FPT	BTS (Bureau of Transportation Statistics)		Prompt Response	Continuous	CapacityV	Sum of vessels weights expressed in DWT (deadweight tonnes = metric tones = 1000kg or 2,205 pounds)
port integration due to interconnection	ES	Lloyd's list repository	M1b	Infrastructure Demand	Binominal	GasPipes	Whether or not the port has industrial gas pipelines infrastructure
	ES	Lloyd's list repository		Infrastructure Demand	Binominal	OilPipes	Whether or not the port has crude oil and oil products pipelines infrastructure
	FPT	Lloyd's list repository		Land Use Patterns	Binominal	FacilityC	Whether or not the port offers container facilities
	FPT	Lloyd's list repository		Land Use Patterns	Binominal	FacilityR	Whether or not the port offers ro-ro facilities
	FPT	Lloyd's list repository		Land Use Patterns	Binominal	FacilityQ	Whether or not the port offers other liquid bulk facilities
The strategic dimension of port integration due to governance concerns	GEP	IMO International Maritime Organization		Reducing Air Emissions	Continuous	Facilities	Number of port reception facilities (be they fixed, floating or mobile) in which final disposal of MARPOL residues/wastes occurs in a manner that protects the environment, the health and safety of workers and general population according with IMO
	GEP	US Army Corps of Engineers	M2	Improving Water Quality	Continuous	DredgeOcean	Amount of dredged ocean material disposed in cubic yards by state according with the US Army Corps
	PSi	United States Geological Survey (USGS)		Minimizing Impacts of Growth	Continuous	GAPSstatus1	Area of a state in acres in which the port is located (georeferencial measure) having permanent protection of natural land and water cover and a mandated management plan in operation to maintain a natural state within which disturbance events (of natural type, frequency, intensity, and legacy) are allowed to proceed without interference or are mimicked through management according with the USGS
	PSi	USCounty.Org		Minimizing Impacts of Growth	Continuous	CountyArea	County land area in square miles
The strategic dimension of port integration due to logistics operations	FPT	Buenaventura Port website	M3	Port Throughput	Continuous	CoffOutBUN	Commodity throughput of coffee (tons) handled in Buenaventura Port
	ES	Department of Customs in Colombia (DIAN)		ForeignTrade	Continuous	CoffExpCol	National exports of coffee (tons)

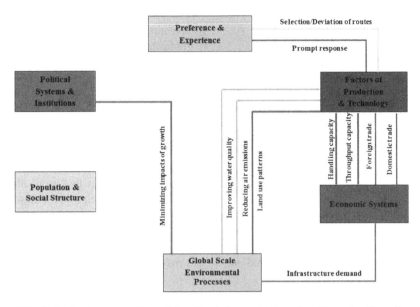

Fig. 3. Systemic composition of data-levels for port integration "Learning Space"

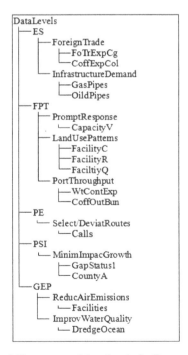

Fig. 4. Taxonomy of data-levels for Port Integration

map each strategy of port integration and also allow a data aggregation scheme. The created ontology uses the systematic approach called "*learning space*" which captures the relevant factors and measurement variables simplified during the data mining activity. The learning space is depicted in Figure 3 in this paper. Five notions or entities illustrate the complexity of the data collection for port integration:

Factors of Production and Technology (FPT), Economic Systems (ES), Global Scale Environmental Processes (GEP), Political Systems & Institutions (PSI) and Preference & Experience (PE). We do not model Population and Social structure for the Port domain because the flows between it and the other systems are unclear from the literature. This ontology also consists of nine disjoint classes and 15 object properties to create the conceptual data hierarchy shown in Figure 4.

What the OWL hierarchy in Figure 4 actually represents, in contrast to the systemic

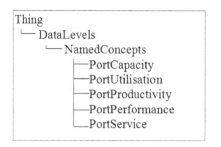

```
Thing
 └─ DataLevels
     └─ NamedConcepts
         ├─PortCapacity
         ├─PortUtilisation
         ├─PortProductivity
         ├─PortPerformance
         └─PortService
```

Fig. 5. Creation of concepts out of data-levels for Port Integration

composition shown in Figure 3, is necessary implication. For instance:

All Foreign Trade and Infrastructure Demand (classes) *isA* type of Economic System (ES)[2] and A Foreign Trade (class) *hasA* amongst other things some Exports of cargo in Monetary and freight units (FoTrExpCg and CoExpCol), etc. The hierarchy assumes that Foreign Trade and Infrastructure Demand are different classes. Also, Figure 4 assumes that each subclass belongs to one superclass; for example,

Foreign Trade *isA* type of Economic System and it is not a type of Factors of Production & Technology System (FPT), Preference & Experience System (PE), Political System and Institutions (PSI), or Global Scale Environmental Process (GEP). In reality, these distinctions may be blurred and a class may belong to more than one macro-level system.

For the purpose of identification, macro-level data from now onwards will be called: Entity, meso-level data: Class, and micro-level of data: Object property. The aim is twofold: create an illustration of the data-level concept for port integration and describe semantically key data contended in the thesis such as: port capacity, port utilization, port productivity, port performance and port service. Note that these five concepts are made from each of the data-levels, using the properties and relationships among them (Figure 5).

In OWL there is a distinction between *primitive* and *defined* classes. "More formally, OWL allows concepts to be defined by sets of necessary and sufficient condition... It is critical to understand that in general, nothing will be inferred to be subsumed under primitive class by the classifier" [17], (p.67). Therefore, an important aspect is to check when classes fail to be classified under a concept, whether or not the description is *primitive* or *defined*. However at this stage, the ontology in this paper is not meant to commit to a definition because each class is only a sample of concepts in the universe for the decision of port integration. Thus, this paper considers leaving the nine disjointed classes as *primitive*.

Rector et al. [17] highly recommend including a paraphrase of any description logic before encoding it in OWL software such as Protégé. Thus, before showing the initial data-level hierarchy using logic-based ontology language, we provide a summary of paraphrases presented by these authors in Table 2 (p. 78).

The purpose of the ontology is to specifically manage a domain of knowledge. It allows us to describe semantically the key decision concepts suggested in this paper, i.e. port capacity, port utilization, port productivity, port performance and port service. The conceptual notion of each term is based on The Tioga Group [4] work that relies

---

[2] *Economic System (ES):* According to Consortium for International Earth Science Information Network (CIESIN) the ES determines how people produce and consume goods and how wealth is distributed and evolves. To find the other systemic definitions, see the Systemic Theory glossary at the beginning of this thesis.

heavily on port industry rules of thumb and a variety of assumptions as well as quantifiable relationships.

The following descriptions are only illustrations of the many possible notions that exist in the literature. To offer more would require a much greater investment in data collection and analysis. Also these illustrations are evidence that "no one measure will suffice, as the differences between ports and the interrelated nature of the metrics create multiple possible interpretations for single data elements" [4, p. 4].

Table 2. Summary of paraphrases. Taken from [17, p.78].

OWL definition	Paraphrase	Rationale
Class(Thing partial …	All Things …	Primitive vs Defined
Class(Thing complete parent …	A Thing is any Parent that …	Defined vs Primitive
(add to all descriptions and definitions)	…amongst other things	Open world hypothesis
allValuesFrom	Only	often misunderstood
someValuesFrom	Some	brevity and clarity
And	both … and also	minimise logic errors
not(…and…)	not all of / not both …and also	minimise logic errors
not(…or…)	neither ….nor ….	minimise logic errors
someValuesFrom not	has some … that are not...	minimise logic errors
not (someValuesFrom …)	does not have … any	minimise logic errors
AllValuesFrom not	has …no…/ has only …that are not …	minimise logic errors
Not (allValuesFrom …)	does not have …only	minimise logic errors
SubclassOf(A,B)	A implies B	Clarify use of subclass for implication

Illustration 1 (description of port capacity): The Tioga Group [4. pp.60–62] shows a regression analysis yielding the relationship between vessels' capacity (CapacityV) and Port Throughput (WtContExp). Note that Port Throughput can be measured with significant differences and variations per port. Thus here, one selected measurement among the options is container shipments for the export activity (WtContExp). The two measurement concepts should illustrate the higher concept of port capacity. The purpose is therefore, to describe the concept of port capacity in terms of understanding the relationship between CapacityV and WtContExp.

In order to minimise the logic error in the description of port capacity three important questions are asked:

1. Does all PortCapacity have CapacityV and WtContExp?
2. Do any DataLevels have CapacityV and WtContExp   types of   PortCapacity?
3. Does PortCapacity have CapacityV and WtContExp and nothing else?

To avoid misunderstanding and errors associated with the use of a universal quantifier for reasoning about the description of port capacity, we use the existential quantifier *amongst other things* and *some*.

Listing 1 illustrates the description presented of port capacity.

Listing 1. Illustration 1: description of port capacity

OWL:
Class (PortCapacity partial
DataLevels
       restriction (***hasA*** amongst other things some values From CapacityV)
       restriction (***hasA*** amongst other things some values From WtContExp)
Paraphrase:
PortCapacity has *amongst other things*, *some* values from vessels' capacity in DWT (CapacityV) and also *some* values from container shipments for the export activity (WtContExp).

Illustration 2 (description of port utilisation): The Tioga Group [4] in principle suggests that every terminal could be developed to its maximum capacity. They make a distinction between low short-term utilization, medium short-term utilization and high short-term utilization. Low short-term utilisation ports have substantial reserve capacity. Most Ro-Ro terminals (Facility R) fall in this category. In medium short-term utilisation, terminals have no immediate need to expand and invest. Most container terminals (FacilityC) fall in this category. Finally, in high short-term utilisation, terminals are at their utilisation limit, intensively liquid bulk terminals (FacilityQ) fall in this category. On the other side, they foresee that the continual pressure for land use may create potential problems for port utilization. These problems seem to relate well with highly politicised projects such as dredging projects in which port utilisation may be seriously affected (p. 88). An interesting variable to observe the previous statement is GAPStatus1, which indicates the area of a state surrounding the port that has protection of natural land and water cover and a mandated management protection plan in operation.

The OWL description of port utilisation, Listing 2 illustrates the use of *not some* to make negation of restrictions.

Listing 2. Illustration 2: description of port utilisation

OWL:
Class (PortUtilisation partial
DataLevels
    restriction (***hasA*** amongst other things some values From FacilityR)
    restriction (***hasA*** amongst other things some values From FacilityC)
    restriction (***hasA*** amongst other things some values From FacilityQ)
    not (restriction (***hasA*** amongst other things some values From GAPStatus1))
Paraphrase:
PortUtilisation has *amongst other things, some* values from Ro-Ro facilities (FacilityR) and/or also *some* values from container facilities (FacilityC) and/or also *some* values from liquid bulk facilities (FacilityQ) but does not have *any* values from a mandated management protection plan area of natural land and water cover of a state surrounding the port (GAPStatus1).

Illustration 3 (description of port productivity): if the port authority perspective must be taken into account, port productivity becomes the factor of growing public interest involving port planning, access, impacts, and emissions as productivity in external contexts. As The Tioga Group (2010) states "criteria for useful productivity measures might include…relevance [as a] measure [that] should document factors that will enter into operational choices, capital investments, and cargo routing decisions…the choice of port productivity metrics should be dictated in large part by their intended use" (p. 24). Therefore, traditional factors such as efficient handling of containers requires far more than just quayside space and labour; it requires for instance, port choice and cargo routing as a factor in which productivity is estimated and used. In these circumstances, port authorities compete for vessel calls (Calls) finding themselves compelled to defend their air emissions through a number of port reception facilities in which final disposal of residues/wastes occur for the sake of environment, safety of workers and population (Facilities).

The OWL description of port productivity, Listing 3 illustrates the logic use of *intersectionOf* (and).

Listing 3. Illustration 3: description of port productivity

OWL:
Class (PortProductivity partial
DataLevels
    restriction (***hasA*** amongst other things some values From Calls)
    restriction (***hasA*** amongst other things some values From Facilities)
Paraphrase:
PortProductivity has *amongst other things, both* has *some* values from calls service of vessels of 10,000 DWT or greater (Calls) and *also some* values from port reception facilities in which final disposal of residues/wastes occur for the sake of environment, safety of workers and population (Facilities).

Illustration 4 (description of port performance): useful metrics are those which enable management to identify the causes of declining performance and choose among possible responses. The Tioga Group [4] notes from Talley 's seminal work [18] that "port performance must transcend the functional engineering relationships of berths, cranes, etc., to examine the mission of the port itself in maximising throughput and profit" (p.107). Port managers with a longer time horizon in mind are typically involved in investments of infrastructure that in consequence require available capital. Therefore, functional relations between for example, output measures such as container throughput —in general or by commodity— (WtContExp; CoffOutBUN) and expected demands such as national exports —in general or by commodity— (FoTrExpCg; CoffExpCol) would match market requirements and positive responses.

The OWL description of port performance, Listing 4 illustrates the logic use of *SubClassOf* and *intersectionOf* (and).

Listing 4. Illustration 4: description of port performance

OWL:
Class (PortPerformance partial
DataLevels
    restriction (***hasA*** amongst other things some values From WtContExp)
Equivalent axiom
    SubClassOf(restriction (***hasA*** amongst other things some values From CoffOutBUN)
    restriction (***hasA*** amongst other things some values From FoTrExpCg)
Equivalent axiom
    SubClassOf(restriction (***hasA*** amongst other things some values From CoffExpCol)
Paraphrase:
PortPerformance has *amongst other things*, *both* has *some* values from container shipments for the export activity (WtContExp), which *implies* having *some* values from commodity shipments of coffee for the export activity (CoffOutBUN) and *also* *some* values from foreign trade exports of cargo (FoTrExpCg), which *implies* having *some* values from foreign trade exports of coffee (CoffExpCol).

Illustration5 (description of port service): generally, port service is associated with port performance; however, it may also depend on specific services provided by the port in its competitive strategy [19]. For instance, common privately operated ports cluster themselves in order to provide marine facilities such as crude oil and gas (Oil-Pipes, GasPipes). Therefore, the loading and unloading performances will depend on the size in DWT of serviced vessels (CapacityV).

The OWL description of port service, Listing 5 illustrates the logic use of *unionOf* (or) and *intersectionOf* (and).

Listing 5. Illustration 5: description of port service

OWL:
Class (PortService partial
DataLevels
     restriction (***hasA*** amongst other things some values From OilPipes)
     restriction (***hasA*** amongst other things some values From GasPipes)
     restriction (***hasA*** amongst other things some values From CapacityV)
Paraphrase:
PortService has *amongst other things*, *some* values from availability of crude oil and oil products pipelines infrastructure at port (OilPipes) and/or *also some* values from availability of industrial gas pipelines infrastructure at port (GasPipes) that have *both also some* values from vessels' capacity in DWT (CapacityV).

5   Conclusion

This paper has sought to develop five novel ontological descriptions of notions contended in the hypothetical *i*-DMSS modules. The ontology sketch model presented in this paper not only provides a vocabulary for the consensual discussion of the port integration decision but also serves to assess the "*learning space*" which captures the relevant factors and measurement variables simplified during the data mining activity and empirical analyses.

According to Engers et al. [12], the first step in the ontological process is to use a rationale of the ontology to learn how it might be structured. Then via an iterative process involving collaboration between experts in the domain, an ontology for that domain will emerge. We have proposed five illustrations that can be executed even manually. However, the key value of the illustrations is to make the concept of an ontology accessible, hopefully leading to major interest in their application within the domain, that is, the illustrations have created situations which hopefully provide a mental model of port integration involving the participation and exchange of individual ports.

The benefits of using an ontology lie in the semantic use of terminology relevant for the port integration decision. Nevertheless, based on the promise of a shared vocabulary provided by an ontology, it is anticipated that knowledge discovery can be performed even when data collection involves combining data from several and disparate repositories.

Some challenges may be envisaged in which modeling the ontology will require consensus among domain experts from many and different port areas and the complexity of reaching consensus when multiple conflicting views may exist can threaten consistency across the systems (macro-levels of data). A work that must be done is to show a prototype system to the port domain based on different scenarios (e.g. through simulations). To observe this kind of system may require, for example, the use of agent-based simulations that would allow decomposing the *learning space* into smaller and simpler parts, which are easier to understand, model and validate.

References

1. Halabi Echeverry, A.X., Richards, D.: Addressing Challenges for Knowledge Discovery from Data in the Domain of Seaport Integration. In: Richards, D., Kang, B.H. (eds.) PKAW 2012. LNCS, vol. 7457, pp. 73–85. Springer, Heidelberg (2012)
2. Burstein, F., McKemmish, S., Fischer, J., Manaszewicz, R., Malhotra, P.: A Role for Information Portals as Intelligent Support Systems: Breast Cancer Knowledge Online Experience. In: Phillips-Wren, G., Ichalkaranje, N., Jain, L.C. (eds.) Intelligent Decision Making: An Ai-Based Approach, vol. 97, pp. 383–389. Springer, Berlin (2008)
3. Pomerol, J.C., Adam, F.: Understanding Human Decision Making - A Fundamental Step Towards Effective Intelligent Decision Support. In: PhillipsWren, G., Ichalkaranje, N., Jain, L.C. (eds.) Intelligent Decision Making: An AI-Based Approach. SCI, vol. 97, pp. 3–40. Springer, Heidelberg (2008)
4. Improving Marine Container Terminal Productivity: Development of Productivity Measures, Proposed Sources of Data, and Initial Collection of Data from Proposed Sources. Technical report. The Tioga Group, Inc., Moraga, CA (2010)
5. Karacapilidis, N.: An Overview of Future Challenges of Decision Support Technologies. In: Intelligent Decision-making Support Systems, pp. 385–399. Springer, London (2006)
6. Kaza, S., Chen, H.: Public Safety Information Sharing: An Ontological Perspective. In: Chen, H., Brandt, L., Gregg, V., Traunmüller, R., Dawes, S., Hovy, E., Macintosh, A., Larson, C. (eds.) Digital Government, vol. 17, pp. 263–282. Springer US (2008)
7. Tiwari, P., Itoh, H.: Containerized cargo shipper's behavior in China: A discrete choice analysis. Journal of Transportation and Statistics 6(1) (2003)
8. Ruth, T., Flach, G., Weitzel, M.: Semantics-based, strategic planning and composition of intermodal freight transport services in sea port hinterlands. In: Proceedings of the 11th International Conference on Knowledge Management and Knowledge Technologies. ACM (2011)
9. Hoxha, J., Scheuermann, A., Bloehdorn, S.: An approach to formal and semantic representation of logistics services. In: Proceedings of the Workshop on Artificial Intelligence and Logistics (AILog), 19th European Conference on Artificial Intelligence (ECAI 2010), Lisbon, Portugal (2010)
10. Adam, N., Janeja, V., Paliwal, A., Atluri, V., Chun, S., Cooper, J., Schaper, J.: Semantics-Based Threat Structure Mining for Homeland Security. In: Chen, H., Brandt, L., Gregg, V., Traunmüller, R., Dawes, S., Hovy, E., Macintosh, A., Larson, C. (eds.) Digital Government, vol. 17, pp. 307–329. Springer US (2008)
11. Gruber, T.R.: Toward principles for the design of ontologies used for knowledge sharing?. International Journal of Human-Computer Studies 43(5), 907–928 (1995)
12. Engers, T., Boer, A., Breuker, J., Valente, A., Winkels, R.: Ontologies in the Legal Domain. In: Chen, H., Brandt, L., Gregg, V., Traunmüller, R., Dawes, S., Hovy, E., Macintosh, A., Larson, C. (eds.) Digital Government, vol. 17, pp. 233–261. Springer US (2008)
13. Kamel, M., Roudsari, A., Carson, E.: Towards a Semantic Medical Web: HealthCyberMap's Dublin Core Ontology in Protege-2000. Paper Presented at the Fifth International Protege Workshop. University of Newcastle (2001)
14. Horridge, M.: A Practical Guide To Building OWL Ontologies Using Protégé 4 and CO-ODE Tools Edition1. The University of Manchester (2011)
15. Preventis, A.: CHRONOS: A Tool for Handling Temporal Ontologies in Protégé. In: IEEE 24th International Conference on Tools with Artificial Intelligence (ICTAI). IEEE (2012)

16. Yu, Y., Hunter, J., Reiter, E., Sripada, S.: An approach to generating summaries of time series data in the gas turbine domain. Paper Presented at the International Conference on Info-tech and Info-net, Proceedings, ICII - Beijing (2001)

17. Rector, A., Drummond, N., Horridge, M., Rogers, J., Knublauch, H., Stevens, R., Wang, H., Wroe, C.: OWL Pizzas: Practical Experience of Teaching OWL-DL: Common Errors & Common Patterns. In: Motta, E., Shadbolt, N.R., Stutt, A., Gibbins, N. (eds.) EKAW 2004. LNCS (LNAI), vol. 3257, pp. 63–81. Springer, Heidelberg (2004)

18. Talley, W.K.: An economic theory of the port. Research in Transportation Economics 16, 43–65 (2006)

19. Fourgeaud, P.: Measuring port performance. The World Bank (2000)

Cultivation Planning Application to Enhance Decision Making among Sri Lankan Farmers

Tamara Ginige[1,2], Deborah Richards[1], and Michael Hitchens[1]

[1] Department of Computing, Faculty of Science,
Macquarie University, Australia
tamara.ginige@students.mq.edu.au,
{deborah.richards,michael.hitchens}@mq.edu.au
[2] Faculty of Business,
Australian Catholic University, Australia
tamara.ginige@acu.edu.au

Abstract. As part of a larger project to develop a Mobile Based Information System (MBIS) to enhance livelihood activities of Sri Lankan farmers, we investigated how farmers access agricultural knowledge and apply the knowledge to do their tasks. As farmers found it difficult to access and find the required information among published knowledge currently available, crop ontology has been developed to query the factual knowledge in the context specific to a farmer. In the interviews that we conducted, we found that providing factual knowledge alone is not sufficient as farmers also lack the procedural knowledge to make use of the factual knowledge. Therefore, we developed a Cultivation Planning Application that has procedural knowledge embedded into several modules that allow farmers to perform tasks that help them in their decision making process.

Keywords: Cultivation Planning Application, Knowledge Management, Decision Making.

1   Introduction

The availability and usage of mobile phones in developing countries have increased rapidly during recent years. Mobile subscription of the developing countries at the end of 2013 was 87.6% [1]. As a result, in many developing countries, mobile-based solutions have been used to improve efficiency, competitiveness, productivity and income in many areas, including agriculture [2-6]. These solutions have brought many benefits in their own context and also provided the user with a high volume of factual knowledge. In order for a user to benefit from the factual knowledge, the user has to know how to use that knowledge to carry out activities. This depends on the competency level of the user. A user who has a low level of competency may be overwhelmed and not feel empowered to apply this factual knowledge to assist his/her livelihood activities. Therefore, mobile-based solutions should be implemented to empower the users by providing factual knowledge as well as the procedural knowledge that enables them to make

Y.S. Kim et al (Eds.): PKAW 2014, LNCS 8863, pp. 180–194, 2014.
© Springer International Publishing Switzerland 2014

informed decisions. Knowledge acquisition researchers have long recognized that the capture of procedural knowledge is important for decision-making [7] and this problem-solving knowledge could be reused for solving similar types of problems using factual knowledge from different domains [8, 9].

To assist Sri Lankan farmers in their decision-making, an international collaborative research project was formed aiming to develop Mobile Based Information Systems (MBIS) to support the livelihood activities of people in developing countries. The international colloborative research group involves researchers from Sri Lanka, Australia, Italy and United States. The current focus of the project is on improving the livelihood of Sri Lankan farmers via a MBIS. One of the reasons why we chose Sri Lanka for our investigation was its high mobile subscription. Currently 95% of the total population in the country are mobile phone subscribers hence supporting the fact that the mobile phone has become a part of their daily lives [1].

In this paper we present our analysis of the knowledge acquisition needs of Sri Lankan farmers and embed the identified factual and procedural knowledge-based processes in the design of an MBIS, focusing particularly on the Cultivation Planning Application module. The paper is organized as follows. The next section presents background information relevant to the current situations of farmers. We then present the design science research approach that we have used to arrive at the Cultivation Planning Application, after developing an information flow model and insights we gained after field testing a profit calculator. The last section contains the conclusions.

2   Background

In the Sri Lankan economy, agriculture is one of the important sectors and approx-imately 33% of the total labor force is engaged in agriculture [10]. Farming rice, veg-etables or other crops is the most important activity for the majority of people living in rural areas of Sri Lanka. Currently there are not many mobile applications that have been developed to address the local needs of the farmers. Depending on the crop cycle, farmers have different information needs. There are six stages of a crop cycle: *deciding* stage where farmers decide what to grow, *seeding* stage where farmers either purchase or prepare seeds, *preparing and planting* stage, *growing* stage where farmers apply fertilizer, pesticides and water, *harvesting, packing and storing* stage and *selling* stage [11].

Farmers often make wrong decisions due to the lack of access to current and rele-vant information. For example, during the deciding stage, many farmers often choose to grow the same crop within a region, and this could cause a potential over supply of crops [12]. Farmers only come to know, or realise, there is an oversupply when they bring their harvest to the market, and the oversupply reduces market price for the crop, disadvantaging the farmers. Neither the farmers nor government agencies are able to make the necessary adjustments for lack of timely information regarding what farmers plan to cultivate, or have cultivated. The yield could be affected by various other factors such as availability of water and unpredictable weather. Some farmers do not have accurate knowledge on diseases and pests and how to treat them. There are similar issues at all the stages of the crop cycle [13]. Most farmers seek advice from agricultural extension officers but in the case of a new disease or a new pest, agriculture officers also take time to find the solutions. This delay in receiving timely information often destroys their crops. Farmers do not have accurate knowledge of the best fertilizers to use and how much they need to apply. This is directly related to the quality of their harvest, hence the selling price and profit achieved.

The majority of farmers depend on their self-knowledge, friends, family and sometimes a village middle-person for advice and information that may not be accurate, up-to-date or complete [13]. Farmers who have a small quantity of produce find it difficult to locate a good space in a physical market to sell their produce as the farmers who produce large quantities dominate the market space. Often the middle-person takes advantage of these situations, as farmers do not have enough information to carry out successful negotiations. This leaves farmers feeling powerless, helpless and desperate, because they do not see that their livelihood is improving. In the past, some very unhappy farmers have attempted to commit suicide in desperation [14]. Some farmers have stopped farming and have started to look for other jobs.

3   Related Work

We present in this section, related work conducted by members of the collaborative research team that we used to learn about the current knowledge management issues in the Sri Lankan farming domain. In the following sub sections, we consider identification of information needs (3.1); implementation of a profit calculator to support decision making process in farming cycles (section 3.2); implementation of a crop ontology for the farmers (section 3.3) and an enhanced crop ontology to provide both factual and procedural knowledge (section 3.4).

3.1   Identification of Information Needs

To understand the existing issues in the farmer domain, in 2012 data collection was carried out involving 25 farmers using interviews and questionnaires. This study is reported in [15].

The data collection process helped us to understand the current information flow in the farming domain (Fig.1). An agriculture extension officer is appointed to each village. This officer visits the farmers often and provides advice and solutions to the issues they are experiencing during their cultivation. This officer is also responsible for gathering farmer data such as the cultivation extent and different crops that the farmers grow. The officer provides this farmer data to the agriculture department. The reports prepared by the agriculture department are provided to other government organisations, research institutes and published on the web. The decision makers use this static information to predict the supply and demand situation, the food security levels in the country and decide on how much to import. However, such important decisions or the data gathered have never been given back to the farmer. This data collection process also revealed that the farmers do not have access to these websites due to the low computer literacy and unavailability. As a result they are unable to access the data that are available on the websites either.

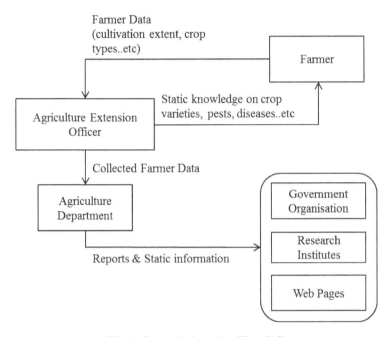

Fig. 1. Current Information Flow [15]

This study of De Silva et al (2012) enabled us to find out the information needs of three major phases of the farming cycle: crop choosing, crop growing and crop selling. It also helped to identify the various stakeholders in each phase. More importantly, the study revealed that there is no proper coordination or information flow among stakeholders. Another important finding was that information is both static and dynamic in nature. For example, there is static information such as fertilizer and pesticide details and dynamic information such as crop selling price and the weather. Therefore to make optimal decisions in this sector, both static and dynamic information are equally important.

Based on the results of the study, a new, farmer-centric information flow model with better interaction and collaboration between all stakeholders of the farming domain was proposed (Fig.2 - [15]). This model lets the farmer input some of the essential information that is required by a different set of stakeholders. As a result, it enables the stakeholders to access both static and dynamic information as needed. This model seeks to increase the information visibility and aid the farmer to take optimal decisions at the right time. The improved understanding provided by the model may lead to better outcomes at the selling stage to improve the financial sustainability of the farmers.

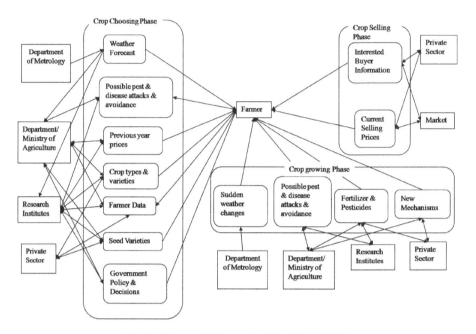

Fig. 2. Proposed Information Flow Model [15]

3.2   Implementation of a Profit Calculator to Support Decision Making Process in Farming Cycles

One of the goals of the farmers is to have financial security. The causal analysis carried out by the Sri Lankan research team has identified that farmers make important decisions at key phases of a crop cycle such as crop choosing, growing and selling with the revenue in mind [15]. Further, in recent ICT application development to support farmers in developing countries, calculators have been included as part of the application. For example, Farmbook is a basic business planning tool and profitability calculator that enables farmer registration to the application, build business plans and evaluate the profitability of specific products in their business plans [16].

For the farmers in developed countries, a profit calculator can be seen as a very basic and simple tool to use. This is not the case for Sri Lankan farmers. The majority of these farmers use basic mobile phones, not smart phones. They haven't seen or used a tool like a profit calculator for decision making before. Therefore we have decided to implement a profit calculator as a tool that is specially developed to calculate farming expenses, expected income and profit/loss. Our aim was to investigate how a tool like this would assist the farmers to make decisions at crucial stages of the crop cycle.

The profit calculator was designed to calculate the expenses of four categories: fertilizer, pesticide, labor and machine hire. To allow the farmer to enter data, each expense category had a drop down menu with four expense items to choose from. For fertilizer and pesticide expense calculations, once the expense item was selected, farmers had to input the quantity required and the unit price. For labor and machine hire expenses, farmers had to enter hiring cost of a machine or a person per day and number of days that service was required. Farmers also needed to enter data to calculate the expected income. Using this data, profit calculator computed the total expenses and displayed the profit/loss.

The profit calculator was field tested with 32 farmers in 2012. The main objective of the 2012 study was to find out how the farmers kept a record of farming expenses, whether a tool like this would help them with their decision making process and further requirements. About 12% of the farmers did not keep any records of their expenses. Another 23% of the farmers did a mental calculation of their expenses and 4% of them used a calculator but did not keep a record. 42% of the farmers did expense calculations manually and recorded them on books. 19% of the farmers used a calculator to compute their calculations and recorded the expenses on books. Farmers who did not carry out an expense analysis properly reported that their expected income and the actual income were different and unexpected expenses as one of the reasons for this difference.

3.3   Implementation of Crop Ontology for the Farmers

Farmers need agricultural information and knowledge to make informed decisions such as seasonal weather, best varieties or cultivars, seeds, fertilizers and pesticides, information on pest and diseases, control methods, harvesting and post harvesting methods, accurate market prices, current supply and demand, and information on farming machinery and practices at various stages of the farming life cycle [13, 17]. The quotes provided above further confirm this. For the Sri Lankan farmers, the majority of farming information is available via government websites, leaflets, agriculture department and mass media. However this information is general in nature, incomplete, heterogeneous and unstructured. It is difficult to search for information when it is presented this way. As the majority of farmers do not use computers, they are unable to access the information available on the websites [18]. This has resulted in a gap between the farmer's current knowledge and required knowledge. Therefore it was important to implement an agricultural knowledge repository that is consistent, well-defined, and provide a representation of the agricultural information and knowledge needed by the farmers within their own context.

3.4   Crop Ontology to Provide Both Factual and Procedural Knowledge

As the first attempt of creating a crop ontology, accurate content knowledge was gathered by interviewing the agriculture experts, reviewing research articles and books [19, 20] and identifying the authoritative online data sources. The information needs were formulated as a set of questions relating to farmer's information needs [21]. *For example: typical questions are: (a) what are the suitable crops to grow? (b) What are the best fertilizers for selected crops?* It was also identified that the way an agriculture expert answers these questions depends on the Sri Lankan farmer context such as *farm environment, types of farmers, farmers' preferences,* and *farming stages.* The next step was to formulate contextualized questions from the user's information needs (Fig. 3 - User Context Model). One example of a contextualized question would be - *What are the suitable fertilizers for the Crops which are grown in specified Location.*

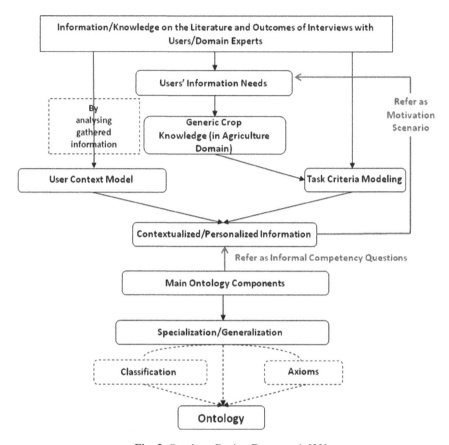

Fig. 3. Ontology Design Framework [22]

4   Approach

As our aim is to design an MBIS to support knowledge management, we have adopted a Design Science Research (DSR) approach [23]. DSR consists of three cycles of activities: relevance cycle, rigor cycle and design cycle. The relevance cycle initiates the DSR process. It identifies the design requirements of the research question, the environment in which the artefact (e.g. an MBIS) can be introduced, how the artefact is to be used in the environment, how it is to be field tested and what metrics are used to demonstrate the successful use of the artefact in that environment. The Rigor Cycle ensures that the design is based on scientific theories and methods to produce a new knowledge base of artefacts that will be useful to the environment. The new knowledge base may contain extensions to the original theories and methods, new artefacts and all experience gained from performing the iterative design cycles and field testing the artefact in the application environment [23, 24].

Below we outline the studies undertaken in the DSR process to implement Cultivation Planning Application within MBIS.

4.1   Relevance Cycle - Understanding the New User Requirements to Support the Decision-Making Process in Farming Cycle

In order to gather user requirements for our future designs, we asked farmers about their additional requirements they would like to have in a tool like a profit calculator. They mentioned that having a better understanding of their expenses in the various stages of the crop cycle and an awareness of different suppliers may help them to better manage their expenses. On average, each farmer has listed at least four expense items that have an effect on their total expenses. In addition they proposed more functional requirements for the future design of the profit calculator: detailed expenses for each stage of the crop cycle and whole cycle, correct units of fertilizer and pesticide as they come in powder, liquid and granular form, history of expenses for future comparison and analysis, profit as a % of expenses, space for farmers to enter new costs and information, and a facility to obtain loans via banks during financial hardships.

4.2   Relevance Cycle - Understanding the Need to Provide Factual and Procedural Knowledge

During the field testing of the profit calculator, it was evident that the majority of farmers did not know how to apply their knowledge to do a task. Around 81% of the farmers agreed that it was beneficial to carry out some analysis on their expenses during the crop cycle and the guidance provided by the tool was helpful.

4.3   Rigor Cycle – Knowledge Gained from Previous Studies

The knowledge that we have gained from the work described in section 3 was helpful for us to understand how to design applications that can provide factual knowledge and procedural knowledge. Studying the current information flow was helpful to understand the information needs of a crop cycle, nature of information, stakeholders and gaps in information flow and sharing. That enabled us to implement a better information flow model (Fig. 2 - [15]. It was evident that the farmers do not have proper access to information to make informed decisions. Therefore to bridge the gap between the farmer's current knowledge and required knowledge, it was important to implement an agricultural knowledge repository that can provide the agricultural information and knowledge needed by the farmers within their own context [21]. Field testing of the profit calculator gave us an understanding of how farmers make decisions, keep their records and what tools they use. This further identified the gap they have in their factual knwledge and procedual knowlegde [18]. In this cycle we also drew on a number of theories including empowerment theory [25] and self-efficacy [26] in our interpretation of the knowledge gained from previous studies, which led us to the next phase, the design of an MBIS that would empower the farmers to improve their livelihood.

4.4   Design Cycle – Preliminary Design of Cultivation Planning Application (CPA)

The knowledge that we have gained in the rigor cycle has enabled us to further improve the design of the profit calculator. In addition to identifying new requirements, our systematic analysis sought to discover much deeper needs of farmers and we further reviewed and revised our current design of the profit calculator. It evolved into a comprehensive "Cultivation Planning Application" (CPA) with a built in expense calculator [18]. The objective of the new design was to create an application that can be used to plan and evaluate the finances when they are in the process of deciding which crop to grow. Cultivation Planning Application has several tools that assist them to make decisions and take necessary actions [18].

4.5   Relevance Cycle – Further Understanding on the Need to Provide Factual and Procedural Knowledge via CPA

Prior to fully implementing our CPA, we needed to further understand the issues the farmers were facing, how they found solutions to their problems and how they make decisions in detail. In 2013, we interviewed 50 farmers at three different locations in Sri Lanka. It was clear from the interviews that knowledge management was an issue for the farmers. One farmer said:

"I would like have a better understanding of my expenses. Every season, things are becoming very expensive, such as fertilizer, pesticide, chemicals etc. I run into debts sometimes. I would like to know how to calculate these expenses properly" (a male farmer from Dambulla, Age: 31 - 40, highest level of education: secondary - year 10, number of mobiles owned: 2)

The above statement reveals the need for factual knowledge concerning costs and procedural knowledge on how to manage their expenses. As further examples, the two quotes below reveal the lack of knowledge and access to it.

"I am a new farmer. My problem is that I do not have much knowledge. I can get the information from the agriculture officers but if I can learn how to grow something new by myself, that would be good. I have access to the Internet and I like to read and learn new ideas" (a male farmer from Pollonnaruwa, Age: 31-40, highest level of education: secondary -year 10, Diploma, number of mobiles owned: 1)

"We are not knowledgeable about the crop diseases. We don't know what chemical to use. We need to depend on the shops that sell them.   Most of the time we have to try more than one, resulting many trips to the shop. We have no choice. This is very expensive for us and in the end our crop gets damaged as we were late to provide a solution" (a female farmer from Dambulla, Age: 41-50, highest level of education: secondary - year 12, no of mobiles owned: 1)

The next quote demonstrates the uncertainty faced by farmers and the need to adapt, revise and update their knowledge in quick response to their environment.

"Last season our crops contracted a new disease. We could not recognize it and even the agriculture officers did not know what that was. By the time we found a solution, it was too late. Our whole crop got damaged. We need to identify them quickly and provide a solution quickly too" (a male farmer from Dambulla, Age: 41-50, highest level of education: secondary - year 10), number of mobiles owned: 1)

The next two quotes demonstrate the need and desire to share and reuse knowledge with others.

"We don't know what others are growing. Most of the time, we all grow the same thing because of the good selling price we received for a crop in the previous season. Then the market becomes saturated with that crop and the selling price goes down. I would like to know what others are growing and receive advice on what else I can grow and how I can grow it" (a male farmer from Dambulla, Age: >51, highest level of education: secondary - year 12, number of mobiles owned: 1)

"I make my own organic fertilizer and would like to sell it to our own community of farmers. I can't compete with big suppliers. It would be good for us to have an avenue via technology to advertise and sell our own products" (a male farmer from Pollonnaruwa, Age: 31 - 40, highest level of education: secondary (year 10, Diploma), number of mobiles owned: 2)

From the results of these interviews, it was evident that some farmers did not know about factual knowledge of some areas of farming well and some did not know how to apply that knowledge to carry out activities that lead to decision making. These observations have further justified our initial claim that mobile-based solutions should be implemented to empower the users by providing factual knowledge as well as the procedural knowledge that enable them to make informed decisions to improve their livelihood activities.

4.6 Design Cycle - Enhanced Crop Ontology to Provide Both Factual and Procedural Knowledge

From the awareness gained after the field trial of the profit calculator and the interviews in 2013, it was evident that both factual and procedural knowledge is very important to the farmers. For example; with regards to a question like *what are the best fertilizers for selected crops,* the names of the fertilizers can be provided. In order to assist the correct application of fertilizer, additional information such as fertilizer quantity and application method is needed. A fertilizer quantity depends on the many other factors such as the fertilizer types (e.g. Chemical, Organic, or Biological fertilizers) and its specific sources (e.g. Nitrogen, Phosphorus, Potassium, etc.) and their ratio, location, water source, soil PH range, time of application, and application method. The amount of fertilizer to apply depends on this additional information. In order to model this information we created a notion of a fertilizer event in the Ontology and a Task Criteria Model. Task Criteria Model and User Context Model (Fig. 3) generate contexualised information that are referred to as the Competency Questions (CQs). These CQs are used to identify the concepts, relationships and axioms to develop the ontology. As a result, the original Crop Ontology was significantly expanded to provide the additional crop information as well as associated fertilizer and pesticide information in the context of farm environment [22].

5   Re-designed Mobile Based Information System (MBIS)

As explained in section 4, we performed several iterations of the Design Science Research cycle. Rigor cycle (section 4.3) has helped us to understand the information needs of a crop cycle, nature of information, stakeholders and gaps in information flow and sharing. The result of this cycle was to understand the need of an agricultural knowledge repository that can provide the agricultural information and knowledge needed by the farmers within their own context. Three relevance cycles (sections 4.1, 4.2 and 4.5) have helped us to understand how farmers can benefit from a tool like a profit calculator to calculate their expenses. This further revealed that a stand-alone profit calculator without any integration to the various parts of the farming process is not sufficient for farmers to plan and evaluate the finances when they are in the process of deciding which crop to grow. We have used the knowledge gained from the rigor and relevance cycles in the two design cycles (sections 4.4 and 4.6) to re-design the MBIS. The profit calculator became a part of an overall business planning process (section 4.3). The design of agricultural data repository – crop ontology - was enhanced to provide both factual and procedural knowledge (section 4.6).

The following section explains in detail how we have re-designed the MBIS with three major areas where activities and decision making take place: Crop Selection (section 5.1), Cultivation Planning Application (section 5.2) and My Offerings (section 5.3) (Fig. 4). Also depicted in Fig. 4 is the need for the farmer to register with the system using the mobile phone when they use the system for the first time. The geo coordinates of the mobile phone identify the location of the farm.

5.1   Crop Selection

The first activity for the farmer after the registration process is to decide on a crop to grow. If the farmer does not know which one, the farmer can use Crop Selection process to look at the crops that are suitable for the area where the farm is. The crop ontology provides the farmer with a list of crops that are suitable for the area and the farmer can decide on a short list of crops to grow. Farmers enter the extent of their crop cultivation to the production database. The aggregation of similar information from a larger cross section of farmers provides them an indication of the future yield of a particular crop in an area, allowing them to make a decision on which crop they should be growing.

5.2   Cultivation Planning Application

Our original profit calculator evolved into a comprehensive "Cultivation Planning Application" with a built-in expense calculator. Rather than the farmers having to enter information, the farmer now can query the crop ontology to receive the required information. This allows farmers to plan and evaluate their finances when they are in the process of deciding which crop to grow. Cultivation Planning Application has several tools that assist them to make decisions and take necessary actions.

- *Expense calculator* of the application helps the farmer to calculate the expense of cultivating a crop for each stage of the farming cycle. The farming cycle has several stages and each stage has a related set of expenses. Crop ontology provides the farmer the details of these expenses such as fertilizer, pesticide, etc. for each stage. It calculates the expense for each stage and also for the whole cycle. Farmers can either use the recommended quantities that the system advises or enter the quantities that they have used in the past to understand the changes in the expenses.
- *Supplier Database* has the details of the suppliers who provide seeds, fertilizer, pesticide, chemicals, packaging, machines, transport and any other expense details. When a farmer selects a certain expense item, the supplier database provides the farmer with a list of suppliers who sells that item with the details such as sale price and contact details.
- *Farmer Expense History Database* will be used to store the past expenses that each farmer has created using Expense Calculator for different products and stages. A farmer can study and compare the history of expenses when making decisions for the current season.

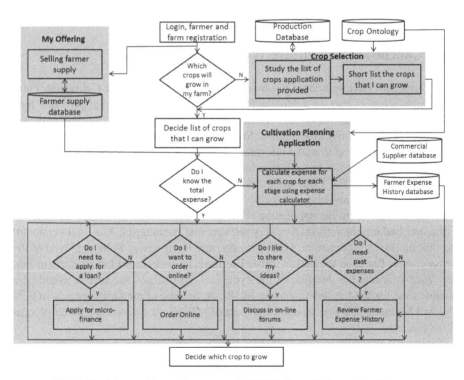

Fig. 4. Decision making and processes in Mobile Based Information System

- *Online ordering* tool will help the farmers to learn the business transactions and banking activities involved in online ordering. This will improve farmers' decision making skills and business skills.
- *Applying for Micro Finance* will help farmers to apply for a loan through state/private owned bank to receive financial support immediately.
- *Discussion Forums* will help farmers to discuss their issues with the other farmers and exchange ideas, become aware of new ideas and alternative solutions. These discussions will provide farmers with confidence to make informed decisions.

5.3   My Offerings

My Offerings is an implementation of a requirement that came from farmers themselves. Other than crops, farmers often produce seeds and/or organic fertilizer that they would like to sell. Rather than competing with larger commercial suppliers, they can benefit if they can sell it directly to their farming community. When farmers are not farming in some seasons, their labor is available for other farmers to use and they have machines that others can hire. My Offering is a place where they can advertise their products and services. Farmers can enter their product and service details into the Farmer Supply database to share their knowledge with others. This information will be available for all farmers to view and make decisions on products and services that they need.

6   Conclusion and Future Work

In this paper we have presented our investigation into developing a Cultivation Planning Application as part of a Mobile Based Information System that provides both factual and procedural knowledge in an integrated manner. Our investigation has revealed that the majority of farmers in Sri Lanka do not have proper access to current agricultural information to make informed decisions at crucial stages of their farming cycles. Providing just the factual knowledge does not guarantee that this information is applied correctly. The Cultivation Planning Application has many tools with embedded procedural knowledge to guide the farmer to apply the factual knowledge correctly. Every tool in the application is designed to provide customized information to the user making the information very relevant and meaningful. The final version of the Mobile Based Information System is currently being tested to be deployed to the farmers in Sri Lanka at the end of 2014. The farming cycle in Sri Lanka starts in January each year and the duration of the cycle is 4-5 months. Therefore it would be a suitable time for the farmers to use the MBIS. At the end of the farming cycle, a field trial will be conducted to evaluate the impact of MBIS in the decision making process of the farmers.

References

1. ITU. ICT Facts and Figures 2014 (2014), `http://www.itu.int/en/ITU-D/Statistics/Pages/stat/default.aspx`
2. mFarms. mFarms (2013), http://mfarm.co.ke/ (cited July 14, 2013)
3. Radhakrishna, R.: e-Choupal transforms Indian agriculture. Appropriate Technology (2011)
4. Farmforce. Foundation for Sustainable Agriculture (2013), `http://www.syngentafoundation.org/` (cited July 17, 2013)
5. Vaswani, K.: Indonesian farmers reaping social media rewards. BBC News: The Technology of Business 2012 (July 8, 2012)
6. UNICEF. Communication for development: Strengthening the effectiveness of the United Nations (2011), `http://www.unicef.org/cbsc/files/Inter-agency_C4D_Book_2011.pdf`
7. Clancey, W.J.: Guidon, DTIC Document (1984)
8. Chandrasekaran, B., Johnson, T.R.: Generic tasks and task structures: History, critique and new directions. In: Second Generation Expert Systems, pp. 232–272. Springer (1993)
9. Studer, R., Benjamins, V.R., Fensel, D.: Knowledge engineering: Principles and methods. Data & Knowledge Engineering 25(1), 161–197 (1998)
10. Agriculture. Department of Agriculture Govenment of Sri Lanka (2011), `http://www.agridept.gov.lk/` (November 28, 2011)
11. De Silva, H., Ratnadiwakara, D.: ICT Policy for Agriculture Based on a Transaction Cost Approach: Some Lessons from Sri Lanka. International Journal of ICT Research and Development in Africa (IJICTRDA) 1(1), 14 (2010)
12. Hettiarachchi, S.: Leeks Cultivators Desperate as Price Drops to Record Low. Sunday Times, Sri Lanka (2011)
13. Lokanathan, S., Kapugama, N.: Smallholders and Micro-enterprises in Agriculture. In: Knowledge-based Economies. LIRNEasia, Colombo (2012)
14. Senaratne, G.G.: More rural suicides in Sri Lanka (2005), `http://www.wsws.org/articles/2005/nov2005/suic-n21.shtml` (cited July 9, 2012)
15. De Silva, L.N.C., et al.: Towards using ICT to Enhance Flow of Information to aid Farmer Sustainability in Sri Lanka. In: 23rd Australasian Conference on Information Systems, Geelong, Victoria, Australia, p. 10 (2012)
16. Ferris, S.: Information and Communication Technologies for Development. In: CRS 2011 ICT4D, Lusaka, Zambia, p. 34 (2011)
17. De Silva, L.N.C., Goonetillake, J.S., Wikramanayake, G.N., Ginige, A.: Farmer Response towards the Initial Agriculture Information Dissemination Mobile Prototype. In: Murgante, B., Misra, S., Carlini, M., Torre, C.M., Nguyen, H.-Q., Taniar, D., Apduhan, B.O., Gervasi, O. (eds.) ICCSA 2013, Part I. LNCS, vol. 7971, pp. 264–278. Springer, Heidelberg (2013)
18. Ginige, T., Richards, D.: Design and Evaluation of a Mobile-based Cultivation Planning Application for empowering Sri Lankan Farmers. In: Lamp, J. (ed.) 24th Australasian Conference on Information Systems, Melbourne, Australia (2013)
19. Narula, S.A., Nainwal, N.: ICTs and Agricultural Supply Chains - Opportunities and Strategies for Successful Implementation Information Technology in Developing Countries. IFIP. Indian Institute of Management, Ahmedabad (2010)
20. Decoteau, D.R.: Vegetable Crops. Prentice-Hall, Upper Saddle River (2000)

21. Walisadeera, A.I., Wikramanayake, G.N., Ginige, A.: An Ontological Approach to Meet Information Needs of Farmers in Sri Lanka. In: Murgante, B., Misra, S., Carlini, M., Torre, C.M., Nguyen, H.-Q., Taniar, D., Apduhan, B.O., Gervasi, O. (eds.) ICCSA 2013, Part I. LNCS, vol. 7971, pp. 228–240. Springer, Heidelberg (2013)
22. Walisadeera, A.I., Ginige, A., Wikramanayake, G.N.: Conceptualizing Crop Life Cycle Events to Create a User Centered Ontology for Farmers. In: Murgante, B., et al. (eds.) ICCSA 2014, Part V. LNCS, vol. 8583, pp. 791–806. Springer, Heidelberg (2014)
23. Hevner, A., Chatterjee, S.: Design Research in Information Systems - Theory and Practice, pp. 9–22. Springer, New York (2010)
24. March, S.T., Smith, G.F.: Design and natural science research on information technology. Decision Support Systems 15, 251–266 (1995)
25. Zimmerman, M.A.: Citizen participation, perceived control and psycological empowerment. American Journal of Community Psychology 16(5), 725–750 (1988)
26. Bandura, A.: Self-efficacy: Toward a Unifying Theory of Behavioral Change. Psychological Review 84(2), 191–215 (1997)

Extracting Conceptual Relations from Children's Stories

Briane Paul Samson and Ethel Ong

Center for Language Technologies, De La Salle University, Manila, Philippines
briane.samson@dlsu.edu.ph, ethel.ong@delasalle.ph

Abstract. Automatic story generation systems require a collection of common-sense knowledge to generate stories that contain logical and coherent sequences of events appropriate for their intended audience. But manually building and populating a semantic ontology that contains relevant assertions is a tedious task. Crowdsourcing can be used as an approach to quickly amass a large collection of commonsense concepts but requires validation of the quality of the knowledge that has been contributed by the public. Another approach is through relation extraction. This paper discusses the use of GATE and custom extraction rules to automatically extract binary conceptual relations from children's stories. Evaluation results show that the extractor achieved a very low overall accuracy of only 36% based on precision, recall and F-measure. The use of incomplete and generalized extraction patterns, insufficient text indicators, accuracy of existing tools, and inability to infer and detect implied relations were the major causes of the low accuracy scores.

Keywords: Natural Language Processing, Text Analysis, Relation Extraction, Commonsense Knowledge.

1   Introduction

People use storytelling as a natural and familiar means of conveying information and experience to each other. During this interchange, people understand each other because we rely on a large body of shared commonsense knowledge. But computers do not share this knowledge, causing a barrier in human-computer interaction in applications requiring computers to understand and generate coherent text. To support this task, computers must be provided with a usable knowledge about the basic relationships between concepts that we find everyday in our world.

Creative text generation systems such as T-PEG [1] have utilized a semantic network representation of commonsense concepts to identify the relationships of words found in human puns. The extracted word relationships are then used as templates to enable computer systems to generate punning riddles, given the same repository of commonsense knowledge. This repository is ConceptNet [2].

Story generation systems, specifically Picture Books [3, 4], on the other hand, generate children's stories of the fable form for children age 4-8 years old by using a semantic ontology of commonsense concepts whose design was patterned after ConceptNet. The manually built knowledge repositories of the story generators contain

Y.S. Kim et al (Eds.): PKAW 2014, LNCS 8863, pp. 195–208, 2014.

binary conceptual relations about objects, activities and their relationships in a child's daily life. Later on, Yu and Ong [5] explored using a two-layer ontology with ConceptNet [6] as one of the major resource utilized to provide the upper story world knowledge about commonsense concepts.

Building knowledge repositories for story generation systems required a lot of manual effort. One way to address this was through the use of crowdsourcing techniques to acquire knowledge from the community, specifically from children [7] in order to learn concepts that are relevant for story generation. Another approach is through relation extraction.

Research works in relation extraction have achieved significant progress in extracting facts and concepts in the domains of newspapers [8], biographies [9], and legal documents [10]. For domain-independent data, systems like KnowItAll [11] extracted entities using generic noun phrase patterns. TextRunner [12], on the other hand, do not rely on predefined relation types but discovers relation triples automatically. These triples represent binary relations (arg1, relation, arg2) that were identified and extracted from a sentence.

However, limited work has been done on stories. Stories contain not only facts and conceptual entities, but also sequences of actions that characters perform or experience at various points in the story world. These descriptions on story events may span multiple sentences. Knowledge about how these events are ordered and the constraints under which they can occur must also be extracted.

This paper presents an approach to extracting binary conceptual relations from children's stories by defining a set of extraction rules that were then fed to GATE[1]. We refer to such relations as assertions representing storytelling knowledge and model them as an ontology of commonsense concepts. Section 2 identifies the types of storytelling knowledge needed by story generation systems with particular emphasis on domain-specific commonsense concepts. This is followed by a description of the process in defining and extracting conceptual relations on commonsense concepts from children's stories in Section 3. An analysis of the quality of the extracted assertions is then presented in Section 4. The paper ends with a discussion of issues and recommendations for future work.

2   Storytelling Knowledge

The knowledge needed by story generators can be classified into two broad categories, namely the operational knowledge about narrative structures and story plots to drive the flow of the story; and the domain knowledge that describes the story characters, the world, and the causal chain of actions and events. In this paper, the commonsense storytelling knowledge we referred to, specifically concepts and events, are classified under the domain knowledge. Concepts include concrete objects and their descriptions. Events include actions that story characters explicitly perform in the story world, the events that occur as a result of these actions, and events that are from

---

[1] GATE: General Architecture for Text Engineering, University of Sheffield.
https://gate.ac.uk

naturally occurring phenomenon. Assertions in the form of binary semantic relations relate two concepts or events.

This section gives a brief overview of the different categories of semantic relations that are used to represent assertions in the commonsense knowledge repository of Picture Books. This serves as the basis for the types of assertions that are targeted by our relation extractor. A more detailed discussion of the knowledge representation of Picture Books and how this was utilized for story planning are beyond the scope of this paper and can be found elsewhere [3, 4].

2.1 Assertions Describing Concepts

A story world is comprised of various objects that interact with one another to achieve some form of a narrative plot. These objects, which include characters and the things that they manipulate, are described as part of the sequence of events that comprise the story flow. Character and object descriptions are two of the major factors that can motivate characters to exhibit certain behaviors, thus prompting them to perform actions in the story.

Character descriptions include roles, physical attributes, physical and mental states, capabilities to execute some actions, and emotions that a character may experience before or after the occurrence of event. Sample assertions for each of these are shown in Table 1.

Table 1. Semantic relations to describe story characters used in Picture Books [3, 4]

Category	Concept1
Concepts describing Character States	IsA(fighting, problem) IsA(itchy, discomfort) IsA(grounded, punishment)
Concepts describing Character Emotions	IsA (happy, emotion) IsA (scared, emotion) Feels(character, scared) Feels(character, sleepy)
Character Reaction to Events	EffectOf (break object, scared) EffectOf (meet new friends, smile)
Character States after an Event	EventsForGoalState(play games, happy)
Character Capabilities	CapableOf(character, hide)
Roles and Responsibilities	HasRole(character, king) ResponsibleFor(king, rule country)

The *IsA*, *EffectOf*, *EventsForGoalState* and *CapableOf* relations are adapted from ConceptNet. The *HasRole* and *RoleResponsibleFor* relations are used to model assertions that describe roles that characters may play in stories as well as the tasks associated with that role. These are currently not included in Picture Books. The rest of the relations in Table 1 were defined by Picture Books based on the requirements of the story planning task.

Objects are described based on their classification, properties and compositions, possible locations and co-located objects, and the actions that they can be used as instruments. Sample assertions for each of these are shown in Table 2. The *IsA*, *Property*, *PartOf*, *UsedFor* and *CapableOf* relations are adapted from ConceptNet. Concepts that model locations can also be associated with other concepts that describe them or their usage, as shown in Table 2.

Table 2. Semantic relations to describe objects used in Picture Books

Category	Concept1
Classification	IsA(doll, toy)
	IsA(ball, toy)
	IsA(marshmallow, food)
Properties and Compositions	HasProperty(lamp, fragile)
	HasProperty(marshmallow, fluffy)
	PartOf(wheel, truck)
	MadeOf(cake, sugar)
Location	LocationOf(toys, toy store)
	LocationOf(swing, park)
	OftenNear(swing, slide)
	HasProperty(camp, far)
	UsedFor(camp, camping)
	UsedFor(park, picnic)
Usage	UsedFor(toy, play)
	UsedFor(food, eat)
	UsedFor(water jug, drink)
Events on Objects	CapableOf(lamp, break)
	CanBe(toys, scattered)

2.2 Assertions Describing Events

Stories are comprised of sequences of events, which include explicit or voluntary events in the form of intentional character actions, and implicit or involuntary events that arise due to the execution of these actions or due to natural causes. Relations between events can be signified in two ways: temporal succession and causality. Temporal succession uses time to show the sequential relationship between two events. For instance, *Event A* happens before *Event B*. On the other hand, causality means *Event B* happened as a result of the occurrence or execution of *Event A*.

ConceptNet provides a number of relations to describe events, namely *EffectOf*, *FirstSubEventOf*, *EventForGoalEvent* and *EventForGoalState*. Table 3 shows sample assertions in Picture Books using these relations as well as additional relations that were defined specifically for story planning. The same set of relations is used to define both events and concepts. The story planner uses some other relations, e.g., *CapableOf* and *CanBe*, to signify that an event concept is an action that a character can perform. In Picture Books 2 [4], the *IsTransition* relation has been defined to model event assertions that describe the appearance, disappearance or movement of an object or character between two scenes in a story. The *negate* relation is used to model complementary events, usually a positive and a negative one.

Table 3. Semantic relations to describe events and actions

Category	Concept1
Causality of Events	EffectOf(hearing sound, scared)
	EffectOf(eating, sleepy)
	EffectOfIsState(become dirty, feel itchy)
Events to Achieve Goals	EventForGoalEvent(go to store, buy food)
	EventForGoalState(clean up, be neat)
Event Components	HasSubevent(sleep, brush teeth)
	HasSubevent(sleep, pray)
	HasSubevent(sleep, read story book)
Usage	UsedFor(toy, play)
	UsedFor(food, eat)
	UsedFor(water jug, drink)
Events on Objects	EventRequiresObject(play, toy)
	CapableOf(lamp, break)
	CanBe(toys, scattered)
Transition	IsTransition(bring, appearance)
	IsTransition(eat, disappearance)
	IsTransition(walk, movement)
Complements	Negate(sleep early, sleep late)
	Negate(eat healthy food, eat junk food)

Since stories are sequences of events, their analysis may necessitate the creation of new relations to represent sequences of events, temporal relations between events, as well as the constraints under which certain events may take place. For example, during testing, evaluators noticed that one of the generated stories of Picture Books occurred at an inappropriate time; specifically, the first segment of the story that introduces the day, the place, and the main character, contained the following text:

> *The evening was warm. Ellen the elephant was at the school. She went with Mommy Edna to the school.*

Although the temporal properties of events can be easily modeled in the Suggested Upper Merged Ontology as shown in the works of Cua et al for SUMO Stories [13], Picture Books' knowledge base currently does not provide relations about when certain events can take place. Furthermore, some granularities may be needed to model various aspects of time, namely season (planting can only occur during spring, snow can only fall during winter), month (Christmas in December, Valentine's in February), or even weeks, days, hours, and minutes. Assertions such as *Happens(Christmas, December)* and *Happens(going to school, morning)* can be defined by adopting the predicates used by Mueller [14] to model event occurrences.

3   Design and Implementation

The extraction process started with the gathering and preprocessing of the input corpus; followed by the creation of extraction templates; and lastly, the extraction of target relations using the open-source tool, GATE.

3.1   Data Gathering and Preprocessing

The input corpus for this research is comprised of 30 children's stories and include titles from the following: five (5) Topsy and Tim stories published by Ladybird Books and written by Jean Adamson and Gareth Adamson about the adventures of twins, and sixteen (16) stories from the Little Life Lessons: A Treasury of Values collection published by Publications International for children age 4-7 year olds; and seven (7) stories from the Jump Start series published by Scholastic, and two (2) Winnie the Pooh stories published by Disney Press for children age 8-10 year olds.

Each story in the corpus was modified to clean the data of any inconsistencies. Dialogues, for instance, show inconsistencies because of different writing styles, its conversational nature, use of informal language and colloquial words, and have incomplete thoughts. Thus, most dialogues were transformed into declarative sentences. The objective of these modifications was to convert the dialogues into complete and coherent sentences in order to yield proper extractions. It is important to note that even though the story has changed in terms of writing, the theme was retained. The intention was to make the actions and facts more apparent to the extraction tool.

Aside from dialogues, other modifications include: changing interjections into the emotions conveyed; expanding of contractions; removing of the punctuation marks (period) that do not denote the end of a sentence; and removing of words made-up by story characters such as *splendiferous* from the Winnie the Pooh titles.

3.2   Target Relations and Extraction Templates

For the purpose of this research, sixteen (16) relations were identified to be extracted; they were deemed relevant and helpful to the development of commonsense knowledge for the children's story domain. Table 4 shows the sixteen conceptual relations targeted in this research.

Extraction templates were defined for each of the target relations; they are the different ways a certain relation is manifested in a sentence or a span of text. Some of the templates were adopted from the ones used by ConceptNet to crowd-source data; the others were manually derived, especially for the *EventForGoalEvent*, *EventForGoalState*, *EffectOf*, *EffectOfIsState*, and *Happens* relations.

Table 4. Target relations

Relation	Description
IsA	Specifies what kind an entity is.
PropertyOf	Specifies an adjective to describe an entity.
PartOf	Specifies the *parthood* of an entity in another entity.
MadeOf	Specifies a component of an entity.
CapableOf	Specifies what an entity can do.
OftenNear	Specifies an entity near another entity in most instances.
LocationOf	Specifies the location of an entity.
UsedFor	Specifies the use of an object in an activity.
EventForGoalEvent	Specifies an event that causes the fulfillment of a goal event.
EventForGoalState	Specifies an event that causes the fulfillment of a goal state.
EffectOf	Represents a cause-effect between two events
EffectOfIsState	Represents a cause-effect between an event and an end state.
Happens	Specifies the time an event/state happens.
HasRole	Specifies the role of a person in the story.
RoleResponsibleFor	Specifies an action done by a role.
Owns	Specifies the ownership of an object.

Table 5 shows the different elements present in an extraction template; all these are tagged by the open-source tool, GATE. The first nine elements (9) in Table 5 can be tagged by default; the others were custom tags created for this research. The *<Indica-*

tor> element tag denotes the presence of a relational structure in a sentence, which is usually identified by the use of a transition word. Transition words are used mainly to aid in identifying explicit relations. The indicators were collated from ConceptNet, Picture Books 2 [4], and sentences from the corpora.

Table 5. Template elements

Default Tags	Custom Tags
<NP>, <NP:JobTitle>, <Noun:Possessive>, <AP>, <Pronoun:Possessive>, <Verb>, <VP>, <VP:Gerund>, <PP:Temporal>	<Event>, <GoalEvent>, <GoalState>, <Cause>, <Effect>, <EffectState>, <Indicator>

Shown in Table 6 are the templates used for the *PartOf* relation which can be extracted within a single sentence.

Table 6. Extraction templates of *PartOf* relation

Templates
<NP> <PartOfIndicator> <NP>
<Noun:Possessive> ... <NP>
<Pronoun:Possessive> ... <NP>

Here is a sample sentence to show the existence of the first template:

A window is a part of a house.
In the example, "A window" is the noun phrase or <NP>, "part of" is the <PartOfIndicator>, and "a house" is the second <NP>. When the extraction tool recognizes these three elements in this order, the *PartOf* relation will be extracted.

Table 5 shows the templates used for the *EventForGoalEvent* relation which can be manifested within a span of 2 sentences. Here are example sentences for this relation:

Kisha wants to buy a car. She saved all her lunch money.
The verb phrase "buy a car" is the <GoalEvent> in the first sentence, while "saved all her lunch money" is the <Event> in the second sentence. These occurrences indicate the existence of an *EventForGoalEvent* across the 2 sentences.

Table 7. Extraction templates of *EventForGoalEvent* relation

Templates
<GoalEvent> ... <Event>
<Event> <MotivationIndicator> <GoalEvent>

3.3   Extraction Tool

The architecture of the system was implemented using the open-source tool GATE. Figure 1 shows the GATE Application Pipeline designed for this research.

Each children's story in the corpora is processed by creating a GATE Document. These are then added to a GATE Corpus. First, the GATE application resets the input of any previous annotations. This applies only if the input has already been annotated before passing through GATE. After cleaning, the input is parsed into tokens. The input was then split into sentences and each token was annotated with their respective part-of-speech tags.

After that, named-entities, like common story character names and locations, were annotated. In resolving unique and story-specific named-entities like *Pooh* and *Tree Fort Island*, new gazetteer resources were used and new characters, locations and roles are added. New gazetteers were also created for indicators, world states and emotions, among others.

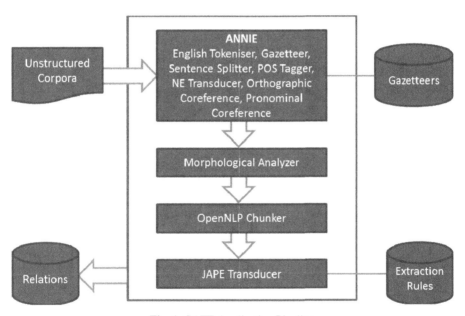

Fig. 1. GATE Application Pipeline

Then, pronouns are matched with the named-entities they are referring to in the text. Then, each token are processed to identify their lemmas, affixes and chunks. Lastly, the input text is run through a transducer to identify all the target relations and create the appropriate annotations for each. The transducer uses the defined templates and allows multiple relation types to be extracted from a single sentence.

4   Extraction Results and Analysis

The extracted relations were evaluated on their accuracy and completeness, and usability in the Picture Books system to generate stories. In evaluating the accuracy and completeness of the relations that were extracted, a gold standard was created where each story was manually tagged with the appropriate relations. Subsequently, precision, recall and F-measure values were computed and analyzed. Table 8 shows the results after comparing the automatically extracted relations from both the raw and modified versions of the stories to the gold standard.

Table 8. Evaluation results based on gold standard

Stories	Gold Standard	Extraction	False Positive	False Negative	Correctly Extracted	P	R	F
Overall (RAW)	663	662	421	422	241	0.36	0.36	0.36
Overall (MODIFIED)	663	615	403	451	212	0.34	0.32	0.33
Everybody Cries (RAW)	456	392	255	319	137	0.35	0.30	0.32
Everybody Cries (MODIFIED)	456	410	254	300	156	0.38	0.34	0.36
Start School (RAW)	139	150	103	92	47	0.31	0.34	0.33
Start School (MODIFIED)	139	173	119	85	54	0.31	0.39	0.35
Hopsalot's Garden (RAW)	68	73	45	40	28	0.38	0.41	0.40
Hopsalot's Garden (MODIFIED)	68	79	48	37	31	0.39	0.46	0.42

Overall, the extraction tool had a precision of 0.34; recall of 0.32; and an F-measure of 0.33. Furthermore, it was able to get relatively high accuracy scores (F-measure) for the *PropertyOf*, *PartOf*, *CapableOf* and *Owns* relations; each having scores of 0.40, 0.42, 0.47, and 0.62, respectively. The high accuracy of the aforementioned extracted relations can be attributed to the simplicity of their most common pattern in a sentence. For example, majority of the stories in the corpus contain the following patterns used to extract the *Owns* assertion:

<Noun:Possessive> ... *<Noun>*
<Pronoun:Possessive> ... *<Noun>*

The *CapableOf* relation looks for a noun and an immediate verb in a sentence, thus, easily extracting assertions from sentences such as the following:

> *Pierre threw a ball to Puppy.*   ==>   *CapableOf(Pierre, throw)*

On the other hand, approximately 64% of the extracted relations were false positives, especially for the *IsA, EffectOf, UsedFor, Happens,* and *HasRole* relations. These are extracted relations not found in the gold standard. Such results suggest that the defined templates were too generalized and all-encompassing. Consider the following pattern for extracting *IsA* relations:

> *<Noun or Gerund> <,>[0,1] <Determiner> + ... <Noun>*

This yielded the assertion *IsA(having, day)* from the following story text:

> *The best thing about having the worst day ever is that tomorrow will be a lot better.*

Some inaccuracies of the part-of-speech tagger and issues with the gazetteer contributed to the extraction of false positives as well. Consider the sentence below:

> *Bear's first game is tomorrow.*

The relation *IsA(game, tomorrow)* was extracted because both the words *game* and *tomorrow* were tagged as noun, which satisfies the template:

> *<Noun> is <Noun>*

In the case of the *HasRole* relation, the assertion *HasRole(he, driver)* was extracted from the following sentence without resolving the pronoun *he*.

> *He cannot tell if the driver sees him, though.*

The *EffectOf* relation also received a number of false positives with the following generic template pattern used more often:

> *<Event:VP> < . > ... <Event:VP>*

The pattern accepts any tagged *Events* from two adjacent sentences, leading to the extraction of the assertion *EffectOf(made the team, gets closer)* from the following pairs of story text:

> *Bear made the team.*
> *As he gets closer, Pig sees that Puppy has been crying.*

Lastly, there were target relations that did not have any extractions at all because of their high dependence on indicators, incorrect part-of-speech tags and limitation on the number of sentences it can extract from. For example, the assertion *Happens(walk to school, today)* was extracted because the system used the word *today* as the time indicator for the given activity.

On the quality of the extraction, it is important to note that for event relations like *EffectOf* and *EventForGoalEvent*, the extracted relations seem to be longer and more specific because the extractor uses whole phrases as concepts. This may be different from the concepts of Picture Books that are more generalized. Here are some example extractions:

> *EffectOf(looked at the map,checked the wind)*
> *EffectOf(pours something into the volcano,stopped him)*
> *EventForGoalEvent(called everyone,go to the ship)*

Out of all the extracted relations, only 6 relations were acceptable to be used by Picture Books, and all of them are *PartOf* relations. The other extracted relations are not aligned with the existing themes, thus generating incoherent story text; or are too specific to the story they were extracted from.

5   Conclusion and Further Work

Researches in the field of natural language processing (NLP) seek to finds ways to make human-computer interaction more fluent. But human-computer communication is hampered by the lack of a shared collection of common sense knowledge that people rely on when they communicate in order to understand each other. In order to make computers achieve the same level of expressiveness as humans, we must provide them "a common knowledge with richness that more closely approaches that of the human language." [15]

Although dedicated IE systems have been developed to extract information from various domains, this research is a first step towards extracting relations from children's stories. And based on the results obtained through the evaluation of the extraction tool, it was proven possible to extract new semantic relations from children's stories and feed them into Picture Books' ontology. However, the extraction tool was found to be inaccurate in doing so. Overall, it only got a precision of 0.34; recall of 0.32; and an F-measure of 0.33. Therefore, the automatically extracted relations were mostly incorrect and the extraction tool was not able to extract all expected relations in a given text. As for their quality, it was greatly affected by the common sentence structures in a story, the quality and accuracy of the part-of-speech tagging, the limitations of the defined extraction templates, and the completeness of the indicators.

After evaluation, it is conclusive that as the sentence structures become more complex and the length of the story increases, the extractions get less accurate. It exposes a limitation on the templates used as they can only successfully handle simpler sentences and simpler manifestations of a relation in a text.

For the extraction rules, an attempt to handle all sentence patterns with the least number of rules has caused exceptional cases to not be covered. Moreover, these rules cannot handle implied and inferred relations, and the different senses of a word. Lastly, the templates were limited to extract event relations from one or two adjacent sentences only.

The prevalent use of indicators in most of the extraction templates posed a limitation on the number and quality of extractions done. First, in most cases, indicators are not always used because of their formality. This also assumes that the concepts constituting a relation are within a sentence. If not, it is assumed that the second concept is in the next sentence, the subject pronoun referring to the first concept, and the whole thing signaled by an indicator.

There are also redundant extracted relations that were not generalized into a single binary relation which made the ontology cluttered. Lastly, the binary nature of the relations caused some to become unusable. Most event relations were too specific, because of the existence of direct and indirect objects, and character names.

To address these deficiencies, it is recommended to incorporate as many patterns as possible to improve the extraction rules. Such patterns should also include those that span more than two sentences. There must be an increased focus on extracting event relations as they are not usually explicitly indicated in a span of text. Such relations also constitute the bulk of a story. Building an accurate cause-effect chain of events would be very beneficial for most creative text generation systems.

And in improving the quality of the ontology, future works should consider storing metadata, like frequency and direct object, with the binary relations to reduce specificity and improve usability. Lastly, relations can be further refined by using a language resource that can supply accurate semantic information.

References

1. Hong, B.A., Ong, E.: Generating Punning Riddles from Examples. In: Proceedings of the Second International Symposium on Universal Communication, Osaka, Japan, pp. 347–352 (2008)
2. Liu, H., Singh, P.: ConceptNet - A Practical Commonsense Reasoning Tool-kit. BT Technology Journal 22(4), 211–226 (2004)
3. Hong, A.J., Solis, C., Siy, J.T., Tabirao, E., Ong, E.: Planning Author and Character Goals for Story Generation. In: Proceedings of the NAACL Human Language Technology 2009 Workshop on Computational Approaches to Linguistic Creativity, pp. 63–70. ACL, Colorado (2009)
4. Ang, K., Yu, S., Ong, E.: Theme-Based Cause-Effect Planning for Multiple-Scene Story Generation. In: Proceedings of the 2nd International Conference on Computational Creativity, Mexico City, Mexico, pp. 48–53 (2011)
5. Yu, S., Ong, E.: Using Common-Sense Knowledge in Generating Stories. In: Anthony, P., Ishizuka, M., Lukose, D. (eds.) PRICAI 2012. LNCS (LNAI), vol. 7458, pp. 838–843. Springer, Heidelberg (2012)
6. Liu, H., Singh, P.: Commonsense Reasoning in and over Natural Language. In: Negoita, M.G., Howlett, R.J., Jain, L.C. (eds.) KES 2004. LNCS (LNAI), vol. 3215, pp. 293–306. Springer, Heidelberg (2004)
7. Chua Jr., R.C., Ong, E.: Commonsense Knowledge Acquisition through Children's Stories. In: Richards, D., Kang, B.H. (eds.) PKAW 2012. LNCS (LNAI), vol. 7457, pp. 244–250. Springer, Heidelberg (2012)
8. Muslea, I.: Extraction Patterns for Information Extraction Tasks: A Survey. In: Proceedings of the AAAI 1999 Workshop on Machine Learning for Information Extraction (1999)
9. Alani, H., Kim, S., Millard, D., Weal, M., Lewis, P., Hall, W., Shadbolt, N.: Automatic Extraction of Knowledge from Web Documents. In: Proceedings of ISWC 2003 Workshop on Human Language Technology for the Semantic Web and Web Services, Florida (2003)
10. Cheng, T.T., Cua, J., Tan, M., Yao, K.: Information Extraction for Legal Documents. Unpublished undergraduate thesis, De La Salle University, Manila (2010)

11. Etzioni, O., Cafarella, M., Downey, D., Popescu, A.M., Shaked, T., Soderland, S., Weld, D.S., Yates, A.: Unsupervised Named-Entity Extraction from the Web: An Experimental Study. Artificial Intelligence 165, 91–134 (2005)
12. Banko, M., Cafarella, M.J., Soderland, S., Broadhead, M., Etzioni, O.: Open Information Extraction from the Web. In: Proceedings of the 20th International Joint Conference on Artificial Intelligence, Hyderabad, India, pp. 2670–2676 (2007)
13. Cua, J., Ong, E., Manurung, R., Pease, A.: Representing Story Plans in SUMO. In: NAACL Human Language Technology 2010 Second Workshop on Computational Approaches to Linguistic Creativity, pp. 40–48. ACL, Stroudsburg (2010)
14. Mueller, E.: Modelling Space and Time in Narratives about Restaurants. Literary and Linguistic Computing 22(1), 67–84 (2007)
15. Niles, I., Pease, A.: Towards a Standard Upper Ontology. In: Proceedings of the International Conference on Formal Ontology in Information Systems, pp. 2–9. ACM, New York (2001)

Interpreting Overlaps in Business Process Mapping via Organisational Soft Knowledge Flows

Alis Keshishi and Peter Busch

Department of Computing,
Macquarie University
N.S.W. 2109
Australia

Abstract. Knowledge Management (KM) as the term implies, is broadly about improving knowledge use within an organisation. At a lower level, Business Process Management (BPM) is the set of management activities related to business processes that can ideally be arranged in a life cycle. Social Network Analysis (SNA) is a technique enabling the researcher to better understand interactions between people. Relatively little research has been conducted with regard to the crossover of social networks and workflows, with the aim of examining workflows as management views them, as opposed to the actual social interactions of staff. Improvements in the overlay of management interpretations of work and real social networks could potentially lead to improvements in business process efficacy. In this study SNA diagrams are examined in order to implement executable models and potentially enable automated analysis of workflows. A means of converting SNA data to Business Process workflows is presented and an example provided.

Keywords: Social Network Analysis, Business Process Management, Knowledge Management, Workflow, Formalisation, Petri Nets, Business Process Modelling.

1   Introduction

Knowledge Management (KM), Business Process Management (BPM), and Social Network Analysis (SNA) as areas of study have well established profiles, particularly the last discipline. Knowledge Management focuses on the efficacy of data, information and particularly knowledge as a resource within the firm and examines how it may be best utilised amongst staff [1]. Business Process Management (BPM) represents a means of "supporting business processes using methods, techniques and software to design, enact, control and analyze operational processes involving humans, organizations, applications, documents and other sources of information" ([2] p. 11). Social Network Analysis (SNA) on the other hand "is an established social science approach of studying human relations and social structures by disclosing the affinities, attraction and repulsions operating between persons and persons, and between persons and objects" ([3] p. 64). What is not well researched is the intersection

Y.S. Kim et al (Eds.): PKAW 2014, LNCS 8863, pp. 209–222, 2014.
© Springer International Publishing Switzerland 2014

of the above disciplines [1], namely examining how well business processes in companies actually match the working relationships of employees as viewed through the 'lens' of Social Network Analysis. This paper provides an approach that could be used to identify the individuals, teams, and units who play central roles; to detect information breakdowns, bottlenecks, structural holes, as well as detect isolated individuals, teams, and units and how these relates to workflow modelling.

2   Background

The application of Social Network Analysis (SNA) is extensive given the length of time this data analysis technique has been in existence. SNA has provided a means of measuring and mapping relationships between employees, but what SNA has not typically been used for is the analysis of business processes in organizations. SNA provides the researcher with a means of interpreting what facilitates or impedes knowledge flows binding interacting organisational units together; that is the "who knows whom, whom shares what information and knowledge with whom by what communication media" ([4] p. 2). In short "SNA is an established social science approach of studying human relations and social structures by disclosing the affinities, attraction and repulsions operating between persons and persons, and between persons and objects" ([3] p. 64). One advantage to applying SNA to business is to provide a more seamless customer service, for customer calls and emails for example can be routed more effectively with an internal social network in place [5], as well as provide the ability to highlight the roles and goals of workers which are not observed through applying other means of analysis [6]. [7] further mentions that knowledge workers typically waste 28% of their time due to poor workflow control mechanisms, claiming a need for a formalised approach to help workers achieve goals to structure the creation, maintenance, and re-use knowledge.

An added advantage to conducting SNA is for a researcher to be positioned external to an organisation in a positivist research-from-a-distance sense, rather than observing workplace relationships through an interpretivist researcher-involved-in-participant-observation sense. It is not enough however to simply observe the relationships of employees, rather what is sought is to compare such relationships with management's view of how processes should be conducted. Applying SNA techniques into business processes, especially workflows, would be a most significant approach to better understand current business process management issues. Furthermore, if there is a method to illustrate relationships in the workplace, then modeling employee work processes could be best represented by workflow modeling [8]. As such, we hereby combine data mining and social network analysis techniques for analyzing social interaction networks in order to improve our understanding of the data, as well as the modeled behavior, and its underlying processes. SNA uses two types of mathematical tools to represent information about patterns of ties among social actors: graphs or sociograms, and matrices [9].

2.1   Sociogram

A graphical model consists of points or nodes to represent actors and lines to represent relations or ties among actors. "When sociologists borrowed this way of graphing things from mathematicians, they re-named their graphics 'sociograms' " ([9] p. 21). Graphs might represent a single type of relation or more than one type of relation among employees. Each tie between a pair of actors may be directed, or represent co-occurrence, co-presence or a bonded-tie. Graphs are a very effective means for presenting information about social networks, however when there are a number of actors or many kinds of relations, they become too complicated to visually display all relationships [9].

2.2   Sociomatrix

Social network information can also be represented in the form of matrices. Matrices are collections of elements in a tabular form of rows and columns. "Representing the information in this way also allows the application of mathematical and computer tools to summarize and find patterns. The most common form of matrix in social network analysis is a very simple one composed of as many rows and columns as there are actors in the data set, and where the elements represent the ties between the actors" ([9] p. 25).

3   Formalising SNA Data

"Once a pattern of social relations or ties among a set of actors has been represented in a formal way (graphs or matrices), we can define some important ideas about social structure in quite precise ways using mathematics for the definitions" ([9] p. 36). There are three main reasons for formalizing SNA data: matrices and graphs are compact and systematic; matrices and graphs allow us to apply computers to analyze data, and; matrices and graphs have rules and conventions. Formalizing SNA data also allows analysts to identify cliques of actors. "At the most general level, a clique is a sub-set of a network in which the actors are more closely and intensely tied to one another than they are to other members of the network" ([9] p.79). Here we use sociograms and sociomatrices to identify cliques of actors for analysis and resource utilization.

3.1   Workflows

What is required is not just observing employees in their working relationships, but understanding how this relates to workflow as management believes it takes place. Workflow systems represent a series of connected interactions between people and the IT systems of an enterprise, typically working towards the automation of a particular business process, supporting the necessary task, document, and information flow, governed in turn by a set of business rules [10] [11]. Accordingly, the key challenges to workflow management are efficient and effective automation of workflows and the ability to agilely handle the change inherent in enterprise transformation [10]. Business Process Management provides us with a means to understand and produce more effective and efficient workflows in many organisations at the operational level, with examples being reported at Toyota and Ford [12]. Business processes are essentially a completely closed, timely and logical sequence of activities which are required to work on process-oriented business objects such as an invoice or a purchase order. The business process which can be arranged as a lifecycle, also acts as an essential interface to the business partners external to the company [13]. The modelling of such work processes are naturally represented through workflow modelling in order to facilitate the coordination and integration of manual and automated processes into a cohesive whole [14] [8].

Data gathered for process models varies from questionnaire data to the use of an event log which records workflow events, whether by email, fax, voicemail, machine instruction and so forth [5]. Event logs may be defined as a chronological record of computer system activities which can be used for identifying users' actions or processes on the system [15]. Logs are often used on email traffic and phone-call records, however [16] note that e-mail is less useful, being difficult to analyse as real effort exists in "distinguishing between e-mails corresponding to important decisions and e-mails representing less relevant operational details" (p. 244). Instead using logs from an enterprise information system is suggested; such logs have relevant event data in a more structured form; for instance the logs in ERP, B2B and CRM systems involve specific operational details. The aforementioned examples represent automated output or steps in a work process. Probably the only alternative to using event logs in one form or another would be asking an employee what they have achieved or who they have collaborated with by way of a questionnaire.

3.2   Petri-Nets and Related Work

Regardless of the means of data acquisition, what is desired is the ability to take working relationships and model them as a means of determining the fit between employees versus management's view of workplace reality. This paper provides a working example of how such a process may be undertaken. Returning to the concept of SNA as a means of mapping relationships amongst employees, the models or sociograms utilised are relatively informal as they are graphical rather than mathematical in the true sense of the word. As such a degree of formalisation of executable models is required first [10]. Workflow nets are one means that provide the researcher with a formal means of modeling workflows based on Petri-nets, and may include 3 tuples (P, T, F). P: place in petri-net, indicates a condition; T: transitions in a petri-net, indicates tasks; where a token is a workflow state of a single case; finally F: is a flow relation between P and T [2]. The approach described is relatively novel, although [17] had used the XML Process Definition Language (XPDL) to similarly describe a related process formally, where the basic structural elements were activities, transitions, and participants. These three elements could be linked with tuples of the intended process model (Transitions -> P, Activities -> T, Participant -> R). [18] had also introduced a similar framework, namely that of workflow-based social network discovery and analysis, which provided ideas to develop automatic workflow to SNA conversion software. [18] had used Information Control Net (ICN) based workflows where ICN was an 8-tuple ($\Gamma = (\delta,\rho,\lambda,\varepsilon,\pi,\kappa,I,O)$) over a set (A) of activities, a set (T) of transition conditions, a set (R) of repositories, a set (G) of invoked application programmes, a set (P) of roles, and a set (C) of actors. From the ICN based workflow, social networks could be discovered using 'workflow-based social network discovery.' Without going in to elaborate detail, Song et al.'s [18] workflow-based social network had 4 tuples; the first tuple describing the social relationship: successors and predecessors, the second tuple represented acquisitions of activities, while the third and fourth tuples described the connections with external workflow-based social networks.

In short, a combination of SNA and Workflow-nets (WF-nets) can play a significant role in aiding the BPM lifecycle. These include the following advantages: the application of SNA techniques could be used to identify the individuals, teams, and units who play central roles; to detect information breakdowns, bottlenecks, structural holes, as well as isolated individuals, teams, and units [4]. The advantage of SNA is that it permits the researcher to compare existing workflows to build a more accurate organisational picture with regard to how work is actually being undertaken, as opposed to how management views processes [16]. The application of SNA techniques to a role-based workflow-net (WF-net) based on Petri-nets, allows for the determination of the centrality of a role or its degree of importance within the process, while identifying relatively disjoint roles. WF-net permits observing the workflow both conditionally and via parallel routing. Parallel routing requires finishing each task simultaneously for eliminating bottlenecks. From such a concept, the priority of assigning resources would be defined. Using Petri-nets as a formalism for BPM and WFM, it is clear that Petri-nets can serve as a solid foundation for BPM/WFM technology.

Workflows can be mapped into Petri-nets. The classic Petri-net consist of two node types called transitions and places. Places are represented by circles, and transitions by rectangles. These nodes are connected to each other via direct arcs. Each workflow task is represented by a corresponding transition, and places are used to display the pre- and post-conditions or resources needed for the flow of the work. Figure 1 (a and b) illustrates the basic properties of a Petri-net and a Petri-net-based workflow in general. The Petri-net illustrated has four places and two transactions. P1 and P3 are input places for transitions T1 and T2 accordingly. A transition node is ready to fire if and only if there is one token at each of its input places. For example a state transition will occur as the token in the input place P1 fires the transition T1 and moves the token to P2 or P3 as its possible output places.

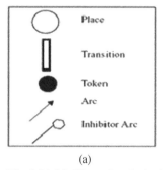
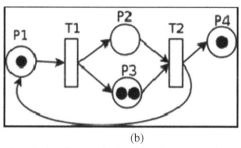

(a)   (b)

Fig. 1 (a) (b): Illustrating the basic properties of a Petri-net and a Petri-net based workflow

4   Example Organisation

To illustrate the mapping of workflow management concepts onto a Petri-net we can consider examining the 'Complaint Handling' process in an organization in which the actors and their overlapping roles are illustrated in figure 2.

Fig. 1. Illustrating overlapping actors and their roles

The 'Complaint Handling' process which is illustrated in figure 3 shows that first the complaint is registered (task: Register), followed by two tasks, which are performed in parallel; a questionnaire is sent to the complainant (task: Send_Questionnaire) and the complaint is evaluated (task: Evaluate). The next step is a conditional routing; if the complainant returns the questionnaire within two weeks, the task process questionnaire (task: Process_Questionnaire) is executed. If the questionnaire is not returned within two weeks, the result of the questionnaire is discarded (task: Time_Out). Based on the result of the evaluation, either the com plaint needs to be processed or not (conditional routing with tasks: Process_Questionnaire or Time_Out). The actual processing of the complaint (task: Process_Complaint) is delayed until the questionnaire is processed or a time-out has occurred. The processing of the complaint is checked via task check processing (task: Check_Processing). If further processing is required then the task; 'process complaint' will be initiated as a result of iterative routing. Finally, task archive (task: Archive) is executed.

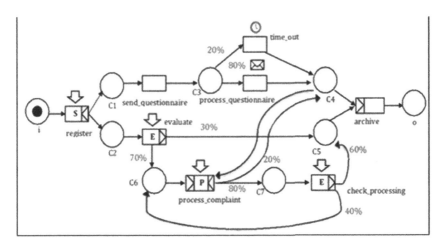

Fig. 2. The processing of complaints with triggering information

The tasks have been modelled by transitions. To model the states between tasks, conditions are added. Each condition has been modelled by a place (circle). For example place C2 corresponds to the condition 'ready to evaluate the complaint'. If a place contains a token then that condition is satisfied. For example C4 is true if the questionnaire is processed or a timeout occurs. In a multi-case model if a place contains many tokens, then this might indicate a bottleneck.

4.1 Applying SNA Techniques to a Role-Based Workflow-Net

To create a role-based workflow-net for handling the complaint process, we assign roles to the tasks or activities. The initials; S, P and E are used for the Support, Processing and Evaluate roles, and are shown in figure 3 above. This figure shows the processing of complaints extended with triggering information and building blocks for workflow modelling. In order to identify the relationship between the roles, their strengths/weaknesses and actors/employees degree of centrality, we need to identify the routings and count the arcs (flows).

There are four different types of routing in this process. *Parallel Routing* {Evaluate(E) and Send_ Questionnaire (S)}; *Conditional Routing* {Process_Questionnaire (80%) or Time_Out (20%); Processing_Required (70%) or No_Processing (30%); Process Complaint (80%) or Re-assessment_Required (or Archive)(20%)}; Processing_Ok (60% If processing is ok) or Processing_NOK (40% - if processing is not ok and requires re-work by the processor); *Sequential Routing* {Process_Complaint then Check_Processing; Process_Questionnaire then Process_Complaint}; *Iteration* {Processing_NOK back to Process_Complaint}. For conditional routings the proportion of possibilities are added as a percentage next to the task in figure 3. These figures represent a theoretical scenario, however in real conditions the figures will be based on the possibility of their occurrences being extracted from system's event logs. An arc is a flow between P(Condition) and T(Task). Every arc is valued at 1 except arcs in conditional routings, which are valued at their proportion, such as 40% or 60%.

The automated system tasks such as 'Time_Out' or 'Send_Questionnaire' are not considered in the routing process, however if a routing is directed to a user in the results of these tasks, the value of the arc is considered for the routing process. For example 80% of questionnaires, which are returned on time, are sent to a processor for processing purposes. This (task: 'Send_Questionnaire') is an automated task however initiated, and followed by support staff and in a successful process it will be routed to a processor. As there might be some re-assessment of the questionnaire, so there will be some contact between the support person and the processors, therefore and for this reason, the value of the arc connecting the tasks are weighted and considered in the calculation.

4.2   Sociomatrix of Roles

In examining the routing process, the results of counting arcs (flow between conditions and tasks) among different roles are shown in the matrix below (table 1). All SNA data begins as either binary, integer or real numerical values in sociomatrix format (table 1), from which point the values are then converted to a sociogram (figure 4) for better visual display.

Table 1. Sociomatrix of Roles

	Support(S)	Process(P)	Evaluate(E)
Support(S)	0	0.8	2
Process(P)	1	0	1.8
Evaluate(E)	0.9	2.1	0

The sociogram for roles which is illustrated in figure 4 shows that the relationship between Evaluate(E) and Process(P) is strongest and between Process(P) and Support(S) is weakest. At the same time Evaluate(E) has the highest worker or actor degree of centrality; that is the most important node or role in the network [19]. For example if a threshold of more than 1 is applied to the sociogram, the relation between E and P, and E and S will remain, while the relationship between P and S will be relatively disjoint.

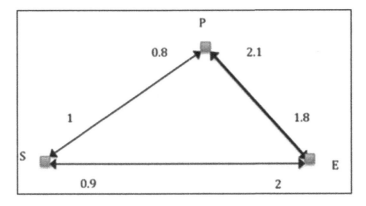

Fig. 3. #: Sociogram of Roles

From such a result, we may recommend actors/employees on the 'Evaluate' team, be placed on more important activities with a higher degree of involvement with other departments.

5   Social Network Analysis and Data Mining

In examining the relational network among employees based on a contact frequency, employees in a company were asked via a questionnaire to choose one of the options below for the frequency of contact with their colleagues. The contact frequencies are: 6.0 hourly contact; 5.0 every few hours; 4.0 daily contact; 3.0 once every couple of days; 2.0 weekly and; 1.0 bi-weekly. The result of the questionnaire is displayed in table 2 below.

Table 2. Sociomatrix of Actors /Employees

	Mike (E)	Marian (E)	Eric (E)	Susan (P)	Peter (P)	John (P)	Harry (PS)	Kate (PS)	Tracy (S)	Bill (S)
Mike (E)	0	2	3	3	4	6	1	1	5	2
Marian(E)	2	0	4	3	5	6	1	1	3	5
Eric(E)	3	4	0	6	4	3	3	3	6	4
Susan(P)	4	3	6	0	4	3	4	6	5	4
Peter(P)	4	5	4	4	0	3	4	5	3	3
John(P)	6	6	3	3	3	0	3	3	2	3
Harry(PS)	1	1	2	4	4	3	0	4	4	6
Kate(PS)	1	1	2	6	5	2	4	0	3	5
Tracy(S)	4	3	6	5	3	2	3	3	0	6
Bill(S)	2	5	3	4	3	3	6	5	6	0

Below are the sociograms (figure 5 a-f), illustrating relationships of actors to one another in terms of threshold. With space limitations it is not possible to illustrate all sociograms clearly. However examining the sociograms, which are derived by the SNA software (UCINET V6) from the sociomatrix (table 2) we can note a number of parameters. The layout of the actors/employees is in an approximate circle shape; meaning employees are roughly the same distance from one another (the SNA software uses Multi-Dimensional Scaling (MDS) algorithms to achieve this based on reported relationship distances of actors to one another). Actor nodes can be identified by their name with different symbolism. In addition a real numerical value appears next to each actor, in this case representing an information centrality value; this parameter is a statistical measure of the likelihood of information transfer between actors [9]. The higher the numerical value the more likely information will be passed from one actor to the other; Eric(E again for Evaluate) is most likely to pass information to Susan(P for Processing) and Tracy(S for support etc.), but share it less with Marian(E) or Mike(E). Furthermore, examining the edges in the sociogram, we may note the edge thickness variation between the actors; high relationship strength is displayed with thicker edges.

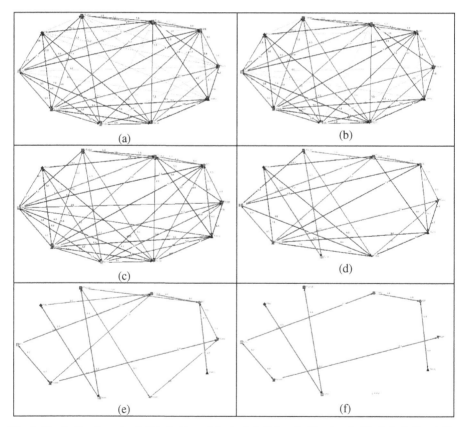

Fig. 4. Illustrating from top left to bottom right (a-f) {all thresholds, thresholds 2, 3, 4, 5 and 6)

At the same time edges are also colour coded; with red being the strongest relationship followed by green, dark blue, grey, light blue, with pink representing the weakest relationship. From figure 5 (a) to (f), by increasing the value of the related threshold, the arcs are progressively removed. In figure (e), the nodes are still connected via a closed loop for the contact frequency of every few hours (green edges), by (f) the remaining illustrated actors contact each other at least hourly. The nodes are connected via linear edges, and one actor; Peter(P) is an isolate. The clique, which has a high volume of frequency, can be found by applying the maximum threshold.

The above process can be formalised to discover the algorithm for ideal social networks among actors/employees. The threshold is increased until the network is disconnected. By increasing the threshold value we can identify the cliques who indicate groups having more frequent and therefore stronger relationships between actors [19].

The network of employees discussed above could be used for allocating resources and aiming to reduce the time lag between activities. We examine the cliques for two thresholds of 5 and 6, beginning with cliques with a threshold =5. The following are the optimal cliques for a threshold of 5: {Eric(E), Tracy(S), Bill(S), Kate(P,S), Susan(P)}, {Susan(P), Tracy(S), Bill(S), Kate(PS)}, {Marian(E), Bill(S), Kate(P,S), Peter(P)}; clique: {Eric(E), Susan(P), Tracy(S)}. As the Evaluate(E) role is the most important role with a higher degree of actor centrality, we examine each of the three evaluators and their relationships with other staff more closely.

Mike(E): Mike from the evaluation team has a contact frequency of a few hours with Tracy from the support team and John from the processing team. So the clique of {Mike(E), John(P), Tracy(S)} will be a good fit for processing a case from initiation until archive.

Marian(E): Marian from the evaluation team has contact frequency of a few hours with Bill from the support team and Peter from the processing team. So the clique of {Marian(E), Peter(P), Bill(S)} will be a good fit for processing a case from initiation until archive.

Eric (E): Eric from the evaluation team has a contact frequency of a few hours with Tracy from the support team and Susan from processing team. So the clique of {Eric(E), Susan(P), Tracy(S)} will be a good fit for processing a case from initiation until archive.

We can also conclude that Tracy(S) from the support team has a regular contact with two of three evaluators and processors. She seems to have a good relationship with many people from different departments.

The following represent the remaining pairs who have a contact frequency of every few hours: Bill(S)-Kate(P,S); Susan(P)-Tracy(S); Peter(P)-Kate(P,S); Tracy(S)-Bill(S); Bill(S)-Harry(P,S); Kate(P,S)-Susan(P). Probably some of these frequent contacts will affect work productivity. For example according to the sociograms of roles, the support and processing team has the weakest relationships, so if there are employees within these roles who have regular contacts of every few hours, then the company needs to re-assess the employee's time or potentially reconstruct their practices.

Next we consider Cliques: Threshold=6; within this threshold the contact frequency is hourly. The following actors/employees have strong contact with each other: Eric(E)-Tracy(S); Tracy(S)-Bill(S); Bill(P,S)-Harry(S); Kate(P,S)-Susan(P); Eric(E)-Susan(P); Mike(E)-John(P); Marian(E)-John(P). According to the sociomatrix of roles, the strongest roles are between Evaluator(E) and Processor(P) following by Evaluator(E) and Support(S). In which case the best pairs for tasks involved in (E,S) is Eric(E)-Tracy(S) and for (E,P) is Eric(E)-Susan(P) followed by Mike(E)-John(P) and Marian(E)-John(P). The following represent the optimal cliques for a threshold of 6. They are better suited for processing a case initiated by the support team to be followed by evaluators and processors. Clique: {Tracy(S), Eric(E), Susan(P)} Clique: {Tracy(S), Mike(E), John(P)}; Clique: {Bill(S), Marian(E), John(P)}. If the organisation can maintain such a network on workflow, the maximum lag between activities would be reduced dramatically.

6   Application of SNA Results to WF- Nets

In this section we integrate the results from WF-nets and SNA data in order to group resources based on the SNA analysis. We then formalise the allocation of resources with regard to parallel routings and conditional routings.

Resources need to be allocated in the order of *parallel*, *conditional* and *sequential* routings. The first task for a Support(S) staff is a parallel routing for sending the questionnaire to the complainant and passing the case to an evaluator. For *parallel* routing we have the paths: Register(S), Evaluate(E), Process_Complaint(P) and Register(S), Send_Questionnaire(S/P) and Process_Questionnaire (P). For parallel routings, tasks need to be done concurrently, so it is important that an employee from the Support(S) team can work productively with employees from both Processing(P) and Evaluation(E) teams in order for the tasks to be completed and the case becomes ready for a 'checking' process without any delay. The reason for this is that the task 'Process_Complaint' cannot be completed until the questionnaire is processed. Beginning with Cliques: Threshold=5, the best clique for threshold 5 is: Clique: {Bill(S), Marian(E), Peter(P)} and for Threshold: 6 are: Clique: {Tracy(S), Eric(E), Susan(P)}, Clique: {Tracy(S), Mike(E), John(P)}, Clique: {Bill(S), Marian(E), John(P)}. For *conditional* routings we examine one of four cases illustrated in figure 3. Process_Complaint (P) then (80%, Check_Processing(E)) or (Process_Complaint(P) then (20% Process_Questionnaire(S), reassess). In this case there is an 80% chance that the case is sent for 'Check-Processing' so the most important roles involved are E and P, therefore the following pair of employees from E and P teams are suitable for undertaking these tasks. If a case needed further clarification between Processors and the Support team in regard to Process_ Questionnaire, then the best matched employees from P and S are identified. For Threshold=5 the best cliques are: {Marian(E)-Peter(P) (80%)},{Peter(P)-Kate(P,S) (20%)} and for Threshold: 6; {Eric(E)-Susan(P) (80%)}, {Mike(E)-John(P) (80%)}, {Marian(E)-John(P) (80%)}, for a 20% possibility of routing: {Susan(P)-Kate(P,S)},{Bill(P,S)-Harry(S)}.

In the process of handling complaints, the sequential routing is either between the Evaluate(E) team and Process(P) team or between the Support(S) and Evaluate(E) teams, which have already been discussed above, and the same cliques mentioned above can also be mapped for this routing.

7   Discussion

A simple working example has been presented through application of SNA to Business Process Management as an example of mapping workplace relationships. The results from WF-nets and SNA data have been integrated to group resources based on the SNA analysis. Then we formalised the allocation of resources with regard to parallel routings and conditional routings. This examines how a simple set of work processes may be mapped in SNA to determine the closeness of fit to work practices. The sociogram of employees clearly illustrates that some employees who need to work closely together on a particular case, appear to have a weakened relationship, and some who do have a strong relationship don't work together. For example Peter(P) does not appear to have a very close relationship with evaluators and the support team, which may be an issue if their task requires them to work closely together. John(P) seems to have a weakened relationship with support staff but strong contact with evaluators, which might be a cause of concern if he needs to follow up the case with the support team. Some employees such as Susan(P) and Kate(P,S) have a very high frequency of contacts, which might be a positive factor as both undertake similar tasks, however Kate(P,S) does not have a good relationship with any evaluators, which may have a negative influence on Susan(P). Furthermore Harry(P,S) who is supposed to be involved in both support and processing jobs, does not have a strong working relationship with employees in the evaluate team; this could be a cause for concern for the company if their task requires them to work closely together. As a result management may choose to re-examine the working relationships and physical placement of staff.

8   Conclusion

We have provided a way of assigning resources to parallel routing and conditional routing based on role-based workflows, assuming all tasks have the same elapsed time. In this paper we have briefly examined a means for combining workflows and Social Network Analysis data as an algorithm in pseudocode. Analysis of workflows can take place through the use of Petri-nets and we have chosen to do likewise. We have examined a hypothetical organisation with certain roles being conducted by particular employees. Through the examination of SNA data relating to the same organisation we have been able to map the most appropriate individuals for a task based on SNA measures such as centrality. Finally we have examined approaches to undertaking workflows, either parallelised or conditionally and in turn which employee cliques would be best suited, given our sample organisation.

References

1. Busch, P.: Business Process Management, Social Network Analysis and Knowledge Management: A Triangulation of Sorts? In: Australasian Conference on Information Systems (ACIS 2010), Brisbane, December 1-3, 10 p. (2010)
2. van der Aalst, W.: The Application of Petri Nets to Workflow Management. Journal of Circuits Systems and Computers 8(1), 21–66 (1998)
3. Hassan, N.: Using Social Network Analysis to Measure IT-Enabled Business Process Performance. Information Systems Management 26(1), 61–76 (2009)
4. Serrat, O.: Social Network Analysis. In: Knowledge Solutions. Asian Development Bank, Mandaluyong (2009)
5. Bonchi, F., Castillo, C., Gionis, A., Jaimes, A.: Social Network Analysis and Mining for Business Applications. ACM Transactions on Intelligent Systems and Technology 2(3), Article 22, 1–37 (2011)
6. Poltrock, S., Handel, M.: Modeling Collaborative Behavior: Foundations for Collaboration Technologies. In: Hawaii International Conference on System Sciences (HICSS), pp. 1–10 (2009)
7. Harrison-Broninski, K.: Dealing with Human-Driven Processes. In: Rosemann, M. (ed.) Handbook on Business Process Management 2, pp. 443–461. Springer, Heidelberg (2010)
8. Papazoglou, M., Ribbers, P.: e-Business: Organizational and Technical Foundations. John Wiley & Sons Ltd., Chichester (2006)
9. Hanneman, R.: Introduction to Social Network Methods (2002), http://faculty.ucr.edu/~hanneman/nettext/ (accessed June 9, 2010)
10. Caverlee, J., Bae, J., Qinyi, W., Ling, L., Pu, C., Rouse, W.: Workflow Management for Enterprise Transformation. Information Knowledge Systems Management 6(1/2), 61–80 (2007)
11. Stohr, E., Zhao, J.: Workflow Automation: Overview and Research Issues. Information Systems Frontiers 3(3), 281–296 (2001)
12. Ko, R.: A Computer Scientist's Introductory Guide to Business Process Management (BPM). Crossroads 15(4), 11–18 (2009)
13. Mendling, J.: Business Process Management. In: Metrics for Process Models. LNBIP, vol. 6, pp. 1–15. Springer, Heidelberg (2008)
14. Deokar, A., Kolfschoten, G., Vreede, G.: Prescriptive Workflow Design for Collaboration-intensive Processes Using the Collaboration Enginnering Approach. Global Journal of Flexible System Management 9(4), 11–20 (2008)
15. Alles, M., Jans, J., Vasarhelyi, M.: Process Mining: A New Research Methodology for AIS. In: CAAA Annual Conference, pp. 1–16 (January 2011)
16. van der Aalst, W.M.P., Song, M.: Mining Social Networks: Uncovering Interaction Patterns in Business Processes. In: Desel, J., Pernici, B., Weske, M. (eds.) BPM 2004. LNCS, vol. 3080, pp. 244–260. Springer, Heidelberg (2004)
17. Delias, P., Doulamis, A., Doulamis, N., Matsatsinis, N.: Optimizing Resource Conflicts in Workflow Management Systems. IEEE Transactions on Knowledge and Data Engineering 23(3), 417–432 (2011)
18. Song, J., Kim, M., Kim, H., Kim, K.: A Framework: Workflow-Based Social Network Discovery and Analysis. In: 13th IEEE International Conference on Computational Science and Engineering, pp. 421–426 (2010)
19. Wasserman, S., Faust, K.: Social Network Analysis: Methods and Applications. Cambridge University Press, Cambridge (1994)

Building a Vietnamese SentiWordNet Using Vietnamese Electronic Dictionary and String Kernel

Xuan-Son Vu, Hyun-Je Song, and Seong-Bae Park[*]

School of Computer Science and Engineering
Kyungpook National University
Daegu, 702-701, South Korea
{sonvx,hjsong,sbpark}@sejong.knu.ac.kr

Abstract. In this paper, we propose a novel approach to construct a *Vietnamese SentiWordNet* (VSWN), a lexical resource supporting sentiment analysis in Vietnamese. A SentiWordNet is typically generated from WordNet in which each synset has numerical scores to indicate its opinion polarities. However, Vietnamese WordNet is not yet available currently. Therefore, we propose a method to construct a VSWN from a Vietnamese electronic dictionary, not from WordNet. The main drawback of constructing a VSWN from a dictionary is that it is easy to suffer from the sparsity problem, since the glosses in the dictionary are short in general. As a solution to this problem, we adopt a string kernel function which measures the string similarity based on both common contiguous and non-contiguous subsequences. According to our experimental results, first, the use of string kernel outperforms a baseline model which uses the standard bag-of-word kernel. Second, the Vietnamese SentiWordNet is competitive with the English SentiWordNet which uses WordNet when it constructed. All those results prove that our methodology is effective and efficient in constructing a SentiWordNet from an electronic dictionary.

Keywords: SentiWordNet, Vietnamese SentiWordNet, Opinion Mining, String Kernel.

1   Introduction

In this paper, we present a Vietnamese SentiWordNet (VSWN). VSWN is a lexical resource supporting for opinion mining in Vietnamese, and it inherits all the principles of English SentiWordNet (ESWN), where ESWN is a lexical resource devised for supporting sentiment classification and opinion mining applications [13]. ESWN is firstly introduced by Esuli et al. [7] and is publicly available for research purposes. It has played a vital role in opinion mining or other sentiment analysis applications [1]. In order to contribute such an important lexical resource for Vietnamese language, We have introduced the first VSWN [15].

---

[*] Corresponding author.

Y.S. Kim et al (Eds.): PKAW 2014, LNCS 8863, pp. 223–235, 2014.
© Springer International Publishing Switzerland 2014

However, this VSWN has suffered from the sparsity problem, since the dataset consists of short text. As a result, the previous VSWN was limited. Therefore, this paper focuses on resolving the sparsity problem of the previous VSWN to achieve more effective VSWN.

This paper proposes a novel method to build a VSWN from an electronic dictionary. The proposed method is based on the our previous work [15]. That is, the core of a VSWN is made by translating the ESWN into Vietnamese, and then expands it by adding new synsets from a Vietnamese dictionary. The sentiment score for the newly added synsets are determined by a machine learning method. That is, the sentiment scores of each synset in VSWN are found by two support vector machines. The scores of a synset are determined by classifying its gloss in the Vietnamese dictionary (Vdict) with two support vector machines called as positivity and negativity classifier. Then, the scores are set as the margins to the hyperplanes of one of the support vector machines.

Note that the sparsity problem which occurs often in document classification also happens in constructing a VSWN. The problem occurs in document classification when the number of features that actually appear in a document vector is much less than the number of all possible features. In constructing a VSWN, a document corresponds to a synset of WordNet. Since the gloss of the synset in the dictionary is short in general, the sparsity problem is observed in our task. As a solution to this problem, we apply the string kernel function [11] to the support vector machines. Unlike other kernel functions such as a linear kernel, the string kernel measures the similarity between strings directly by taking into account information about not only their common contiguous substrings, but also their common non-contiguous substrings. As a result, we can overcome the shortness of the glosses in the dictionary.

We perform two kinds of experiments to evaluate the proposed method. The first one is to check how well the string kernel solves the sparsity problem. The task of classifying a given synset into positive or negative class is used to show the effectiveness of string kernel. The performance of sentiment classification using the string kernel is compared with a baseline model which uses the linear kernel. The string kernel achieves up to 5.2% higher F1-score than the baseline. The second one is to see the quality of the resultant VSWN. The VSWN is first regarded as a synset list in which all synsets are ordered by their positive (or negative) score, then it is compared with a gold standard positive (or negative) synset list [15] made manually. These two positive (or negative) lists contain the same synsets in different order. Thus, the performance of the VSWN is measured with the Kendall tau distance (τ_p distance) [1,9]. The average τ_p distance between two positive (or negative) synset lists measures the agreement of synset ordering in terms of rank correlation. Our experimental results show that the proposed method achieves up to 2.6% higher performance than previous VSWN [15] in terms of τ_p distance. These results imply that the proposed method which solves sparsity problem well constructs a VSWN effectively.

The rest of the paper is organized as follows. Section 2 introduces some current studies of building SentiWordNet. Section 3 addresses our method to generate

VSWN using a Vietnamese dictionary (Vdict). The string kernel along with feature selection to overcome the sparsity problem is deeply demonstrated in Section 4. The experimental results are shown in Section 5. Finally, Section 6 gives conclusions and our future studies.

2   Related Work

There has been a long journey for opinion mining in English with various available English resources including English WordNet, English SentiWordNet, subjectivity word list [6], and so on. SentiWordNet among them is the most well-known and essential resource for opinion mining. However, there are few researches that focus on building a SentiWordNet especially for minor languages such as Vietnamese. It is a difficult task to build a SentiWordNet. Thus, there have been just a few researches on this task. For English, Esuli et al. first introduced ESWN [7], and then some other researchers released its improved versions [8,5,1]. Das et al. presented the SentiWordNet for Indian language [3] and one more contribution towards a global SentiWordNet [4]. The reason why there have been just little studies on SentiWordNets for minor languages can be explained in two folds. The first one is about availability of WordNet. Even if WordNet is one of the most critical resources for constructing a SentiWordNet, there are no WordNet for most minor languages. The other is related with human labour. If a SentiWordNet is made only by human labor from scratch, it would be too expensive. Thus, it is necessary to have a method to overcome these two primary difficulties.

Due to the unavailability of human labor, SentiWordNet is usually generated automatically. English SentiWordNet (ESWN) is generated from English Word-Net, and then the sentiment polarities of each synset is obtained by a machine learning method [8,1]. Moreover, by taking advantages of WordNet, random-walk step [1] on WordNet improved the resultant SentiWordNet considerably. Another way to generate a SentiWordNet is to use ESWN. An Indian SentiWordNet is generated using a machine translator [3]. The machine translator translated the synsets in ESWN into Indian, and then copies the sentiment scores for synsets directly from ESWN. This approach is a first approach for minor languages which do not have a WordNet, however, it heavily depends on the performance of machine translation.

We have proposed a Vietnamese SentiWordNet (VSWN) [15]. This VSWN inherits the advantages of both ESWN and ISWN. We adopt the translation method of ISWN to build a VSWN core that overcome the availability of Word-Net. Then, we applied a machine learning method to expand the VSWN core as in ESWN. However, since the VSWN is solely based on a Vietnamese dictionary, it has a problem of sparsity in its learning step.

3   Generating a Vietnamese SentiWordNet

Vu and Park have proposed the process of generating a Vietnamese SentiWord-Net (VSWN) [15]. It consists of two steps as shown in Figure 1. The first step is

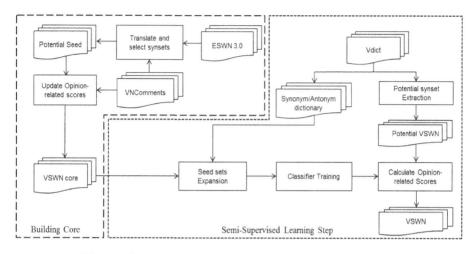

Fig. 1. The process of building a Vietnamese SentiWordNet

to build a VSWN core, and the second step is a semi-supervised learning to expand the VSWN core. Turney and Littman have found the subjectivity seed sets (TLSeeds) in a WordNet [14]. The TLSeeds play a role of sentiment core of Word-Net, since they contain positive and negative core synsets. However, there exists no lexical sentiment resource that is publicly available for Vietnamese. Thus, a translation method is used to build the VSWN core instead of TLSeeds. This VSWN core is expanded to a final VSWN through a semi-supervised learning step. In this step, the VSWN core is also used to generate a sentiment dataset for the semi-supervised learning step, and the dataset is used to expand the VSWN core.

The process of building a VSWN core can be explained in more detail with two sub-steps: (1) synset selection and translation using Google Translator and human annotators and (2) updating opinion-related scores. The first sub-step is to translate ESWN into Vietnamese. The quality of machine translator is, however, limited in general. Thus, several human annotators are employed to select well-translated synsets. Note that sentiment polarities of a word are different in different languages. Therefore, the second sub-step updates opinion-related scores of selected synsets so as to be closer to Vietnamese context. As a result, the VSWN core contains 1,017 synsets of 1,206 terms, where 1,093 terms are adjectives and the remaining 113 terms are verbs.

In the second step, a machine learning method is used to expand the VSWN core. This step is composed of four substeps: (1) seed set expansion, (2) classifier training, (3) potential synset extraction, and (4) calculation of opinion-related scores for each synset. The expansion of the VSWN core begins by preparing three sentiment seed sets for the machine learning method. All synsets in the core of which positive score is higher than 0.3 belong to a positive seed set. In the same way, all synsets of which negative score is higher than 0.3 become a negative seed set, and remaining synsets become a neutral seed set. Due the

Table 1. A simple statistic on the number of words used in the glosses of the Vietnamese dictionary

The number of words	Value
the longest gloss	69
the shortest gloss	3
average number of words per gloss	23
total words used in glosses	2,735

limited number of synsets, the synsets are added additionally by synonym and antonym relation in the Vietnamese dictionary at the substep (1). After this addition, the seeds are combined to create training data for training positivity and negativity classifiers in the substep (2). These classifiers are used to generate opinion-related scores in the substep (4).

It is well known that a synset in SentiWordNet is composed from six fields [7,15]. In this work, four of them are generated from Vietnamese dictionary to be a potential VSWN. The fields are *POS* (part-of-speech of the term), *ID* (synset identifier), *term* (a word representing a concept), and *gloss* (a definition about the term which comes along with sample sentences of the term). This is the substep (3). The result of this substep is a potential VSWN. This potential VSWN contains all information as a SentiWordNet except the opinion-related scores of synsets. Therefore, the substep (4) fills up the opinion-related scores for all synsets of the potential VSWN using the classifiers trained in the substep (2). The margin of the support vector machines is used as the scores in this work. After normalizing scores of a synset (i.e. positive and negative score) to be located within the interval [0,1], they are used as the final scores. Then, the resultant VSWN becomes our final VSWN.

The sparsity problem is observed during the training of the classifiers at the substep (2). In Vietnamese there is a number of compound words of which meaning is different from those of their base words. For example, the compound word *đánhbại* "*win*" is composed of two base words *đánh* "*fight*" and *bại* "*lose*". Even if the sentiment of base words *đánh* and *bại* are negative, that of *đánhbại* is positive. For this reason, the result of sentiment classification could be different according to the level of word model used. That is, the result of base-word level would be different from that of compound-word level. In addition, the glosses in the dictionary are in general a short text. Table 1 shows a statistics on the number of words used in the glosses. According to this table, a gloss uses just about 0.84% of vocabulary on average. That is, if the gloss is expressed as a word vector, it would be extremely sparse. The worse is that the problem still remains even after feature selection to decrease the vocabulary size. As a solution to this sparsity problem, we adopt the string kernel [11].

Table 2. The 2-character features of the words *xấu* *"ugly"*, *xinh* *"pretty"*, and *xịn* *"high quality"*

Word \ Features	x-i	x-n	x-h	i-n	i-h	n-h	x-ấ	x-u	ấ-u	x-ị	ị-n
ϕ(xinh "pretty")	λ^2	λ^3	λ^4	λ^2	λ^3	λ^2	0	0	0	0	0
ϕ(xấu "ugly")	0	0	0	0	0	0	λ^2	λ^3	λ^2	0	0
ϕ(xịn "high quality")	0	λ^3	0	0	0	0	0	0	0	λ^2	λ^2

4   Overcome of Sparsity Problem

4.1   String Subsequence Kernel

A standard bag-of-word (BoW) model [10] or bag-of-token (BoT) model (especially in Vietnamese) are commonly used for training a classifier in generating a SentiWordNet. However, they suffer from the sparsity problem. The string subsequence kernel (SSK) proposed by Lodhi et al. [11] is one solution to the sparsity. SSK is an inner product between two strings in the feature space generated by all subsequences of length k. The basic intuition of SSK is that if two strings share more substrings in common, they are more similar. The advantage of SSK is that the substrings need not contiguous. If the appearances of substrings are coherent, they receive a higher weight than appearances with larger gaps. This is done by penalizing the lengths of the gaps exponentially with a decay factor $\lambda \in (0,1)$. Let us consider Table 2 as an example. The similarity between xinh "pretty" and xịn "high quality" is K(xinh "pretty", xịn "high quality") $= \lambda^6$. On the other hand, that between xinh "pretty" and xấu "ugly" is K(xinh "pretty", xấu "ugly") $= 0$. Thus, xinh "pretty" is more similar to xịn "high quality" than to xấu "ugly".

The SSK is formalized as follows. A string s is any finite sequence of symbols from an alphabet $\sum$ including an empty sequence. The string $s = s_1, ...s_{|s|}$ has length $|s|$ and st is the concatenation of two strings s and t. The string $s[i : j]$ is the substring $s_i, ..., s_j$ of s. We say that u is subsequence of s if there exist indices $\mathbf{i} = (i_1, ..., i_{|u|})$ with $1 \leq i_1 < ... < i_{|u|} \leq |s|$, such that $u_j = s_{i_j}$ for $j = 1, ..., |u|$ or $u = s[\mathbf{i}]$ for short. $\sum^n$ is the set of all finite strings of length n, and the feature mapping ϕ for a string s is given by defining the u coordinate $\phi_u(s)$ for each $u \in \sum^n$. Then $\phi_u(s)$ becomes

$$\phi_u(s) = \sum_{\mathbf{i}:u=s[\mathbf{i}]} \lambda^{i_u - i_1 + 1},$$

and the string subsequence kernel for two string s and t can be computed as,

$$K_n(s,t) = \sum_{u \in \sum^n} \phi_u(s)\phi_u(t)$$

$$= \sum_{u \in \sum^n} \sum_{\mathbf{i}:u=s[\mathbf{i}]} \sum_{\mathbf{j}:u=t[\mathbf{j}]} \lambda^{i_{|u|} + j_{|u|} - i_1 - j_1 + 2}.$$

The direct computation of this kernel is highly expensive. Lodhi et al. [11] proposed a recursive computation of K_n that is computed in $O(kn|s||t|)$ time.

The problem of this kernel is that it is not normalized. That is,

$$K(\text{xinh, xinh}) \neq K(\text{xấu, xấu}).$$

Therefore, we use the normalized version of the string kernel given as

$$K'(s,t) = \frac{K(s,t)}{\sqrt{K(s,s) \cdot K(t,t)}}.$$

4.2   Training Classifiers with SSK for Expanding VSWN Core

Before training classifiers for determining synset sentiment, a feature selection is applied first to this task. There are two primary reasons for feature selection. First, it is known that there are always noisy features in managing texts. The feature selection can exclude noisy features which result in poor classification performance. Even short text such as a dictionary gloss suffers from noisy features. In a natural language sentence, there are some grammatical words. They exist to increase the readability of human readers, not for machines. Thus, they should be excluded in processing the contents of a text. In addition, most machine learning methods suffer from the curse-of-dimensionality [2]. Thus, the exclusion of some non-informative features helps the performance improvement of machine learning methods. As a result, feature selection is applied prior to training classifiers.

Second, feature selection has good effect in classification tasks, when the number of features is larger than that is actually needed for finding a good hyperplane. Since SSK maps a string into a high dimensional space, feature selection is effective with SSK. We compare four feature selection methods for constructing a Vietnamese SentiWordNet. The methods compared are document frequency threshold (DF), the χ^2 statistics (CHI), information gain (IG), and mutual information (MI).

5   Experiments

5.1   Experiments on Classification

Experimental Settings. In Figure 1, the VSWN core is expanded into a final VSWN. In this step, two support vector machines are used to determine the opinion-related score of synsets. Therefore, we show empirically that the uses of support vector machines with string kernel are appropriate for this task.

After the seed sets expansion step in the second phase, the total number of glosses extracted from a Vietnamese dictionary is 2,528. Among them, 847 are positive, 449 are neutral, and the remaining 1,232 glosses are negative. These glosses are divided into three sets: (i) a training set, (ii) a development set, and (iii) a test set. Their ratio in the number of glosses is 3:1:1. In preparing data

Table 3. Classification accuracy of SSK with different value of k for both BoW and BoT models on development data

# feature Method	100	200	300	400	500	600	700	800
BoW, k = 3	**0.637**	**0.636**	**0.672**	**0.663**	**0.652**	**0.678**	**0.656**	**0.668**
BoW, k = 5	0.463	0.484	0.521	0.535	0.533	0.527	0.539	0.518
BoT, k = 3	**0.636**	**0.641**	**0.672**	**0.672**	**0.668**	**0.665**	**0.677**	**0.674**
BoT, k = 5	0.475	0.478	0.529	0.531	0.526	0.51	0.522	0.528

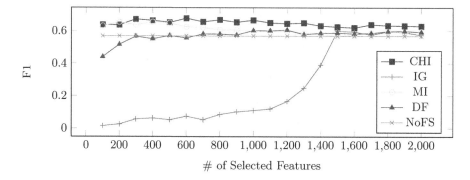

Fig. 2. The performance feature selection methods with SSK for BoW model

for BoT model, JvnTextPro tool from Nguyen et al. [12] is used for tokenizing the glosses. We perform 4-fold validation on training set and development set to select the feature selection method and the number of selected features.

SSK has two parameters of the length k and the decay factor λ. We perform with different values of λ within an interval $[0, 1]$. However, it does not have any effect in our experiments. Thus, we set λ as 0.5, the medium value. Table 3 shows that the classification performance changes according to the value of k. All the results in this table are obtained through 4-fold cross validation. That is, the results are reliable. According to this table, SSK with $k = 3$ gives always better results than that with $k = 5$ in both BoW and BoT models. Therefore, $k = 3$ is selected for further experiments below.

Experimental Results of Feature Selection. Figure 2 and 3 show the classification performance of feature selection methods. For all feature selection methods, the support vector machine with SSK is used as a classifier, but it is used with BoW model in Figure 2 and with BoT model in Figure 3. Since CHI shows the best performance in both figures, its effect in the linear kernel (LK) is also verified. Figure 4 depicts the performances of LK. In this figure, it is observed that CHI is not helpful in LK. LK with CHI achieves worse performance than LK without CHI for most cases.

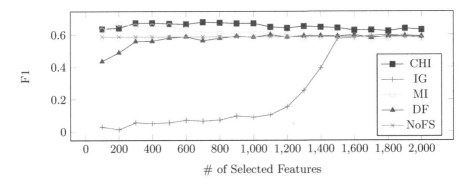

Fig. 3. The performance feature selection methods with SSK for BoT model

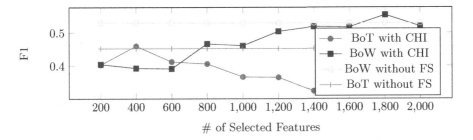

Fig. 4. The performance of linear kernel (LK)

The summary of feature selection is as follows.

1. The combination of SSK and CHI achieves always the best performance for both BoW and BoT models.
2. According to Yang and Pedersen [16], DF, IG, and CHI are strongly correlated. However, this is not true in our experiments, and IG is always worst until 1,500 features.
3. The feature selection for the linear kernel is not helpful, while it is useful with string kernel.
4. The string kernel achieves the best performance with 600 features in BoW model, while it achieves the best performance with 700 features in BoT model.

Evaluation of Classifiers. Table 4 and 5 show the classification performances of support vector machines in BoW and BoT models respectively. From these tables, four conclusions can be drawn.

1. The combination of feature selection and LK does not help improve the classification. This is mainly due to the sparsity problem. Evidently, F1-scores of with top 1800 features in BoW and top 400 features in BoT are less than LK without feature selection. The F1-scores are 7.2% and 7.5% lower than those without feature selection respectively.

Table 4. Performance comparison between SSK and LK in BoW model

Method	Feature Selection	Precision	Recall	F1
LK-BoW	χ^2 1800	0.534	0.425	0.473
	None	0.5	0.599	0.545
SSK-BoW	χ^2 600	0.650	0.614	**0.632**
	None	0.725	0.468	0.569

Table 5. Performance comparison between SSK and LK in BoT model

Method	Feature Selection	Precision	Recall	F1
LK-BoT	χ^2 400	0.589	0.377	0.460
	None	0.520	0.551	0.535
SSK-BoT	χ^2 700	0.604	0.608	**0.606**
	None	0.740	0.486	0.587

2. SSK outperforms LK in our task. Without feature selection, SSK achieves 2.4% and 5.2% higher performance than LK in BoW and BoT model respectively.
3. The combination of SSK and CHI achieves better performance than SSK without CHI. With CHI, the performance of SSK is improved by 1.9% and 6.2% in BoT and BoW model respectively.
4. Due to the sparsity problem, BoW model is very similar to BoT model if any feature selection is not applied to them. This results proves that the use of SSK is important in our task.

5.2   Resultant VSWN

As illustrated from beginning, available lexical resources for Vietnamese are limited except Vdict which is useful to generate VSWN. Vdict is a well form constructed dictionary by using XML language. It consists of 39,561 terms in which each term has essential information about morphology, syntactic, and semantic that are sufficient for deriving synset information. A detailed description about Vdict is reported in [15]. We previously used Vdict to generate a VSWN [15], however it was suffered from the sparsity problem. Thus, our main purpose in this work is to overcome the problem by introducing the string kernel. Our experiments shows that the string kernel can improve our resultant VSWN effectively. Eventually, VSWN in this work consists of 38,578 synsets. This number of synsets is less than that of our previous work [15]. It is because of a number of synset that are removed automatically by the feature selection process. They are too sparse to perform the classification step. Obviously this method is applicable only when we found the advantages of the string kernel. It effectively solves the sparsity problem that occurs in computing the sentiment scores of new synsets.

Table 6. τ_p values for the positivity and negativity orderings of the proposed VSWN, the previous VSWN, and ESWN 3.0

	Positivity	Negativity
ESWN 3.0	0.281	0.231
VSWN [15]	0.297 (+1.6%)	0.283 (+5.2%)
The proposed VSWN	**0.274 (-2.3%)**	**0.257 (-2.6%)**

5.3   Evaluation of VSWN

In order to see the appropriateness of the resultant VSWN, a gold standard of sysset ordering is prepared manually. That is, the gold standard enumerates the synsets in the VSWN by their sentiment strength. Thus, if the resultant VSWN is perfect, the synset ordering would be the same with that of the gold standard. As a measure of the appropriateness of the resultant VSWN, Kenddall tau (τ_p) distance is employed. The τ_p distance between two orderings is defined as the number of pairwise disagreement between the two orderings [1]. Therefore, the lower value indicates a better performance.

Table 6 reports the τ_p values for the positivity and negativity orderings of SentiWordNets. It compares our VSWN with the first version of VSWN [15] and ESWN. The main difference between our VSWN and the previous VSWN is that our VSWN overcomes the sparsity problem. According to the table, our VSWN is much better than the previous VSWN for both positivity and negativity orderings. Evidently, our work has better performance of 2.3% for positivity and 2.6% for negativity compared with those of our previous work [15]. In addition, it is better than ESWN 0.7% in positivity ordering. The negative numbers (i.e -2.3% and -2.6%) in the table 6 represent for the improvment of our VSWN compared with the previous VSWN. Therefore, our SentiWordNet for minor language without much lexical resources is competitive to English SentiWordNet originated from WordNet.

6   Conclusion

In this paper, we have presented an approach to generate SentiWordNet for minor languages. Vietnamese like other minor languages suffers from non-existence of lexical resources. Therefore, we have proposed a method to build a Vietnamese SentiWordNet (VSWN) without Vietnamese WordNet. The method first builds the VSWN core by translating English SentiWordNet and updating sentiment scores of synsets. Then, it expands the VSWN core to the resultant VSWN by adding new synsets from Vietnamese dictionary.

The major problem of building VSWN is a sparsity problem since the gloss of the synset in Vdict is short in general. To solve this problem, we adopt the string kernel and the feature selection method to support vector machines. In our experiments, the combination of feature selection and string kernel is appropriate to determine sentiment strength.

Compared to other SentiWordNets, the number of sysnsets in our VSWN is small because of the limitation of the Vietnamese dictionary. In the future, we will extend our VSWN using massive data of user comments available on the Internet.

Acknowledgments. This work was supported by ICT R&D program of MSIP/IITP. [10044494, WiseKB: Big data based self-evolving knowledge base and reasoning platform]

References

1. Baccianella, S., Esuli, A., Sebastiani, F.: SentiWordNet 3.0: An enhanced lexical resource for sentiment analysis and opinion mining. In: Proceedings of the 7th Conference on International Language Resources and Evaluation, pp. 2200–2204 (2010)
2. Bellman, R.E.: Adaptive Control Processes: A Guided Tour. Princeton University Press (1961)
3. Das, A., Bandyopadhyay, S.: SentiWordNet for indian languages. In: Proceedings of the 8th Workshop on Asian Language Resources, pp. 56–63 (2010)
4. Das, A., Bandyopadhyay, S.: Towards the global SentiWordNet. In: Proceedings of the 24th Pacific Asia Conference on Language, Information and Computation, pp. 799–808 (2010)
5. Esuli, A.: Automatic Generation of Lexcial Resources for Opinion Mining: Models, Algorithms, and Application. PhD thesis, University of Pisa (2008)
6. Esuli, A., Sebastiani, F.: Recognizing contextual polarity in phrase-level sentiment analysis. In: Proceedings of Human Language Technology Conference and Conference on Empirical Methods in Natural Language Processing, pp. 347–354 (2005)
7. Esuli, A., Sebastiani, F.: SentiWordNet: A publicly available lexical resource for opinion mining. In: Proceedings of the 3rd Conference on International Language Resources and Evaluation, pp. 417–422 (2006)
8. Esuli, A., Sebastiani, F.: SentiWordNet: A high-coverage lexical resource for opinion mining. Technical Report 2007-TR-02, Istitutiodi Scienza e Technologie dell'Informazione, University of Pisa (2007)
9. Fagin, R., Kumar, R., Mahdian, M., Sivakumar, D., Vee, E.: Comparing and aggregating rankings with ties. In: Proceedings of ACM International Conference on Principles of Database Systems, pp. 47–58 (2004)
10. Gusfield, D.: Algorithms on Strings, Trees and Sequences: Computer Science and Computational Biology. Cambridge University Press (1997)
11. Lodhi, H., Saunders, C., Shawe-Taylor, J., Cristianini, N., Watkins, C.: Text classification using string kernels. Journal of Machine Learning Research 2, 419–444 (2002)
12. Nguyen, C.-T., Phan, X.-H., Nguyen, T.-T.: JVnTextPro: A java-based vietnamese text processing tool (2010), http://jvntextpro.sourceforge.net/
13. Pang, B., Lee, L.: Opinion mining and sentiment analysis. Foundations and Trends in Information Retrieval 2(1-2), 1–135 (2008)
14. Turney, P.D., Littman, M.L.: Measuring praise and criticism: Inference of semantic orientation from association. ACM Transaction on Information Systems 21(4), 315–346 (2003)

15. Vu, X.-S., Park, S.-B.: Construction of vietnamese SentiWordNet by using viet-namese dictionary. In: Proceedings of the 40th Conference of the Korea Information Processing Society, pp. 745–748 (2014)
16. Yang, Y., Pedersen, J.O.: A comparative study on feature selection in text catego-rization. In: Proceedings of the 14th International Conference on Machine Learning, pp. 412–420 (1997)

Estimating Network Structure
from Anonymous Ego-centric Information

Takayasu Fushimi[1], Kazumi Saito[1], and Kazuhiro Kazama[2]

[1] Graduate School of Management and Information of Innovation,
University of Shizuoka
52-1 Yada, Suruga-ku, Shizuoka 422-8526, Japan
takayasu.fushimi@gmail.com, k-saito@u-shizuoka-ken.ac.jp
[2] Faculty of Systems Engineering, Wakayama University
Sakaedani 930, Wakayama-city, Wakayama 640-8510, Japan
kazama@ingrid.org

Abstract. We address a problem of estimating the whole structure of
an actual social network of people from only their two types of anonymous ego-centric information, personal attributes like sex and relational
ones like the numbers of female and male friends, obtained as answers to
questionnaires in a social survey. From these attribute values, we can obtain the degree of each node, which corresponds to the number of friends
of each person, together with some macroscopic information about the
network, like the ratio of links between female and male nodes to the
total number of links, as the mixing matrices. However, we cannot directly know the actual connections between two nodes only from these
observed mixing matrices. Thus, we propose a new method for estimating
the whole structure of the hidden network by minimizing the Kullback-
Leibler divergence between each pair of the observed and estimated mixing matrices, under the constraints with respect to the degree of each
node. In our experiments using three types of networks, we show that the
proposed method can produce much better estimation results, in comparison to a random baseline which is assigned arbitrary links under the
degree constraints, especially for the cases of highly assortative, where
each node has a tendency to connect to nodes with the same attribute
values.

1   Introduction

In recent years, there have been many studies on complex networks which analyze their essential structures and/or phenomena happened over them (Leskovec
et al. 2007; Wu et al. 2008). It has been widely known that many complex
networks have common characteristics such as a small-world nature (Watts et
al. 1998) and a scale-free nature, and many social networks have an assorta-
tive/homophily nature (Newman et al. 2003) which means a tendency that lots
of linked pairs of nodes are likely to have same or similar properties. Furthermore, in order to investigate real world phenomena such as information diffusion
and opinion formation over social networks, the Independent Cascade model, the

Y.S. Kim et al (Eds.): PKAW 2014, LNCS 8863, pp. 236–245, 2014.
© Springer International Publishing Switzerland 2014

Linear Threshold model (Kempe et al. 2003; Saito et al. 2009), and the voter model (Even-Dar et al. 2007) have been studied, under an implicit assumption that the whole structure of a target network is already given. In real world problems, however, it is not always easy to obtain a whole network structure because of the privacy issue, even for on-line social networks mainly due to a rate limitation of accessing data resources. In such cases, we can obtain partial information about the target network. By collecting some statistical or macroscopic information about a network, we need to estimate the whole structure as accurately as possible. Even for an estimated network, we can know some important nodes such as influential ones (Kimura et al. 2010) with a reasonable accuracy by using the above-mentioned models for information diffusion or opinion formation, if the precision of the estimated network is sufficient high.

In this paper, basically supposing that a social survey provides the source ego-centric information, we propose a method of estimating the whole structure from only anonymous ego-centric information. The ego-centric information consists of two types of information, personal attributes like sex and relational ones like the numbers of female and male friends. By collecting and aggregating these pieces of information, we can obtain some macroscopic information like the ratio of links between female and male nodes to the total number of links, as the mixing matrices. However, we cannot directly know the actual connections between two nodes only from these observed mixing matrices. Thus, we propose a new method for estimating the whole structure of the hidden network by minimizing the Kullback-Leibler divergence between each pair of the observed and estimated mixing matrices.

As existing studies on estimating network structure or predicting missing links, a variety of techniques have been proposed such as topological scores (Nowell et al. 2003), feature-based classification (Oyama et al. 2004), kernel-based methods (Kato et al. 2005), hierarchical property (Clauset et al. 2008), and matrix factorization (Menon et al. 2011). These methods attempt to learn link tendencies from observed linked pairs and predict the link existence or non-existence for the remaining node pairs. On the other hand, our method attempts to estimate all links from only ego-centric information, therefore these existing methods and our method differ in the problem settings.

In our experiments, in order to evaluate the precision of the estimated network obtained by our proposed method we utilize three networks each of whose link structure is completely known. For these networks, we assign artificial attributes to all the nodes, where the associated values of some attributes are determined by using the voter model, so that we can quantitatively evaluate the relation between assortativity of networks and estimation precisions.

This paper is organized as follows: after formalizing our problem framework in Section 2, we describe a detail of our proposed method in Section 3. Then, by using three networks, we compare the estimation precisions and representative network statistics with those of a random baseline in Section 4. Finally, we describe our conclusion in Section 5.

2   Problem Framework

Formally, we regard the N answerers of a social survey as nodes and define the node set as V. Let K be the number of categorical attributes we focus on. Let $S^{(k)}$ be the number of categories of the k-th attribute, and we assign each categorical attribute value to an integer ranging from 1 to $S^{(k)}$, i.e., $\{1, \ldots, S^{(k)}\}$. For each node u, we consider the K-dimensional attribute vector $\mathbf{f}_u = (f_u^{(1)}, \ldots, f_u^{(K)})$ whose k-th element is $f_u^{(k)} \in \{1, \ldots, S^{(k)}\}$.

Now, for each pair of node u and attribute k, we also consider the $S^{(k)}$-dimensional vector $\mathbf{g}_u^{(k)}$ whose t-th element $g_u^{(k)}(t)$ corresponds to the number of u's friends with the categorical value t for this attribute, where note that $t \in \{1, \ldots, S^{(k)}\}$ and $d_u = \sum_{t=1}^{S^{(k)}} g_u^{(k)}(t)$. Then, for the k-th attribute, we can define the following mixing matrix element $m_{s,t}^{(k)}$ with respect to a pair of categorical values s and t:

$$m_{s,t}^{(k)} = \frac{1}{L} \sum_{\{u:f_u^{(k)}=s\}} g_u^{(k)}(t) \qquad k = 1, \ldots, K$$

where L stands for the total number of links, i.e., $L \sum_{u \in V} d_u$. Thus, we can obtain the observed mixing matrix $\mathbf{M}^{(k)} = [m_{s,t}^{(k)}]$ for each attribute k. From each mixing matrix, we can calculate the assortative coefficient according to the Newman's method (Newman 2003), so that we can discriminate whether a certain attribute is assortative or not.

In order to derive our objective function, we construct an $N \times S^{(k)}$ projection matrix for the k-th attribute as follows:

$$\mathbf{W}^{(k)} = [w_{u,s}^{(k)}] = \begin{cases} 1 & \text{if} \quad f_u^{(k)} = s \\ 0 & \text{otherwise} \end{cases}$$

Now, we suppose that an adjacency matrix $\mathbf{A} = [a_{u,v}]$ is given where $a_{u,v}$ means the (u,v)-th element, i.e., $a_{u,v} \in \{0,1\}$. Then, for a given projection matrix $\mathbf{W}^{(k)}$ of the k-th attribute, we can calculate an $S^{(k)} \times S^{(k)}$ estimated mixing matrix from an adjacency matrix $\mathbf{A}$, denoted by $\hat{\mathbf{M}}^{(k)}(\mathbf{A}) = [\hat{m}_{s,t}^{(k)}(\mathbf{A})]$, as follows:

$$\hat{m}_{s,t}^{(k)}(\mathbf{A}) = \frac{1}{L} \sum_{u \in V} \sum_{v \in V \setminus \{u\}} a_{u,v} w_{u,s}^{(k)} w_{v,t}^{(k)}.$$

Then we can define the optimal adjacency matrix $\hat{\mathbf{A}}$ which minimizes the KL divergences between the observed and estimated mixing matrices, $\mathbf{M}^{(k)}$ and $\hat{\mathbf{M}}^{(k)}(\mathbf{A})$, as follows:

$$\hat{\mathbf{A}} = \arg \min_{\mathbf{A}} \left\{ \sum_{k=1}^{K} \mathrm{KL}\left(\mathbf{M}^{(k)} || \hat{\mathbf{M}}^{(k)}(\mathbf{A})\right) \right\}$$

under the condition that $\sum_{v \in V \setminus \{u\}} a_{u,v} = d_u$ for each node $u \in V$. Note that $\mathrm{KL}(P||Q)$ means the KL divergence between probabilistic distributions P and

Q. The calculation of the optimal adjacency matrix $\hat{\mathbf{A}}$ can be transformed as follows:

$$\hat{\mathbf{A}} = \arg\min_{\mathbf{A}} \left\{ \sum_{k=1}^{K} \sum_{s=1}^{S^{(k)}} \sum_{t=1}^{S^{(k)}} m_{s,t}^{(k)} \log \frac{m_{s,t}^{(k)}}{\hat{m}_{s,t}^{(k)}(\mathbf{A})} \right\}$$

$$= \arg\max_{\mathbf{A}} \left\{ \sum_{k=1}^{K} \sum_{s=1}^{S^{(k)}} \sum_{t=1}^{S^{(k)}} m_{s,t}^{(k)} \log \hat{m}_{s,t}^{(k)}(\mathbf{A}) \right\}$$

$$= \arg\max_{\mathbf{A}} \left\{ \sum_{k=1}^{K} \sum_{s=1}^{S^{(k)}} \sum_{t=1}^{S^{(k)}} m_{s,t}^{(k)} \log \sum_{u \in V} \sum_{v \in V \setminus \{u\}} a_{u,v} w_{u,s}^{(k)} w_{v,t}^{(k)} \right\}$$

Therefore, we can solve our problem by finding the optimal $\mathbf{A}$ which maximizes the following objective function:

$$J(\mathbf{A}) = \sum_{k=1}^{K} \sum_{s=1}^{S^{(k)}} \sum_{t=1}^{S^{(k)}} m_{s,t}^{(k)} \log \sum_{u \in V} \sum_{v \in V \setminus \{u\}} a_{u,v} w_{u,s}^{(k)} w_{v,t}^{(k)}, \tag{1}$$

under the condition that $\sum_{v \in V \setminus \{u\}} a_{u,v} = d_u$ for each node $u \in V$.

3   Solution Algorithm

In order to maximize the objective function Eq.(1), we employ the EM algorithm by defining the following posterior probability on the link between nodes u and v.

$$\bar{q}_{s,t,u,v}^{(k)} = \frac{\bar{a}_{u,v} w_{u,s}^{(k)} w_{v,t}^{(k)}}{\sum_{x \in V} \sum_{y \in V} \bar{a}_{x,y} w_{x,s}^{(k)} w_{y,t}^{(k)}}$$

where $\bar{a}_{u,v}$ means the current value of (u, v)-th element of the adjacency matrix. Then, we define the expectation value of log-likelihood of complete data on posterior probability referred to as Q function as follows:

$$Q(\mathbf{A}|\bar{\mathbf{A}}) = \sum_{k=1}^{K} \sum_{s=1}^{S^{(k)}} \sum_{t=1}^{S^{(k)}} m_{s,t}^{(k)} \sum_{u \in V} \sum_{v \in V \setminus \{u\}} \bar{q}_{s,t,u,v}^{(k)} \log a_{u,v}.$$

In our problem framework, due to the degree constraints, we add the following Lagrange multiplier terms.

$$\tilde{Q}(\mathbf{A}|\bar{\mathbf{A}}) = Q(\mathbf{A}|\bar{\mathbf{A}}) + \sum_{u \in V} \lambda_u \left(d_u - \sum_{v \in V \setminus \{u\}} a_{u,v} \right)$$

where λ_u means the Lagrange multiplier on node u.

Although the actual value of each adjacency matrix element is $a_{u,v} \in \{0, 1\}$, we relax our problem by allowing each value to be a real number $a_{u,v} \in [0, 1]$. and we refer to this matrix as a relaxed adjacency matrix.

The proposed method estimates the $\tilde{Q}$ function as the E step of the EM algorithm, and maximizes the $\tilde{Q}$ function by updating the relaxed adjacency matrix as the M step as follows:

$$
a_{u,v} = \frac{d_u \sum_{k=1}^{K} \sum_{s=1}^{S^{(k)}} \sum_{t=1}^{S^{(k)}} m_{s,t}^{(k)} \bar{q}_{s,t,u,v}^{(k)}}{\sum_{k=1}^{K} \sum_{s=1}^{S^{(k)}} \sum_{t=1}^{S^{(k)}} m_{s,t}^{(k)} \sum_{v \in V \setminus \{u\}} \bar{q}_{s,t,u,v}^{(k)}}.
$$

The proposed method repeats the E and M steps until convergence. Furthermore, since this relaxation problem is a convex optimization problem over a convex set, it is guaranteed that we can always obtain the unique global optimal solution from any initialized values. Let $\mathbf{A}_t$ be the relaxed adjacency matrix at t-th iteration of our algorithm. For a small value ε, we define the convergence criterion as $|(J(\mathbf{A}_t) - J(\mathbf{A}_{t-1}))/J(\mathbf{A}_{t-1})| < \varepsilon$. Finally, our proposed method selects the largest top-d_u values from $\{\hat{a}_{u,v} : v \in V\}$ for each u. and constructs an estimated link set $\hat{E}$. Then, the method outputs the estimated link set $\hat{E}$.

Consequently given the node set V and K categorical attributes, we propose a method to estimate all the links between actual nodes of their hidden social network by the following steps:

STEP1 For each node u, extract K categorical attribute values and then construct K-dimensional attribute vector $\mathbf{f}_u$. For each user u, extract the number of friends d_u and its breakdown by values of attribute k, and then construct observed mixing matrix $\mathbf{M}^{(k)}$;

STEP2 Estimate a relaxed adjacency matrix $\hat{\mathbf{A}} = [\hat{a}_{u,v}]$ by minimizing the KL divergence between each pair of the observed and estimated mixing matrices, and select the largest top-d_u values from $\{\hat{a}_{u,v} : v \in V\}$ for each u, then outputs an estimated link set $\hat{E}$;

4   Experimental Evaluation

Our goal is estimating the whole structure using only ego-centric information obtained from a social survey. However, in this paper, in order to quantitatively evaluate the precision of estimated network obtained by our proposed method, we utilize three networks each of whose link structure is completely known. Furthermore, it is naturally considered that the estimation precision depends on the numbers of attributes and categories, and the levels of assortative coefficients. Then, we evaluate the relations between estimation precisions and these conditions of utilizing attributes. Therefore, at the STEP1 of our method, as substitute for extracting K attributes from a social survey, we assign K artificial attributes by the method described in the subsection 4.2.

4.1   Network Data

We describe a detail of three networks used in our experiments.

First one is a synthetic network with a hierarchical property, just like employee relationships. In this network, we can assume two types of nodes, central and peripheral nodes. The central nodes are characterized by relatively high degree and low clustering coefficients, while the peripheral nodes by relatively low degree and high clustering coefficients. We generated this network according to Ravasz et al. (Ravasz et al. 2003). This network has 125 nodes and 410 links. Hereafter, this network is referred to as Hierarchical network.

Second one is a hyperlink network of a Japanese university Web site, where we obtained this network by crawling the Web site as of August 2010. This network has 600 nodes and 1,299 links. Hereafter, this network is referred to as Web network [2].

Last one is a co-author network of the international conference NIPS (Neural Information Processing Systems). We define an author as a node and add a link between two nodes who have at least one joint paper. There exist some researcher communities of similar research topics. This network has 1,036 nodes and 2,044 links. Hereafter, this network is referred to as Nips network.

4.2   Artificial Attributes

We describe the method for assigning attribute values to each node via the voter model. The voter model is one of the most basic stochastic process models, which simulates opinion formation processes over networks. Let $h_t(u)$ be the opinion value of node u at time t and $\Gamma(u)$ be the set of parent/adjacent nodes of u. For a given a network $G = (V, E)$, we assign categorical values of an attribute k for each node as follows:

VM1 Initialize $t \leftarrow 1$ and assign the initial opinion value as $h_0(u) \leftarrow s$ by selecting an atrribute value $s \in \{1, \ldots, S^{(k)}\}$ uniformly at random for each node $u \in V$;

VM2 Update the opinion value as $h_t(u) \leftarrow h_{t-1}(v)$ by selecting a parent node $v \in \Gamma(u)$ uniformly at random for each node $u \in V$;

VM3 Terminate if the assortative coefficient $r > 0.8$, otherwise update $t \leftarrow t+1$ and go back to VM2;

In our experiments, this algorithm terminated within 10 iterations for all the trials.

4.3   Experimental Settings

In order to evaluate how assortativity of attributes on a network affects to the performance of our proposed method, we prepare two types of sets of K attributes, assortative ones and non-assortative ones. By repeating the trials of

---

[2] The site name and its address are "Faculty of Computer and Information Sciences, Hosei University" and http://cis.k.hosei.ac.jp/, respectively.

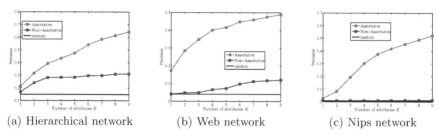

(a) Hierarchical network   (b) Web network   (c) Nips network

Fig. 1. Precision with respect to the number of attributes

the voter model, we obtain the assortative attribute for each pair of node u and attribute k, $f_u^{(k)} \leftarrow h_T(u)$, where T means the final step of our voter model process. On the other hand, by simply assigning an initial random attribute value, we obtain the non-assortative attribute for each pair of node u and attribute k, $f_u^{(k)} \leftarrow h_0(u)$. Hereafter, for a convenience, our proposed method is reffered to as the assortative method in the case that a series of assortative attributes are available, while it is reffered to as the non-assortative method in the case that only a series of non-assortative attributes are available.

We set each initial value of the relaxed adjacency matrix element to $a_{u,v} = d_u/N$, and the convergence criterion of our algorithm is specified by $\varepsilon = 10^{-4}$. Then, we estimate the whole structure of each network by our proposed method using a set of attributes, and evaluate the performance as the average precision of 10 estimation results obtained by 10 sets of attributes generated independently.

4.4   Estimation Precisions with Respect to the Number of Attributes

In order to evaluate our proposed method, we employ a precision measure which has been widely used in the information retrieval field. More specifically, we define the sets of the true and estimated links as E and $\hat{E}$, respectively, and calculate the precision of $\hat{E}$ to E as $F(E, \hat{E}) = |E \cap \hat{E}|/|E|$.

Fig. 1 shows the precisions of the assortative and non-assortative methods with respect to the number of attributes K ranging from 1 to 9, where the number of categories $S^{(k)}$ is set to 5 for each attribute. In these figures, we plot the estimation precisions obtained by the assortative method, the non-assortative method and random baseline. with a line with filled circles, a line with filled squares, and a simple line, respectively. Here, the random baseline is the performance obtained by arbitrary assigning links under the degree constraints.

From Fig. 1, we can observe the following characteristics. First, as expected, for each network, the performance of the assortative method streadly improved when the number of attributes increases in comparison to the random baseline. This fact suggests that the proposed method generally works well by using an enough number of attributes with high levels of assortataive coefficients. Here we should emphasize that a person has a tendency to connect to people with

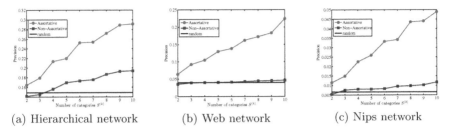

(a) Hierarchical network   (b) Web network   (c) Nips network

Fig. 2. Precision with respect to the number of categories

the same attribute value in general. Second, unlike the assortative method, the performance of the non-assortative method did not improve sufficiently even for a case of large number of attributes. Especially, the performance improvement was almost nothing for the Nips network with the largest size. This fact indicates that our proposed method works well only for networks with a relatively small size in case that only a series of non-assirtative attributes are available.

4.5 Estimation Precisions with Respect to the Number of Categories

We evaluate relations between precisions and the number of categories of attributes used in estimation. Fig. 2 shows the precisions of the assortative and non-assortative methods with respect to the number of categories $S^{(k)}$ ranging from 2 to 10 and the number of attributes K is set to 1 for each result of estimation.

From Fig. 2, we can observe the following characteristics. First, similar to the previous experimental results as shown in Fig. 1, for each network, the performance of the assortative method streadly improved in comparison to the random baseline, when the number of categories increases. This fact also suggests that the proposed method generally works well by using even only one assortative attribute if it has large numbers of specific categories. Second, unlike the assortative method, the performance of the non-assortative method did not improve sufficiently even for a case of large number of categories, except for the small scale Hierarchical network. This fact also indicates that our proposed method works well only for networks with a relatively small size in case that only one non-assirtative attribute is available. Therefore, when combining our results observed in Fig. 1 and 2, by preparing an enough number of assortative attributes, each of which has a relatively large number of specified categories, we can expect that our proposed method is promising to estimating the whole structure of networks from only anonymous ego-centric information.

4.6 Estimation Performances in Terms of Network Statistics

We evaluate the structure of the obtained networks in terms of network statistics. To this end, we focus on the average clustering coefficient $\bar{C}$, the standard

Table 1. Statistics of true, proposed and random networks

(a) Hierarchical network	$\bar{C}$	$C_{\text{S.D.}}$	$\bar{D}$	(b) Web network	$\bar{C}$	$C_{\text{S.D.}}$	$\bar{D}$	(c) Nips network	$\bar{C}$	$C_{\text{S.D.}}$	$\bar{D}$
true	0.837	0.164	2.128	true	0.540	0.413	4.219	true	0.582	0.427	6.213
proposed	0.623	0.211	2.826	proposed	0.340	0.390	14.433	proposed	0.420	0.394	15.923
random	0.063	0.087	2.499	random	0.004	0.031	4.650	random	0.001	0.013	5.060

deviation of the clustering coefficient of each node $C_{S.D.}$, and the average short-est path length $\bar{D}$ as the representative network statistics. Note that the average of shortest path length is calculated by harmonic average to cope with discon-nected networks. In this experiment, we used 9 assortative attributes each of which consists of 5 categories ($K = 9$, $S^{(k)} = 5$).

Table 1 compares the statistics of the true networks, the estimated networks by the assortative method, and random ones. From Table 1, we can see the following similar characteristic. First, the average values of clustering coefficient $\bar{C}$ of the estimated networks by the assortative method are significantly close to those of the true networks, in comparison to those of random networks. We can also see that the standard deviations of clustering coefficients $C_{S.D.}$ of the estimated networks are also reasonably close to true ones. Existing assortative attributes means that the neighborhood nodes in the network are also likely to have same attribute values. Thus, our method can estimate the local relationships and deviation of clustering coefficients more accurately.

Moreover, in case of the relatively small networks like the Hierarchical net-work, we observe that the average shortest path length $\bar{D}$ of the estimated net-work is also close to that of the true network. In contrast, in each case of the relatively large networks such as the Nips and Web networks, we observe that the average shortest path length of the estimated network is not close to that of the true network. This is because our proposed method occasionally produced disconnected network in the case of large scale netowrks. On the other hand, the random network shows the small shortest path length because of random links like small-world model (Watts et al. 1998). From these results, we conjecture that our proposed method can estimate more accurately the local structure like communities.

5   Conclusion

We addressed the problem of estimating the whole structure of a network. In this paper, we proposed a method of estimating the whole structure from only anonymous ego-centric information by minimizing the Kullback-Leibler diver-gence between each pair of the observed and estimated mixing matrices.

In our experiments using several types of synthetic and real networks, we evaluated the estimation precisions with respect to the numbers of attributes and categories and assortativity of attributes. From our experimental results, our proposed method generally works well by using an enough number of attributes with high levels of assortataive coefficients, and the method can estimate more accurately the local structure like communities.

In future, we plan to evaluate the performance of our proposed method by using several types of attributes such as non-assortative but non-random ones, numerical ones like age, and so forth.

Acknowledgments. This work was partly supported by Asian Office of Aerospace Research and Development, Air Force Office of Scientific Research under Grant No. AOARD-13-4042, and JSPS Grant-in-Aid for Scientific Research(No. 25.10411).

References

Clauset, A., Moore, C., Newman, M.E.J.: Hierarchical structure and the prediction of missing links in networks. Nature 453, 98–101 (2008)

Even-Dar, E., Shapira, A.: A note on maximizing the spread of influence in social networks. In: Deng, X., Graham, F.C. (eds.) WINE 2007. LNCS, vol. 4858, pp. 281–286. Springer, Heidelberg (2007)

Kato, T., Tsuda, K., Asai, K.: Selective integration of multiple biological data for supervised network inference. Bioinformatics 21(10), 2488–2495 (2005)

Kempe, D., Kleinberg, J., Tardos, E.: Maximizing the spread of influence through a social network. In: Proceedings of the Ninth ACM SIGKDD International Conference on Knowledge Discovery and Data Mining, KDD 2003, pp. 137–146. ACM, New York (2003)

Kimura, M., Saito, K., Nakano, R., Motoda, H.: Extracting influential nodes on a social network for information diffusion. Data Min. Knowl. Discov. 20(1), 70–97 (2010)

Leskovec, J., Adamic, L.A., Huberman, B.A.: The dynamics of viral marketing. ACM Trans. Web 1(1), 5 (2007)

Menon, A.K., Elkan, C.: Link prediction via matrix factorization. In: Gunopulos, D., Hofmann, T., Malerba, D., Vazirgiannis, M. (eds.) ECML PKDD 2011, Part II. LNCS (LNAI), vol. 6912, pp. 437–452. Springer, Heidelberg (2011)

Newman, M.E.J.: Mixing patterns in networks. Physical Review E 67(2), 026126+ (2003)

Nowell, D.L., Kleinberg, J.: The link prediction problem for social networks. In: CIKM 2003: Proceedings of the Twelfth International Conference on Information and Knowledge Management, pp. 556–559. ACM, New York (2003)

Oyama, S., Manning, C.D.: Using feature Conjunctions across examples for learning pairwise classifiers. In: Boulicaut, J.-F., Esposito, F., Giannotti, F., Pedreschi, D. (eds.) ECML 2004. LNCS (LNAI), vol. 3201, pp. 322–333. Springer, Heidelberg (2004)

Ravasz, E., Barabási, A.L.: Hierarchical organization in complex networks. Physical Review E 67(2), 026112+ (2003)

Saito, K., Kimura, M., Ohara, K., Motoda, H.: Learning continuous-time information diffusion model for social behavioral data analysis. In: Zhou, Z.-H., Washio, T. (eds.) ACML 2009. LNCS (LNAI), vol. 5828, pp. 322–337. Springer, Heidelberg (2009)

Watts, D.J., Strogatz, S.H.: Collective dynamics of 'small-world' networks. Nature 393(6684), 440–442 (1998)

Wu, F., Huberman, B.A.: How public opinion forms. In: Papadimitriou, C., Zhang, S. (eds.) WINE 2008. LNCS, vol. 5385, pp. 334–341. Springer, Heidelberg (2008)

Evolution Strategies with an RBM-Based Meta-Model

Kirill Makukhin

The University of Queensland, Brisbane, Australia
mailto:k.makukhin@webage.net.au

Abstract. Evolution strategies have been demonstrated to offer a state-of-the-art performance on different optimisation problems. The efficiency of the algorithm largely depends on its ability to build an adequate meta-model of the function being optimised. This paper proposes a novel algorithm RBM-ES that utilises a computationally efficient restricted Boltzmann machine for maintaining the meta-model. We demonstrate that our algorithm is able to adapt its model to complex multidimensional landscapes. Furthermore, we compare the proposed algorithm to state-of the art algorithms such as CMA-ES on different tasks and demonstrate that the RBM-ES can achieve good performance.

Keywords: evolution strategies, restricted Boltzmann machine, meta-model, surrogate model, estimation of distribution algorithm.

1 Introduction

Evolution Strategies (ES) are a sub-set of genetic algorithms that use only mutation operator for generating offspring. The ES have been demonstrated to offer a state-of-the-art performance on different optimisation problems with discontinuous, non-differential, noisy and multimodal environments, often outperforming gradient-based techniques (e.g. [1]).

In general, a well acceptable solution to a problem can be found by an ES algorithm after a large number of fitness evaluations. However, such evaluations in many real-world applications are not trivial and/or resource-wise expensive. Various approaches has been proposed to reduce this cost by exploiting the history of previously evaluated exemplars. One of successive approaches is focused on building an approximate probabilistic meta-model of the target function (or surrogate function) that allows to sample offspring only in promising areas.

There is a large variety of meta-models used in conjunction with ES. One kind of algorithms are using Gaussian centring the peak to the global (hopefully) extremum [2, 3]. Other algorithms tries to estimate the target function landscape, or its fraction around the global extremum. They include statistical models with local regression [4], radial basis function interpolation [5], covariance matrix adaptation [6], Gaussian process model [7], Kriging interpolation [8], and adaptive Gaussian mixture models [9] to name a few; see also [10] for a comprehancive review.

In this paper, we propose a new algorithm that utilises a product of Gaussians in a form of a restricted Boltzmann machine that is well-suited for the approximation of

Y.S. Kim et al (Eds.): PKAW 2014, LNCS 8863, pp. 246–259, 2014.

complex *multimodal* target functions, thus improving the performance of (μ,λ) ES in such environments.

This paper first briefly describes the concept of restricted Boltzmann machines, then it introduces the RBM-ES algorithm. Afterwards, the algotithm is analised on an artificial multimodal landscape, compared with other ES algorithms on the BBOB platform [11], and it is finally evaluated on a 'real' cart-pole nalancing control problem in a simulated environment.

2   Product of Gaussians

Combining tractable models (such as Gaussian) to a mixture seems to be beneficial, because the mixture can approximate complex objective functions much better than individual models, especially in a multimodal case. However, mixtures of models seem to be inefficient in high-dimentional spaces [12].

Another way of combining models is by taking the product of individual models followed by renormalisation. If the models are Gaussians with one or more latent variables, then their product becomes a powerfull tool for modelling complex distributions with nearly arbitrary shape and sharpness, and the sharpness is not limited by the width of each individual kernel [13]. A well-know example of such a product is a restrictred Boltzmann machine (RBM). RBMs and their modifications have been excessively studied for the last decade, and they have been shown to be very efficient in many classification, recognition and dimensionality reduction tasks [14–22].

Generally speaking, a binary RBM is a two-layer network of visible and hidden units that are bi-directionally connected to each other with no lateral connections within layers, Fig. 1. An RBM layout. The units make stochastic decisions about whether to be "on" or "off" with probability defined by their net input [12, 23].

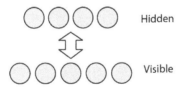

Fig. 1. An RBM layout

Specifically, the probability of turning a unit "on" is:

$$p(h_j|\mathbf{v}) = \frac{1}{1 + e^{-z_j}},$$ (1)

$$z_j = b_j + \sum_i v_i \cdot w_{ij},$$

where w_{ij} is the weight of the connection between the *i-th* visible and *j-th* hidden units, b, c are visual and hidden units' biases respectively.

The binary RBM could be extended to encode real-valued variables in few different ways [16]. In our implementation we have used an RBM with Gaussian visible and binary hidden units [24, 25], where Gaussian units denote linear units with added Gaussian noise.

Under this real-valued model, the conditional probabilities become:

$$p(v_i|h) = \mathcal{N}\left(c_i + \sum h_j w_{ij}, \sigma^2\right),$$ (2)

$$p(h_j|v) = \frac{1}{1 + \exp\left(-\frac{z_j}{\sigma^2}\right)},$$ (3)

where $\mathcal{N}(m, \sigma^2)$ denotes Gaussian noise with mean m and variance σ^2.

The model is trained to minimise the joint probability of visible and hidden units $P(v,h)$. For improving the efficiency of ES, we want to learn $P(v,h)$ in a way that makes it as close as possible to the target function.

In [12] has been proposed a fast method of trining RBMs, namely contrastive divergence (CD), where the weight are updated according to the following equation:

$$\Delta w_{ij} = \langle v_i h_j \rangle^{data} - \langle v_i h_j \rangle^{equilibrium}.$$ (4)

In this equation, $\langle \rangle^{data}$ denotes the expected value of the input multiplied with the inferred hidden states while the input is clamped on the data points, and $\langle \rangle^{equilibrium}$ is the expectation of $v_i h_j$ when the alternating Gibbs sampling of the hidden and visible units was (infinitely) iterated to get samples from the equilibrium distribution. Fortunately, it was shown that the learning could be acceptably efficient even if the Gibbs sampling chain has been stopped after the first update.

Importantly, an RBM is a generative model. That is, by alternating Gibbs sampling steps until equilibrium state [26], it is possible to obtain an unbiased exemplar from the model's probability density distribution [16] that allows efficiently produce offspring for ES. Similarly to the learning stage, the Gibbs sampling chain in practice could be stopped after a few iterations.

3   RBM-ES Algorithm

The proposed RBM-ES algorithm enhances the efficiency of evolution by generating offspring from a meta-model that mimics a target function.

The algorithm is conceptually derived from the simplest form of the real-valued ES, namely PBIL-C [3]. Unlike the PBIL-C, in our algorithm the meta-model is built upon a Gaussian-binary RBM that allows to perform efficiently both the adaptation of the model to the objective function, and the sampling from the learned probability distribution.

A naïve version of the algorithm pseudo-code is listed in Alg. 1. The first population of μ individuals is uniformly randomly generated keeping in mind that it should cover the whole search space. Afterwards, the best λ individuals are used as parent samples to train the RBM. Since then, every new offspring is generated by Gibbs sampling from the meta-model. It usually helps to add some exponentially decaying noise to the step of sampling of visual units to enforce more exploration at the beginning, and also to improve initial search space coverage:

$$p(v_i|h) = \mathcal{N}\left(c_i + \sum h_j w_{ij}, \sigma^2\right) + \mathcal{N}(0,T) .$$ (5)

Alg. 1. The RBM-ES algorithm

1	**initialise** $RBM(w, b, c, \sigma^2), T$
2	**generate** first population X^0 with uniform distribution
3	**repeat** until converge or other stop criteria
4	**select** best λ individuals X^{best} from population X^t
5	**train** RBM with CD algorithm on X^{best}
6	**for** $k = 1$ **to** μ *% generate new population X^t*
7	$v = \mathcal{N}(0,1)$
8	**for** $n = 1$ **to** g *% Gibbs sampling*
9	**calculate** h, eq. (3)
10	**calculate** v, eq. (5)
11	**end**
12	$x_k = v$ *% update offspring with the new individual*
13	**end**
14	$T = \varepsilon T$ *% decay the added noise*
15	**end**
16	**return** individual with the best fitness

The RBM is trained to minimise joint probability of data and hidden units with CD method described earlier. We have found that updating weighs with momentum $\alpha = 0.7 .. 0.9$ improves stability and increases the speed of the learning of the meta-model [16]:

$$w^t = \alpha w^{t-1} + \Delta w .$$ (6)

The variance σ^2 in eq. (5) is set to 0.4 (see Discussion section for more information on the choice of this parameter). The noise decay value ε is set to 0.99, but it might require to be adjusted to account for the complexity and dimensionality of the target function.

The Gibbs sampling chain (lines 8-11 in Alg. 1) in theory should be repeated until the system reaches its equilibrium. However in practice, small number of iterations is usually sufficient. That is, we use $g = 6$ iterations in all our experiments.

The learning rate should be set to a small value; otherwise it might lead to the explosion of the RBM's weights. The value of 0.0005 seems to be a good starting point.

4   Experimental Study

This section describes three experiments. First, we evaluate the adaptation of the meta-model probability distribution on a non-linear multimodal function, illustrating that the RBM is indeed a powerful tool for modelling complex probability density functions (pdf). Next, we run a benchmark test in order to compare the RBM-ES performance to other algorithms. Specifically, we use the BBOB (black-box optimisation benchmarks) platform [11]. Finally, we evaluate the proposed algorithm on a practical task and compare it with other algorithms belonging to the ES family.

4.1   The Adaptation of the Meta-Model's Probability Density to a Target Function

This study illustrates the adaptation of an RBM-based meta-model to a target function. Specifically, a variation of the Gallagher 101 Gaussian peaks function from the BBOB platform was used.

The experiment uses the naïve version of the algorithm listed in Alg. 1 with the parameters described in the section above. The number of RBM's hidden units was 10. We run the algorithm to minimise the target function and plot the probability density function of the meta-model every few dozen generations.

The results are presented in Fig. 2. The fine line contour map (magenta in colour version) shows a 2D crossection of the target function with three deep optima, where the central minimum is the global one. Theoverlaping solid line contour map shows the RBMs pdf. Thus, the four consequent plots (A-D) show the evolution of the meta-model pdf with training.

The problem of finding the global minimum of functions like Gallagher 101 seems to be difficult for many black-box optimisation algorithms, because it has multiple local extremes and valleys. Intuitively, having an algorithm with a meta-model that is able to explore multiple peaks at the same time seems to be advantageous comparing to uni-modal meta-models. Indeed, the RBM-ES demonstrates such an ability. Plot A shows the initial pdf that has a bowl-like shape. With RBM learning, the probability distribution shape gradually changes (Plots B and C) to account for the target function landscape, covering all deepest minima. This allows to localise the sampling of the offspring to promising areas. Finally, the pdf become centred over the global minimum, Plot D.

Although this experiment does not explicitly evaluates the performance of the proposed algorithm, it does uncover the important process underlying the algorithms strength – its ability to handle multimodal functions. The following experiments will compare the performance in more challenging environments.

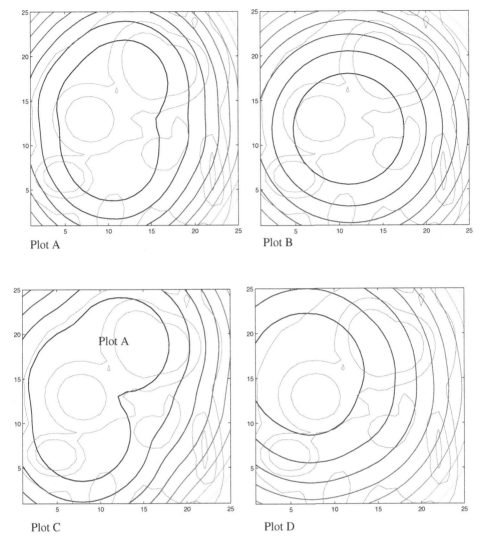

Plot A

Plot B

Plot C

Plot D

Fig. 2. The adaptation of the meta-model's probability density to the target function in 2D projection. Plot A shows the initial pdf of the meta-model. Plots B and C shows the adaptation of the meta-model in order to account the deepest minimum. Plot D shows the final shape of the pdf that has became centred over the global minimum. The fine-line contour map (magenta in colour version) is the target function, and the solid-line contour is the model pdf. The global minimum is located approximately at (7,15). Best viewed in colour.

4.2   Comparing the RBM-ES with other Algorithms on the BBOB Black-Box Optimisation Benchmark Platform

The following experiment evaluates the performance of the RBM-ES algorithm on the BBOB 2013 platform with noiseless functions. The platform allows comparing results with many algorithms presented on GECCO conferences.

The testbed contains 24 real-valued functions that have high complexity and are known to be difficult to minimise. The benchmarking procedure measures how many times problems were solved by an algorithm within limited budged (the number of function evaluations) for different dimensions and for different target precision values.

Fig. 3 presents results for 5-D and 20-D problems for all functions (right plots), as well as for a multimodal subgroups of functions (left plots) that appears to be more difficult to optimise [27]. The charts also show the performance of few other algorithms belonging to the ES family: BayEDAcG [9], Bipop-CMAES [28], Lmm-CMAES [1]. In addition, the top curve with a diamond-shaped marker (in gold on the colour version) shows the best performance achieved on the BBOB'2009 workshop.

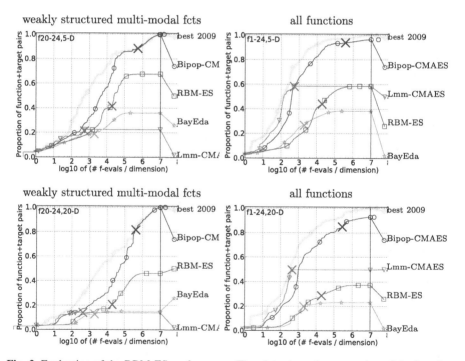

Fig. 3. Evaluation of the RBM-ES performance. The plots show the proportion of the function optimised w.r.t. the number of function evaluations divided by the dimension of the problem. Higher curves represent better performance. Best viewed in colour.

The plots show the number of solved problems with respect to the runtime measured as the number of function evaluations divided by dimension. The number of problems include all functions (right plots) or only multi-model weakly structured functions (left plots). Every function is optimised several times with different target precisions from 10^2 to 10^{-8}. For detailed testbed setup, please refer to [11].

The variant of the proposed RBM-ES algorithm demonstrates high performance on the BBOB testbed and is able to achieve comparable results with other ES algorithms, outperforming some of them, especially on the multimodal subclass of functions. In the next experiment we will evaluate the RBM-ES on a more practical multidimensional.

4.3   The Evaluation of Performance on a Practical Task

In this experiment we evaluate the proposed algorithm for more practical purposes and compare it with other algorithms belonged to the ES family. Specifically, in this experiment ES algorithms are compared on the task of evolving weights of a feed-forward neural network that is used as a controller for the classical cart-pole balancing problem.

The idea of using genetic algorithms to train artificial neural networks for reinforcement learning (RL) tasks is not new, and it has been around for few decades. Resent research has shown that often this approach is superior comparing to plain reinforcement learning, especially for complex tasks, because RL algorithms tend to suffer from the curse of dimensionality [29–32].

The purpose of the controller is to balance the pole, keeping the cart in the centre of the available area as long as possible by applying forces to the cart. The simulator math and sample code for the problem are readily available, i.e. as described in [33]. The task is episodic, and it ends either after 800 successive iterations or when the pole angle exceeds the critical value of ±15 degrees. In the case of losing balance, the controller is penalised with a negative reward -1. Every successive iterations is rewarded by +0.01, thus the total maximum reward is equal to 8. Keeping the cart position close to the centre is reinforced by adding s negative reward in proportion to the offset with a coefficient -0.005.

In this experiment we used a feed-forward network with one hidden layer that has four input units, ten hidden and two output logistic units, Fig. 4. Thus, the dimensionality of the problem, as the number of weights and biases, is equal to 72, which makes the problem relatively hard to solve.

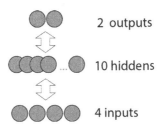

Fig. 4. The controller neural network layout

The input units receive the following pole and cart parameters:

x – cart position;

$\dot{x}$ – cart velocity;

φ – pole inclination;

$\dot{\varphi}$ – pole angular velocity.

The weight of the cart is 1kg, the weight and length of the pole are 0.1kg and 1m respectively. The simulation time step is 0.02 s. The force applied to the cart can be ±10N and the sign depends on weather the output of the first unit is larger than the second one.

We evaluated three different algorithms on the problem: PBIL-C [3], CMA-ES [34], and our RBM-ES. We have picked the CMA-ES algorithm for comparison, because it can be considered as a state-of-the-art algorithm and its Octave/Matlab code is available. Conversely, we included the PBIL-C, the simplest algorithm in the family of ES, as a unitary reference point. Every individual (as the set of controller network's weights) was tested on the cart-pole task five times with slightly different initial cart and pole position to get accurate fitness estimates.

First, we tested the basic ES algorithm PBIL-C. The PBIL algorithm is known to have a good performance, but it's application is limited to separable problems [35]. Thus not surprising, it was able to find a solution to the problem only occasionally, see Fig. 5. In contrast, the CMA-ES has demonstrated much better performance and was able to find a solution at almost every run, Fig.6. Finally, we evaluated the proposed RBM-ES algorithm, Fig. 7. Noticeably, this algorithm was able to find a solution every run.

Our results are inline with the previous work that evaluates different algorithms, including the CMA-ES, on the pole balancing problem [31, 32].

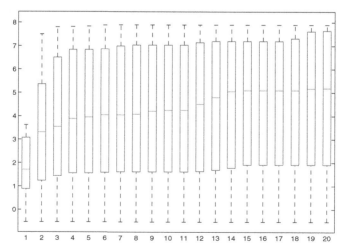

Fig. 5. The evaluation of the PBIL-C algorithm. The vertical axis represents the total average reward, the horizontal is the iteration number $^{\times}10$. The maximum possible reward is 8. The central mark is the median, the edges of the box are the 25th and 75th percentiles, the whiskers extend to the most extreme values.

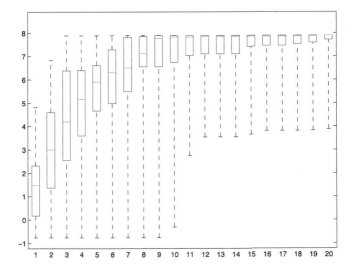

Fig. 6. The evaluation of the CMA-EC algorithm, a naïve version without restarts. See description of Fig. 5.

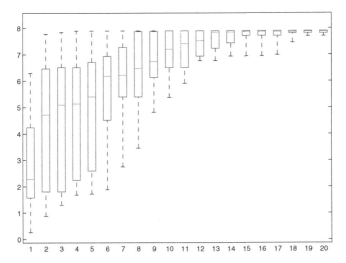

Fig. 7. The evaluation of the RBM-ES algorithm. See description of Fig. 5.

5   Discussion

Apparently, the efficacy of the adaptation of a meta-model to a target function is one of the most important properties of any ES algorithm. The first experiment shows that the proposed approach provides an effective tool for such adaptation. The complex meta-model allows to sample candidate solutions from the most promising areas.

Interestingly, the problem of being trapped in a local minimum seems to be less severe for the RBM-ES comparing to algorithms that maintain a uni-modal model of the target function. Fig. 2 provides an example of the adaptation of the pdf to a function with multiple local extrema. Noticeably, the RBM tries to cover every good candidate to the global solution, thus decreasing the chance of being attracted by one of the local minima instead of the global one.

The second experiment compares the performance of the propose algorithm with several state-of-the art algorithms from the same class of evolution strategies. The RBM-ES demonstrates comparable results and even outperform some algorithms, especially on the multimodal class of problems.

It is worth mentioning that we used a naïve variant of the RBM-ES in this experiment, while other algorithms were specifically tuned for the competition (e.g. multiple restarts, adaptive learning rate, etc.). In addition, the BBOB problems are typically designed with the goal of achieving a very low residual error up to 10^{-8}. This magnitude of error is hardly achievable with a stochastic model based on the RBM with Gaussian-binary units. Although such low error is not always desired in practical tasks, it seems that it is possible to further improve the algorithm performance by proper scaling of the data, and we leave this to the future work.

The final experiment with the pole balancing controller explores a relatively complex optimisation problem with large dimensionality, but presumably simple landscape. Nevertheless, the simplest algorithm from the ES family PBIL-C has not shown good performance, being able to find a solution only occasionally. In contrast, a naïve version of the RBM-ES algorithm achieved the performance slightly better than the CMA-ES, demonstrating relatively quick and robust convergence to a solution.

This cart-pole balancing experiment did not imply noisy environments. However, all the algorithms evaluated are stochastic in nature, and our preliminary tests do not show any significant difference with the addition of a moderate level of noise to the position and velocity "readings" from the cart-pole simulator. Thus, we believe that the RBM-ES algorithm would have shown good results on noisy problems as well.

Comparing to the CMA-ES, our algorithm has more parameters to tune. First, the RBM's hidden layer unit number must be chosen depending on the complexity of the target function. Although there is no a precise recipe for choosing the RBM layout, all common sense methods dealing with the trade-off between complexity and possible overfitting apply here. These methods may also include the addition of a regulariser such as weight decay or sparsity regulation [16].

Another RBM parameter, the variance of the Gaussian visual units σ^2, has a great effect on the shape and sharpness of the learned distribution. The influence of this parameter is discussed in the recent work [25], and a few practical advises are given in [16].

There are also two evolution-specific meta-parameters, λ and μ. Clearly, the parameters must satisfy $\lambda \leq \mu$. We were using $\lambda=3$ and $\mu=9$ in our experiments, an we found that the common approach of changing these values depending on the dimensionality of the problem (e.g. [1]) does not seem to noticeably improve the efficiency, measured as the number of target function evaluations.

While approaches for optimising both RBMs and evolution strategies are well explored separately and described in the literature, it seems also beneficial to implement self-adaptation mechanisms, i.e. as discussed in [36, 37]. This would allow to make the algorithm more robust for accommodating a wider range of different tasks and we will be working in this direction in future.

6   Conclusion

The paper proposed a new algorithm RBM-ES from the evolution strategies family, where the offspring are generated from the probability distribution function of a meta-model, formed by a restricted Boltzmann machine.

The RBM-based meta-model seems to be highly efficient in learn functions with complex landscapes. Specifically, there are two appealing properties of the RBM that are exploited in the proposed RBM-ES algorithm. First, it is able to model *multimodal* distributions that allows doing parallel search in multiple modes. This property helps dealing with the problem of being trapped in a local minimum that is a typical issue for algorithms that maintain a uni-modal model of the target function.

Second, the RBM is able to model distributions that are narrower than its each expert, thus easing another important problem – choosing the initial sigmas. Unlike the RBM-ES, it is know that some algorithms can become unstable and diverge if the initial the deviation was chosen incorrectly [38].

Finally, the RBM-ES is computationally efficient, because RBMs offer a simple and efficient mechanism for sampling from the model's distribution and training.

Acknowledgments. The author thanks Marcus Gallagher and Gleb Yakubov for fruitful discussions, and anonymous reviewers for useful comments that helped to improve this paper. This work was funded by auPilot project.

References

1. Auger, A., Brockhoff, D., Hansen, N.: Benchmarking the Local Metamodel CMA-ES on the Noiseless BBOB'2013 Test Bed. In: GECCO 2013 (2013)
2. Baluja, S., Caruana, R.: Removing the genetics from the standard genetic algorithm. In: ICML, pp. 1–11 (1995)
3. Sebag, M., Ducoulombier, A.: Extending population-based incremental learning to continuous search spaces. Parallel Probl. Solving from Nat. 5, 418–427 (1998)
4. Branke, J., Schmidt, C., Schmec, H.: Efficient Fitness Estimation in Noisy Environments. In: Proceedings of Genetic and Evolutionary Computation (2001)
5. Gutmann, H.-M.: A Radial Basis Function Method for Global Optimization. J. Glob. Optim. 19, 201–227 (2001)
6. Olhofer, M., Sendhoff, B.: A framework for evolutionary optimization with approximate fitness functions. IEEE Trans. Evol. Comput. 6, 481–494 (2002)
7. Büche, D., Schraudolph, N.N., Koumoutsakos, P.: Accelerating Evolutionary Algorithms With Gaussian Process Fitness Function Models. IEEE Trans. Syst. Man, Cybern. Part C Appl. Rev. 35, 183–194 (2005)
8. Runarsson, T.P.: Constrained evolutionary optimization by approximate ranking and Surrogate models. In: Yao, X., et al. (eds.) PPSN VIII. LNCS, vol. 3242, pp. 401–410. Springer, Heidelberg (2004)

9. Emmerich, M., Giotis, A., Özdemir, M., Bäck, T., Giannakoglou, K.: Metamodel-Assisted Evolution Strategies. In: Guervós, J.J.M., Adamidis, P.A., Beyer, H.-G., Fernández-Villacañas, J.-L., Schwefel, H.-P. (eds.) PPSN VII. LNCS, vol. 2439, pp. 361–370. Springer, Heidelberg (2002)

10. Gallagher, M.: Black-box optimization benchmarking: Results for the BayEDAcG algorithm on the noiseless function testbed. In: GECCO 2009, p. 2383. ACM Press, New York (2009)

11. Forrester, A., Sobester, A., Keane, A.: Engineering Design via Surrogate Modelling A Practical Guide. Wiley (2008)

12. Hansen, N., Auger, A., Finck, S., Ros, R.: Real-Parameter Black-Box Optimization Benchmarking 2009: Experimental Setup (2009)

13. Hinton, G.E.: Training products of experts by minimizing contrastive divergence. Neural Comput. 14, 1771–1800 (2002)

14. Martens, J., Chattopadhyay, A., Pitassi, T., Zemel, R.: On the Representational Efficiency of Restricted Boltzmann Machines. In: NIPS, pp. 1–21 (2013)

15. Hinton, G.E.: To Recognize Shapes, First Learn to Generate Images. Prog. Brain Res. 165, 535–547 (2007)

16. Nair, V., Hinton, G.E.: Rectified linear units improve restricted boltzmann machines. In: Proceedings of the 27th International Conference on Machine Learning. ACM Press (2010)

17. Hinton, G.E.: A Practical Guide to Training Restricted Boltzmann Machines (2010)

18. Desjardins, G., Courville, A.: Parallel tempering for training of restricted Boltzmann machines. In: AISTATS, pp. 145–152 (2010)

19. Larochelle, H., Mandel, M.: Learning Algorithms for the Classification Restricted Boltzmann Machine. J. Mach. Learn. Res. 13, 643–669 (2012)

20. Desjardins, G., Bengio, Y.: Empirical evaluation of convolutional RBMs for vision (2008)

21. Luo, H., Shen, R., Niu, C.: Sparse Group Restricted Boltzmann Machines. Arxiv Prepr. arXiv1008.4988, pp. 1–9 (2010)

22. Cho, K., Ilin, A., Raiko, T.: Improved learning of Gaussian-Bernoulli restricted Boltzmann machines. In: Honkela, T., Duch, W., Girolami, M., Kaski, S. (eds.) ICANN 2011, Part I. LNCS, vol. 6791, pp. 10–17. Springer, Heidelberg (2011)

23. Cho, K., Raiko, T., Ilin, A.: Enhanced gradient and adaptive learning rate for training restricted Boltzmann machines. Neural Computation 25(3) (2011)

24. Welling, M.: Product of Experts, http://www.scholarpedia.org/article/Product_of_experts

25. Welling, M., Rosen-Zvi, M., Hinton, G.E.: Exponential family harmoniums with an application to information retrieval. In: Adv. Neural Inf. Process. Syst. (2005)

26. Wang, N., Melchior, J., Wiskott, L.: An analysis of Gaussian-binary restricted Boltzmann machines for natural images. In: ESANN (2012)

27. Bengio, Y.: Learning Deep Architectures for AI. Found. Trends Mach. Learn. 2, 1–127 (2009)

28. Hansen, N., Auger, A., Ros, R., Finck, S., Pošík, P.: Comparing results of 31 algorithms from the black-box optimization benchmarking BBOB-2009. In: Proceedings of the 12th Annual Conference Comp. on Genetic and Evolutionary Computation, GECCO 2010, p. 1689. ACM Press, New York (2010)

29. Hansen, N.: Benchmarking a BI-population CMA-ES on the BBOB-2009 function testbed. In: Proceedings of the 11th Annual Conference Companion on Genetic and Evolutionary Computation Conference, GECCO 2009, p. 2389. ACM Press, New York (2009)

30. Taylor, M.E., Whiteson, S., Stone, P.: Comparing evolutionary and temporal difference methods in a reinforcement learning domain. In: GECCO 2006, p. 1321. ACM Press, New York (2006)
31. Heidrich-Meisner, V., Igel, C.: Similarities and differences between policy gradient methods and evolution strategies. In: ESANN, pp. 23–25 (2008)
32. Riedmiller, M., Peters, J., Schaal, S.: Evaluation of Policy Gradient Methods and Variants on the Cart-Pole Benchmark. In: 2007 IEEE ISADPRL, pp. 254–261 (2007)
33. Hansen, N.: The CMA Evolution Strategy: A Comparing Review. In: Lozano, J.A., Larrañaga, P., Inza, I., Bengoetxea, E. (eds.) Towards a New Evolutionary Computation. STUDFUZZ, vol. 192, pp. 75–102. Springer, Heidelberg (2006)
34. Dorigo, M., Stützle, T.: Ant Colony Optimization. MIT Press (2004)
35. Whitacre, J.M.: Adaptation and Self-Organization in Evolutionary Algorithms (2007)
36. Meyer-Nieberg, S., Beyer, H.: Self-adaptation in evolutionary algorithms. In: Lobo, F.G., Lima, C.F., Michalewicz, Z. (eds.) Parameter Setting in Evolutionary Algorithms. SCI, vol. 54, pp. 47–75. Springer, Heidelberg (2007)

A Comparison of Graph-Based and Statistical Metrics for Learning Domain Keywords

Alexandre Kouznetsov and Amal Zouaq

Department of Mathematics and Computer Science,
Royal Military College of Canada, CP 17000, Succursale Forces, Kingston,
Canada K7K 7B4
akouz086@uottawa.ca, amal.zouaq@rmc.ca

Abstract. In this paper, we present a comparison of unsupervised and supervised methods for key-phrase extraction from a domain corpus. The experimented unsupervised methods employ individual statistical measures and graph-based measures while the supervised methods apply machine learning models that include combinations of these statistical and graph-based measures. Graph-based measures are applied on a graph that connects terms and compound expressions through conceptual relations and represents a whole corpus about a domain, rather than a single document. Using three datasets from different domains, we observed that supervised methods over-perform unsupervised ones. We also found that the graph-based measures Degree and Reachability generally over-perform (in the majority of the cases) the standard baseline TF-IDF and other graph-based measures while the co-occurrences based measure Pointwise Mutual Information over-performs all the other metrics, including the graph-based measures, when taken individually.

1   Introduction

Automatic keyword (key-phrase) extraction is the task that identifies a set of key phrase from a document for the purpose of describing its meaning [Hulth, 2003]. Several automatic key phrases extraction techniques have been proposed in the literature. Statistical methods [Matsuo et al., 2004] tend to focus on statistical features such as TF-IDF (term frequency - inverse document frequency) and the position of a keyword (for instance) to identify keywords in a document. Recently, there have been several approaches that use graph-based measures calculated on words Collocation Networks [Mihalcea and Tarau, 2004], [Lahiri et al., 2014], [Boudin, 2013] and semantic graphs [Zouaq et al., 2011]. Keyword extraction generally targets the extraction of keywords from single documents and these keywords reflect the main content of documents. In this work, our focus is on keyword extraction from a domain corpus (rather than from individual documents) for the purpose of building a domain terminology. In fact, extracting a terminology that reflects domain knowledge from a specialized corpus cannot rely solely on the keywords extracted from each document. Keywords that emerge from documents might not be the keywords chosen to reflect the domain as a whole. Thus a more generic approach is needed that aggregates the information

Y.S. Kim et al (Eds.): PKAW 2014, LNCS 8863, pp. 260–268, 2014.

contained in all documents to identify the relevant items that describe the domain. In this work, our objective is:

i)   To compare a set of unsupervised graph-based measures and statistical measures for keyword extraction from a graph that emerges from the corpus as a whole; and

ii)   To compare the prediction performance of these unsupervised key-phrase extraction methods with the performance of supervised methods that combine the identified graph-based and statistics-based measures in the same machine learning model.

One new aspect of our work, compared to the state of the art, is that graph measures are applied on a graph that emerges after a semantic analysis process on the whole corpus. This graph relates terms and compound expressions through conceptual relations extracted using the tool OntoCmaps [Zouaq et al., 2011] and aggregates all the information coming from all the documents of the corpus. Another contribution of our work is the use of graph-based, statistical and co-occurrence measures to train a keyword extraction classifier and the comparison between unsupervised and supervised approaches for keyword extraction.

The rest of the paper is structured as follows: Section 2 describes the ranking measures used for keyword identification. Section 3 presents unsupervised and supervised keywords extraction methods based on the selected measures. Section 4 reports obtained results with our conclusions in Section 5.

2   Ranking Measures

Our approach to keyword extraction aims at identifying keywords from document collections around a particular domain. In this paper, the graph, which is extracted using the ontology learning tool OntoCmaps [Zouaq et al., 2011], connects words and phrases that are identified using syntactic patterns that extract relations from texts. A relation is described as a triple with a label (a predicate), subject (candidate keyword) and object (candidate keyword). Thus a graph is represented by a set of relations where labels represent edges and subjects and objects represent graph nodes. Candidate keywords are then ranked using various measures to identify the most relevant items. For space reasons, the graph extraction process is not described in this paper but a good description is available in [Zouaq et al., 2011].

Several measures were experimented in this study for keywords identification. These measures can be divided into statistical and graph-based measures.

2.1   Statistical Co-occurrence Measures

Frequency of co-occurrence measures have been successfully applied in the state of the art for computing the semantic relatedness and similarity between two expressions [Washtell and Markert, 2009] [Turney, 2001]. In this project, our hypothesis is that these measures can also indicate important keywords when they are computed on relations extracted by our syntactic patterns. Our intuition is that candidate phrases occurring as subjects and objects in our relations are important phrases if their frequency of co-occurrence score is high. We calculated two features that represent the strength of relatedness between the subjects and objects in the graph relations. These two features are Point-Wise Mutual Information (PMI) [Church and Hanks, 1989] and a variant of PMI, Semi-Conditional Information (SCI) [Washtell and Markert, 2009]. These two features are calculated as follows:

$$PMI(t1, t2) = \log\left(P(t1, t2)/p(t1)p(t2)\right) \tag{1}$$

$$SCI\ (t1, t2) = P(t1, t2)/p(t1)\sqrt{p(t2)} \tag{2}$$

Where $P(t1,t2)$ represents the frequency of predicates between terms $t1$ and $t2$ in the corpus, and $P(t)$ (with $t=t1,t2$) represents the frequency of t in the corpus. The result is then assigned as a weight to the subject $(t1)$ and object $(t2)$ participating in the triple. As there might be several relations where the same subject and/or object participate, we assign to a term t the maximum PMI/SCI weight of all the relations in which t participates.

We also used two standard statistical features to assign a score to candidate phrases: the Term Frequency (TF) and the well-known Term frequency–inverse document frequency (TFIDF) measure [Salton and Buckley, 1988]. These features represent our baselines.

2.2   Graph-Based Measures

Based on the generated graph, we also applied several graph-based measures. All these measures were computed using JUNG (Java Universal Network/Graph Framework) [http://jung.sourceforge.net/]:

— Degree [Deg] measures the number of edges incident upon a node.
— HITS Hubs [HITS (Hubs)] is based on the HITS algorithm [Kleinberg, 1999]. Hub scores measure the importance of a node as a hub (pointing to many others).
— HITS Authority [HITS (Auth)] measures the importance of a node as an authority (referenced by many others).
— PageRank [Prank] is based on the Eigen-vector centrality and computes the number of important nodes that are connected to the current node [Page et al., 1998].
— Node Betweenness [Betw] quantifies the number of times a node acts as a bridge along the shortest path between two other nodes [Brandes, 2001].
— Reachability [Reach] computes the shortest distance between the term of interest T and any other reachable term in the graph based on the Dijkstra algorithm. Each edge weights 1 and the shortest distance (D) between T and any other term is equal to 1 over the distance to reach it. The final score is the sum of these shortest distances to related terms.
— Edge Betweenness [BETWREL] computes the edge betweenness of each link in the graph and assigns the weight of the edge to its source and destination nodes. Similarly to PMI and SCI, the intuition here is that an edge with a high score would connect important nodes.

3   Methodology

3.1   Datasets

Our experiments to identify domain keywords from a corpus were run on three domains:

— Artificial Intelligence (AI): the corpus includes Wikipedia pages around AI and related topics;
— BIOLOGY: the corpus is extracted from Wikipedia based on the recommendation of experts from the Oregon Health & Science University;
— SCORM: it includes manuals of the Sharable Content Object Reference Model available online.

The descriptive statistics about these domains are shown in table 1. For each domain, the performance of the ranking measures was evaluated against a golden standard provided by domain experts (these experts were different from a domain to another). The experts classified each keyword candidate into two classes, namely (1) real keywords (positive class) and (2) Non-keywords (negative class) for the given domain.

Table 1. Some statistics on our datasets

Domain	Number of words in the corpus	Number of candidate keywords	Number of real keywords (positive Instances)	Positive Instances ratio
AI	~10000	1601	695	0.434
BIOLOGY	~15000	2628	358	0.136
SCORM	~30000	2385	1231	0.516
Total	~55000	6614	2284	-

3.2   Measures for Keyword Identification

Our experiments consisted in testing the performance of individual measures for keyword extraction (section 2) against the human golden standard. All the instances in our datasets, which consist of pairs of candidate keywords associated to the score of the metric under consideration, were sorted in descending order.

Supervised learning methods were used to test the interest of the graph-based and statistical metrics for training a domain keyword classifier. For the purpose of comparing the classifiers' results to individual measures' ranked lists, we also had to order the results of the classifiers. We used the positive class probability estimates assigned by the selected classifiers to each test instance. The objective was to identify if a combination of the metrics presented in section 2, powered with supervised learning, would improve the keyword identification task, compared to each individual metric. Examples provided to the classifiers (instances) consisted of candidate keywords combined with all our metrics.

We applied the following two classifiers from WEKA [Weka, 2013]: Rotation Forest [Rodriguez et al., 2006] and Logistic Regression [Cessie and Houwelingen, 1992][1]. A 10 fold cross-validation was applied to evaluate the classifiers.

4   Results

4.1   Evaluation Metrics

We evaluated our results based on the following standard evaluation metrics: R-precision and Average R-precision. R-precision is the precision at a given cut-off point based on a fixed recall value. We used 10 fixed recall values, thus producing 10 cut-off points and 10 precision values for each data set. We consider R-precision as our main measure since our main concern is about increasing precision in our practical tasks, especially at the top of the ranked list. At the same time, as cut-off points are established based on a set of fixed recall values, recall is also considered in our evaluation. The Average R-precision is the arithmetic mean of the R-precision values.

4.2   Unsupervised Measures Results

Table 2 summarizes the results of our unsupervised measures on the three data sets based on Average R-precision. The top-2 values are highlighted for each domain corpus.

Table 2. Average R-precision over 10 Recall cut off points for unsupervised methods

Ranking system	AI	BIOLOGY	SCORM
Unsupervised Statistical Features			
TFIDF	0.51	0.192	0.614
TF	0.5	0.185	0.609
PMI	**0.590**	**0.229**	**0.669**
SCI	0.582	0.206	0.618
Unsupervised Graph-based Features			
Betw	0.456	0.175	0.613
BETWREL	0.477	0.183	0.620
HITS(Hubs)	**0.591**	0.185	0.641
HITS(Auth)	0.453	0.138	0.590
Deg	0.555	0.192	**0.658**
Reach	0.559	**0.214**	0.652
Prank	0.468	0.149	0.601

The details of the R-precision results are not presented due to space considerations. However we can report that overall, in this experiment, PMI over-performs the other

---

[1] While we tried several classifiers from WEKA, those two were selected as they demonstrated relatively high performance on all considered datasets.

statistical measures on the majority of recall points. In fact PMI obtains the best results at the first recall points where the highest precision scores are achieved (i.e. on cut off points close to the top of ranked lists). Even in our most difficult dataset, the BIOLOGY dataset, PMI shows the most consistent results. As far as graph-based measures are concerned, Degree (Deg), Reachability (Reach) and Hits-hub seem to demonstrate a quiet good performance. In particular, Degree has high results at the first recall points while Reachability either outperforms degree or has comparable results after the first recall points. It can also be observed that Hits-hub follows closely Reachability at some recall points. Moreover, on one data set (AI), Hits-hub overperforms all other measures (including Degree and Reachability) on the majority of recall points.

4.3   Supervised Method Experiment Results

As previously indicated, we built two classifiers based on Rotation Forests and Logistic Regression. These supervised machine learning algorithms are compared to the best statistical and graph-based measures, that is: PMI, Degree, Reachability and HITS (Hub). Due to the somewhat similar (but lower) performance of SCI compared to PMI, we kept only PMI in the figure. We also included TFIDF that is considered as a baseline. Fig. 1 represents the results measured in R-precision. (The X Axis represents the recall cut-off point. The Y Axis represents the precision at the given cut off point.)

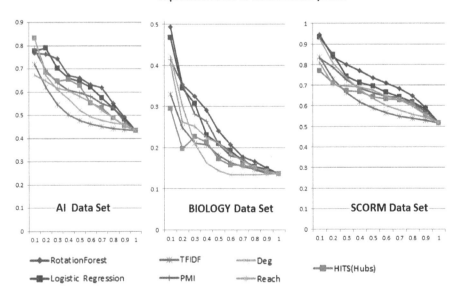

Fig. 1. R-Precision results for AI, BIOLOGY and SCORM data sets

As shown in Fig. 1, machine learning models over-perform individual measures on the majority of recall points. However, HITS (Hub) over-performs both ML Algorithms at the first recall points on the AI dataset and PMI over-performs Logistic Regression in the middle range of recall points on the BIOLOGY dataset.

Regarding the comparison between best graph-based metrics (Degree, Reachability and HITS(Hub)) and best statistical metrics (PMI, TFIDF), one can observe that graph-based metrics over-perform statistical metrics on several cut-off points in the SCORM and AI datasets. When only SCORM and AI data sets are taken in account, Degree tends to over-perform the other metrics on the first recall points but Reachability demonstrates a better stability on the middle range of recall points. HITS(Hub) demonstrates good results only for the AI data set.

When all the three datasets are considered, the number of cut off points where PMI over-performs the graph-based metrics is greater than the number of cut off points where the graph-based metrics over-perform PMI. PMI demonstrates a better performance compared to the other metrics on the BIOLOGY data set which is the dataset with the lowest positive instances ratio.

Degree over-performs TFIDF on all recall points on the SCORM and AI datasets as well as on the first recall points on the BIOLOGY dataset. Reachability over-performs TFIDF on the BIOLOGY dataset (at all the recall points) as well as on the SCORM and AI datasets (in all the recall points except one per dataset).

The results measured in Average R-precision are presented in Table 3 (the best results are in bold).

Table 3. Average R-precision over 10 Recall cut off points. Supervised /Unsupervised methods

Ranking system	AI	BIOLOGY	SCORM
Unsupervised Statistical Features			
TFIDF	0.51	0.192	0.614
PMI	0.590	0.229	0.669
Unsupervised Graph Based Features			
Deg	0.555	0.192	0.658
Reach	0.559	0.214	0.652
Supervised (10 folds cross validation)			
Rotation Forest	**0.634**	**0.254**	**0.724**
Logistic Regression	**0.622**	**0.236**	**0.696**

The Average R-Precisions results confirm our previous finding, that is, the considered supervised methods over-perform unsupervised individual metrics on all the considered datasets. PMI seems to be the best performing metric overall, which is an original result (to our knowledge). Graph-based measures including Degree and Reachability are also good indicators for the "key-phrasedness" of an expression especially when we compare them to standard measures used for keyword identification (TF-IDF).

5   Conclusion

In this paper, we presented a comparison of unsupervised and supervised methods for key-phrase extraction. The experimented unsupervised methods employ statistical measures and graph-based measures to identify important candidate terms while the supervised methods apply machine learning models that include combinations of these statistical and graph-based measures. Using three datasets from different domains, we observed that:

1. In the majority of the observed cases, supervised methods that use combinations of graph-based and statistical measures over-perform unsupervised methods based on single measures. When combined together to build machine learning classifiers, graph-based measures and statistical measures can improve the key-phrase identification task;
2. As only individual metrics are considered, the graph-based measures Degree and Reachability tend to over-perform the standard baseline TF-IDF and other graph-based measures in terms of average R precision. In particular, Degree seems to be a good indicator of top keywords and Reachability seems more stable at highest recall points;
3. One metric of co-occurrence, point-wise mutual information (PMI), is a good indicator of keywords in this experiment and over-performs all the other metrics in the majority of the cases when taken individually. This result is of particular interest as it seems to indicate that when two nominal expressions are related through high PMI-weighted links, then these expressions are themselves highly important for the domain.

One limitations of this work is the somewhat small size of the sample used to train the classifiers. In fact, while competitions such as SemEval [Su Nam Kim et al., 2010] offer standard datasets for the identification of keywords in single documents, there isn't any similar initiative (to our knowledge) for a whole corpus in a specialized domain. In future work, our objective is to continue our experiments on the interest of co-occurrence metrics and graph-based metrics for identifying keywords in graphs extracted using natural language processing tools. One important research direction will be to evaluate the domain independence of classifiers built using these graph-based and statistical metrics.

Acknowledgments. This research was funded by the Royal Military College of Canada Academic Research Program and Short Term Research Program. The authors would like to thank Melissa Haendle, Matthew Brush, Nicole Vasilevsky and Carlo Torniai from the Oregon Health and Science University for the biology dataset.

References

[Boudin, 2013] Boudin, F.: A Comparison of Centrality Measures for Graph-Based Keyphrase Extraction. In: Proceedings of the Sixth International Joint Conference on Natural Language Processing (October 2013)

[Brandes, 2001] Brandes, U.: A Faster Algorithm for Betweenness Centrality. The Journal of Mathematical Sociology 25(2), 163–177 (2001)

[Cessie and Houwelingen, 1992] le Cessie, S., van Houwelingen, J.C.: Ridge Estimators in Logistic Regression. Applied Statistics 41(1), 191–201 (1992)

[Church and Hanks, 1989] Church, K.W., Hanks, P.: Word association norms, mutual information and lexicography. In: ACL, pp. 76–83 (1989)

[Hulth, 2003] Hulth, A.: Improved Automatic Keyword Extraction Given More Linguistic Knowledge. In: Proceedings of the 2003 Conference on Empirical Methods in Natural Language Processing, Sapporo, Japan, pp. 216–223 (2003)

[Kleinberg, 1999] Kleinberg, J.M.: Authoritative Sources in a Hyperlinked Environment. J. ACM 46(5), 604–632 (1999)

[Matsuo et al., 2004] Matsuo, Y., Ishizuka, M.: Keyword extraction from a single document using word co-occurrence statistical information. International Journal on Artificial Intelligence Tools (2004)

[Lahiri et al., 2014] Lahiri, S., Choudhury, S.R. Caragea, C.: Keyword and Keyphrase Extraction Using Centrality Measures on Collocation Networks. Cornell University Library, http://arxiv.org/abs/1401.6571 (submitted on January 25, 2014)

[Mihalcea and Tarau, 2004] Mihalcea, R., Tarau, P.: TextRank: Bringing Order into Texts. In: Proceedings of EMNLP 2004, Barcelona, Spain, pp. 404–411 (July 2004)

[Page et al., 1998] Page, L., Brin, S., Motwani, R., Winograd, T.: The PageRank Citation Ranking: Bringing Order to the Web. In: Proceedings of the 7th International World Wide Web Conference, Brisbane, Australia, pp. 161–172 (1998)

[Rodriguez et al., 2006] Rodriguez, J.J., Kuncheva, L.I., Alonso, C.J.: Rotation Forest: A new classifier ensemble method. IEEE Transactions on Pattern Analysis and Machine Intelligence 28(10), 1619–1630

[Salton and Buckley, 1988] Salton, G., Buckley, C.: Term-weighting approaches in automatic text retrieval. Information Processing and Management 24(5), 513–523 (1988)

[Su Nam Kim et al., 2010] Kim, S.N., Medelyan, O., Kan, M.-Y., Baldwin, T.: SemEval-2010 Task 5: Automatic Keyphrase Extraction from Scientific Articles, http://www.aclweb.org/anthology/S10-1004

[Turney, 2001] Turney, P.D.: Mining the Web for Synonyms: PMI-IR versus LSA on TOEFL. In: Flach, P.A., De Raedt, L. (eds.) ECML 2001. LNCS (LNAI), vol. 2167, pp. 491–502. Springer, Heidelberg (2001)

[Washtell and Markert, 2009] Washtell, J., Markert, K.: A comparison of windowless and window-based computational association measures as predictors of syntagmatic human associations. In: EMNLP, pp. 628–637 (2009)

[Weka, 2013] Weka 3: Data Mining Software in Java, http://www.cs.waikato.ac.nz/ml/weka/index.html

[Zouaq et al., 2011] Zouaq, A., Gasevic, D., Hatala, M.: Towards Open Ontology Learning and Filtering. Information Systems

Using Generic and Generated Components to Create Static Software Analysis Tools Faster

Edward Tippetts

University of Canberra, Canberra, Australia
`eddie.tippetts@canberra.edu.au`

Abstract. In today's software engineering tool landscape, many sophisticated imperative static source code analysis tools exist. However the implementations of these analyses are normally tied to specific languages, so must be recreated for any new or lesser-known languages. It can be burdensome for small groups of language developers or third party tool authors to devote the necessary resources to creating an analysis tool suite specifically for their language, so a number of less popular languages lack such automated tool support to the detriment of their users. As a solution this paper argues that multiple analysis algorithms exist which are applicable to almost any high-level imperative programming language, and that support for them can be added to a language cheaply with a high degree of automation. Pursuit of these would provide a new way of gathering knowledge about application structure for languages that have not previously enjoyed strong tool support.

Keywords: Software Engineering, Code analysis, Code generation, Fact extraction, Imperative programming.

1   Introduction

Users of top-tier programming languages such as Java, C#, JavaScript are well supported by a wide range of powerful source code analysis tools that provide answers to various queries a software developer may have. However new or more obscure languages, such as Rocket Software's Model 204 [1] and Gupta Technologies' TeamDeveloper [2] often do not enjoy such strong support despite ongoing real-world application. An example of this in a new language is Java, which now enjoys broad market penetration and excellent tool support, yet in its early years the Java ecosystem featured limited automated support for developers [3]. These situations can unnecessarily raise the cost of developing and maintaining software systems created in newer or less popular languages when compared with other mainstream languages that have achieved greater popularity. It also prevents software engineers using these languages from obtaining knowledge of their software that could be useful in maintenance efforts.

This problem has much in common with the analysis of multi-language systems, as in both cases the solution must deal with a variety of languages that may have marked differences.

Y.S. Kim et al (Eds.): PKAW 2014, LNCS 8863, pp. 269–278, 2014.

This paper outlines the theoretical basis for a toolkit that can help to alleviate the problem of disparity in tool support for languages by making it cheaper and easier to provide a basic set of analysis tools to include in the software development kit for an imperative language that can be expressed with a BNF [4] or EBNF [5]grammar. To achieve this some example analysis techniques are identified, and these techniques are used to inform the design of a fact extractor which gathers the required details for generic analysis tools.

2   Background and Rationale

A number of domains are closely related to the task of creating a generic fact extractor. Firstly, parser generators are well studied and there are numerous highly capable examples, such as ANTLR [6, 7] and SableCC [8]. These tools prove the concept of automatic tool generation as they are able to accept a standardized EBNF-style input and generate source code ready for compilation into a functional parser.

Source markup is another area of research that contributes to this solution. Source markup involves augmenting input source code with tags to transform it in to a common 'language' which also aids in basic fact extraction tasks. Some examples such as SrcML use source code wrapping markup that is very easily adapted to other purposes [9] such as basic fact extraction. Therefore techniques available in the source markup domain are invaluable in the search for a means to generate a fact extractor.

Inspiration is also drawn from the domain of multi-language systems analysis. XLL (Cross Language Linker) [10] and XDevelop [11] and MMT [12] take varying approaches to modelling varying input languages to a common model or language of practical use, some of which are similar to the approach described below.

2.1   The Source Code Analysis Workflow

Fact extraction or source code analysis is somewhat related to software compilation, and can be said to follow a similar process. A typical workflow for source code analysis follows the steps of parsing, fact extraction, graph construction and finally high-level analysis. Parsing when performed by a generated parser reads the program source code in to an abstract syntax tree that models the source code in a hierarchical model that is derived from the language grammar. The syntax tree is then fed to the graph constructor to identify and extract information that is of use to the analysis tools. Analysis tools can cover a wide range of purposes, from aiding a programmer to understand and improve knowledge of program code [13], to error detection and automated refactoring. The remainder of this paper focuses on basic error detection and code understanding.

2.2   The Opportunity

A practical opportunity exists to offer better automated tool support for less popular languages in a low cost yet effective way. As noted some languages have poor support beyond compilers, so it would be of benefit to users of those languages if a common set of analysis tools could be applied to their situation. Initially these tools would be separate to tools the language users do their day-to-day development in, but in future could be incorporated in a more integrated fashion. This could lead to some potentially powerful analysis systems being developed for languages that have only a small following, resolving one of the problems that can hamstring newer languages or marginalize some.

2.3   Language Similarity

Source Markup
Often these less popular languages can be considered members of existing programming paradigms and display considerable similarity to other languages within those paradigms. A classic example of this similarity is Java compared to C# in which many of the same concepts are implemented in two distinct languages [6]. As an example of a less well known language, Model 204 'User Language' was originally based on BASIC's syntax, and has over time had new features implemented to make it into a hybrid structured/object-oriented language. Similarly D [7] is a newer language that is descended from C and C++, implementing a similar syntactic structure and conceptual framework. All of these languages are similar enough that a developer who understands one language has a head-start in learning the next due to a basic set of shared concepts. However the standard of software engineering tool support varies markedly between these languages.

A notable amount of work on generic or cross-language software analysis tools has been completed toward varying goals. It is relatively common to use an intermediate general model to express the relevant details of the source code [11, 14] which can be used for multiple purposes, an approach adopted by this author.

Example Analysis Techniques
Three analysis techniques were chosen as examples to test the feasibility of generic tools with broad applicability across many languages. All three can work on static source code alone and can be genuinely useful to software engineers in day-to-day programming tasks.

Unreachable procedure detection [15] is commonly included in contemporary analysis tools, and is also performed by some compilers for the purpose of optimization. To support this analysis, two main types of information are required: the reachability of individual statements within a block of code or function, and the relationships between called functions and their callers. **Unused variable detection** [16] identifies variables that are never read, rendering their creation and assignment unnecessary. The algorithm to determine this is simple, if the dependencies between variables are known.

A type of **ripple analysis,** the logical ripple effect [17] aims to automatically locate the affected sections of code in a program should a given module or subroutine be modified by following inter-function and inter-module relationships. It is present in many software engineering support tools available today. The data required by this type of analysis is limited, and is extractable from almost any high-level imperative language.

Data Required for Analysis
To carry out these analyses three types of graph across a program or system are required, as noted below. The graphs selected to provide the information upon which the analyses are based are quite well established in the literature, with the exception of the static variable dependence graph which is itself a variation on an existing model.

A **static call graph** [18] models the relationships between function call statements within a program and the functions that are invoked. At its simplest, such a graph contains a node for each function defined within a program, and a directed edge for each call from one function to another. A **control flow graph** is [19] a more fine-grained view of an application, which breaks a program down in to atomic blocks. This type of graph has a block at each node, with directed edges indicating a possible flow of control from one block to the next. Finally a **static variable dependence graph** models the relationships between various value-holding elements within a program based on the source code with a directed graph. It is related to a data dependency graph [20] however inverts the positions of the active components (operators) and passive components (data or variables) to capture slightly different details. Each distinct piece of data including variables, literals and constants is represented as a node.

Source Markup and Semantic Analysis
As far as the author is aware there is no published academic literature that discusses the idea of creating generic fact extractors, but there is a sound body of literature on fact extractors, source markup and semantic analysis in general. Of relevance here is Lin, Holt & Malton's discussion of fact extractor completeness [21], in which degrees of completeness are laid out for fact extractors with the reasonable implication that an extractor of quality will produce complete results. However, if the goal of the fact extraction exercise is known ahead of time as in this case, some completeness in the output can be sacrificed in the name of cross-language compatibility, provided the details required are retained. This is because while it is impossible to cater for every possible language feature, only a predictable subset of language features will be required for the desired models and analyses.

Due to the marked differences between the semantics of different languages, it is difficult (if not impossible) to provide a single generic semantic analyzer which is capable of dealing with all realistic general purpose programming languages. Whereas EBNF and similar descendants are now in common use to describe the syntax of a language, no semantic description framework has gained such popularity [22]. This situation may change in future as tools improve and awareness of semantic modeling spreads, but the lack of a standard makes it unattractive to create a semantic model for any particular language, given it may see limited use in the short term. A compromise used for the method of this paper is to exploit the similarities between languages within paradigms and provide generic semantic analysis modules that apply common rules. This is possible because each major paradigm usually applies a consistent philosophy to the organization of programs and their features, leading to consistent algorithms for the location of referenced variables, functions or other objects.

3   Proposed Application of Generic and Generated Components

3.1   Overview of Proposed Solution

To realize and test the idea that generic and generated components may be used to significantly hasten development of analysis tools, a working prototype was built. GenFact is an experimental fact extractor generator based on the principles outlined in section 2. It is designed to work in tandem with the SableCC parser generator [8], and provides a GUI for the user, typically a language writer, to mark up their grammar with additional information related to fact extraction. After the required information has been supplied, the user may generate a fact extractor specific to their language, which can generate graphs using a standard format as illustrated in figure 1. This allows a single set of analysis tools to be applied across any language supported by the tool.

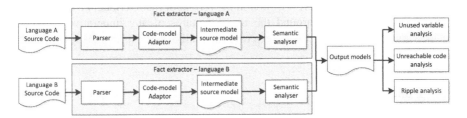

Fig. 1. GenFact source code analysis workflow

The generated fact extractor contains both a source code transformation module based on the marked-up grammar and a collection of semantic analysis modules. The source transformation module builds a low-level fact tree known as the Intermediate Source Model from the input source code which can be processed by the semantic analyzer. The semantic analyzer chosen by the user is then responsible for applying the semantic rules specific to the language being processed, resolving all explicit calls and building data flow relationships. It is important to note that some completeness as per the definition of Lin, Holt and Malton [21] is sacrificed in this design in the name of expedience. The design goal of the system is to allow a basic set of analysis to be set up very fast, and as a consequence not every type of analysis will be possible with the model emitted.

Generated Classes
GenFact uses a template based system to generate the code for the language's fact extractor. The supplied templates emit C# language specification 4 code that compiles against the .Net 4.0 client framework, but may be re-written to emit code in a

different language without recompilation of GenFact. The main output of the generation process is source code for a master processing class, which contains all necessary functions to process each fact type, as well as control functions to manage traversal across the model emitted by SableCC. Additionally a number of support classes describing the data model for the extracted facts are supplied.

The support classes include generic semantic analysis modules for object-oriented and functional paradigms. Support for pure procedural languages is necessarily included in both modules, as function bodies form procedural code. This generic approach is based on the premise noted above that the majority of languages fall into a common set of paradigms. When applying a generic module some accuracy may be sacrificed for expedience, but it allows a working tool be constructed quickly. For languages that have unusual semantics it is possible to create entirely bespoke semantic analysis modules and integrate them into the model provided by GenFact via a common interface, or extend the generic modules provided through inheritance.

The code model adaptor
The code model adaptor is the primary output of the GenFact UI, and consists of code in C# that can be compiled to provide a library ready to interface with a SableCC AST model. The code model adaptor is responsible for traversing a given AST and extracting the features of interest from it in the format of the intermediate data model.

The model is designed around the major features of any imperative language: blocks, variables, function calls (inter-procedure calls), and expressions to work with values.

3.2   Example Program

The contrived language Tiny uses a simple function call resolution mechanism as it requires function names to be unique within their scope. Figure 2 illustrates a static variable dependence graph for the example Tiny program in figure 3. Dark, solid lines indicate a direct dependence on a value while lighter, dashed lines indicate a dependence that has is due to a variable's use as a parameter during a function call. Darker ellipses represent variables that have been explicitly declared, while white ellipses indicate the return-value of a function. This graph provides sufficient information for unused variable detection, as can be seen by the absence of any edges to or from the variable unusedVal. Control flow and static call graphs were still produced, but are not shown as much of the same data is incorporated into the static variable dependence graph.

When coupled with an appropriate front-end UI, this graph is also useful in helping software developers to answer the question "How did this value come to be in this variable?". It also provides the information required to drive unused variable and function analysis. It is worth noting that the node '4' and 'otherFunc' form an island in the graph, separate from the main flow. Similarly the 'unsedVal' variable is an island with no connection to other parts of the graph, indicating that it is irrelevant to the function of the program.

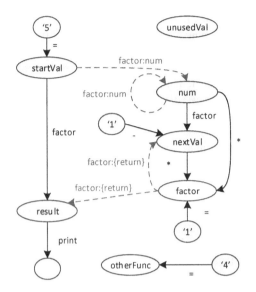

Fig. 2. Example static variable

4 Evaluation

For the purpose of evaluation, the GenFact tool was considered a reference implementation of the proposal in section 3.1, and therefore the evaluation of the tool is considered to cover the underlying theory as well. To support the evaluation, sample programs were written in Java and JavaScript and then run through the tool. The programs were of similar size, and implemented similar logic though varied in their construction to take advantage of features specific to their implementation language. These languages were selected as they take considerably different approaches to many aspects of language design, including type rules, function declaration, call resolution and others. As such these made good test cases for the flexibility of the solution.

The GenFact tool was evaluated for completeness on two binary criteria: its ability to generate ready source code accurately reflecting the model entered by the user and the ability of the generated code to create the graphs identified (static call graph, control flow graph & static variable dependence graph) accurately. This was performed through manual comparison of the output models to the sample programs, ensuring that all features and relationships were present, and that no erroneous relationships had been established.

```
#class testClass
   #func factor ( num )
      #var nextVal
      #var unusedVal
      #if num < 1
            factor = 1
      #else
            nextVal = factor ( num ) - 1
            factor = * ( nextVal , num )
      #endif
   #end_func
   #func main ( )
      #var startVal
      startVal = 5
      result = factor ( startVal )
      print ( result )
   #end_func
#end_class
#class otherClass
   #func otherFunc ( )
      otherFunc = 4
   #end_func
#end_class
```

Fig. 3. Tiny Language program

The flexibility of the solution to cater for different languages was also evaluated, using two major criteria relating to the two language-specific elements of the system. Firstly, the ability of the Intermediate Source Model to hold details important to the semantic analysis and graph construction process was evaluated by considering firstly whether all necessary details could be included, and then whether the facts that had to be associated with various grammar features were a good fit. Secondly, the ability of the generic semantic analysis modules to correctly resolve references to variables and functions were evaluated.

To begin with Gagnon's Java 1.5 grammar for SableCC was marked up with GenFact to describe which elements of the grammar should be copied into the intermediate source model. No critical information was unable to be mapped, and the elements that did need to be mapped were able to be tagged in a manner that was appropriate to their original purpose. A semantic analysis module for mainstream object-oriented languages was used to resolve references.

JavaScript being a simpler language, could be tagged for mapping to the intermediate source model quite quickly. The functional nature of the language was catered for by searching for variables in addition to explicit function declarations. In some cases searching variables made it possible to statically determine which anonymous function would be called via a variable reference, in cases where exactly one function is assigned to a given local variable through the life of the program.

The output from GenFact for both languages was tested and verified. A limitation encountered and shared among most static analysis tools was the inability to predict the state of the program, particularly when executable code was to be evaluated at run-time. An additional limitation of the parser was that JavaScript automatic semicolon insertion could not be implemented as it is in modern web browsers. When this feature was avoided, the resulting graphs match the actual execution flow successfully.

Based on these results the prototype implementation GenFact is considered to be an improvement on other techniques that are available for rapid fact extractor and analysis tool development. It saves considerably on the amount of hand coding required to implement basic analyses for a new language, allowing information to be extracted from existing codebases sooner. This will contribute to the knowledge of software engineers charged with maintaining software implemented in unusual languages.

5   Conclusion and Future Work

In this paper it has been shown that it is feasible to use code generators and generic language technology to reuse a set of analytical tools for multiple languages. The cost of adding support to automated analysis tools was put forward as a contributing factor to the ongoing poor support for some languages, and automated fact extractor generation identified as a potential mechanism to reduce the labor cost of supporting said languages. It was identified that imperative languages have at their core a common set of features which can be used to drive three common types of analysis for automated software development support tools. Those languages expressible in EBNF make good candidates for automated generation of tooling due to the existing support in the area of parser generation, especially in the context of the typical workflow for source code analysis tools. This was demonstrated with GenFact, which allows a SableCC-based grammar to be flagged with a graphical user interface to indicate elements of importance to the analysis process, and then for a generic language markup library to be generated. It was also shown that the call resolution rules in a language can be roughly simulated with generic modules. With this technology, language developers will be one step closer to providing sophisticated development tools for languages with currently lack them. In future further analysis types may be added to provide further utility to programmers across a range of languages.

References

1. O'Neil, P.: MODEL 204 architecture and performance. In: 2nd International Workshop on High Performance Transaction Systems, Pacific Grove, CA, USA (1989)
2. Gupta Technologies: Welcome to Team Developer 6.2, http://www.guptatechnologies.com/Products/App_Dev/TeamDeveloper/default.aspx (accessed 2014)
3. Knight, C.: Smell the Coffee! Uncovering Java Analysis Issues. In: SCAM 2001: 1st International Workshop on Source Code Analysis and Manipulation, pp. 161–167 (2001)
4. Backus, J., Bauer, F., Green, J., Katz, C., McCarthy, J., Perlis, A., Rutishauser, H., Samelson, K., Vauquois, B., Wegstein, J., Wijngaarden, A., Woodger, M., Naur, P.: Report on the algorithmic language ALGOL 60, New York, NY, USA (1960)
5. International Standards Organisation: ISE/IEC 14977:1996, http://www.cl.cam.ac.uk/~mgk25/iso-14977.pdf
6. Parr, T., Quong, R.: ANLTR: A Predicated-LL(k) parser generator. Software Practice and Experience 25(7), 789–810 (1995)
7. The ANTLR Project: About The ANTLR Parser Generator, http://www.antlr3.org/about.html (accessed 2014)
8. Gagnon, E., Hendren, L.: SableCC, an Object-Oriented Compiler Framework. In: Proceedings of the Technology of Object-Oriented Languages, TOOLS 26, Santa Barbara, CA, USA, pp. 140–154 (1998)
9. Collard, M., Decker, M., Maletic, J.: Lightweight Transformation and Fact Extraction with the srcML Toolkit. In: SCAM 2011 - 11th International Working Conference on Source Code Analysis and Manipulation (2011)
10. Mayer, P., Schroeder, A.: Cross-Language Code Analysis and Refactoring. In: SCAM 2012: IEEE 12th International Working Conference on Source Code Analysis and Manipulation, pp. 94–103 (2012)
11. Stein, D., Kratz, H., Lowe, W.: Cross-Language Program Analysis and Refactoring. In: SCAM 2006: Proceedings of the 6th IEEE International Workshop on Source Code Analysis and Manipulation (2006)
12. Linos, P., Lucas, W., Myers, S., Maier, E.: A Metrics Tool for Multi-language Software. In: 11th IASTED International Conference on Software Engineering and Applications, pp. 324–329 (2007)

13. Boerboom, F., Janssen, A.: Fact Extraction, Querying and Visualization of Large C++ Code Bases Design and Implementation, Eindhoven, Germany (2006)
14. Deruelle, L., Melab, N., Bouneffa, M., Basson, H.: Analysis and Manipulation of Distributed Multi-Language Software Code. In: SCAM 2001: First International Workshop on Source Code Analysis and Manipulation, Florence, pp. 43–54 (2001)
15. Strivastava, A.: Unreachable Procedures in Object Oriented Programs. ACM Letters on Programming Languages and Systems, 355–364 (1992)
16. Taylot, R., Osterweil, L.: Anomoly Detection in Concurrent Software by Static Data Flow Analysis. IEEE Transactions on Software Engineering SE-6(3), 265–278 (1980)
17. Yau, S., Collofello, J., MacGregor, T.: Ripple effect analysis of software maintenance. In: COMPSAC 1978: Procedings of the IEEE Computer Society's Second International Computer Software and Applications Conference, pp. 60–65 (1978)
18. Graham, S., Kessler, P., Mckusick, M.: Gprof: A call graph execution profiler. In: SIGPLAN 1982 Proceedings of the 1982 SIGPLAN Symposium on Compiler Construction (1982)
19. Allen, F.: Control flow analysis. In: Proceedings of a Symposium on Compiler Optimization (1970)
20. Kavi, K., Buckles, B., Bhat, U.: A Formal Definition of Data Flow Graph Models. IEEE Transactions on Computers 35(11), 940–948 (1986)
21. Lin, Y., Holt, R., Malton, A.: Completeness of a Fact Extractor. In: Proceedings of the 10th Working Conference on Reverse Engineering (2003)
22. Zhang, Y., Xu, B.: A Survey of Semantic Description Frameworks for Programming Languages. ACM SIGPLAN Notices 39(3), 14–30 (2004)

Author Index